HISTORIC PHOTOS OF
JACKSONVILLE

TEXT AND CAPTIONS BY CAROLYN WILLIAMS

TURNER
PUBLISHING COMPANY

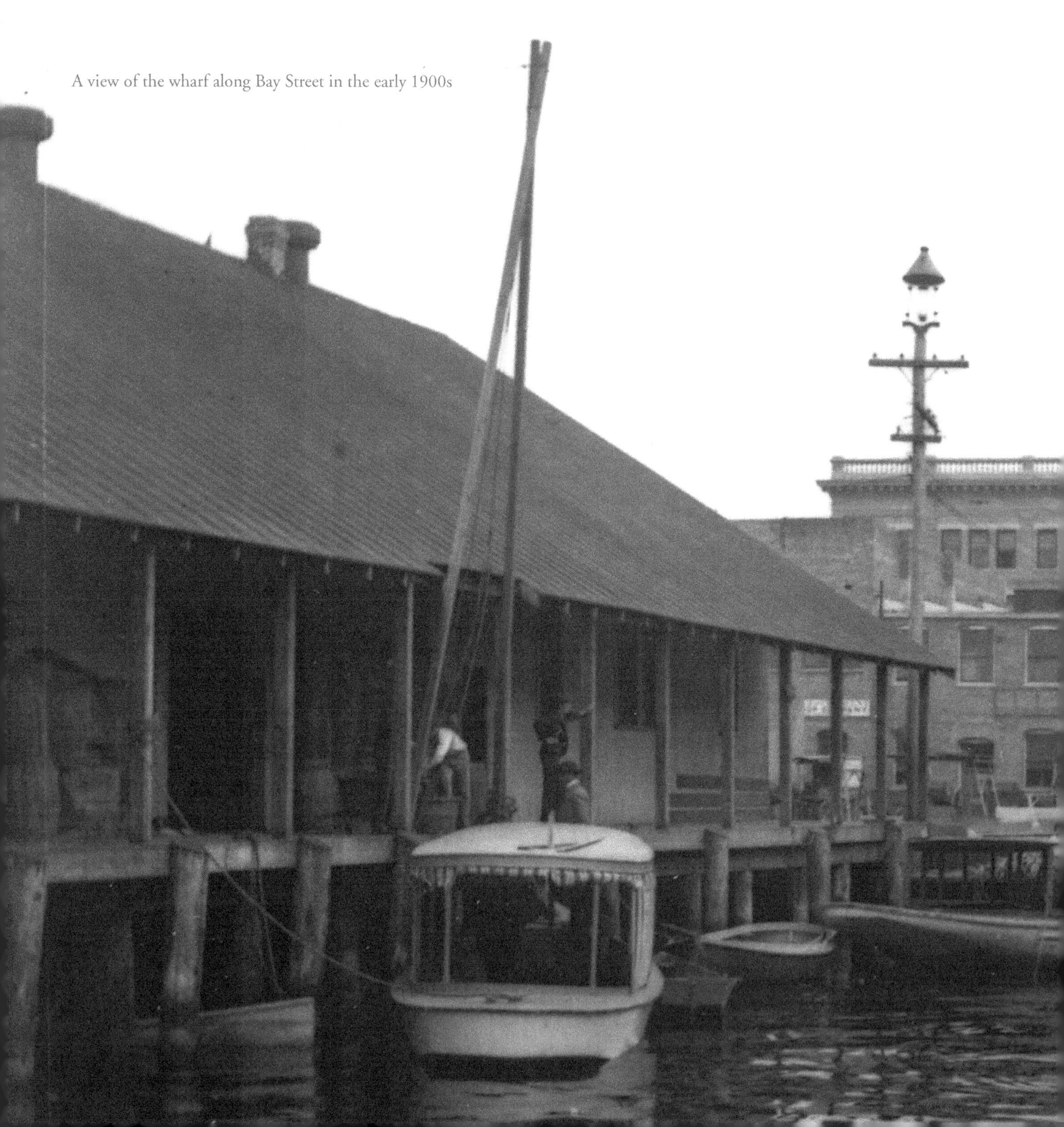

A view of the wharf along Bay Street in the early 1900s

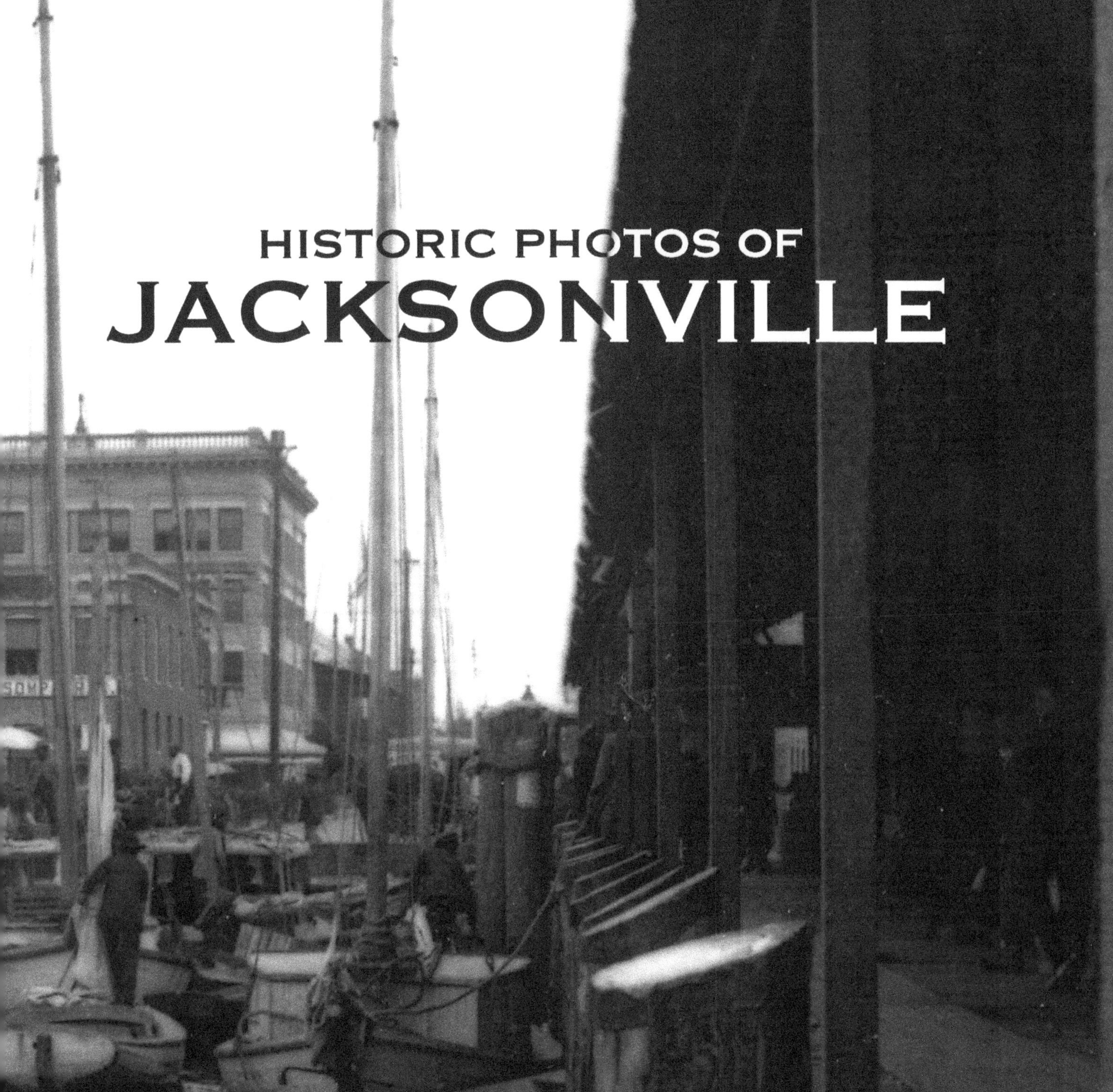

HISTORIC PHOTOS OF
JACKSONVILLE

Turner Publishing Company
www.turnerpublishing.com

Historic Photos of Jacksonville

Library of Congress Control Number: 2006935406

ISBN-13: 978-1-59652-311-1
ISBN: 1-59652-311-5

Printed in the United States of America

ISBN 978-1-68336-928-8 (hc)

Contents

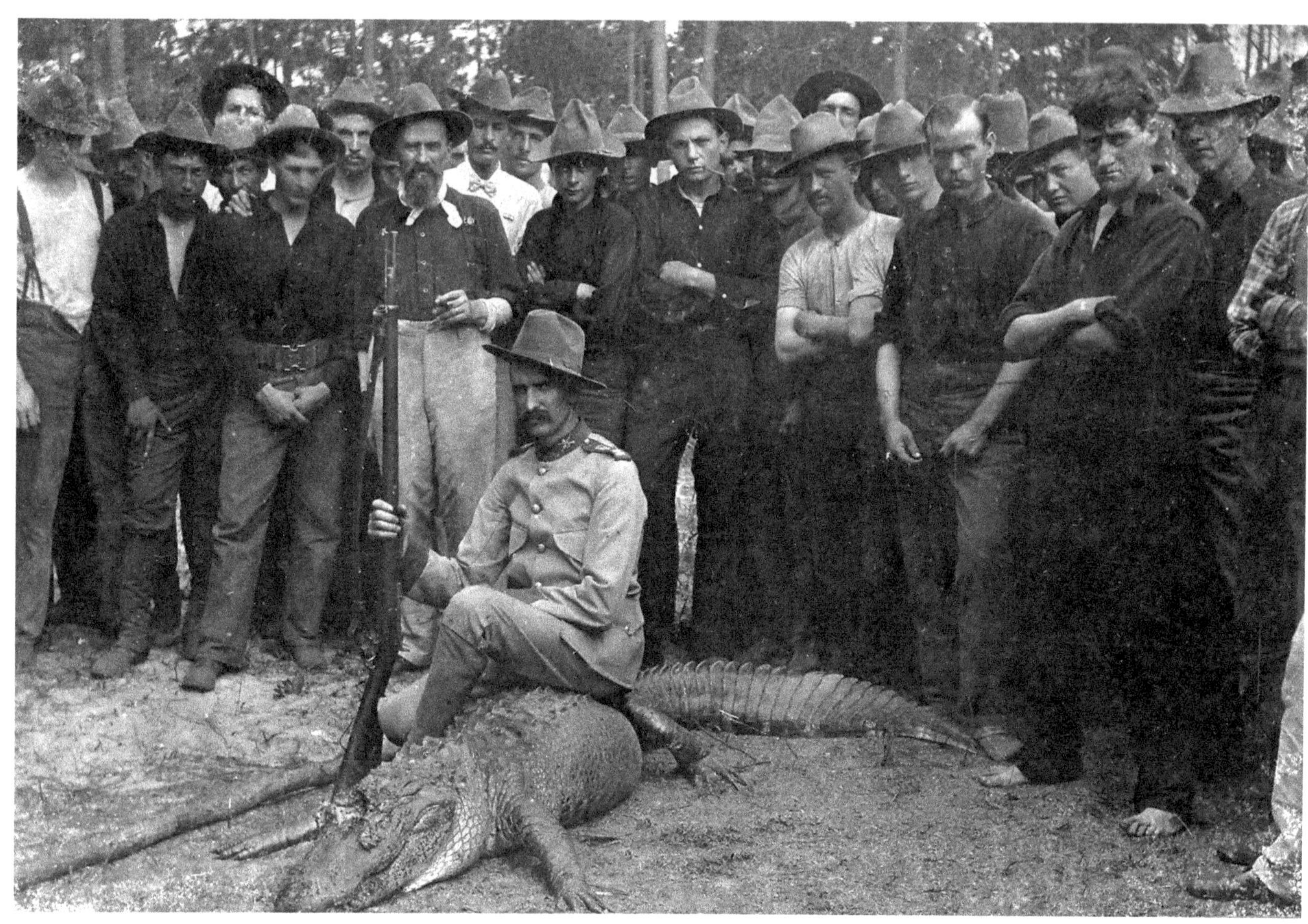

From May 29 to October 24, 1898, the 4th Illinois regiment was stationed here at Camp Cuba Libre, in East Springfield on Ionia Street.

Acknowledgments

This volume, *Historic Photos of Jacksonville*, is the result of the cooperation and efforts of many individuals and organizations. It is with great thanks that we acknowledge in particular the generous assistance of the State Archives of Florida

We would also like to thank the following individuals for their valuable contributions and assistance in making this work possible:

N. Adam Watson, Photographic Archivist, State Archives of Florida
Carolyn Williams, our writer, Associate Professor of History, University of North Florida in Jacksonville

Preface

Jacksonville has thousands of historic photographs that reside in archives, both locally and nationally. This book began with the observation that, while those photographs are of great interest to many, they are not easily accessible. During a time when Jacksonville is looking ahead and evaluating its future course, many people are asking, "How do we treat the past?" These decisions affect every aspect of the city—architecture, public spaces, commerce, infrastructure—and these, in turn, affect the way that people live their lives. This book seeks to provide easy access to a valuable, objective look into the history of Jacksonville.

The power of photographs is that they are less subjective than words in their treatment of history. Although the photographer can make decisions regarding subject matter and how to capture and present it, photographs do not provide the breadth of interpretation that text does. For this reason, they offer an original, untainted perspective that allows the viewer to interpret and observe.

This project represents countless hours of review and research. The researchers and writer have reviewed thousands of photographs in numerous archives. We greatly appreciate the generous assistance of those listed in the acknowledgments of this work, without whom this project could not have been completed.

The goal in publishing this work is to provide broader access to this set of extraordinary photographs which seek to inspire, provide perspective, and evoke insight that might assist people who are responsible for determining Jacksonville's future. In addition, the book seeks to preserve the past with adequate respect and reverence.

With the exception of touching up imperfections that have accrued with the passage of time and cropping where necessary, no other changes have been made. The focus and clarity of many images is limited to the technology and the ability of the photographer at the time they were taken.

The work is divided into eras. Beginning with some of the earliest known photographs of Jacksonville, the first section records photographs from before the Civil War through the end of the nineteenth century. The second section spans the beginning of the twentieth century to the beginning of the 1920s. Section Three moves from the Roaring Twenties to the eve of World War II. The last section covers the war era to the 1960s.

In each of these sections we have made an effort to capture various aspects of life through our selection of photographs. People, commerce, transportation, infrastructure, religious institutions, and educational institutions have been included to provide a broad perspective.

We encourage readers to reflect as they go walking in Jacksonville, strolling through the city, its parks, and its neighborhoods. It is the publisher's hope that in utilizing this work, longtime residents will learn something new and that new residents will gain a perspective on where Jacksonville has been, so that each can contribute to its future.

—Todd Bottorff, Publisher

Schooners like the *Lillie* of Key West shown here transported cargo to and from the docks of Jacksonville. Since there were no railroads south of the city, these vessels played an important role in economic development. The St. Johns River was the main artery of trade, providing the only channel of transport for freight and people.

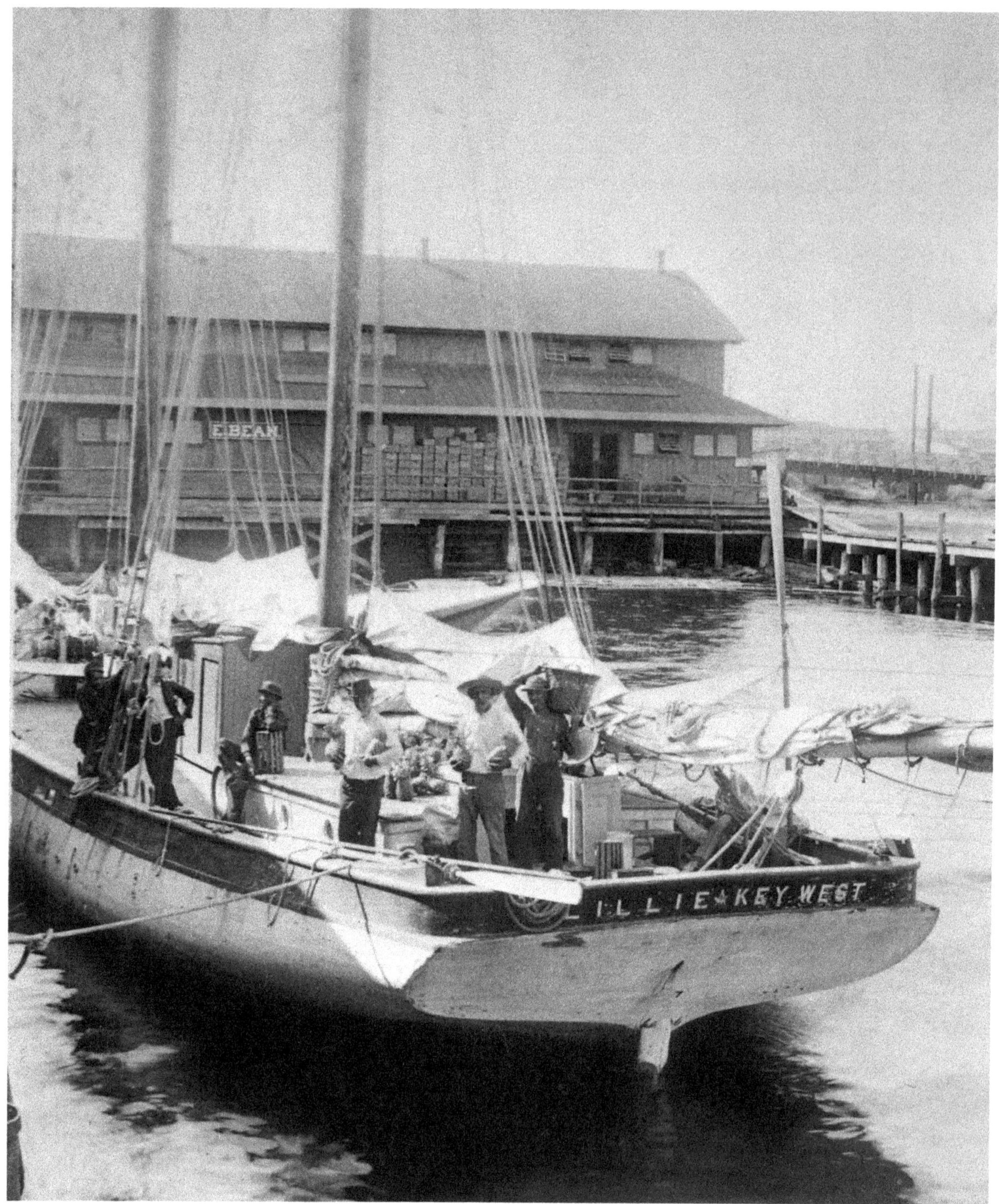

From a Long and Slow Beginning to the Great Fire of 1901

(1850–1901)

Jacksonville begins with the river that is known today as the St. Johns. The various names by which the river and city have been known reflect the many and varied human settlers who have occupied and shaped them. The Timucuans, the indigenous people that Europeans encountered upon arrival, called the region "Wileka," meaning "land of lakes" because of the many springs and marshes collected by the river over thousands of years. The French dubbed the river "River de May" to mark the date of their arrival on May 1, 1562, and named the settlement they established Fort Caroline in honor of their king, Charles IX.

The presence of the French Huguenots in the land they had claimed and named "La Florida" motivated the Spanish Catholics to form their own settlement, St. Augustine, in 1565. From their fort the Spanish launched an attack that resulted in the removal of the French and yet another name for the fort and the river, San Mateo, for St. Matthew, whose feast day was celebrated the day of the conquest.

The Spanish managed to hold on to the region for more than two centuries (with the brief interruption of a British occupation from 1763 to 1783, when the river received the name it bears today, the St. Johns River). The Seminoles, who had replaced the long-vanished Timucuans, called the settlement "Wacca Pilatka" or "Cowford" (as the English translated it) until the early 1800s.

After the second and final war between Britain and the United States (the War of 1812), the most famous hero from that war, Andrew Jackson, headed an expedition that culminated in the transfer by Spain of Florida to the United States in 1821. The following year Jacksonville was named by Isaiah Hart, its main founder, for Old Hickory, who served as the first governor of Florida under U.S. control, from March 10 to December 31, 1821.

During the territorial stage of Florida (1821–1845) until the Civil War era, Jacksonville, like the state as a whole, grew slowly. The area was home to plantations, introduced during the British period, where Sea Island cotton, indigo, and sugar were grown, and which became a permanent part of the economic and social landscape. The timber industry was another mainstay of the economy. Throughout this period Jacksonville evolved from a trading post to a city as the residents grappled with wars, fires, and other disasters.

Because of the river (just 25 miles away and providing the most direct access to the Atlantic Ocean), Jacksonville became a center of Civil War activity. Although no major battles took place, the town was invaded four times by the Union army. The Union forces served as a magnet to slaves, who believed that freedom was "as close as the river," and who fled the farms and plantations in northeast Florida and Georgia. Many former soldiers, black and white, stayed in the area after the war, when Jacksonville experienced its first major stage of city building until the early twentieth century and a yellow fever epidemic in 1888. By the end of the century, in addition to serving as the state's main port, Jacksonville was the center of state tourism. All this growth came to an abrupt end on May 3, 1901, when the city succumbed to a massive fire.

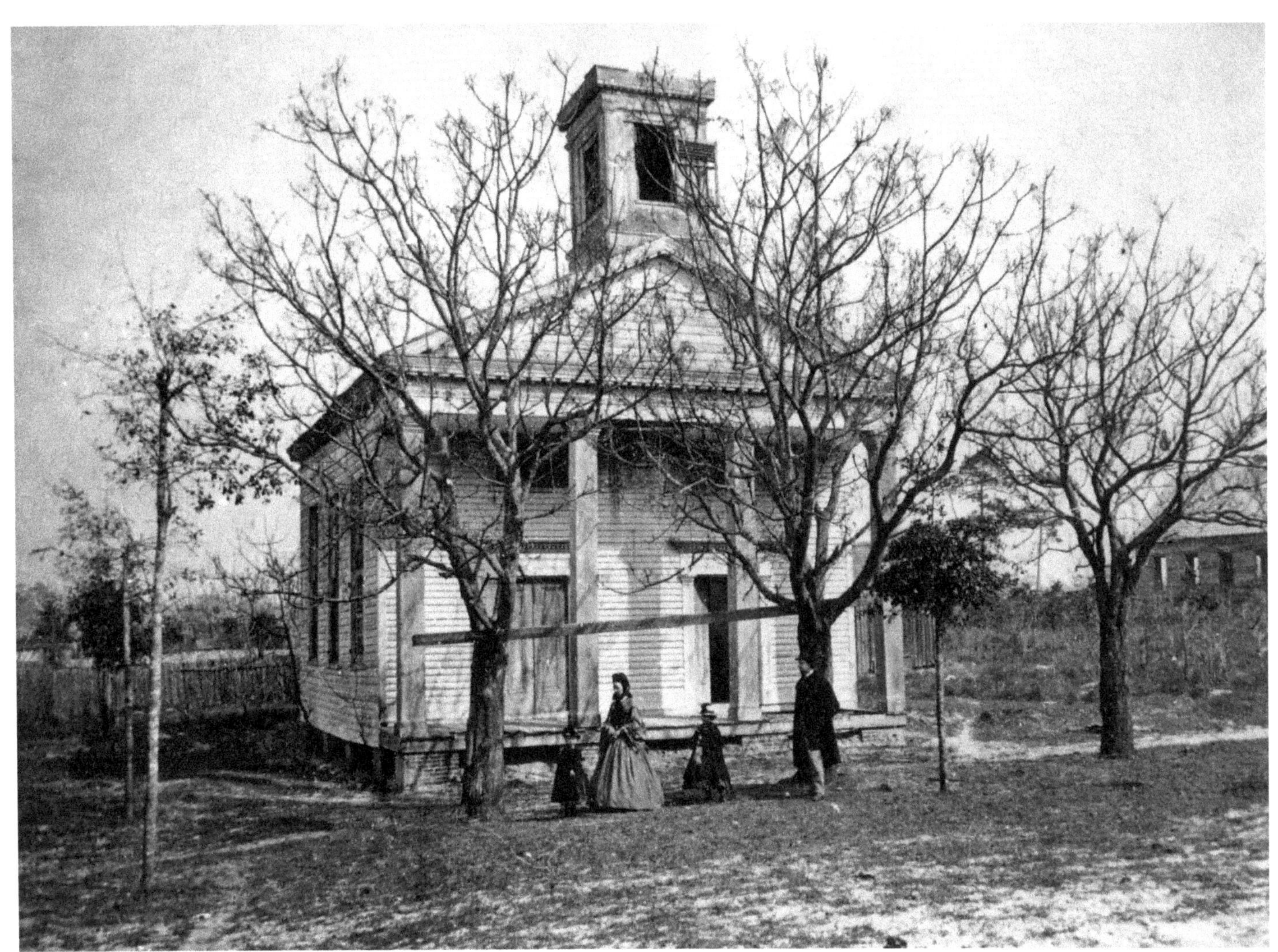

This building is probably St. Paul's Methodist Church, constructed in 1858 and serving the congregation until 1890, when it was sold to Catholics. The structure was later moved across the street to the corner of Newnan and Duval and used as a hall. It was destroyed by the fire of 1901.

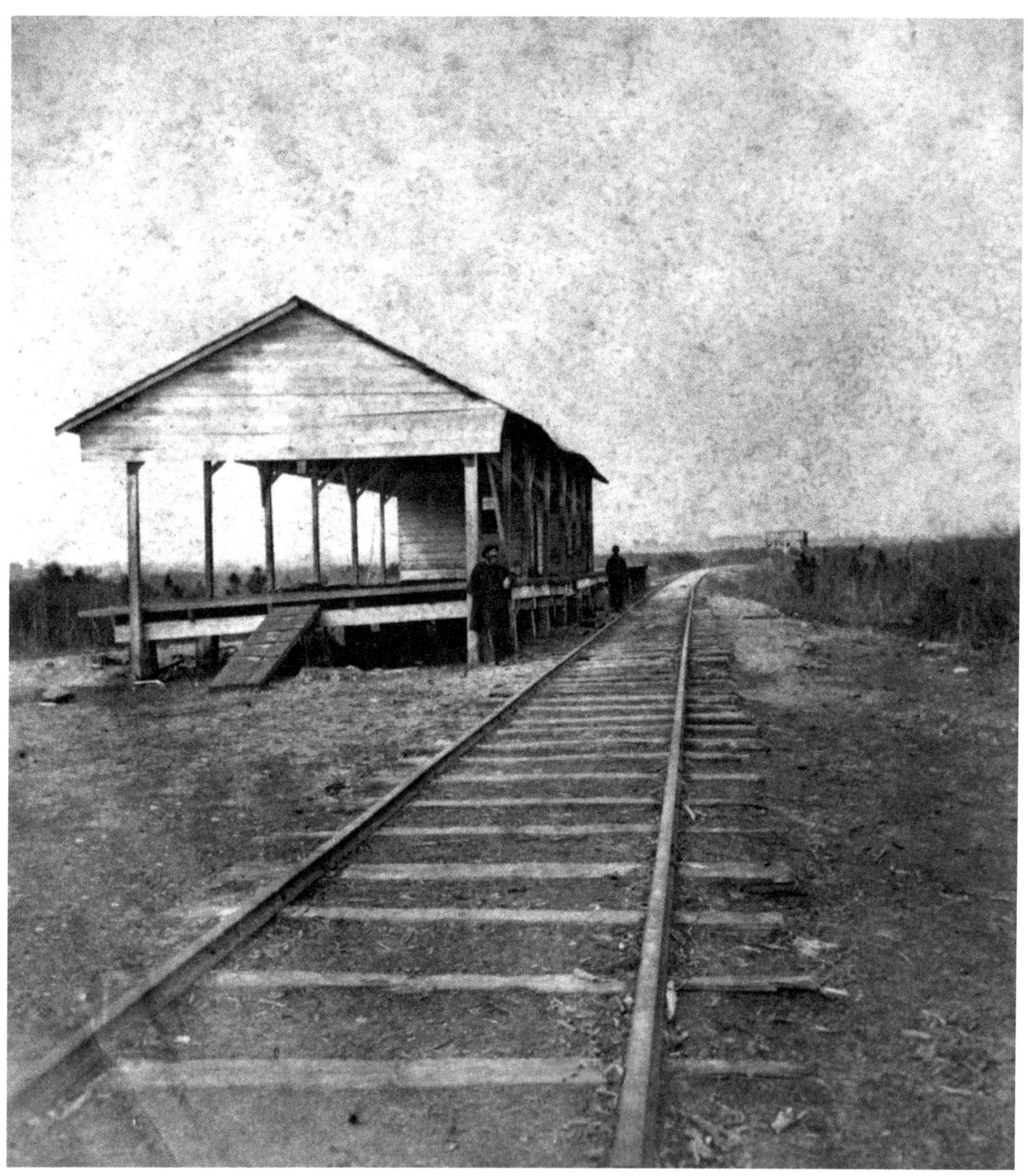

This depot belonged to the Florida Atlantic Gulf Coast Railroad, which ran from Jacksonville to Lake City. The structure was mainly a platform without a shed. Only one train arrived and departed every 24 hours.

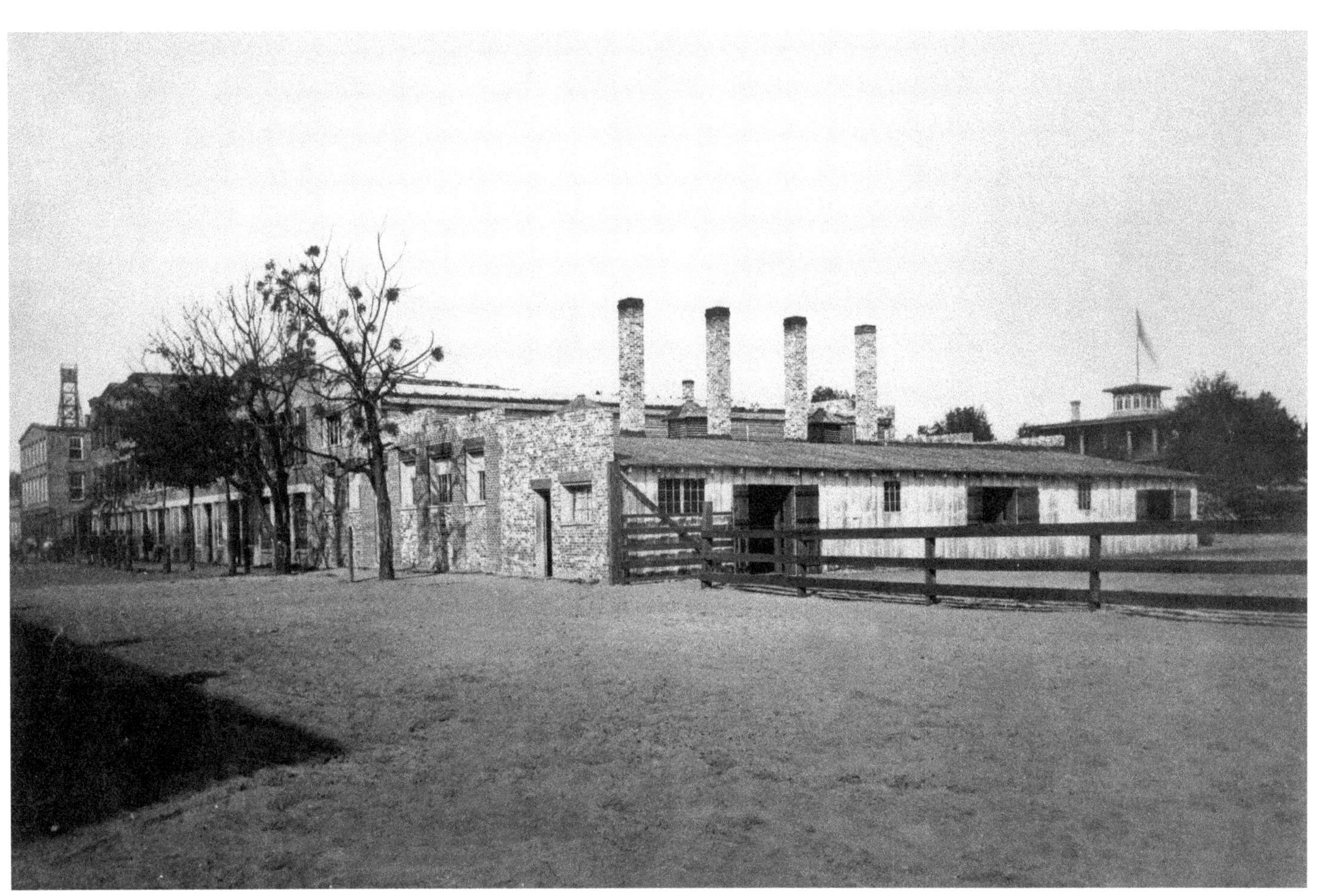

By the time of the war, Jacksonville (incorporated as a city in 1859) was bounded by Hogan's Creek on the north and west Pine Street (today's Main Street) and the St. Johns River on the south. Although much of the fledgling commercial district was destroyed during the four invasions of federal troops, some stores survived the end of the war. This bakery, probably Rivas and Koghman, was located on the north side of Bay Street, between Ocean and Newnan streets.

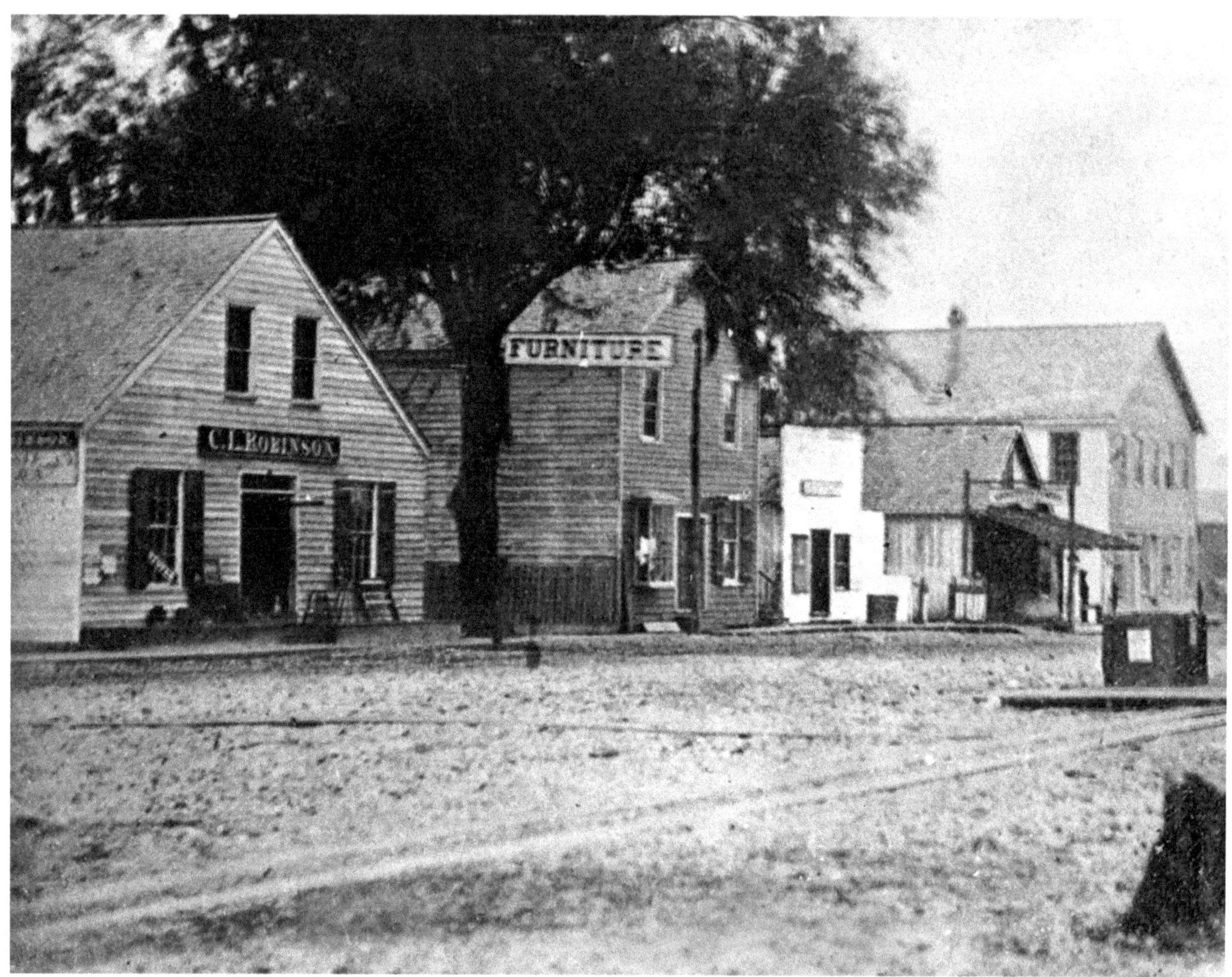

The store at left, at the corner of Bay and Hogan streets, was owned by local entrepreneur Calvin Lewis Robinson. The building burned in 1865.

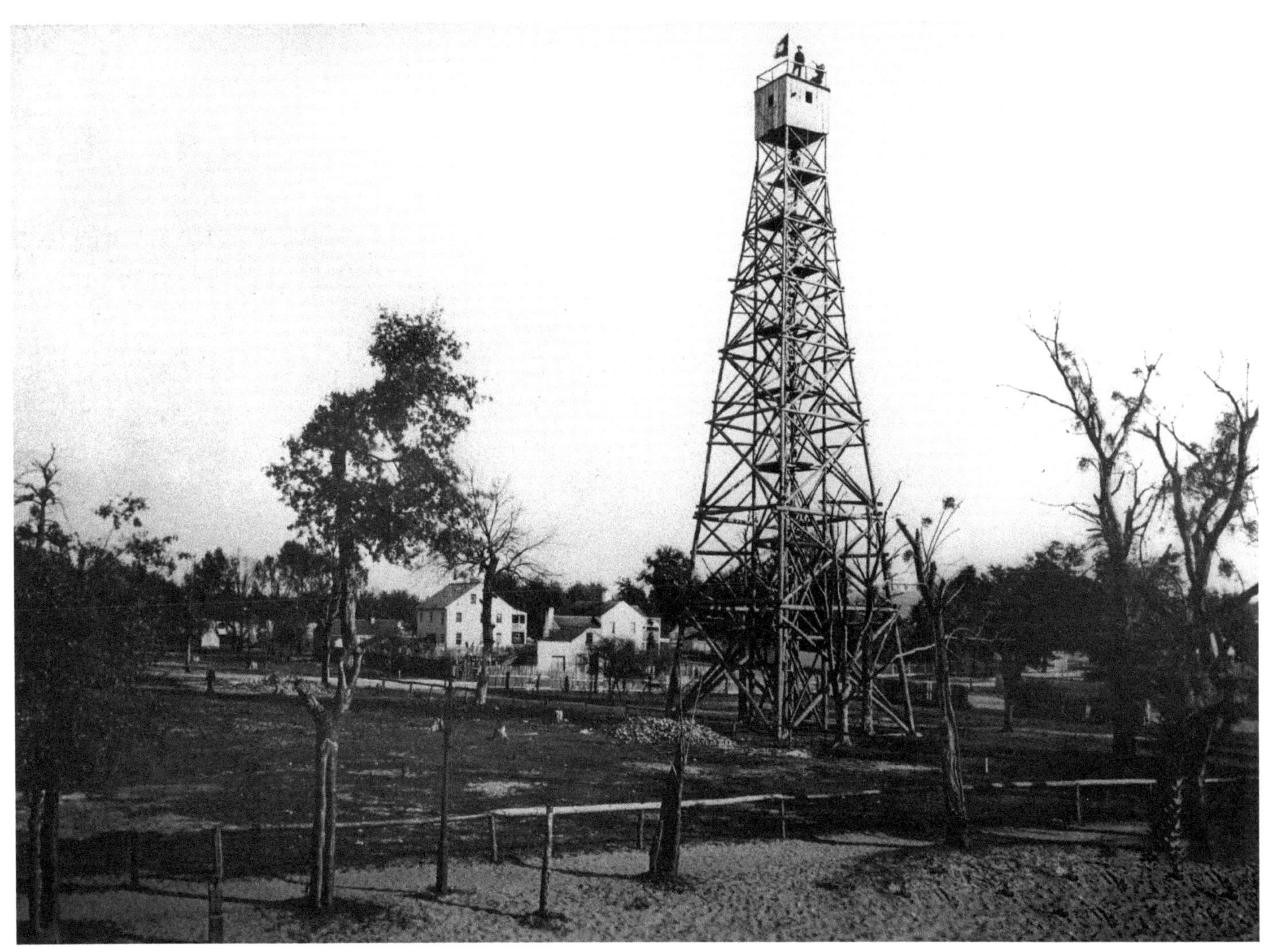

Union troops built signal towers like the one pictured here to communicate with each other and with ships offshore. This tower was located in what was then called the public square (today Hemming Park). The top of the tower was enclosed to protect the signalmen from Confederate snipers.

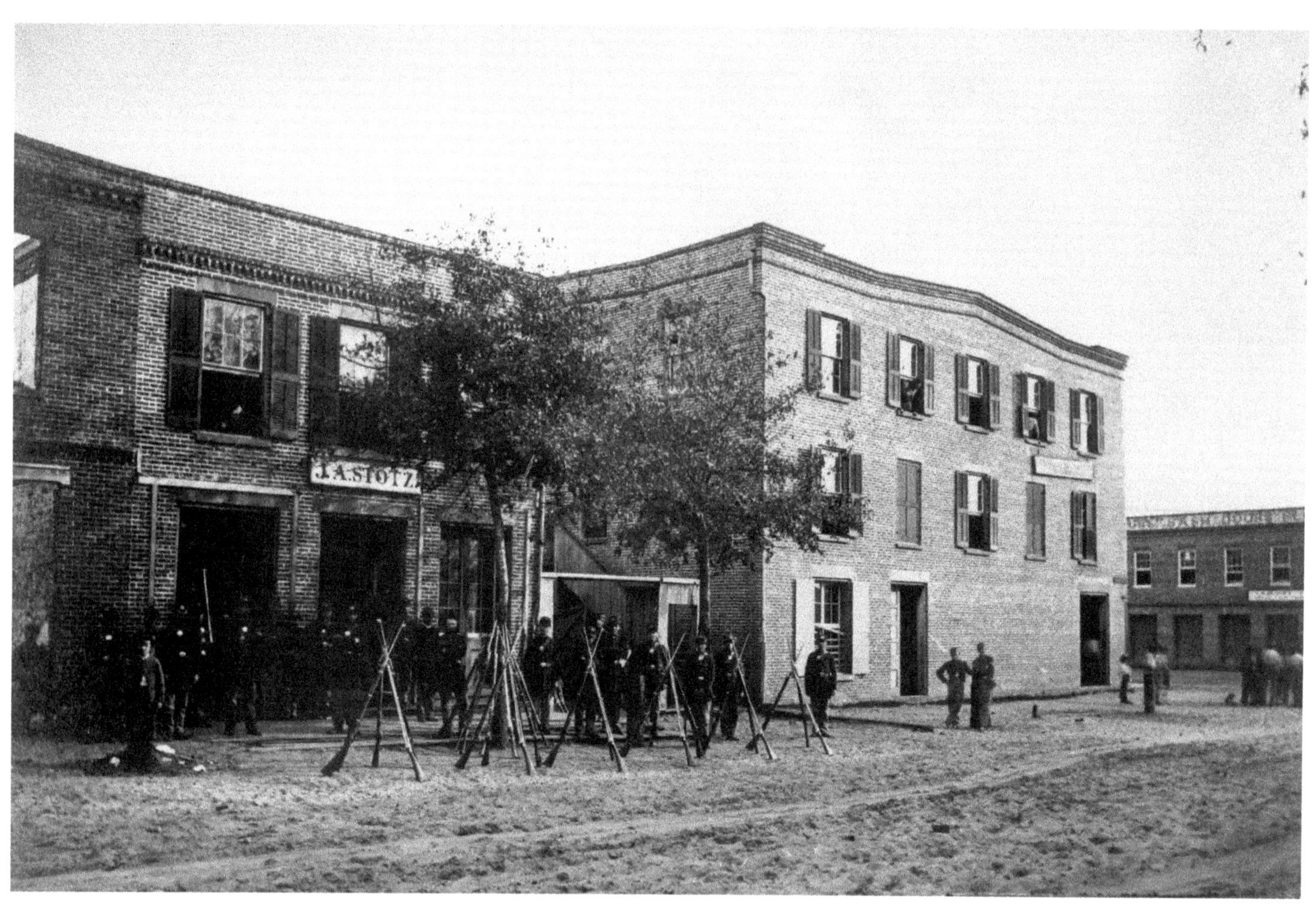

After the Battle of Olustee, the most significant Confederate victory in Florida, many of the surviving Union forces retreated to Jacksonville. The federal army continued to occupy the town until federal troops were withdrawn from the state in 1869. During the period of military rule a provost marshal and guard in command handled court cases. The marshal's house stood at the northwest corner of Bay and Ocean streets.

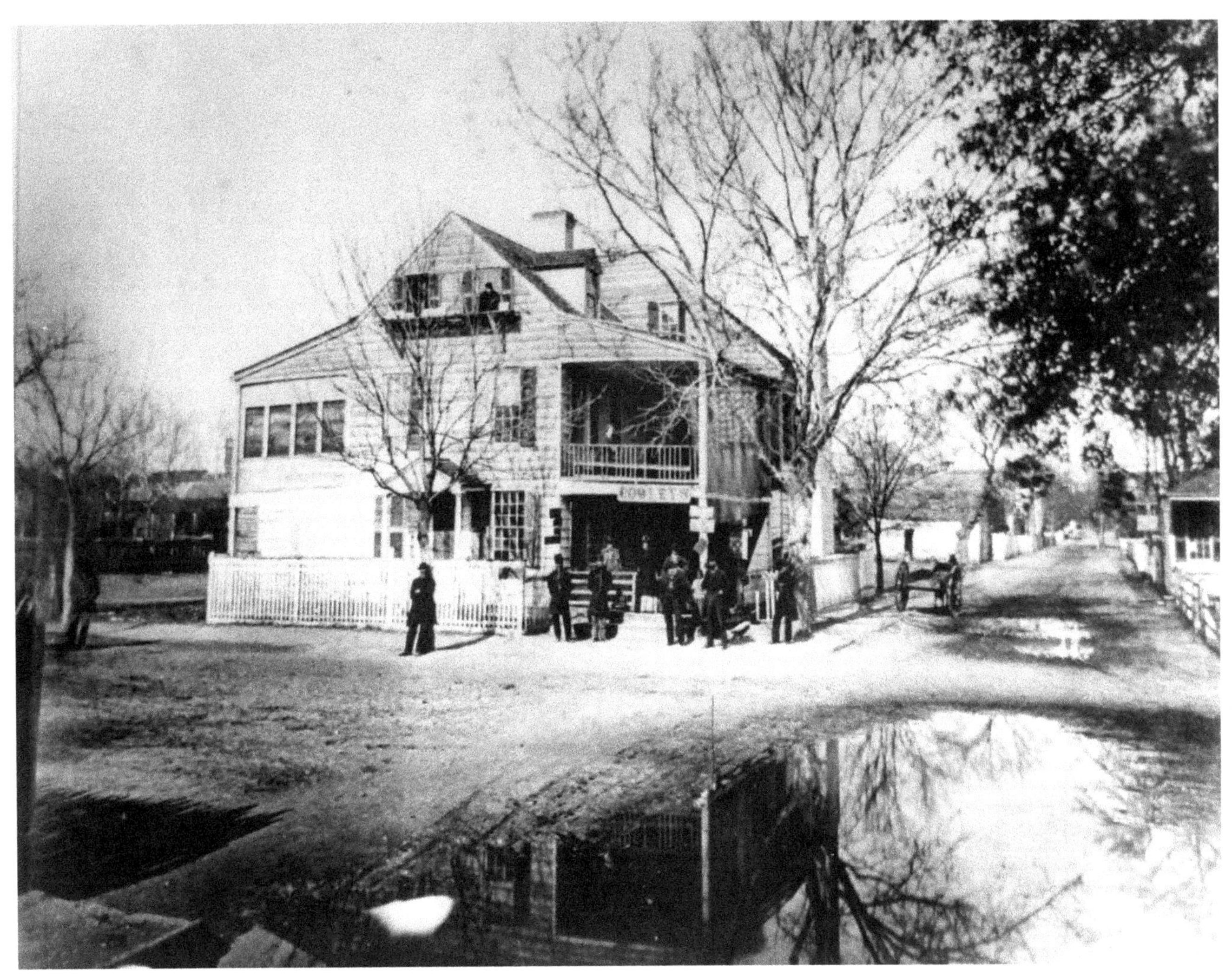

This photo shows Union soldiers gathered at Cooley's commercial establishment.

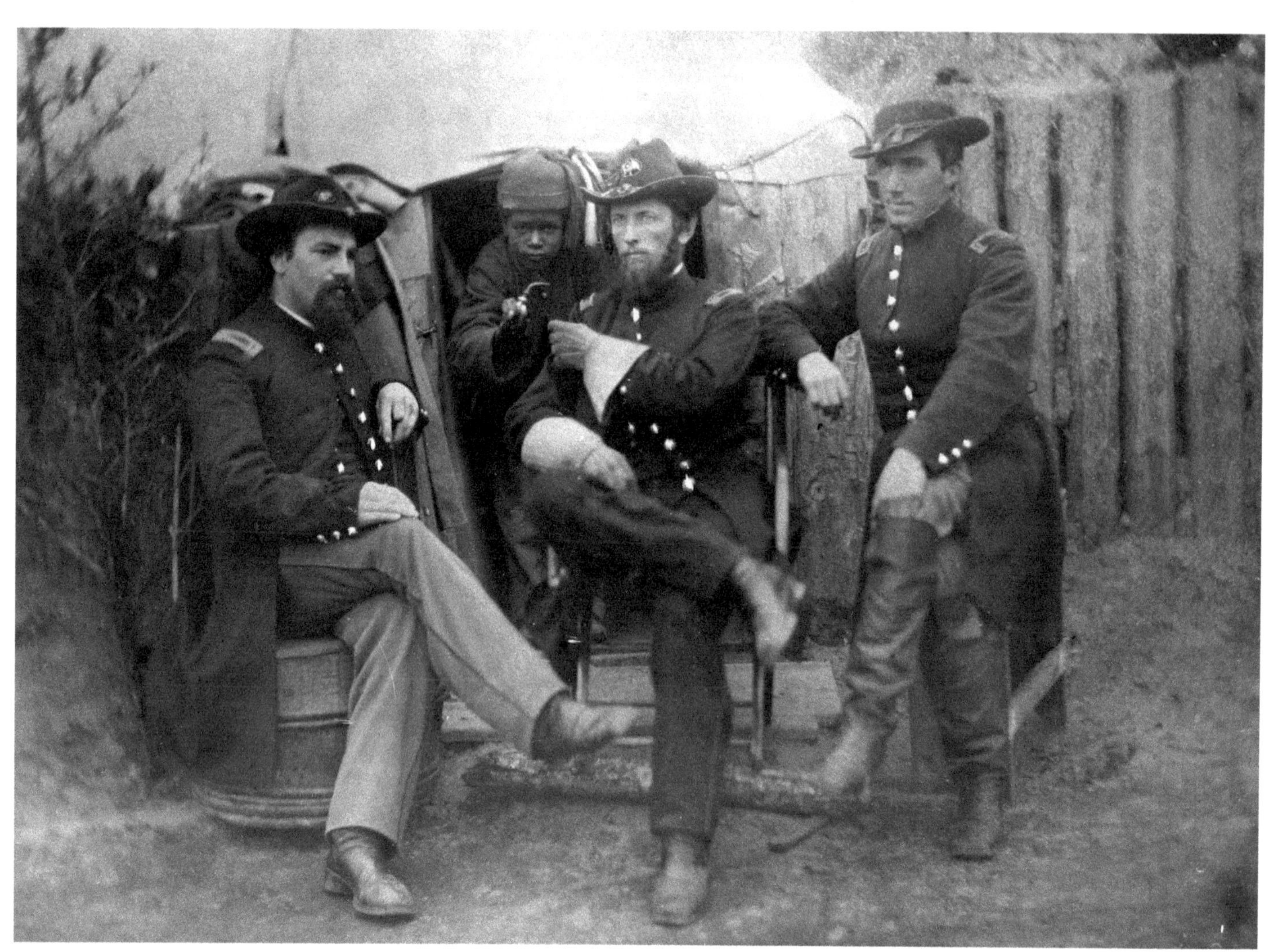

Members of the 75th Ohio Infantry shown here were among the federal troops in the city until the state surrendered in the spring of 1865.

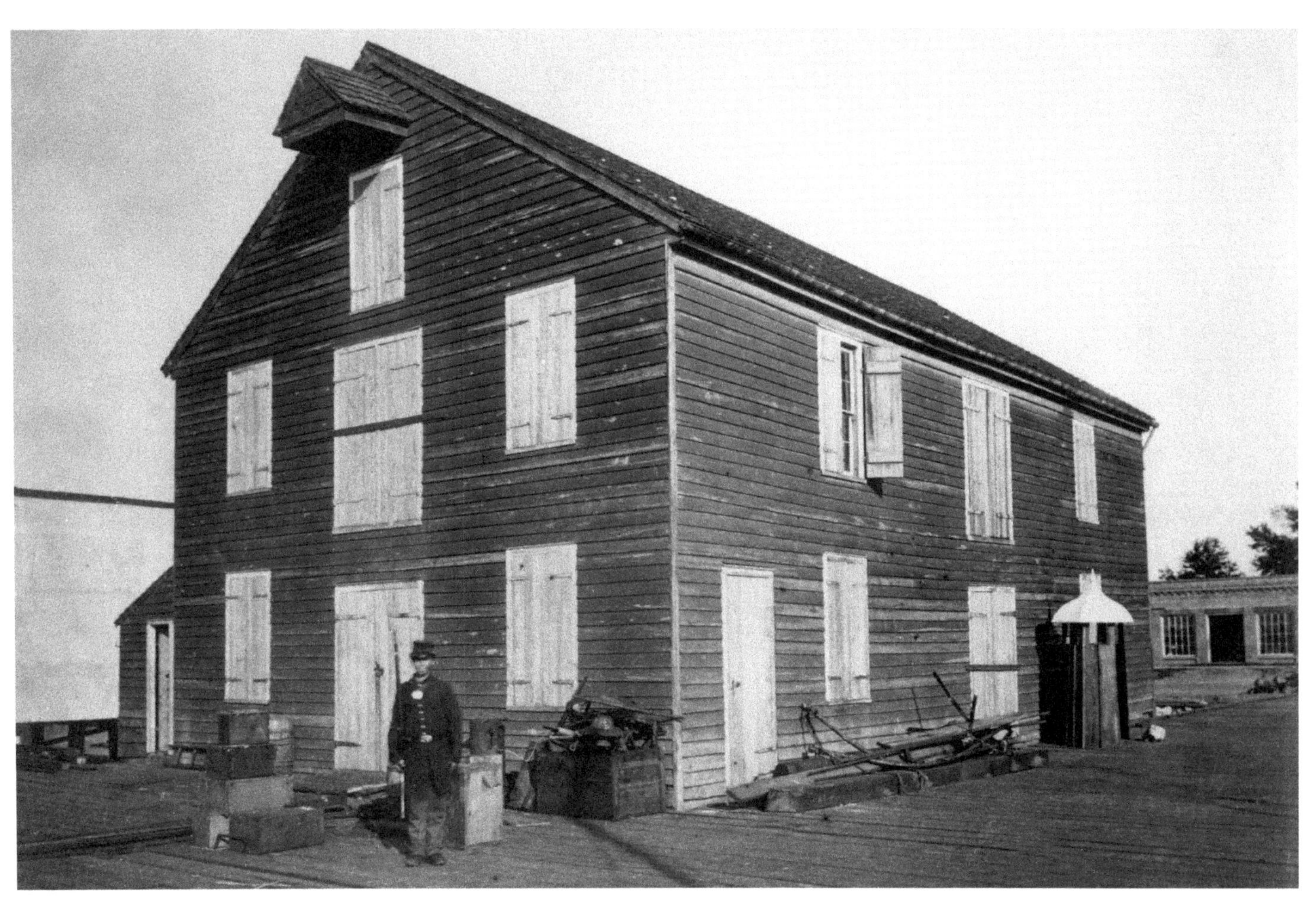

This U.S. boat house was located at the docks at the foot of Ocean Street.

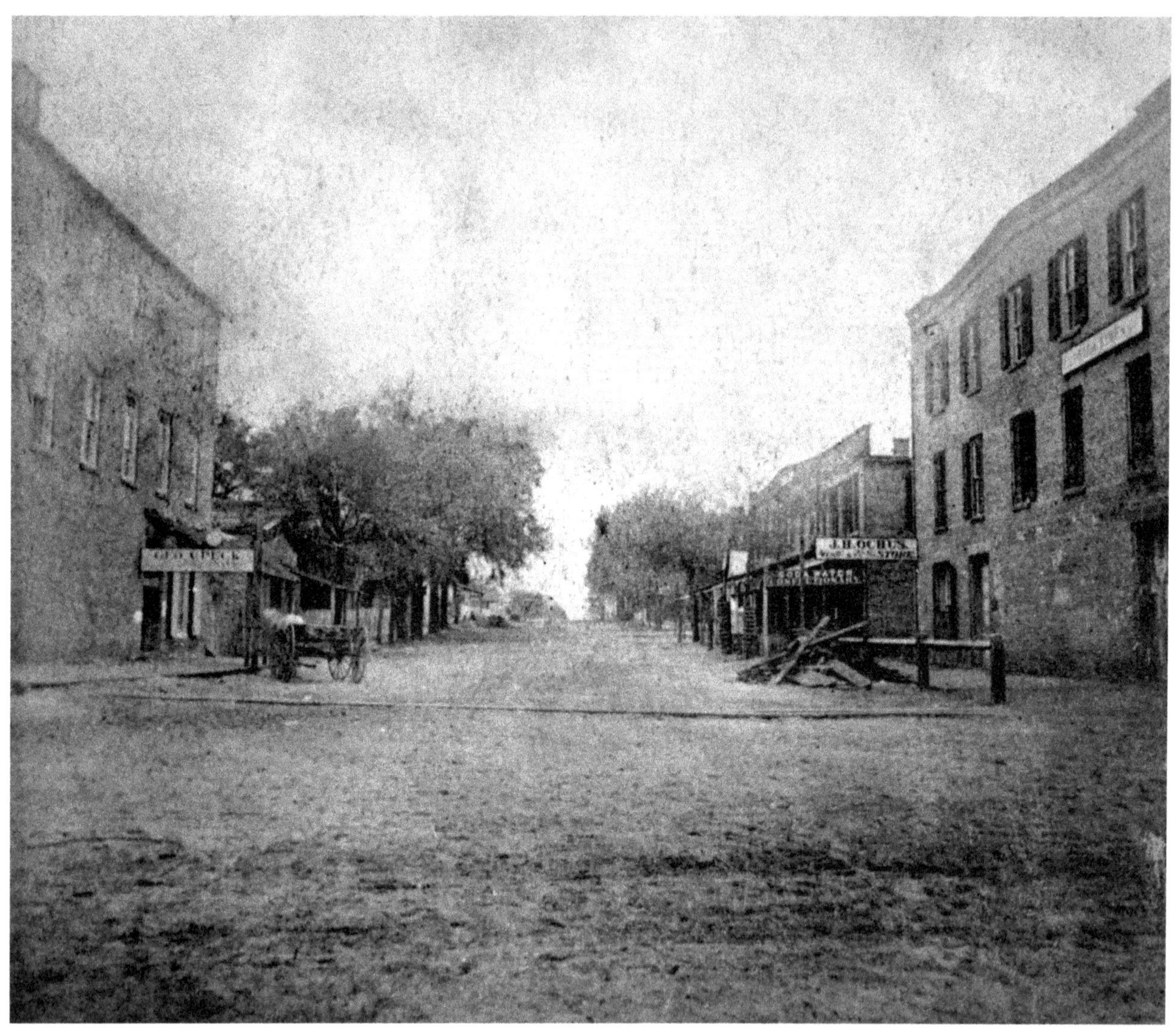

Soon after the war ended the commercial district began to grow in the streets close to the river. Pictured is a view of Ocean Street looking north from Bay.

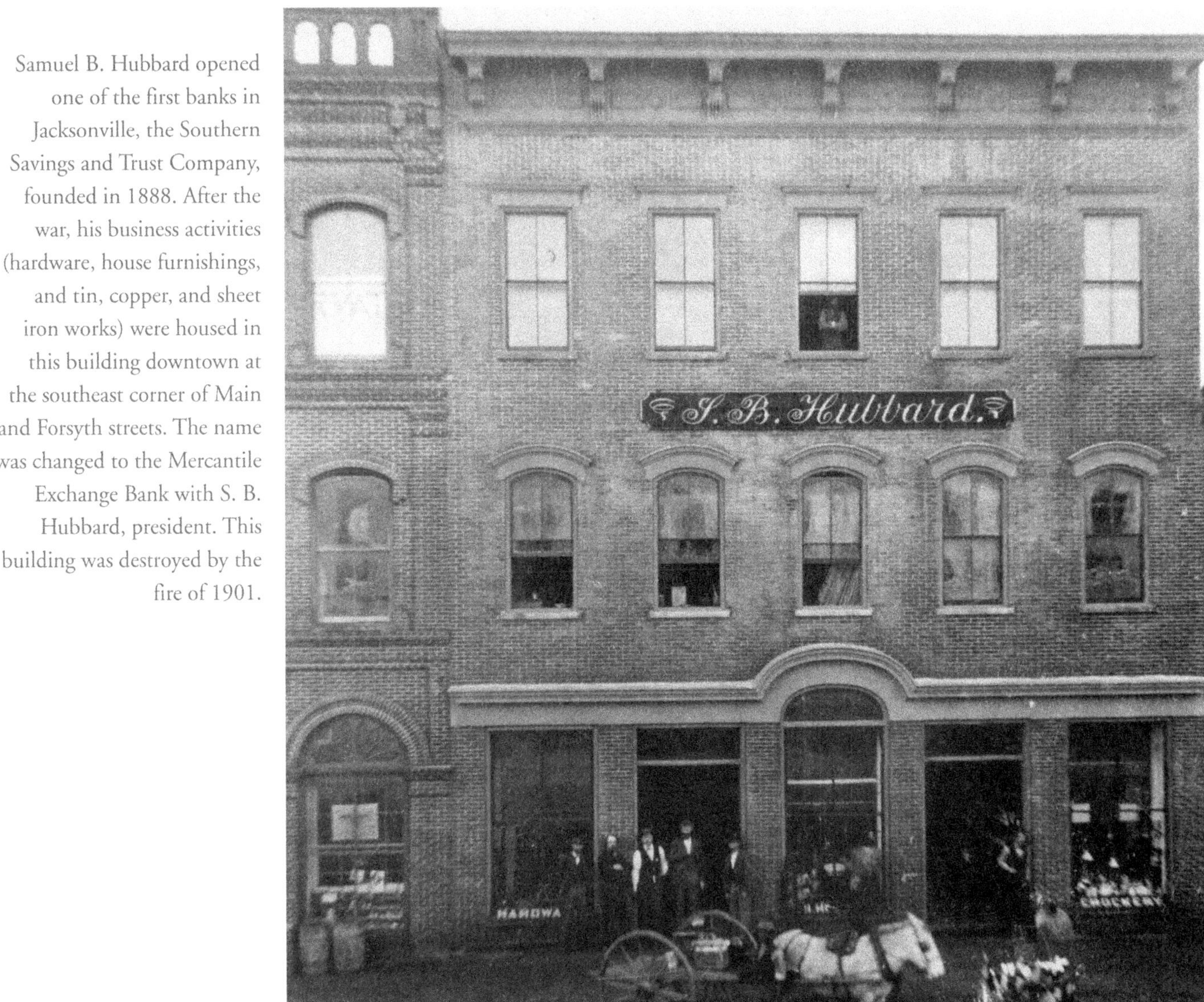

Samuel B. Hubbard opened one of the first banks in Jacksonville, the Southern Savings and Trust Company, founded in 1888. After the war, his business activities (hardware, house furnishings, and tin, copper, and sheet iron works) were housed in this building downtown at the southeast corner of Main and Forsyth streets. The name was changed to the Mercantile Exchange Bank with S. B. Hubbard, president. This building was destroyed by the fire of 1901.

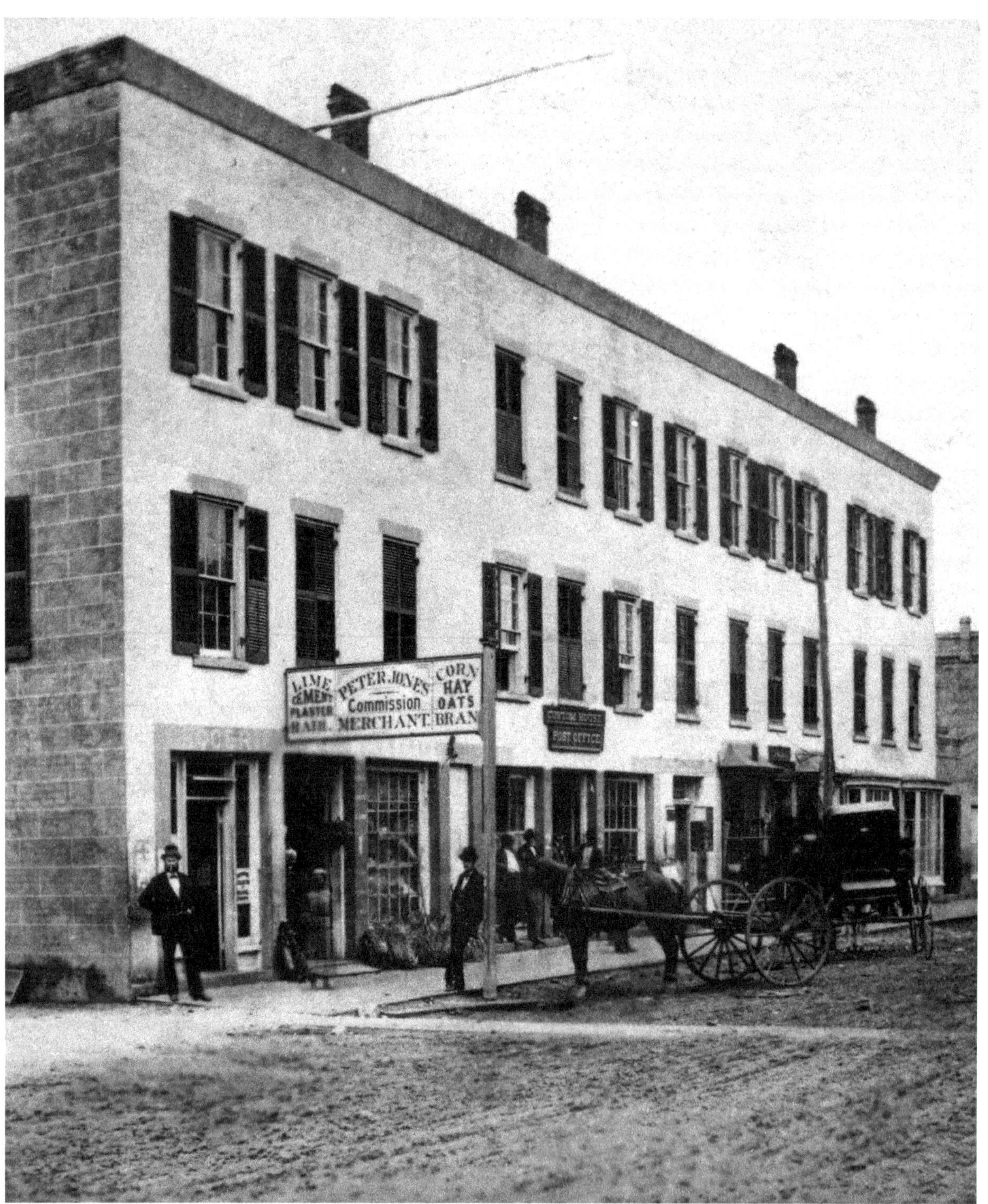

Until 1895, when its permanent headquarters was constructed at Forsyth and Hogan streets, the location of the post office changed with the postmaster. In the 1880s the post office shared quarters with the custom house at the corner of Bay and Union.

The sawmill and lumber business, which characterized Jacksonville early on, became a very lucrative industry in the period after the Civil War.

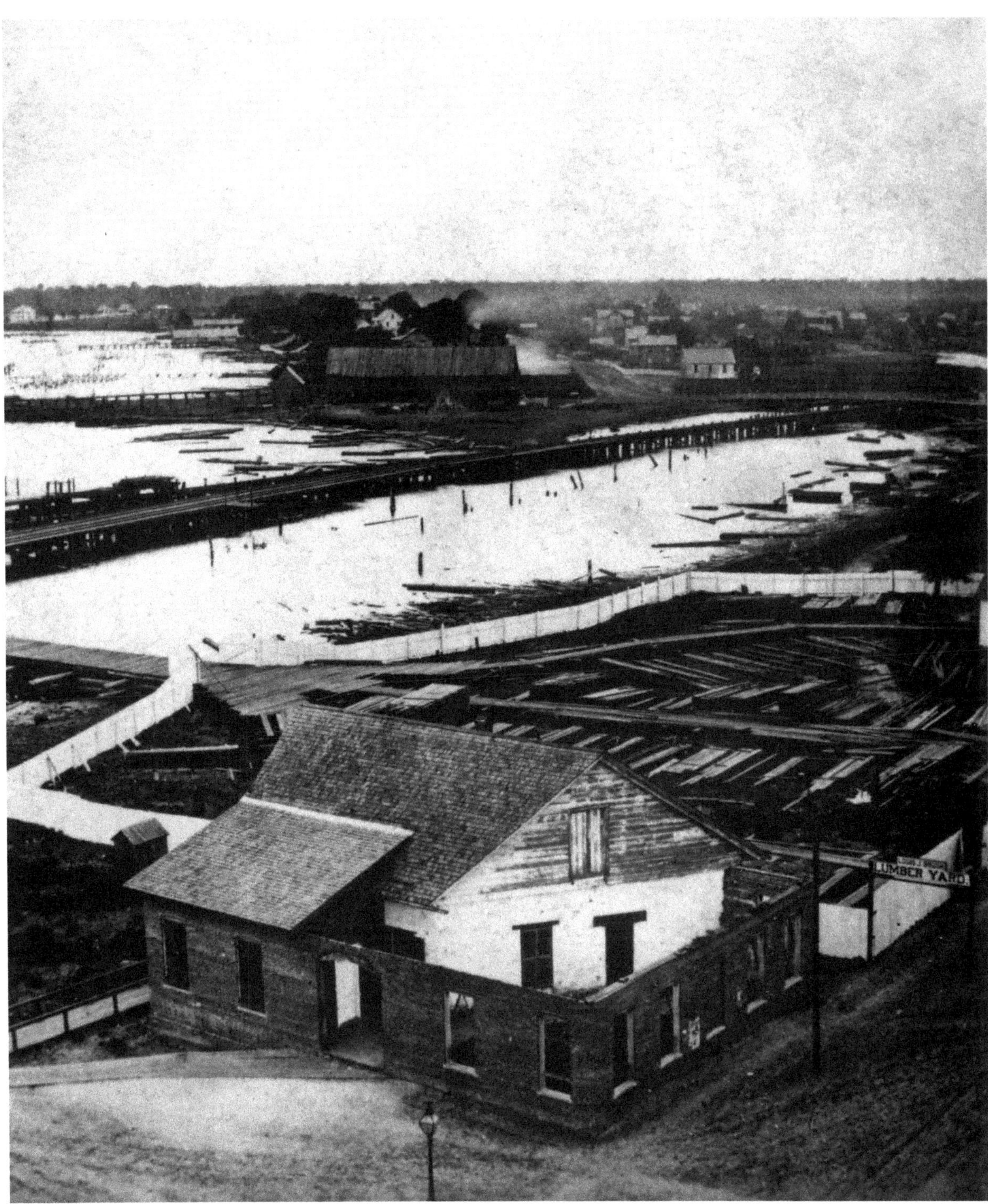

The first mule-drawn trolley cars began operating in Jacksonville in 1880, and the city's first electric streetcar line was introduced 13 years later. Workers like these ones laid tracks as the service expanded.

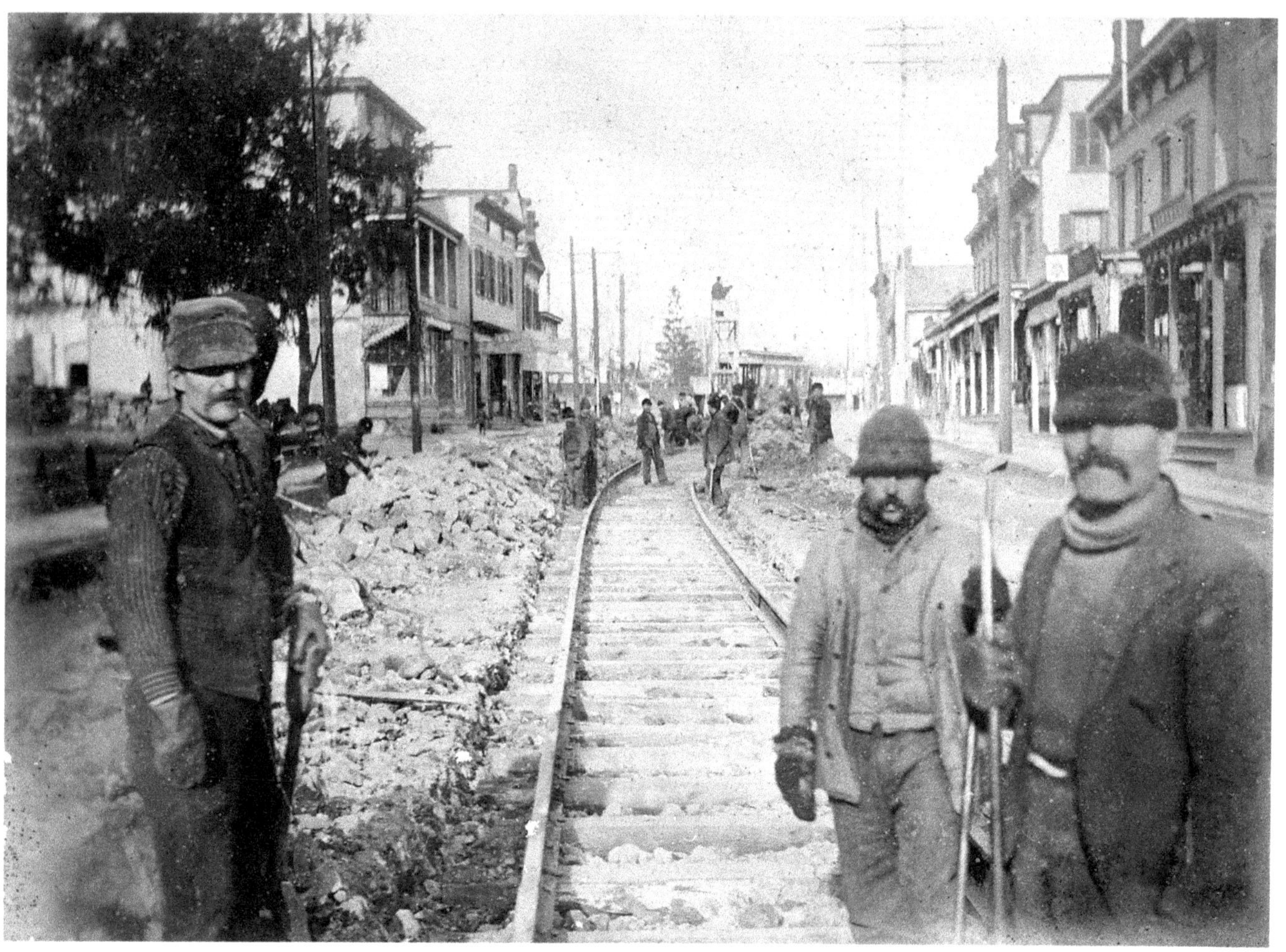

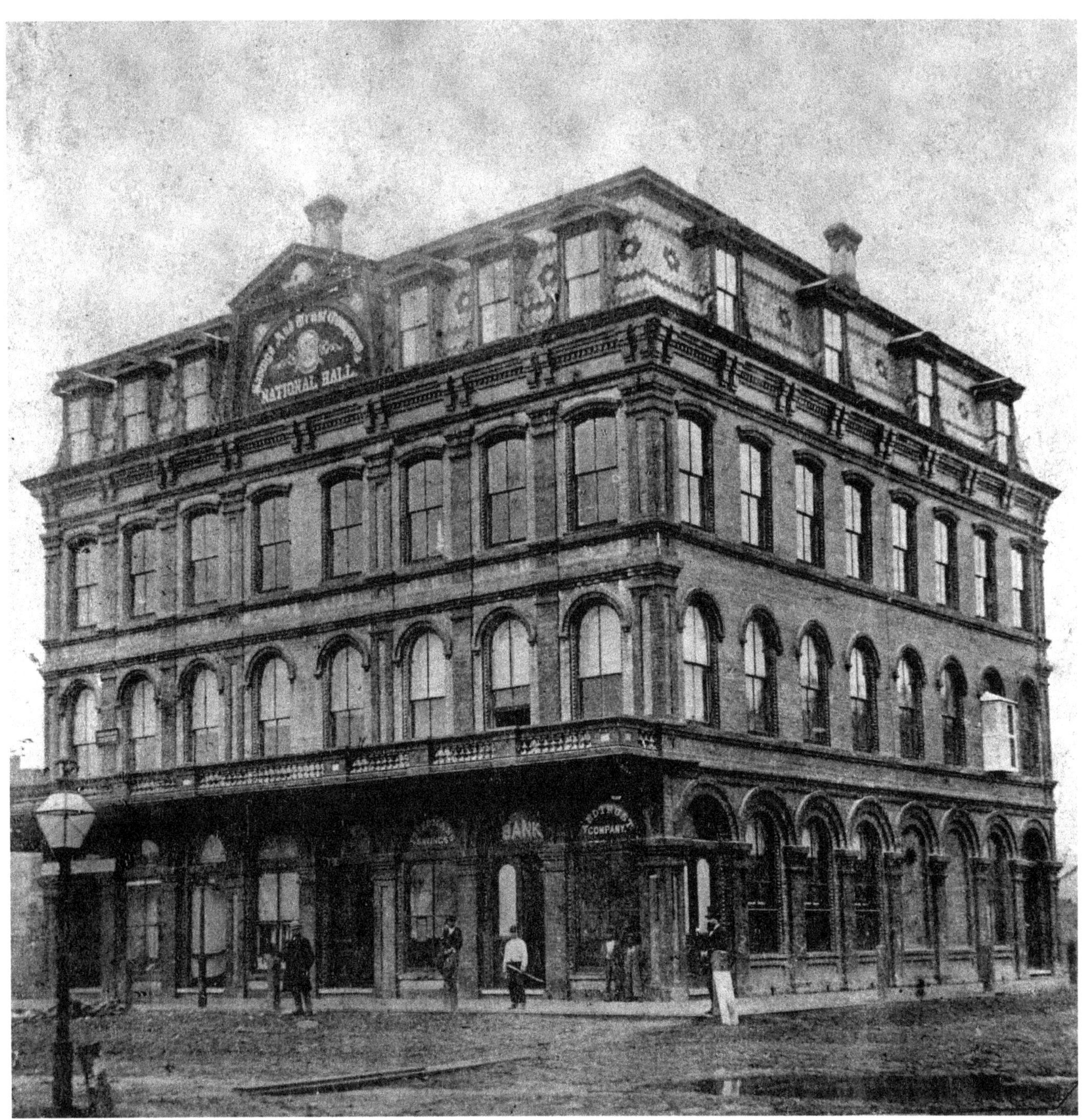

Several banks were established before the Civil War, but none lasted. In 1866 this Freedman's Bank was established for the former slaves in the area. First located at the corner of Bay and Ocean streets, in 1870 the bank operations were moved to this four-story brick building on Forsyth Street. The bank lasted until 1874. This building was destroyed by fire in 1891.

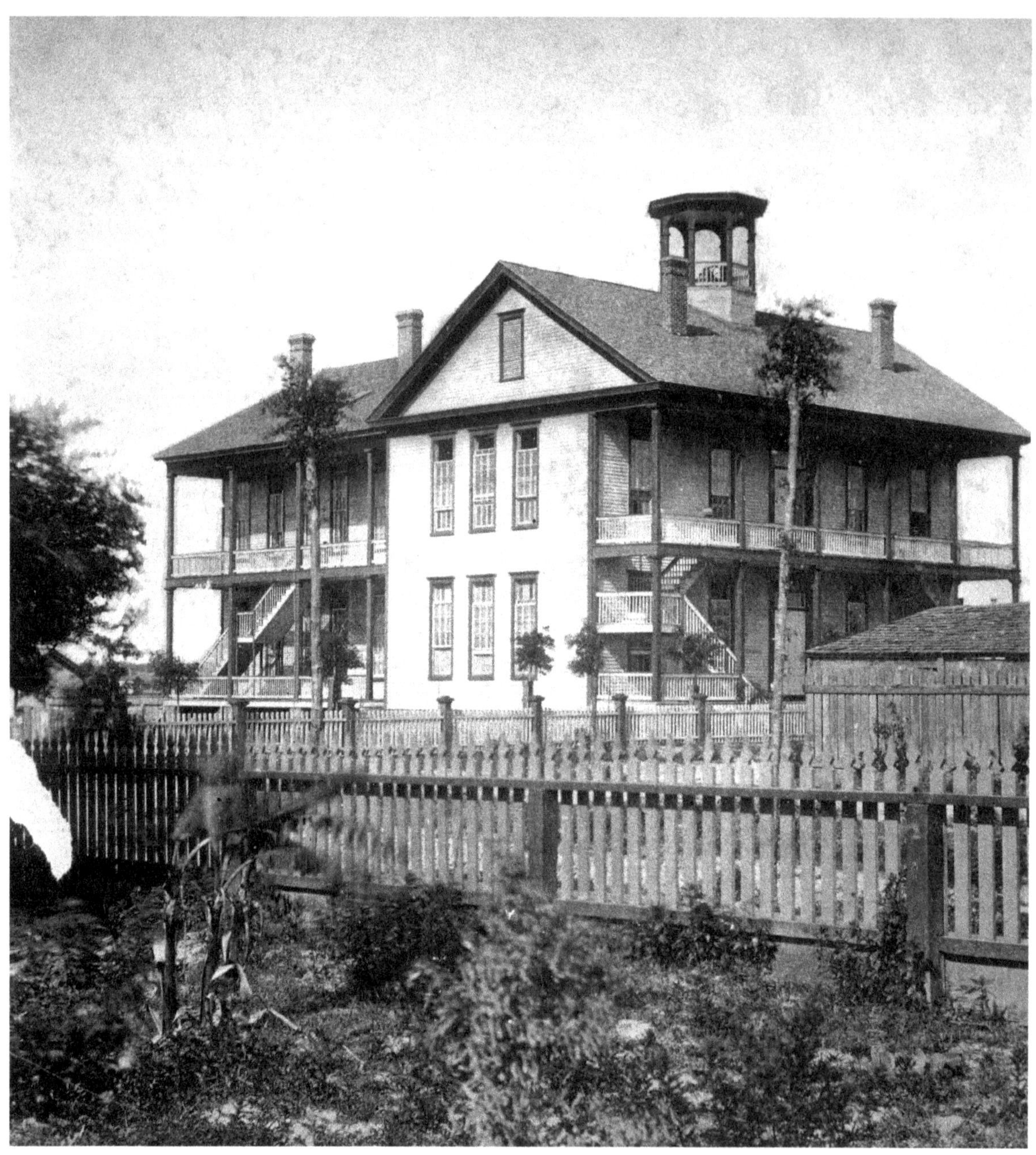

Stanton Institute was established in 1868 by the Freedmen's Bureau and a group of local black citizens to educate African American children in the area. It was named after Edwin Stanton, who served as President Abraham Lincoln's Secretary of War. The school, pictured here in 1870, provided a grammar school education and was incorporated into the Duval County schools that year.

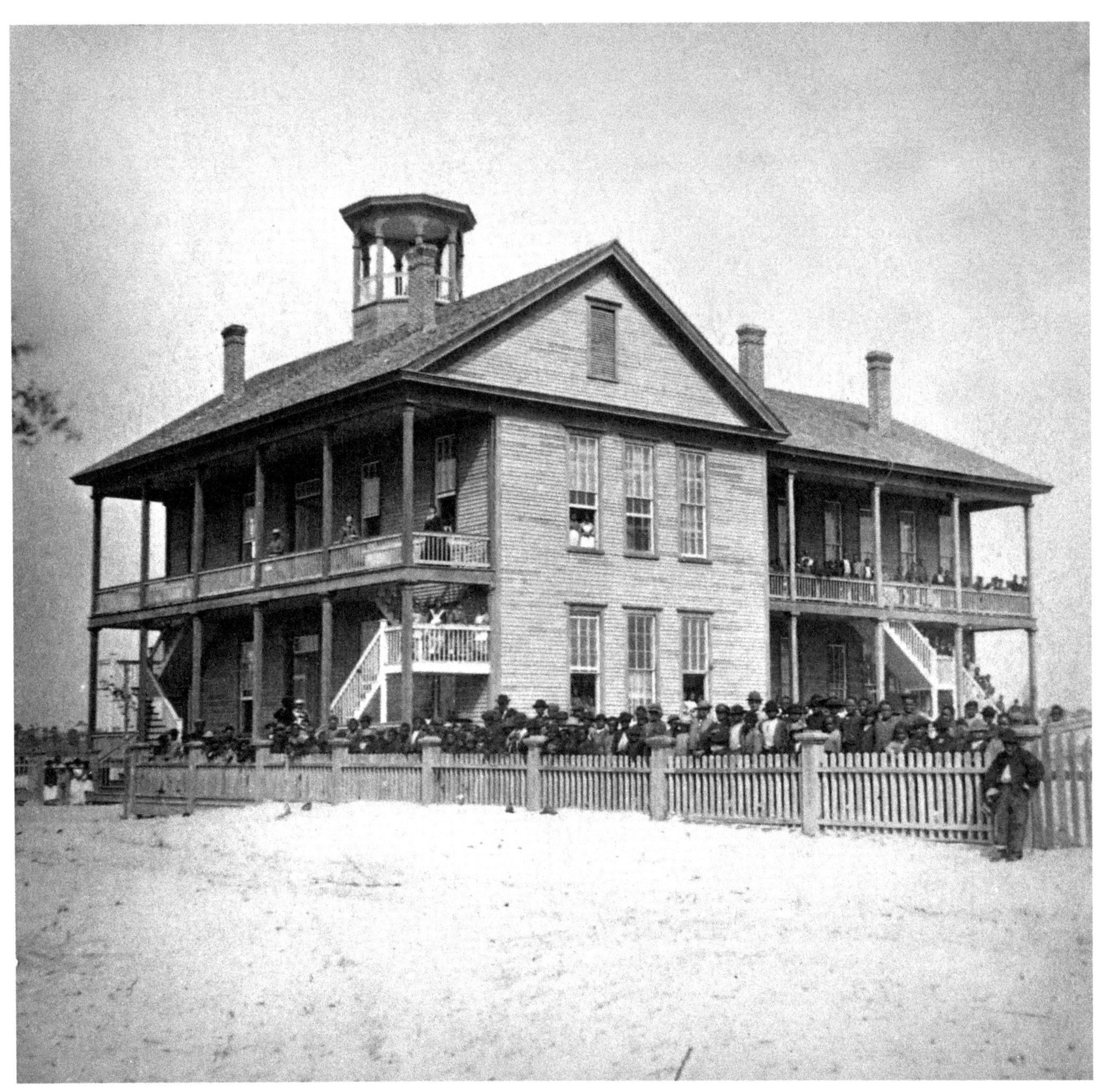

Among the pupils shown here in front of Stanton Institute in 1880 may have been James Weldon and John Rosamond Johnson. Their mother, Helen Dillet Johnson, taught at the school.

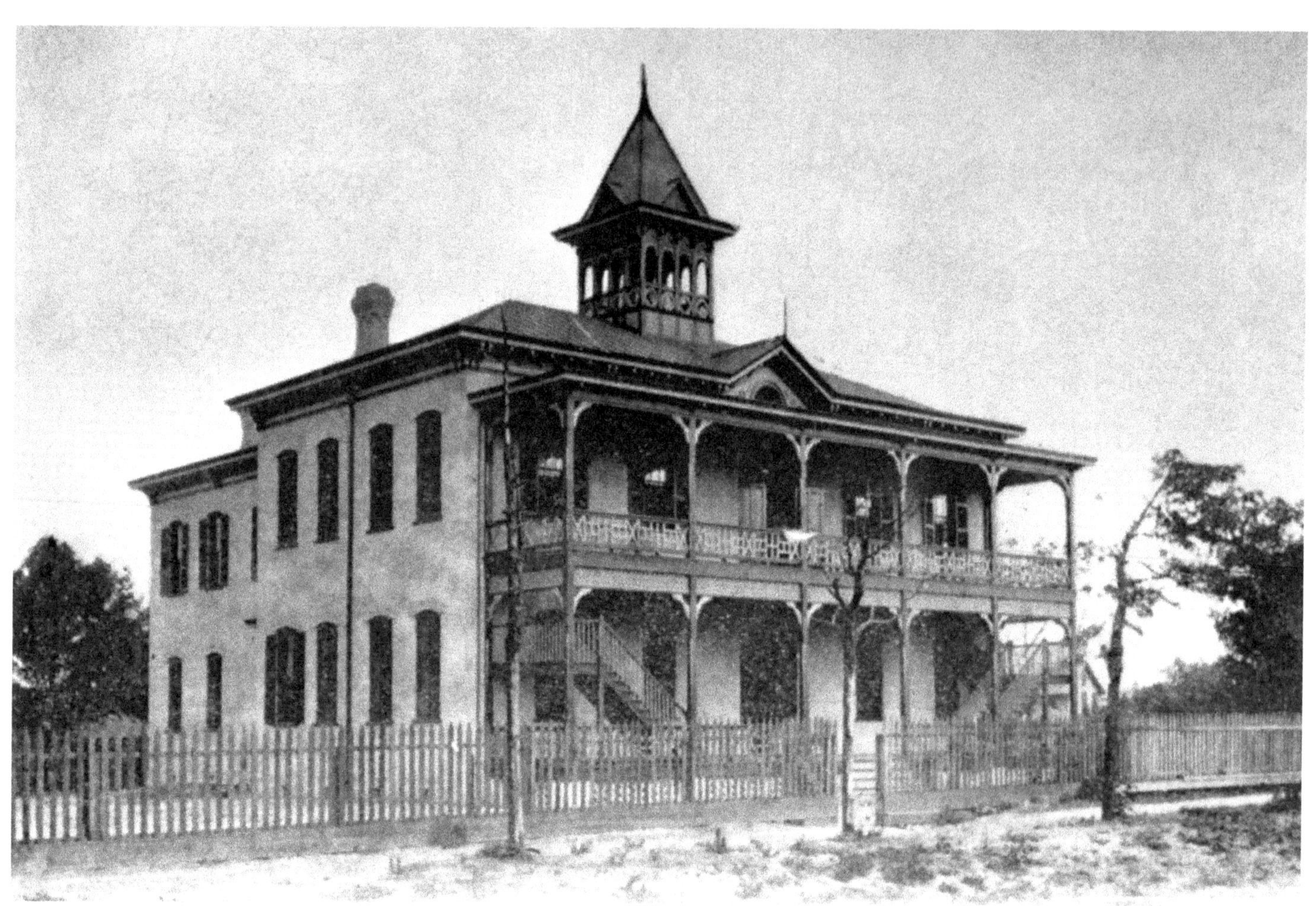

By the 1890s, when this picture was taken, James Weldon Johnson had returned to the school as principal. Under his supervision, the Stanton became the first public institution to offer secondary education for black youth.

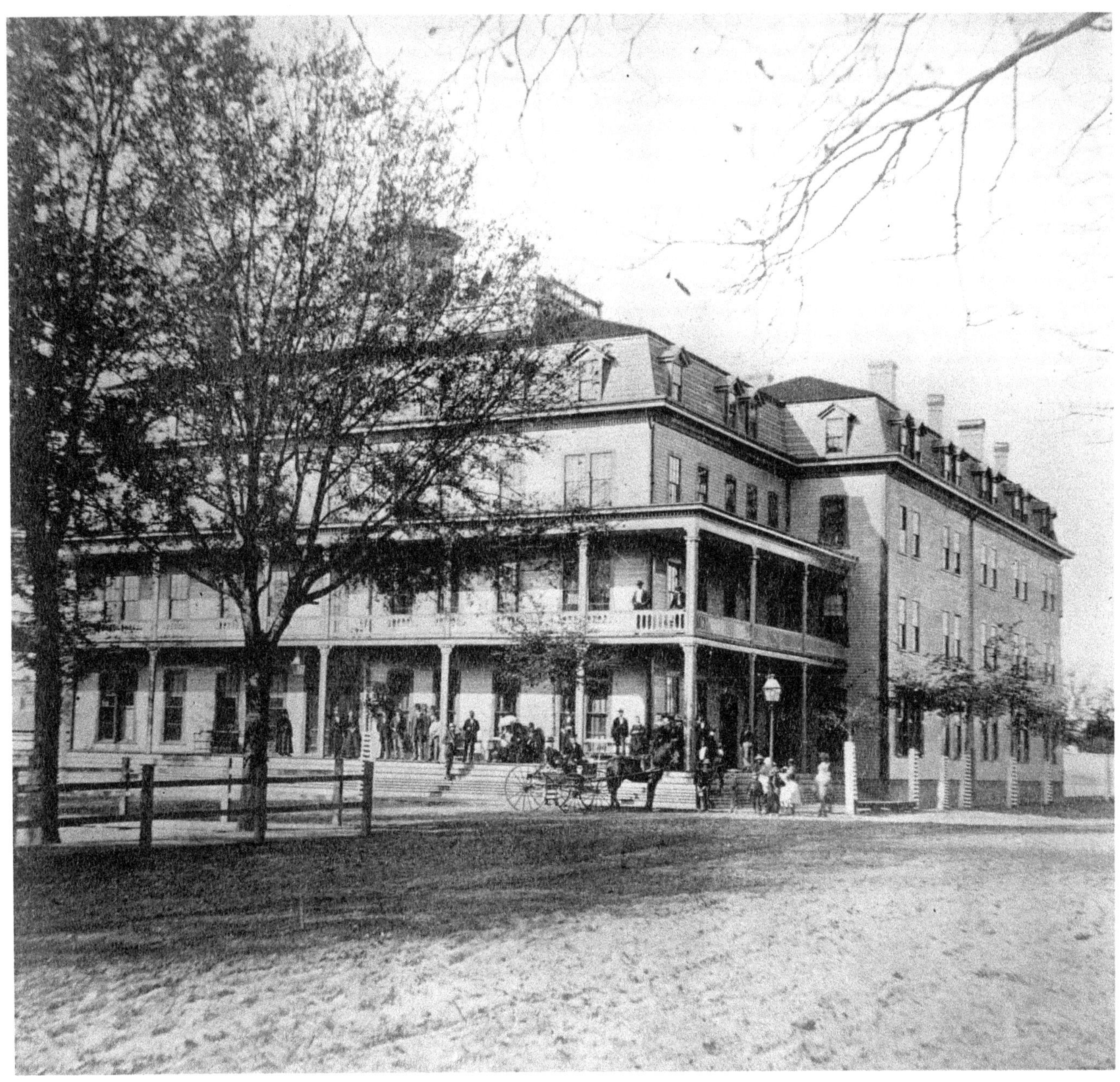

The St. James Hotel was built in 1869, financed by northern capitalists. It grew to be the most famous hotel in the South and was a mecca for wealthy tourists in Florida. The hotel was among the architectural casualties of the Great Fire of 1901. It stood across from Hemming Park.

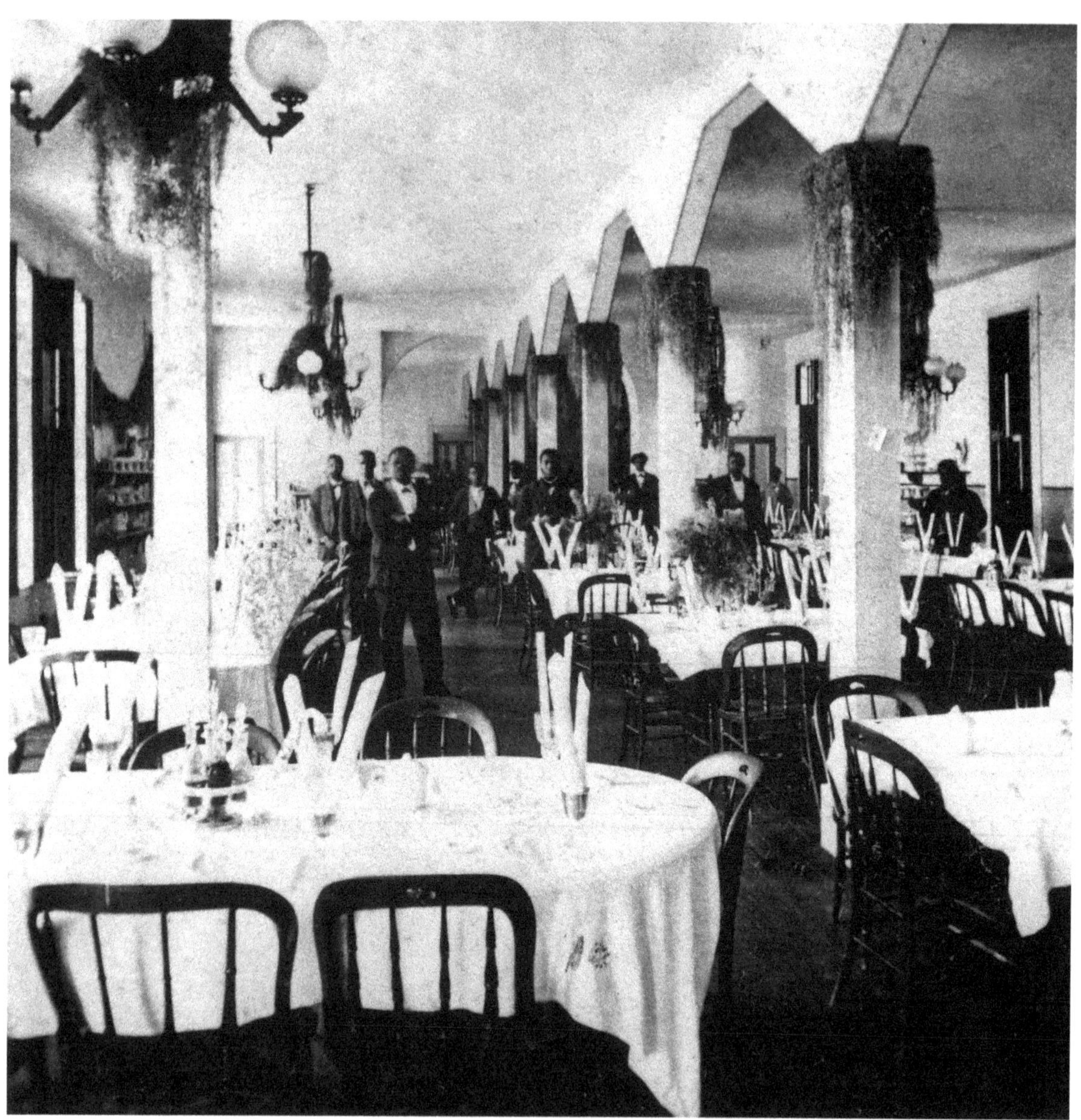

James Johnson, the father of James Weldon and John Rosamond, served as the head waiter of the St. James Hotel. The wait staff is shown here in the hotel's dining room. It was mainly a winter hotel, catering to guests during that season.

The residence of S. H. Stowe is shown here in 1875.

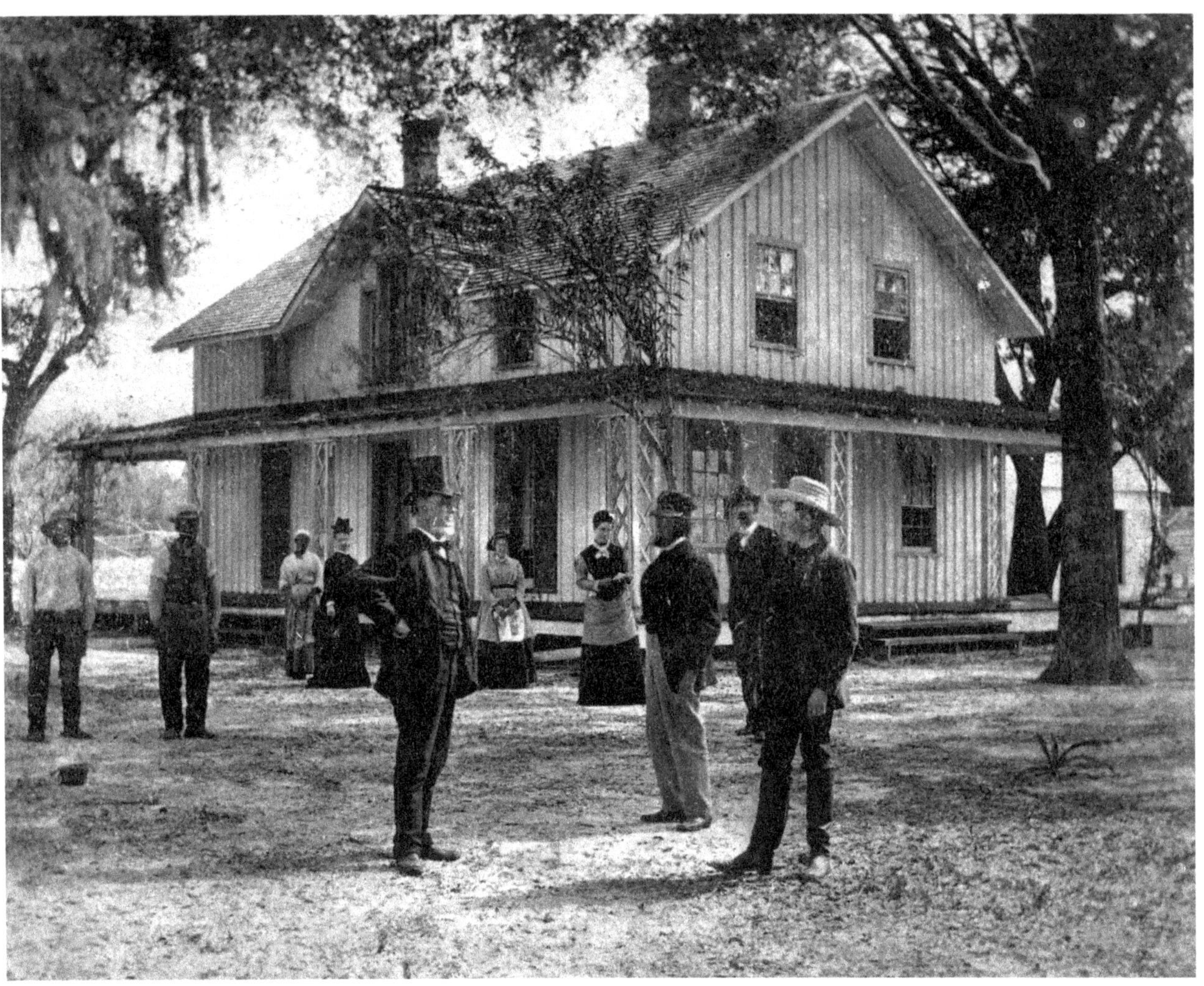

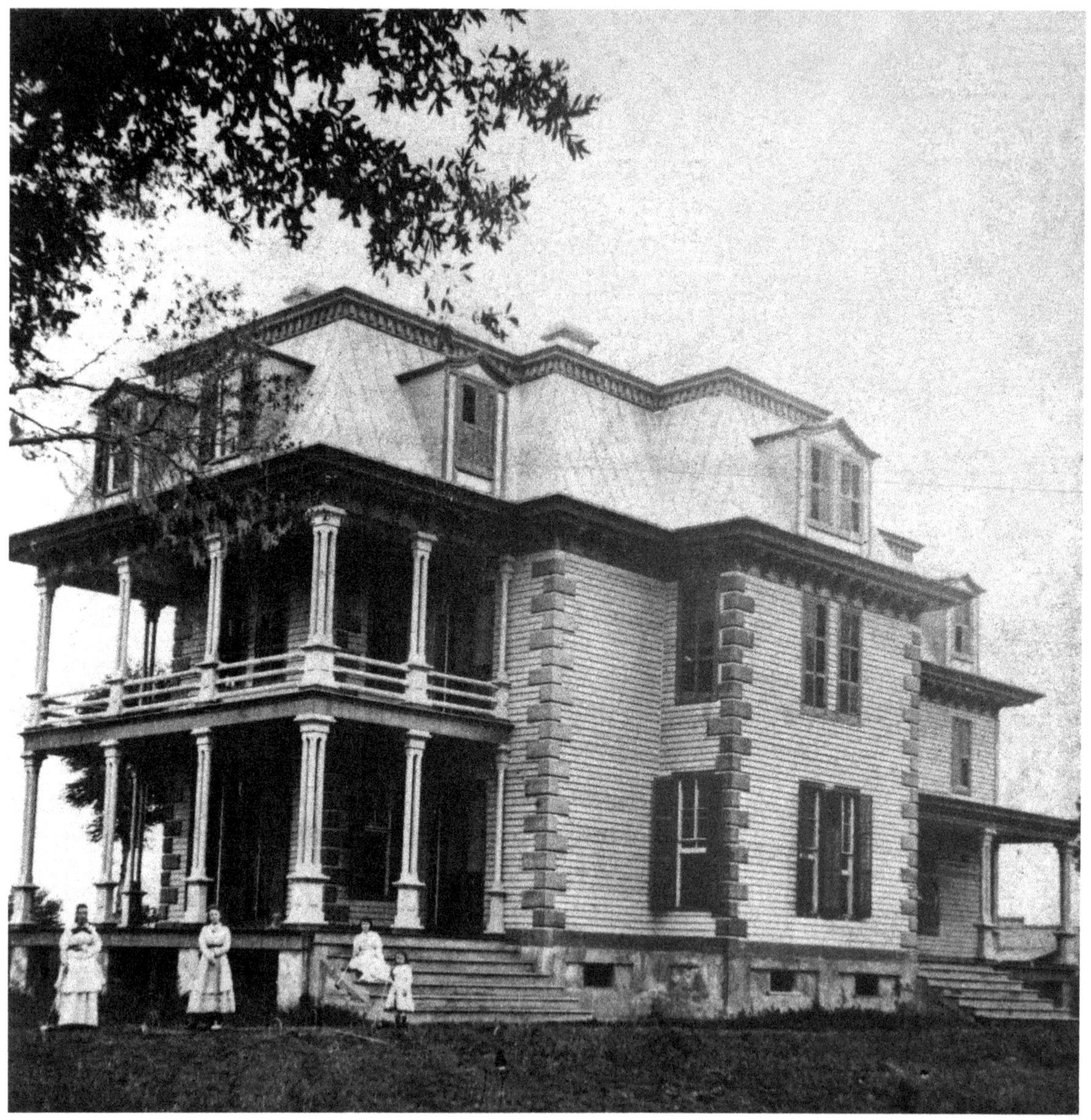

Riverside, located along the river, in 1869

Hotels like the Ocean House, pictured here, enjoyed a lucrative business in the winter season in the late nineteenth century, when Jacksonville was known as the "Winter City of Summerland."

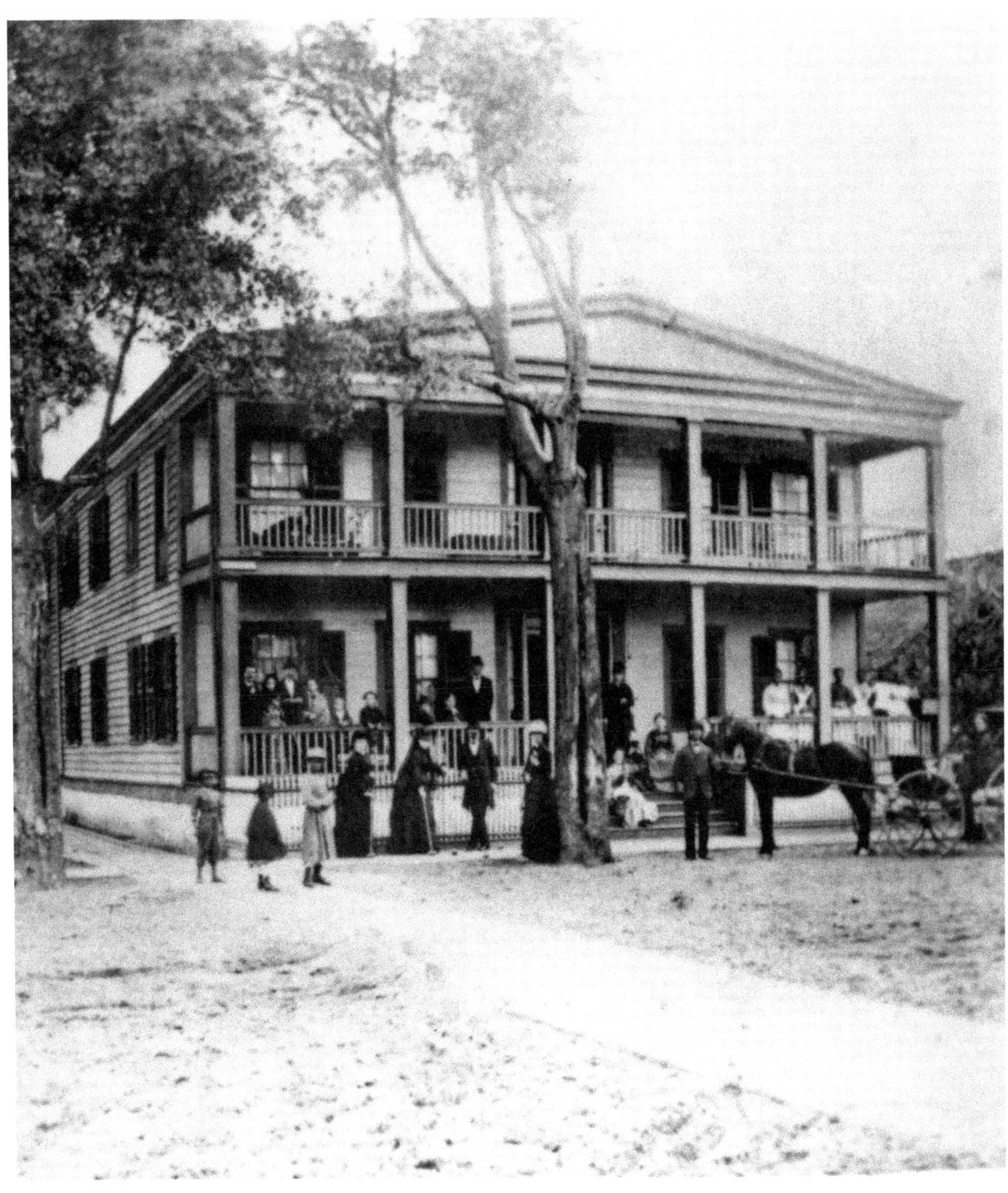

At the end of the nineteenth century, California rose to rival Florida as a place to visit, and began to siphon off tourists. Another blow to Jacksonville's tourism industry was the yellow fever epidemic in 1888. The city weathered the storms and businessmen continued to invest in the hotel industry. The Grand National Hotel, pictured here in 1890, is proof of confidence in the continued appeal of the city. The Grand National was located at the corner of West Bay and Julia streets.

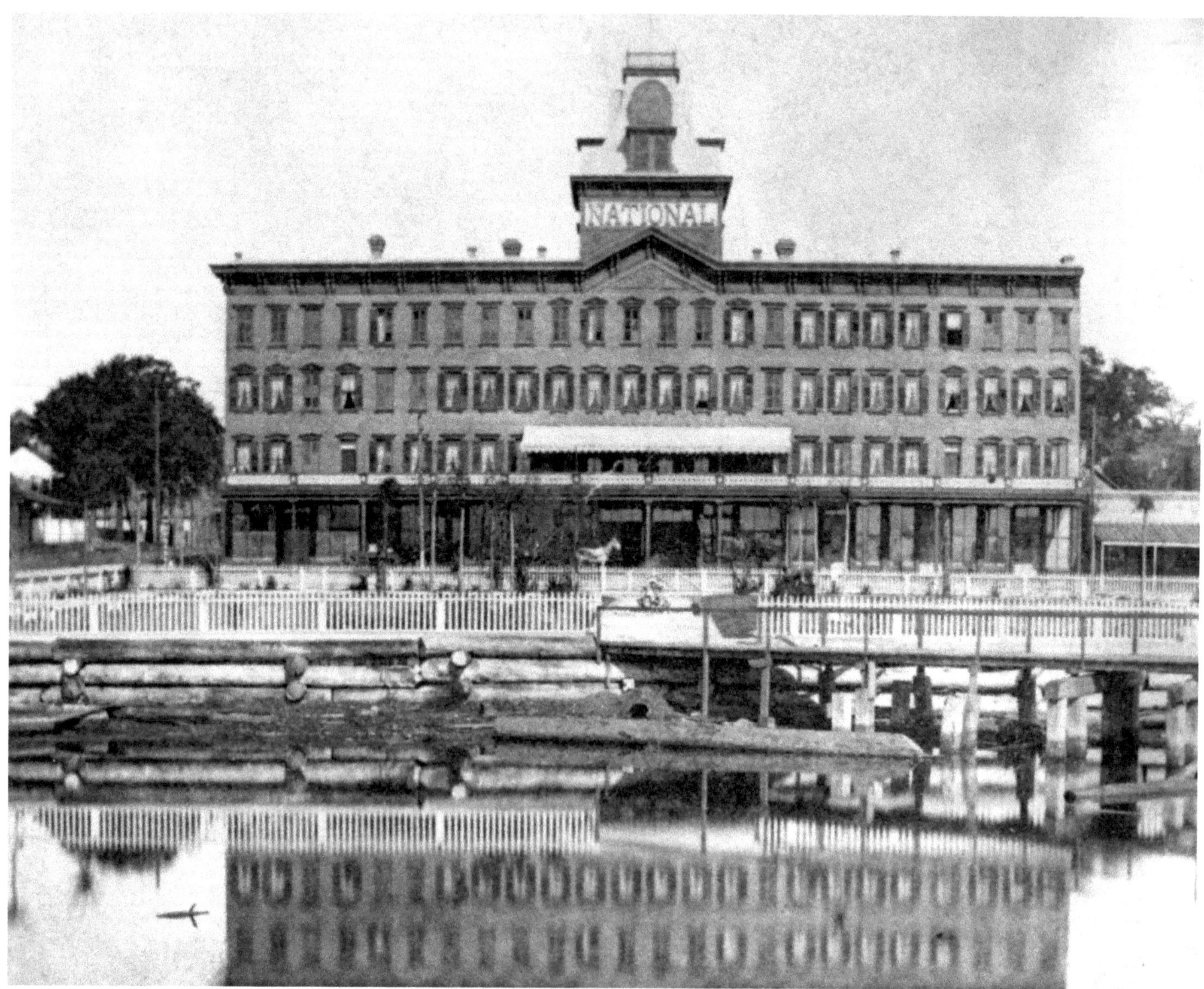

The Florida Atlantic and Gulf Central Railroad was acquired by Henry Plant and combined with other Florida lines in the 1870s. By the following decade, Henry Flagler had replaced Plant as the chief railroad magnate in Florida. Plant and Flagler helped develop Jacksonville into the state's most important distribution center.

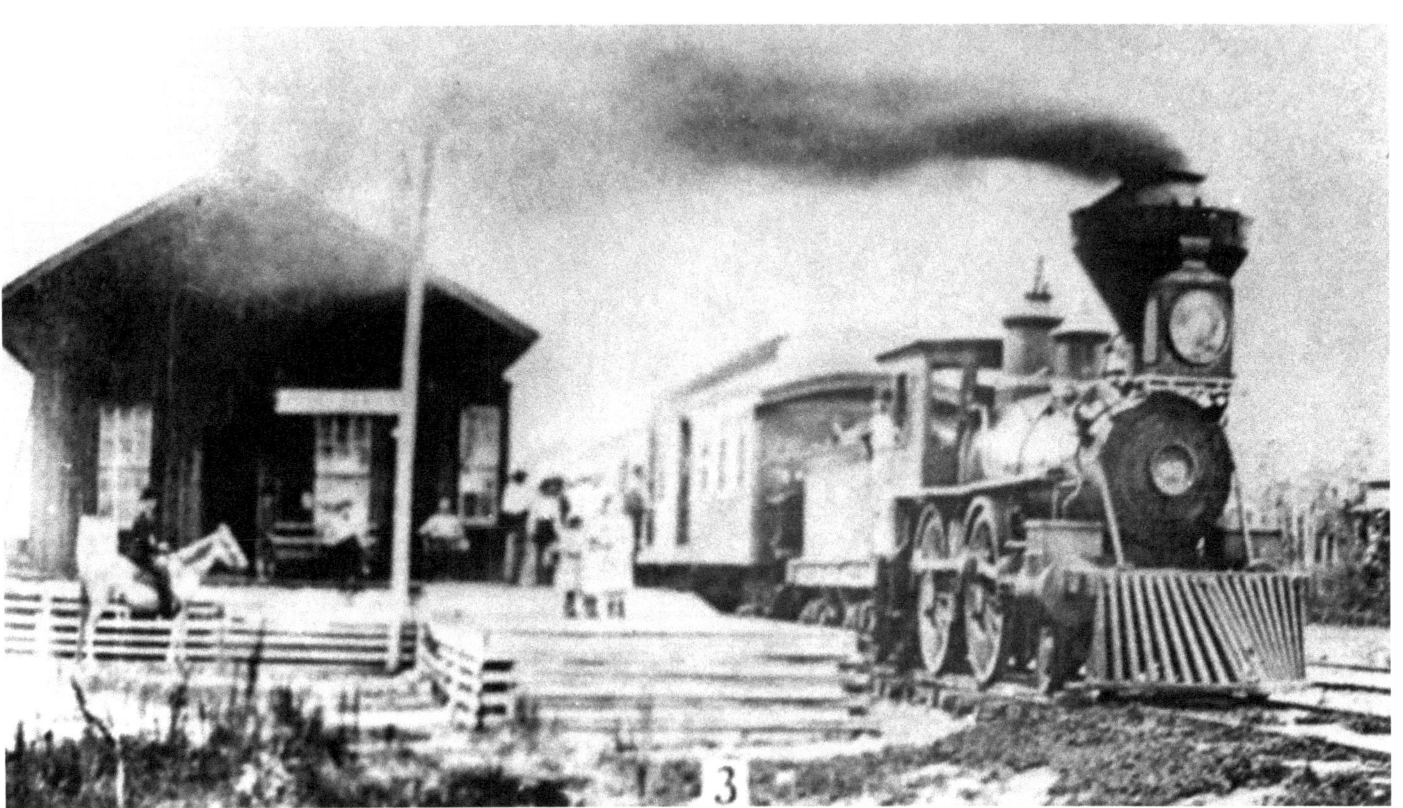

A view of Bull Street

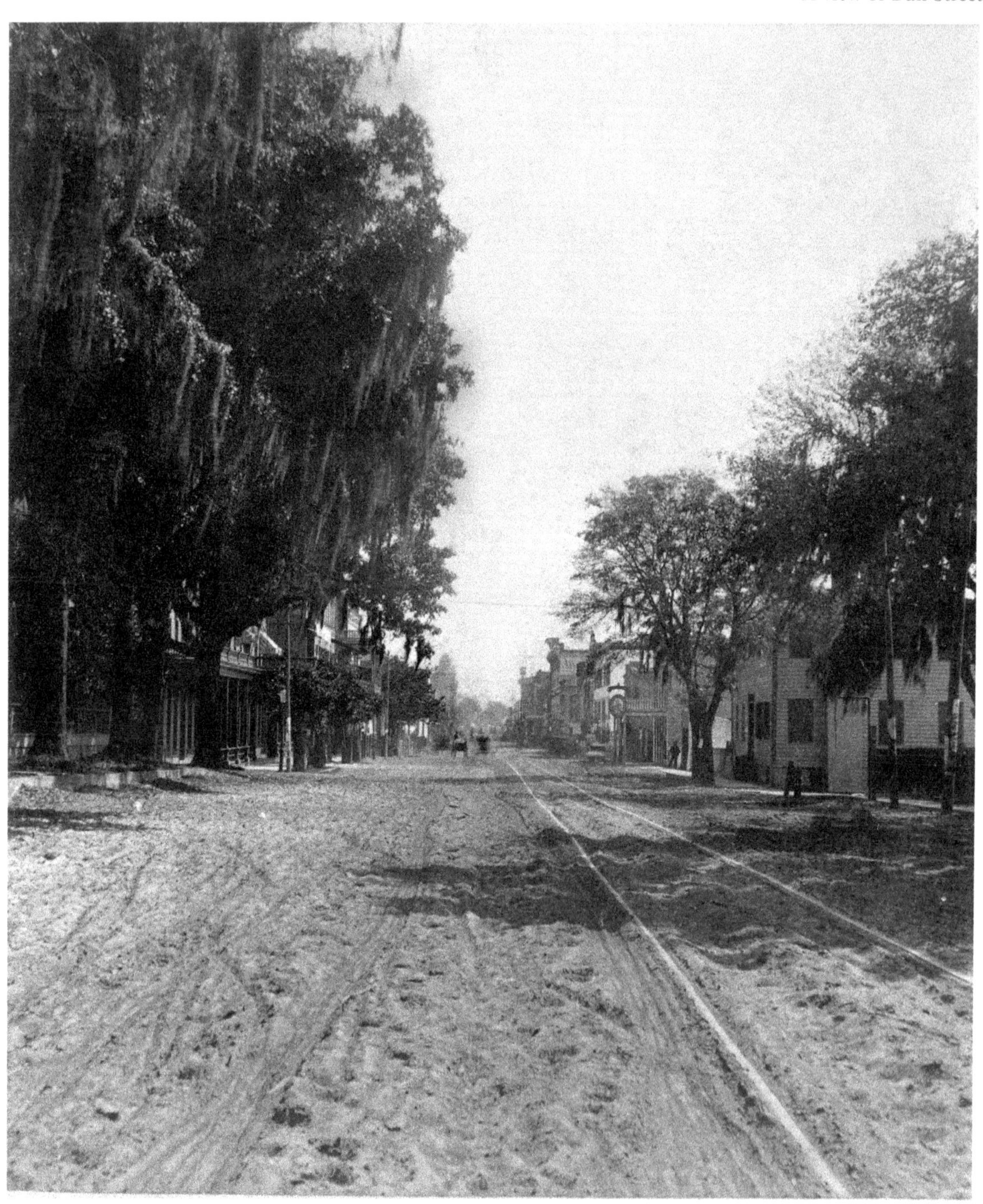

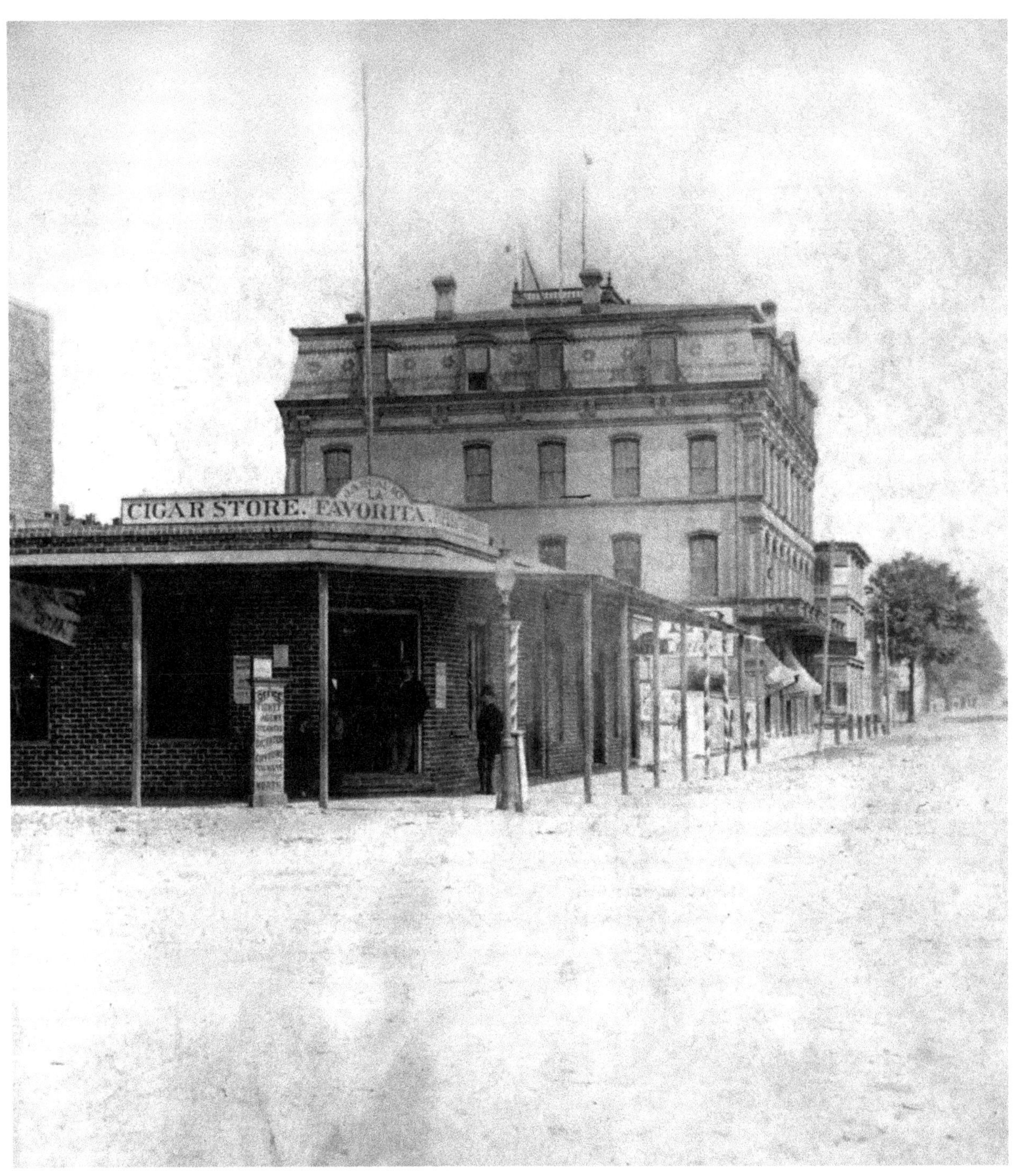

An early view of Main Street (then called Pine Street) from Bay in 1880

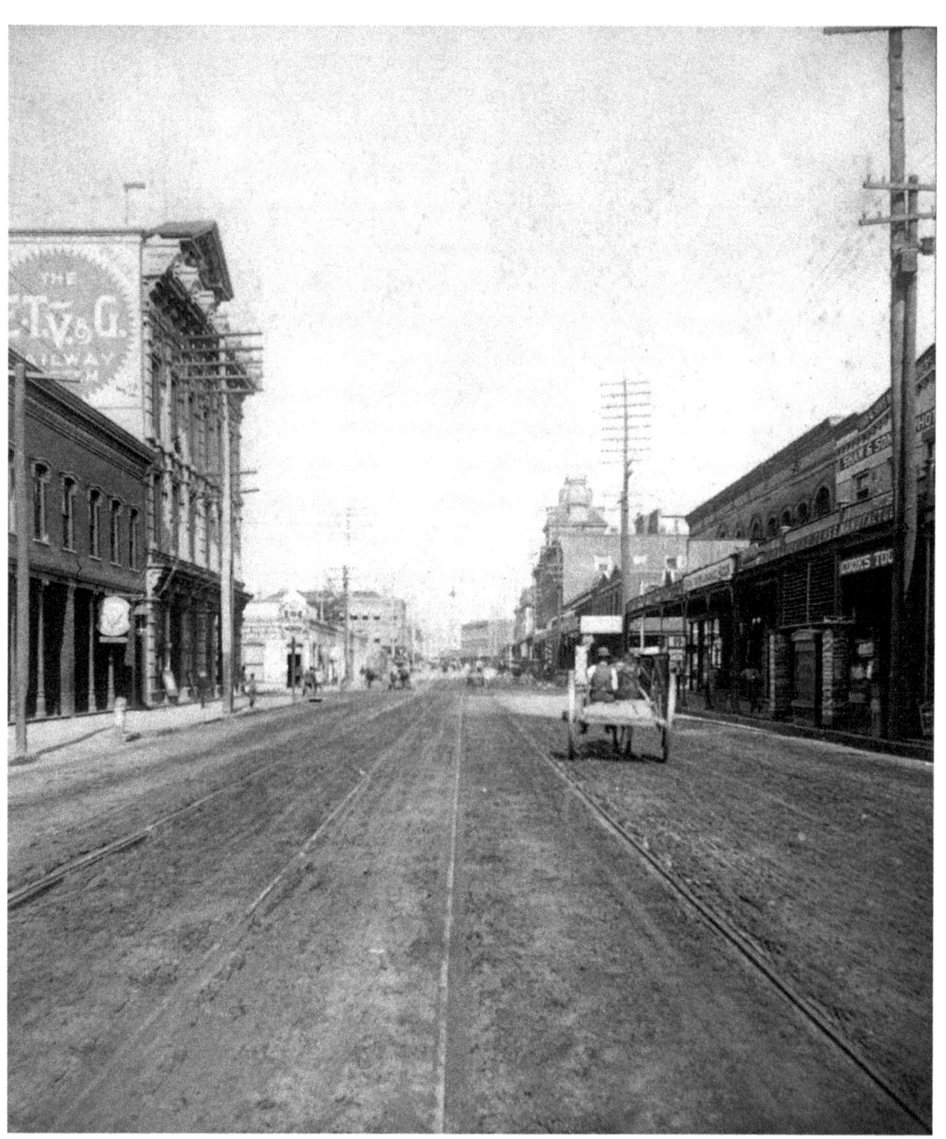

View of Bay Street, a central business district

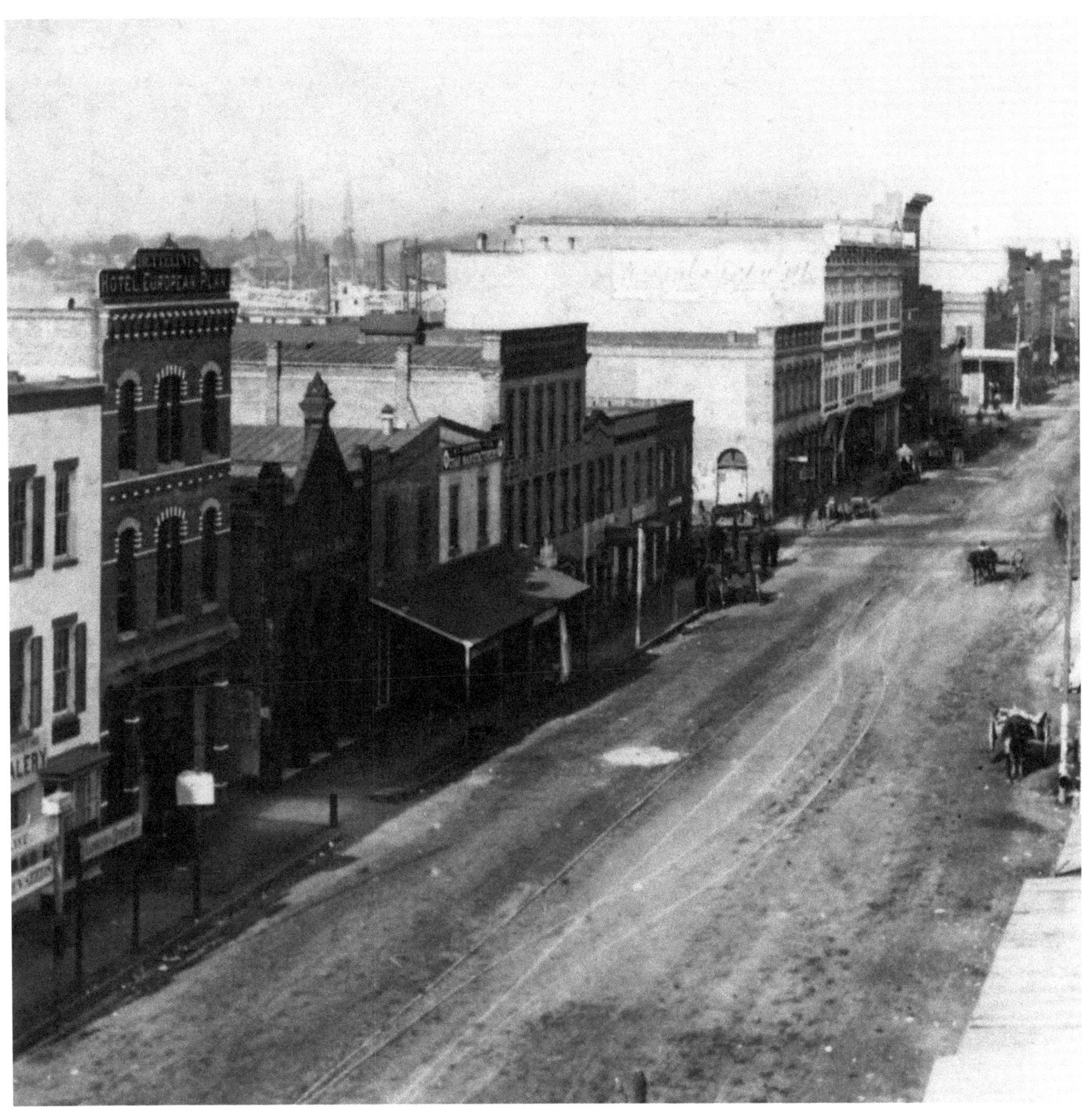

Bay Street from above

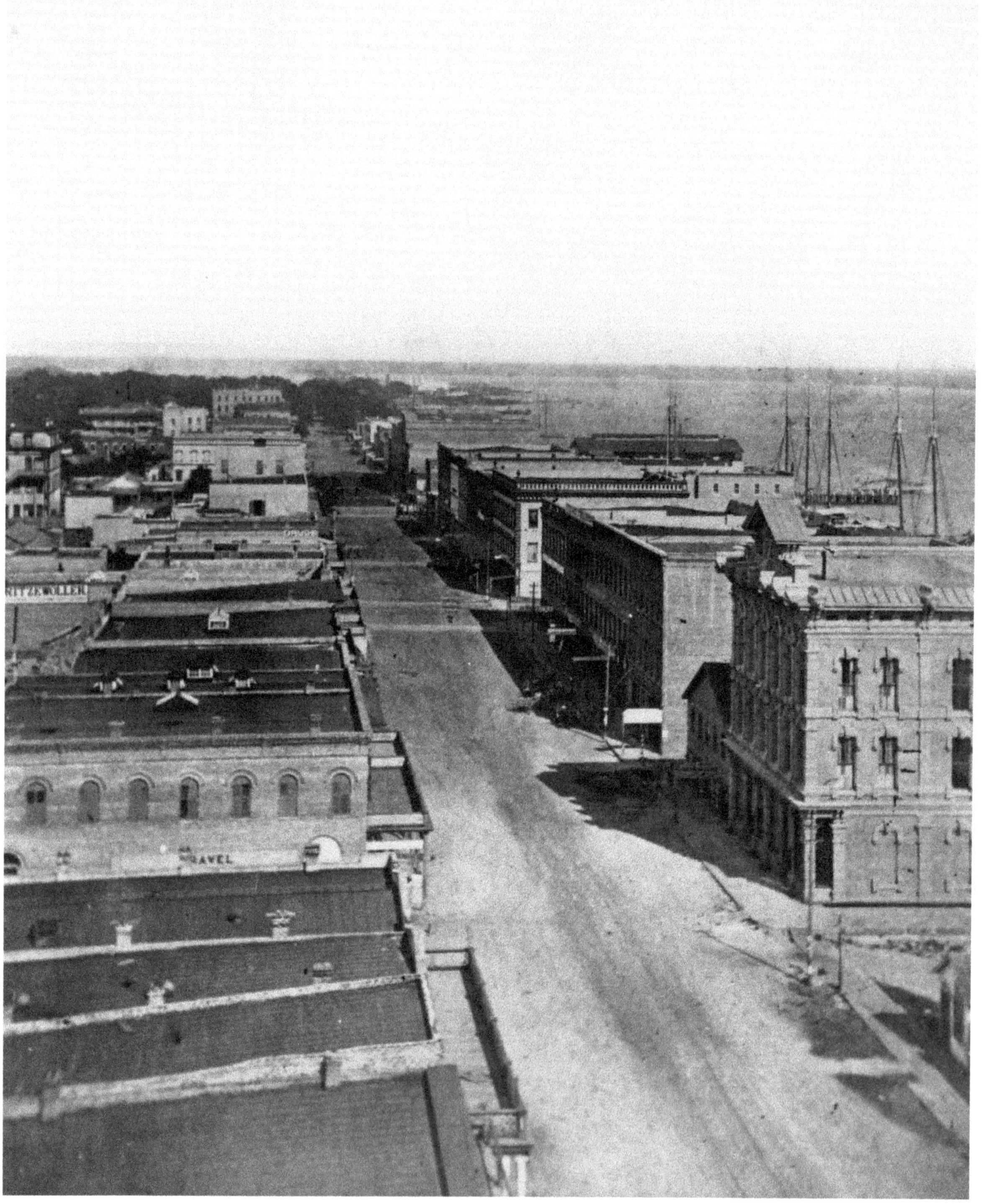

Bay Street rooftops, with the St. Johns River visible in the distance

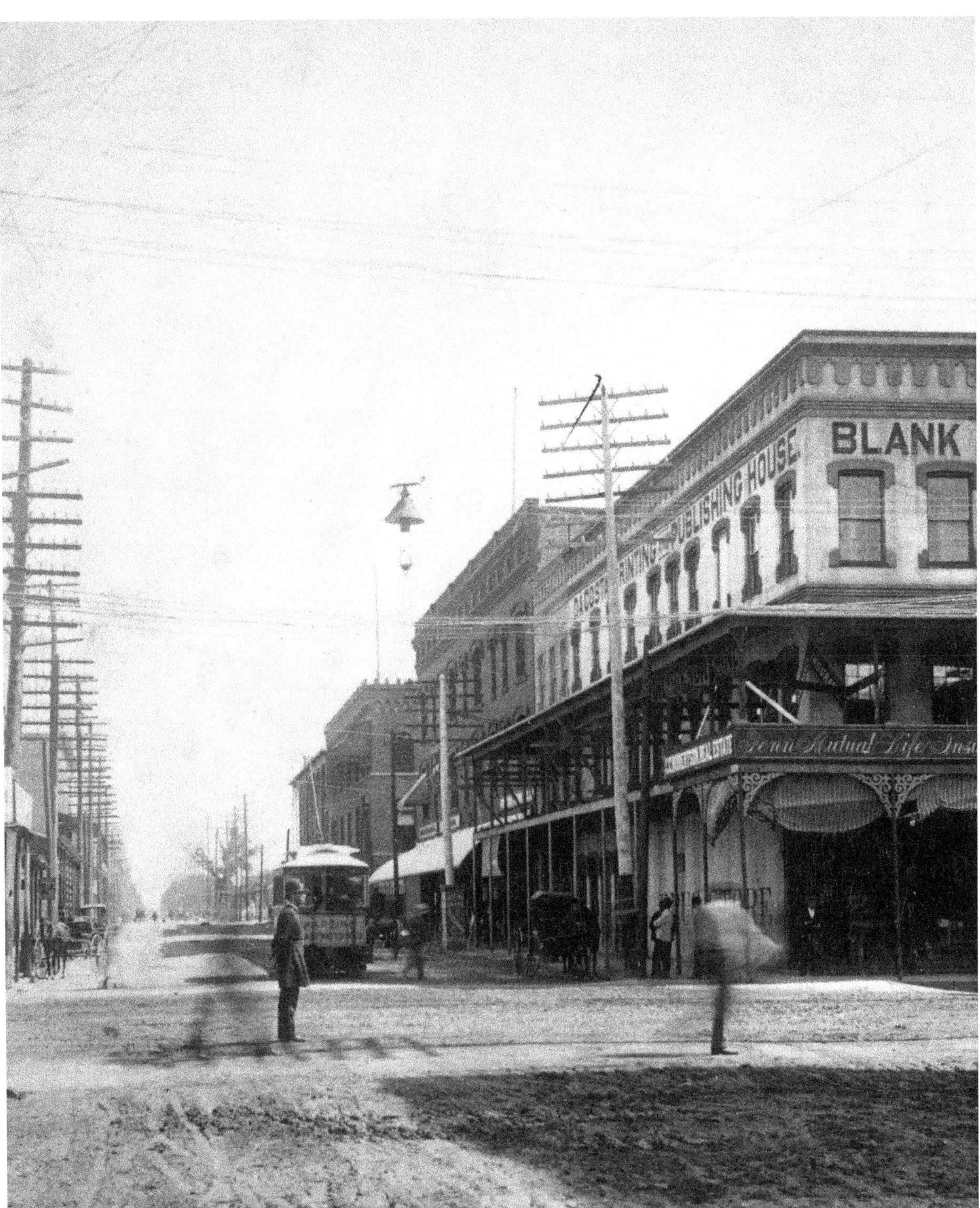

The commercial district eventually expanded onto Main Street, as shown here.

To draw tourists from its chief rival California, city officials decided to hold a "great exposition" of subtropical and tropical products and resources. Entries for the exposition came from all Florida counties, as well as the West Indies and South America. The Subtropical Exposition, held in Springfield, ran from January through May 1888. Among the highlights was a visit by President Grover Cleveland on February 22.

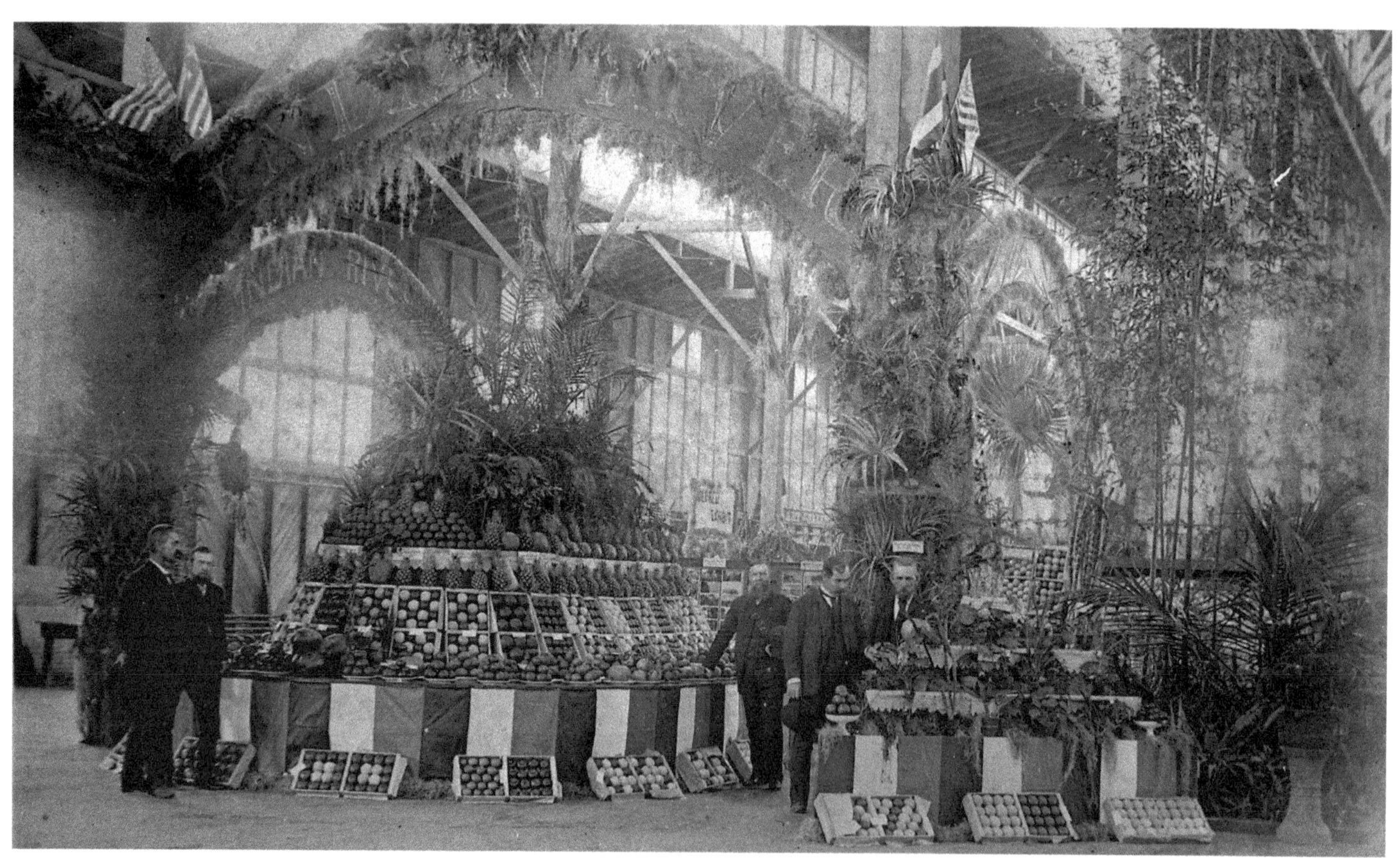

Outdoors at the Subtropical Exposition of 1888

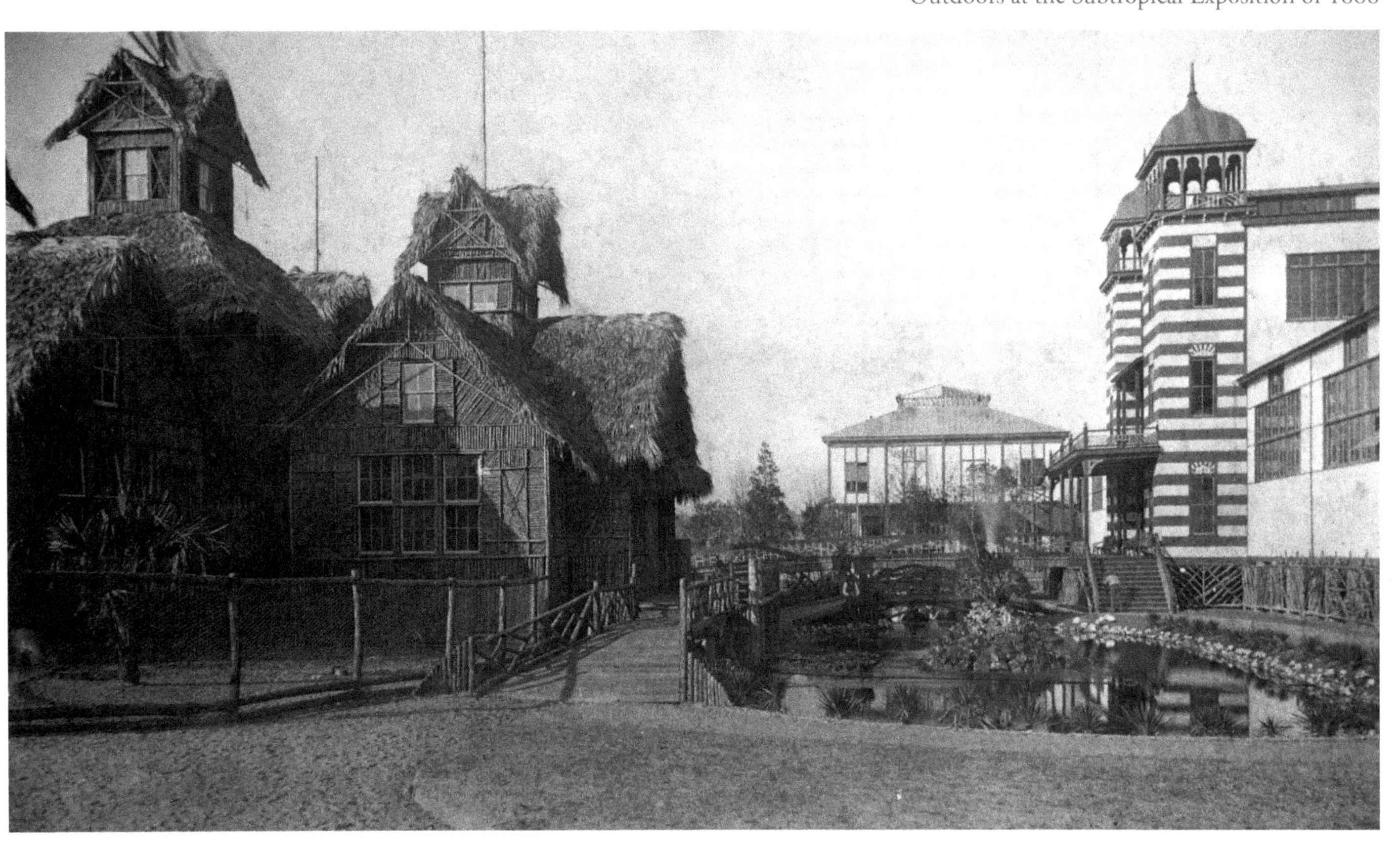

Before shoe polish there was boot blacking, in Jacksonville as elsewhere.

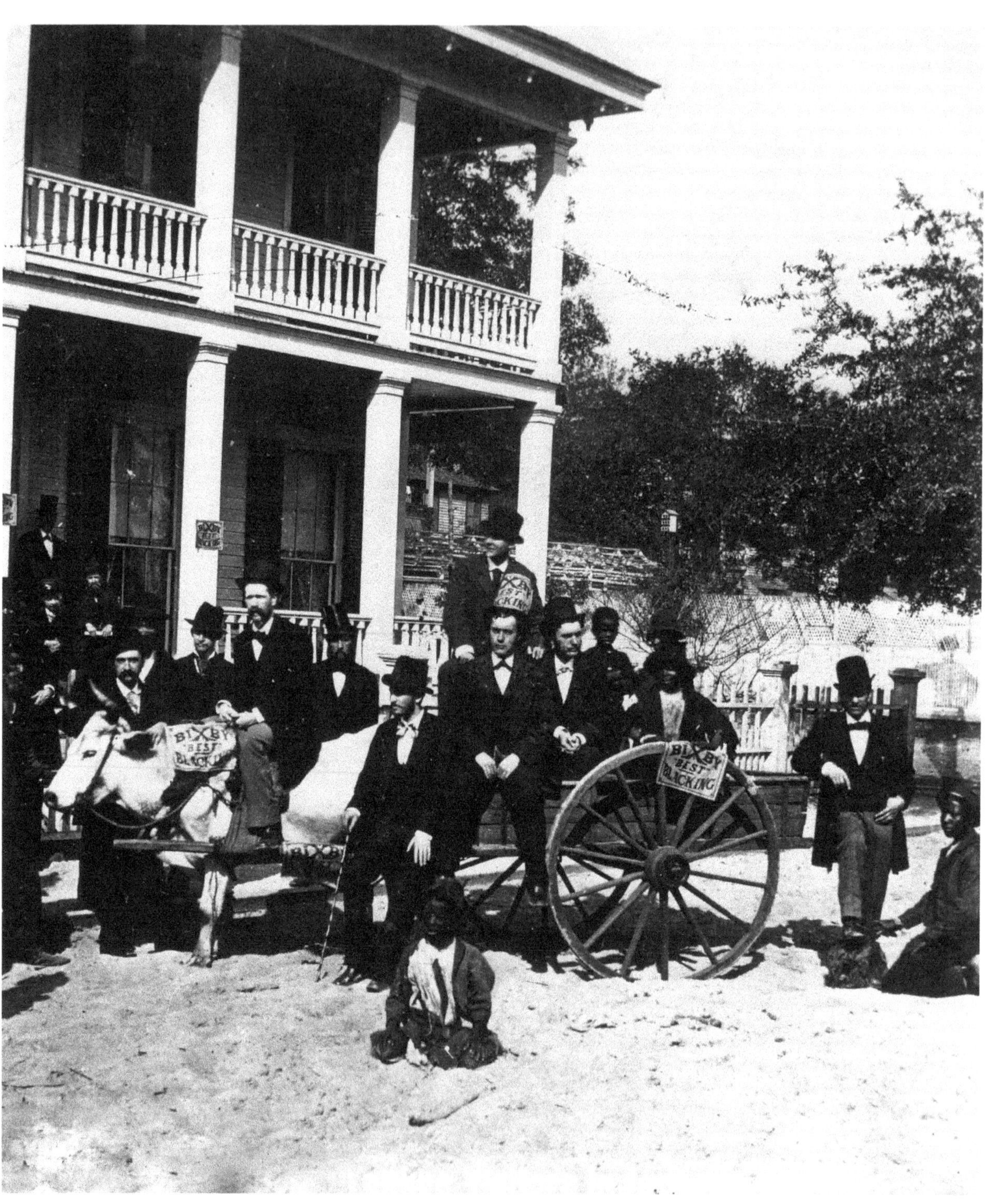

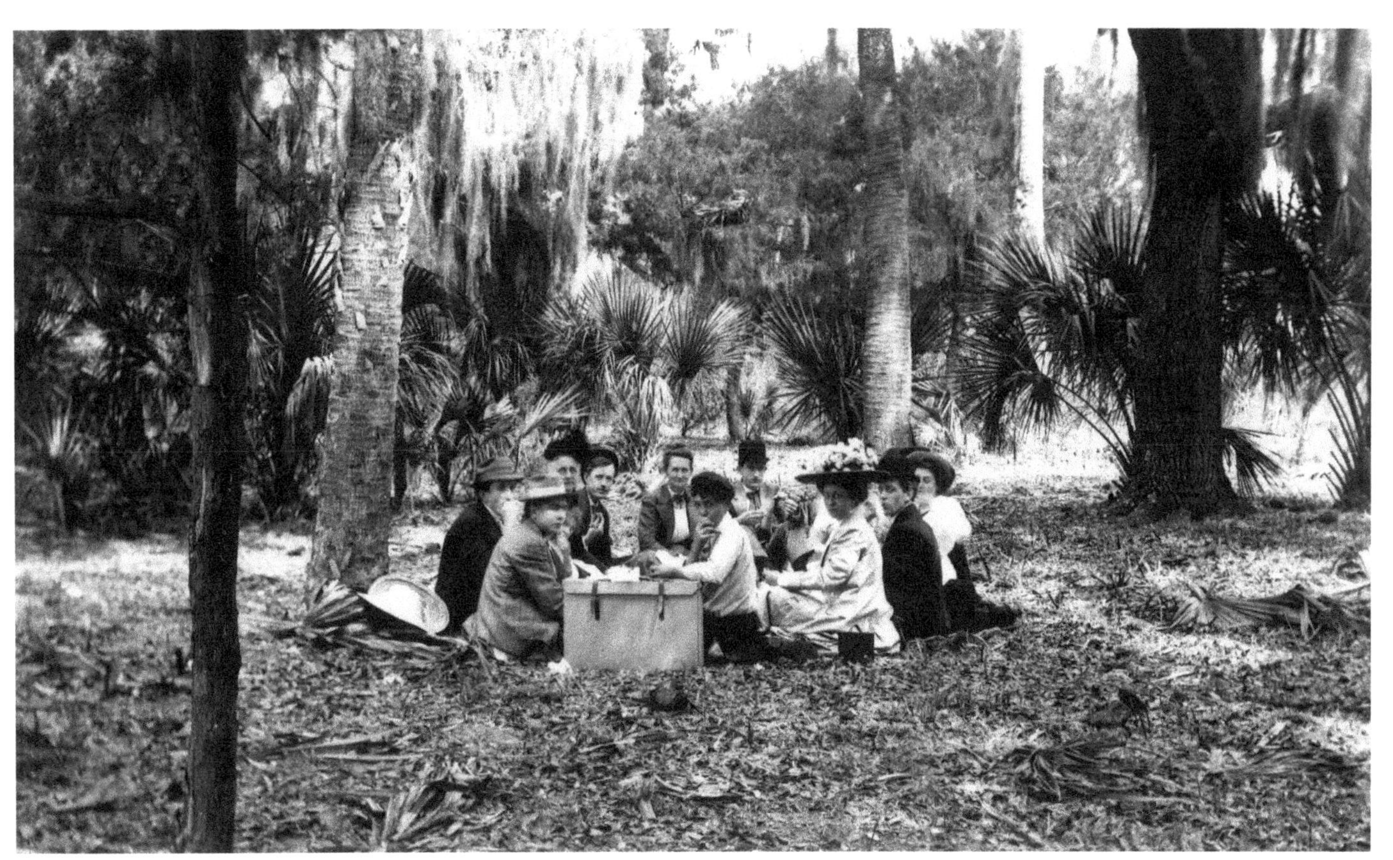

This group engages in a common leisure activity, picnicking.

Public school developed slowly in the city in the decades following the war. By the 1890s a number of schools for white and black children had been created in Brooklyn, LaVilla, East Jacksonville, North Jacksonville (Springfield), and Riverside. Horse-drawn school buses like this one transported the children.

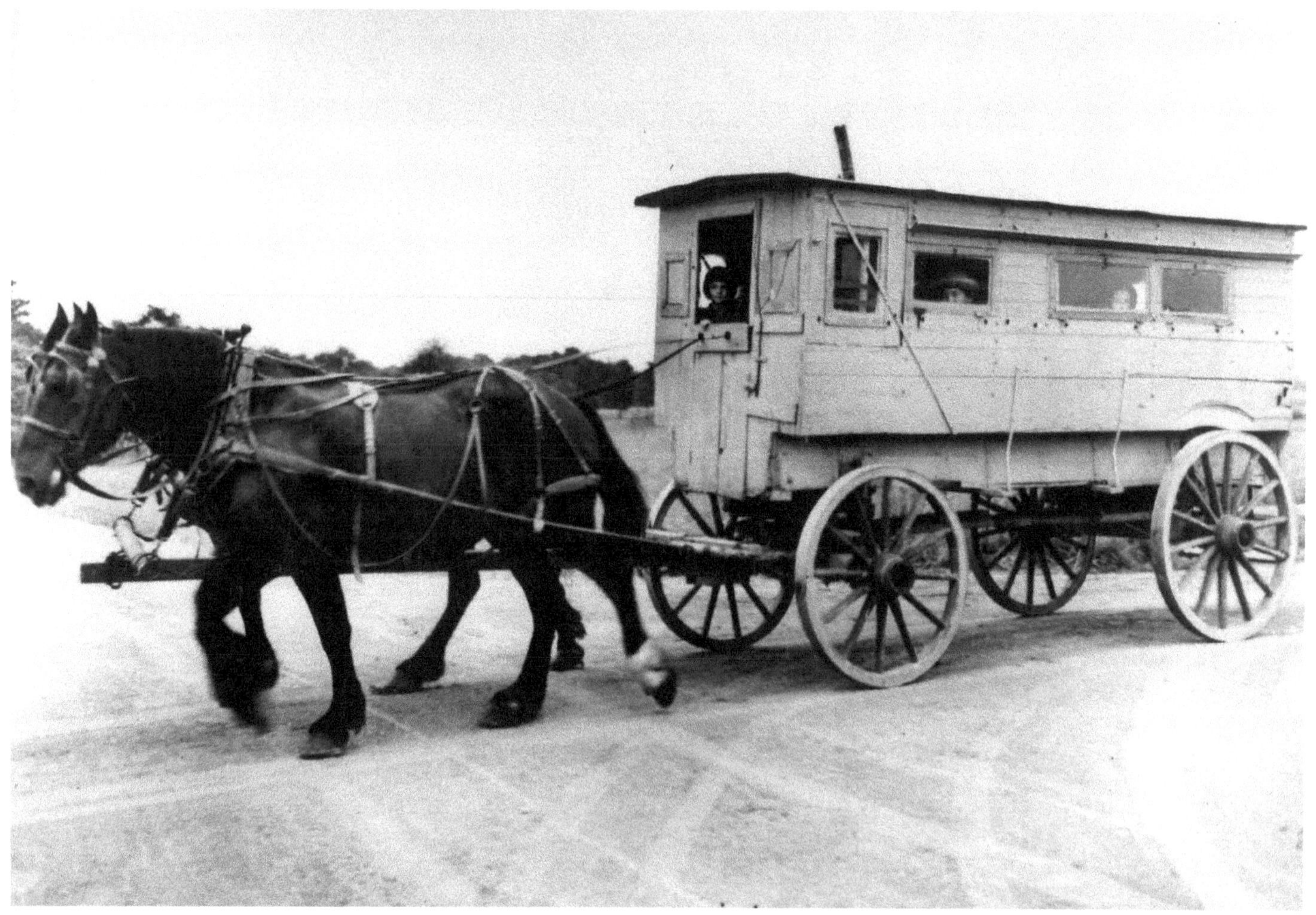

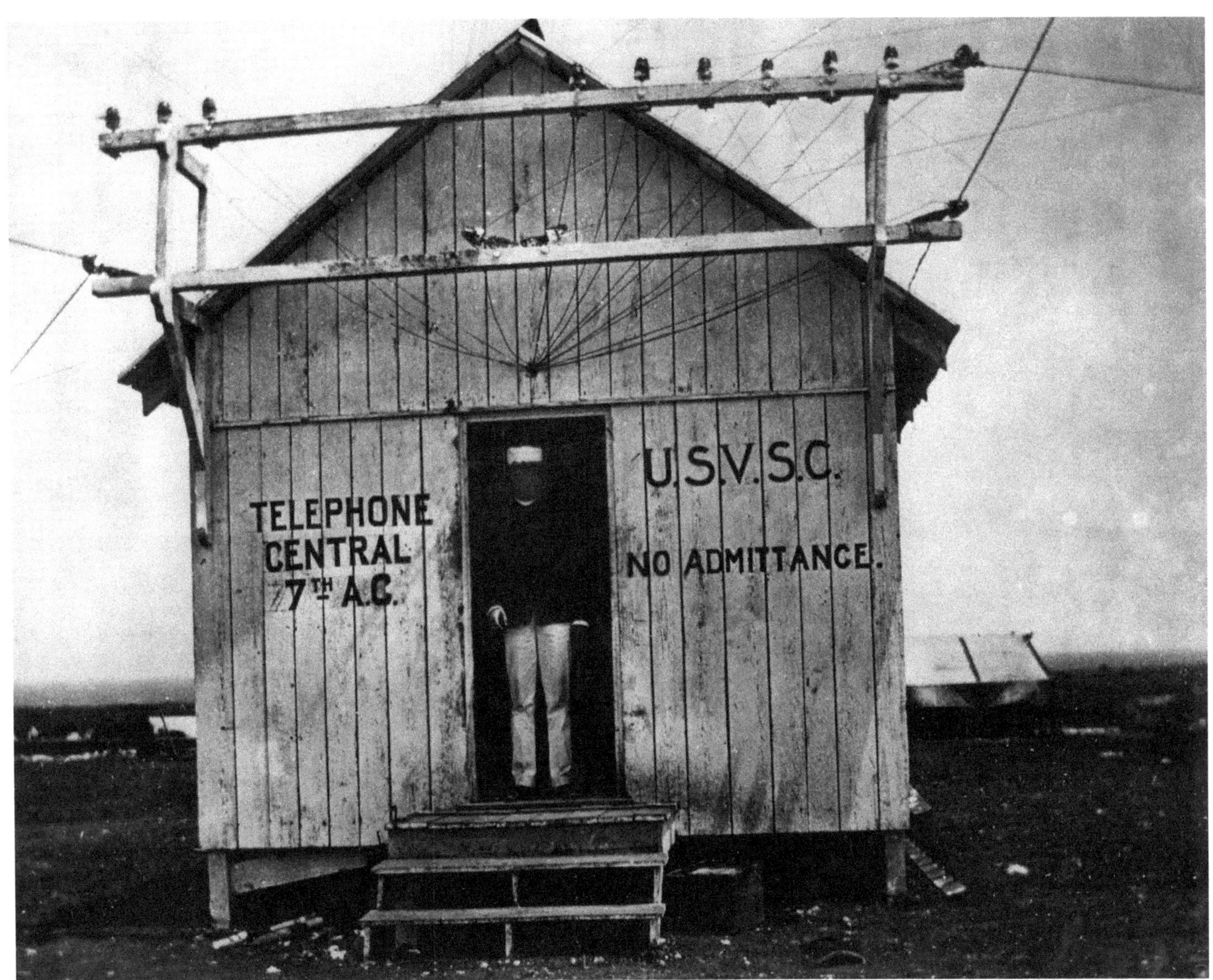

On June 13, 1898, Jacksonville was designated the commissary depot of the 7th Army Signal Corps.

Soldiers at the Signal Corps Camp in 1898

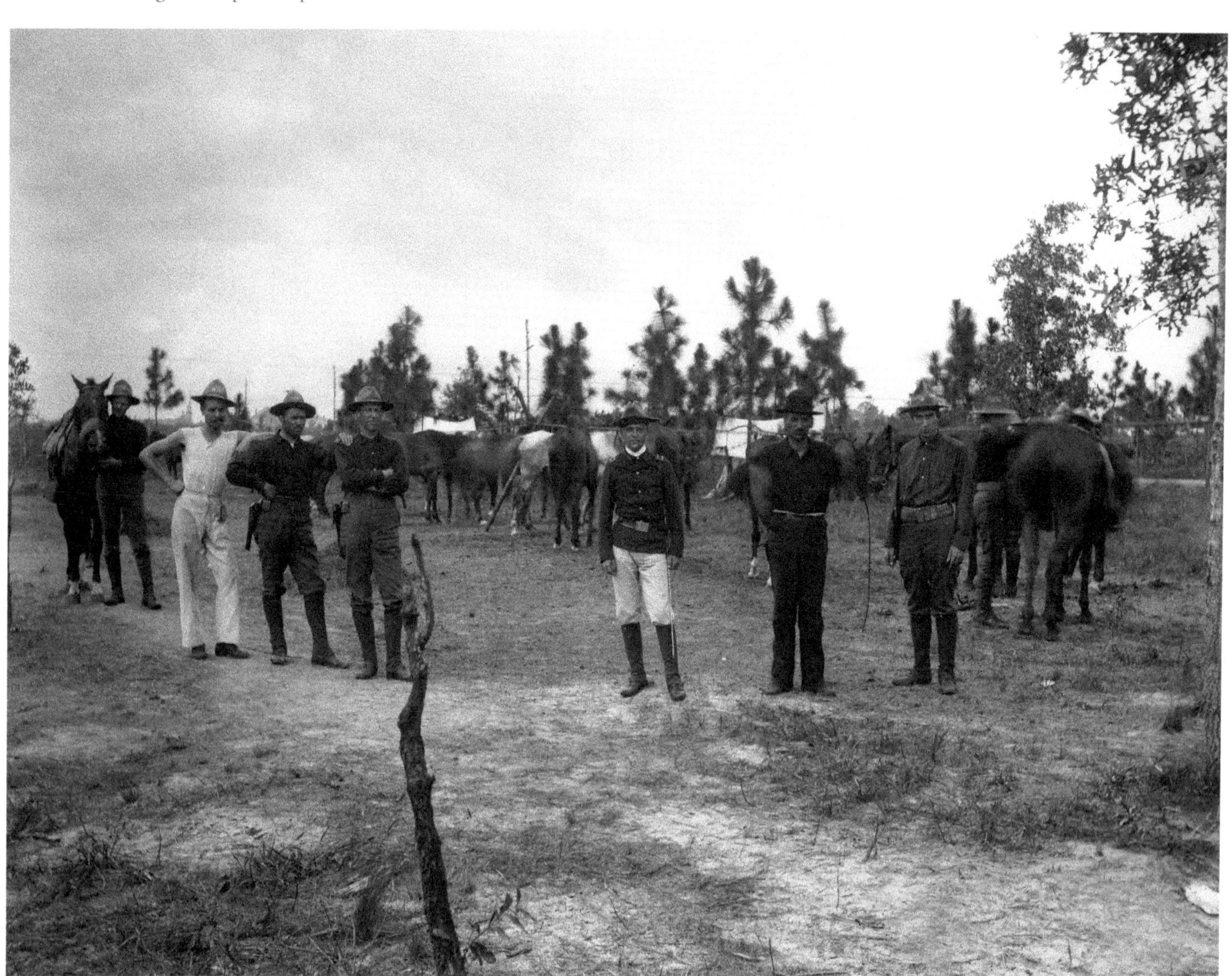

The whole community was infused with patriotism during the Spanish-American War, as these children demonstrate by staging their own parade.

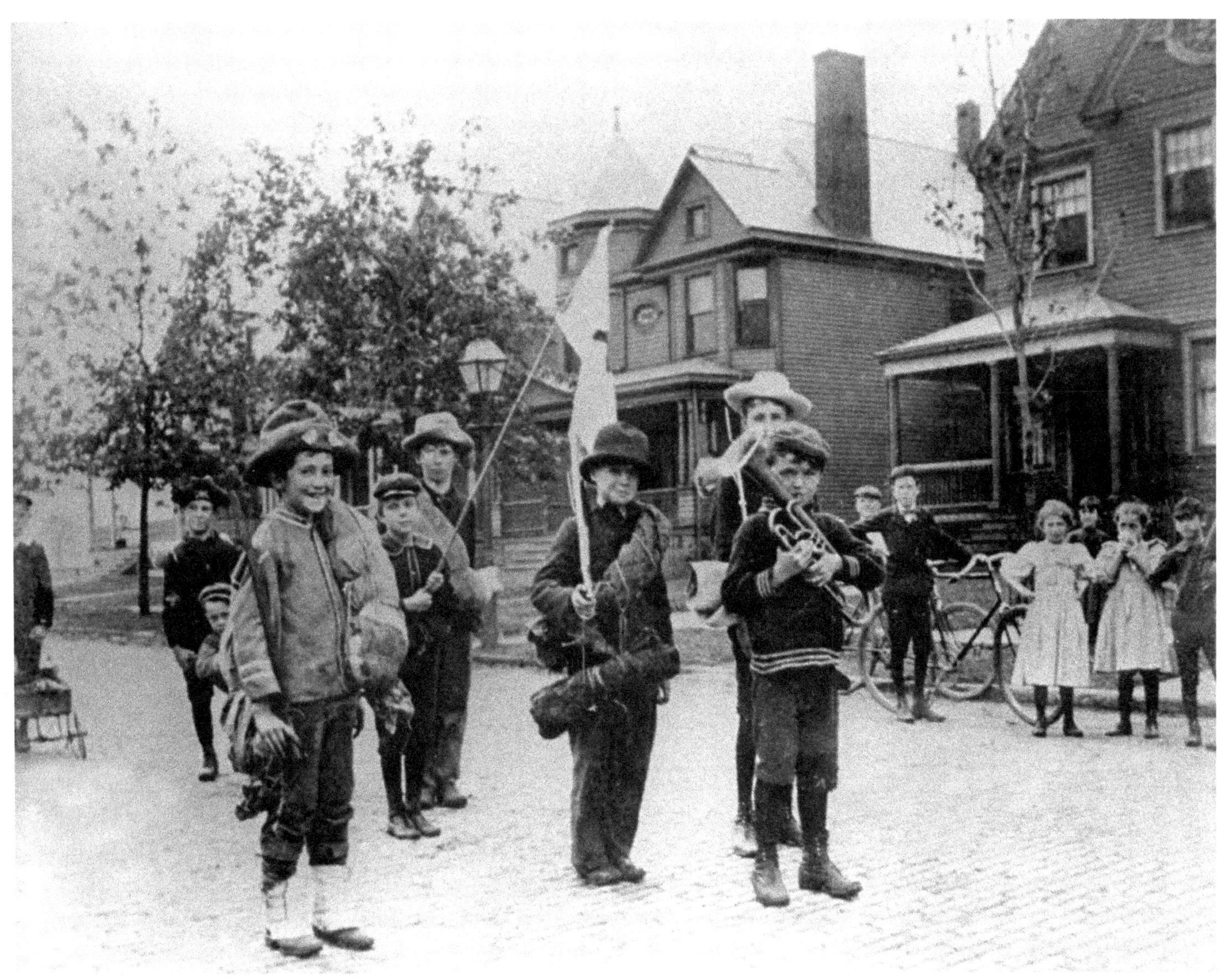

After the excitement of war receded, community life progressed and recovered stability. The congregation of the Elizabeth Swaim United Methodist Church is shown here in 1900.

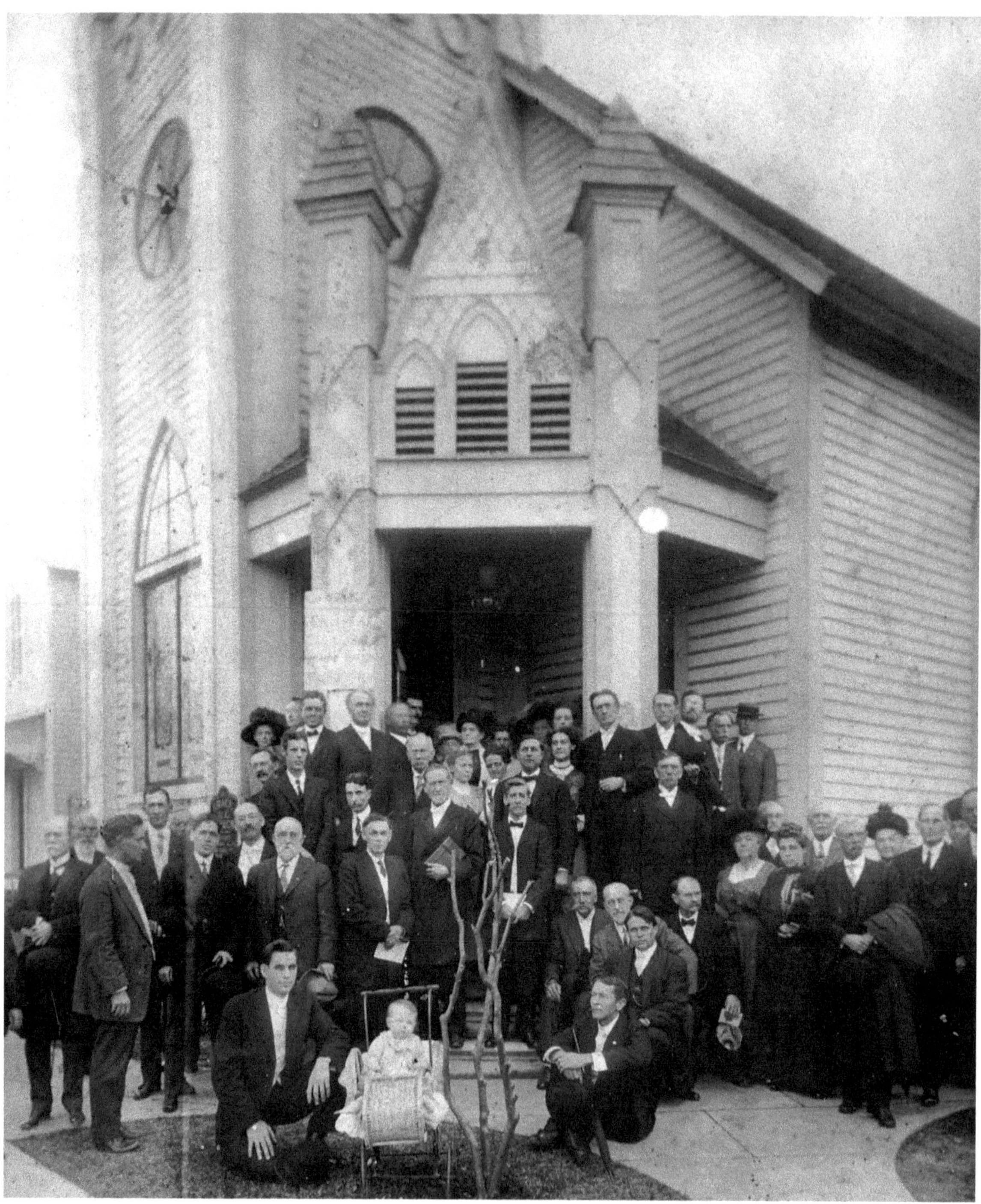

The home of prominent citizen Charles E. Garner is shown here in 1900. Garner was the president and general manager of the Independent Line Steamer Company. His residence was on East Duval Street.

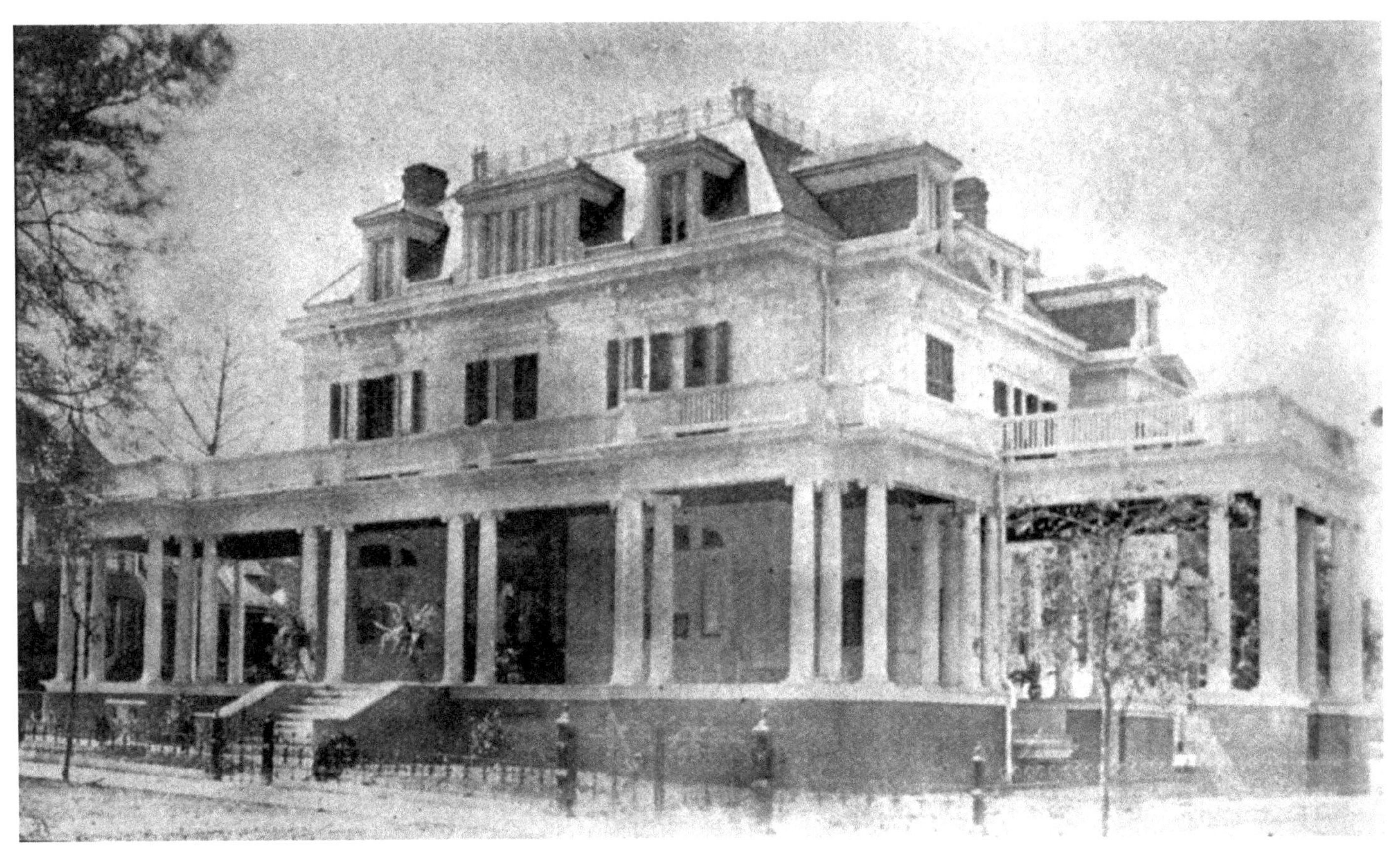

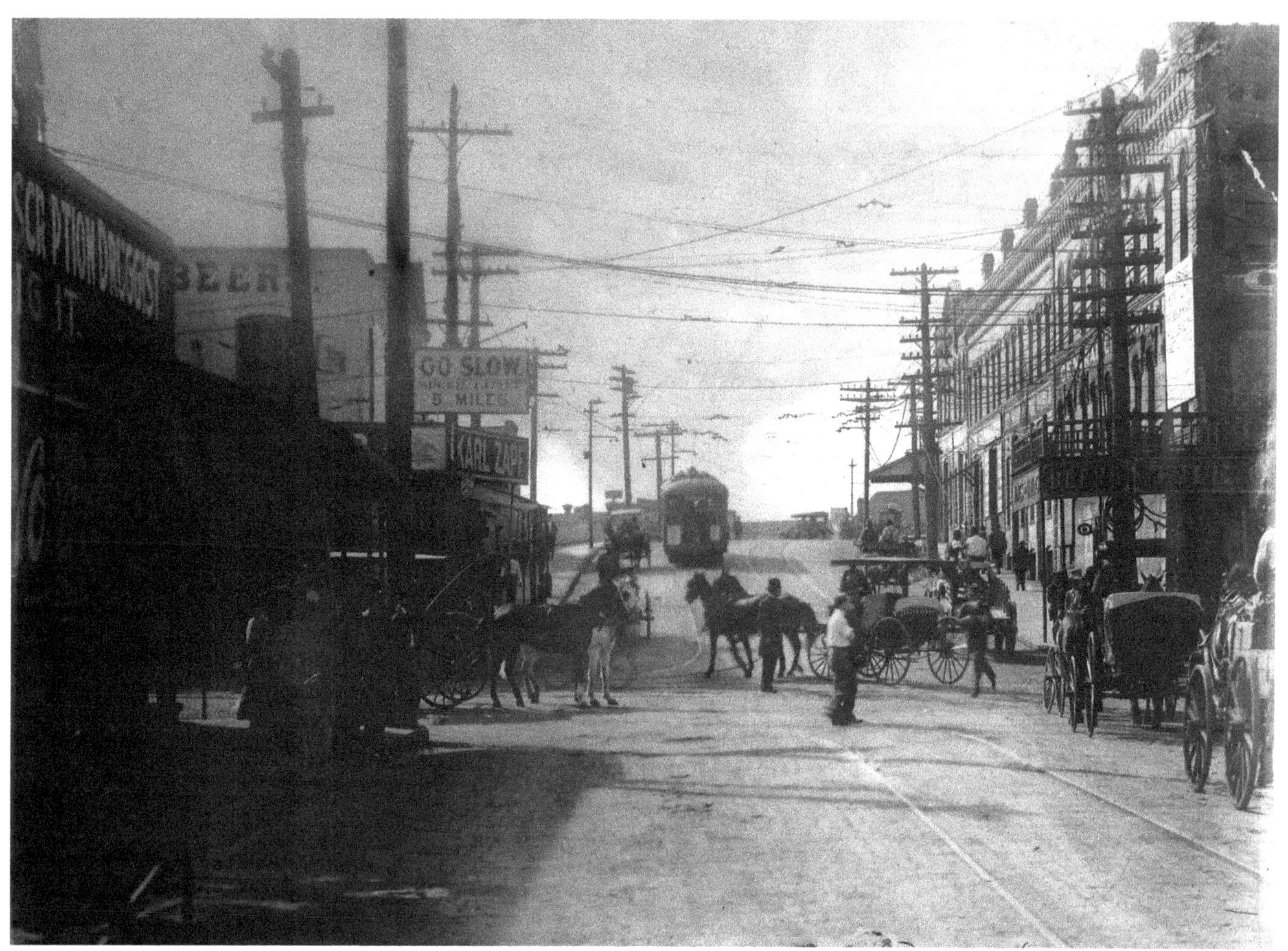

Street scene around 1900

Jacksonville, like the rest of the post–Civil War South, was a predominantly Democratic city. On June 19-22, 1900, the last Democratic state convention was held in the city.

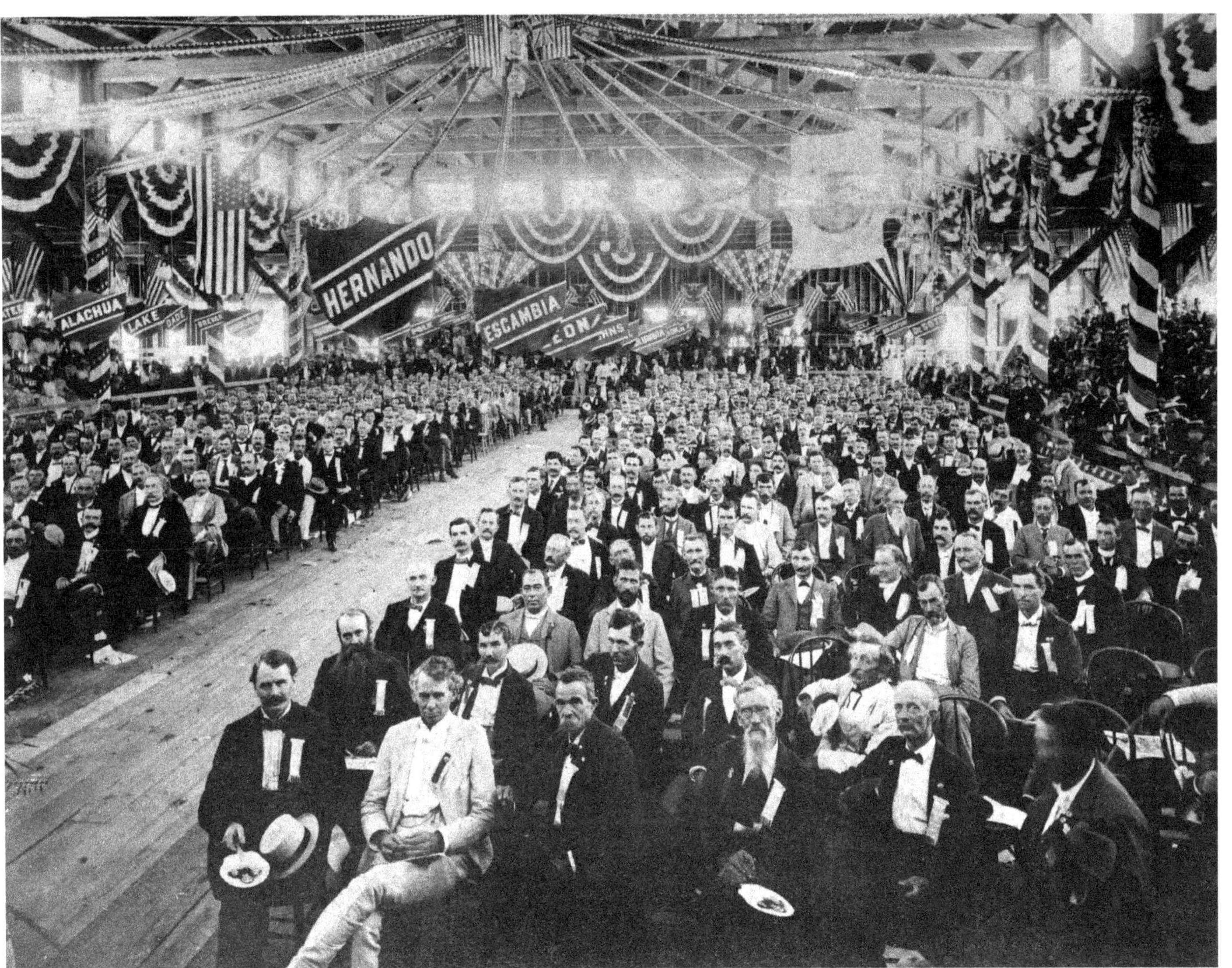

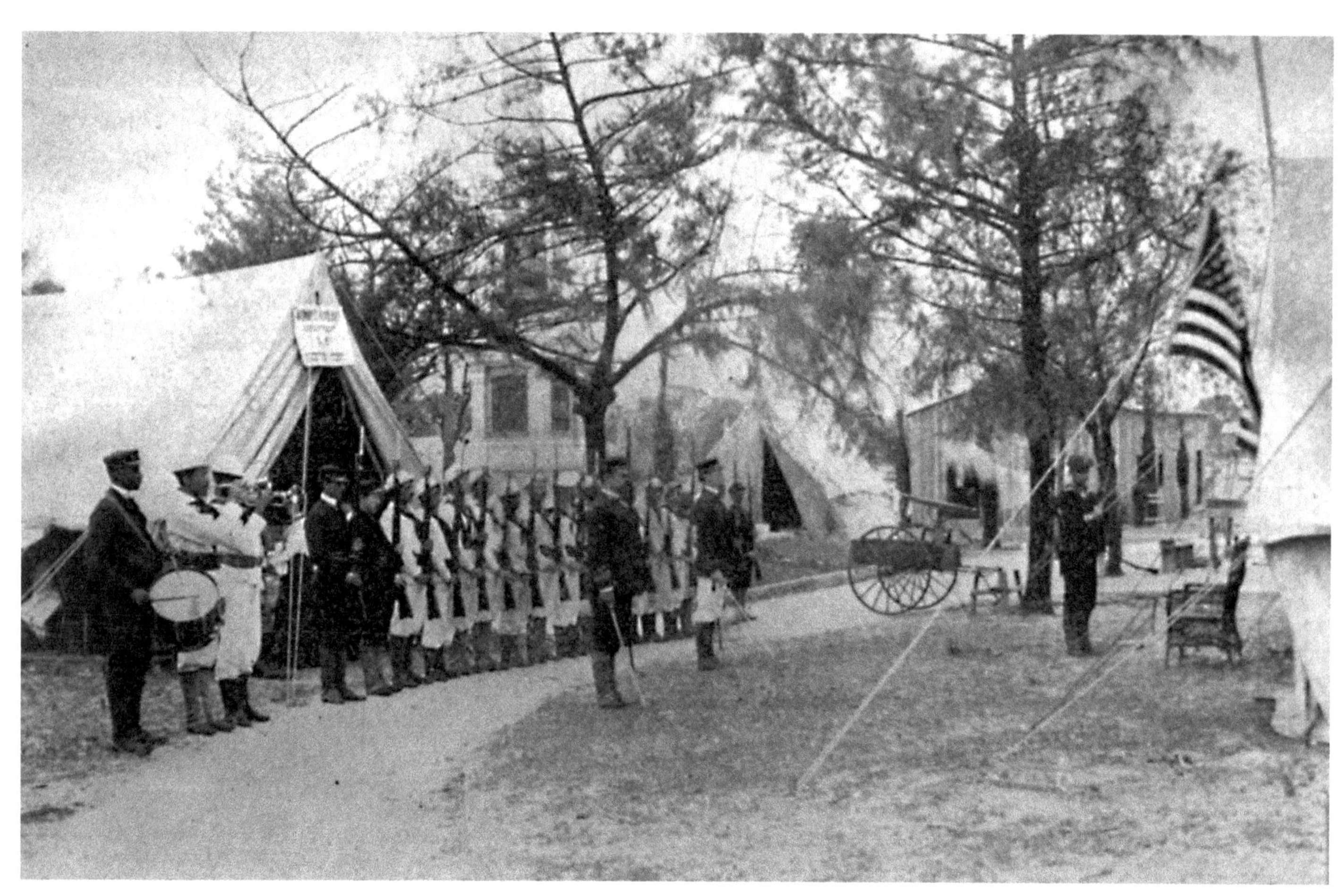

Marine guards in Hemming Park. The park was named in honor of Charles Hemming, who donated a Confederate monument to the city in 1899.

Jacksonville went up in smoke May 3, 1901. More than 2,000 buildings were consumed by the flames, which raged for eight hours. Miraculously only seven people lost their lives. In view are city residents fleeing the fire.

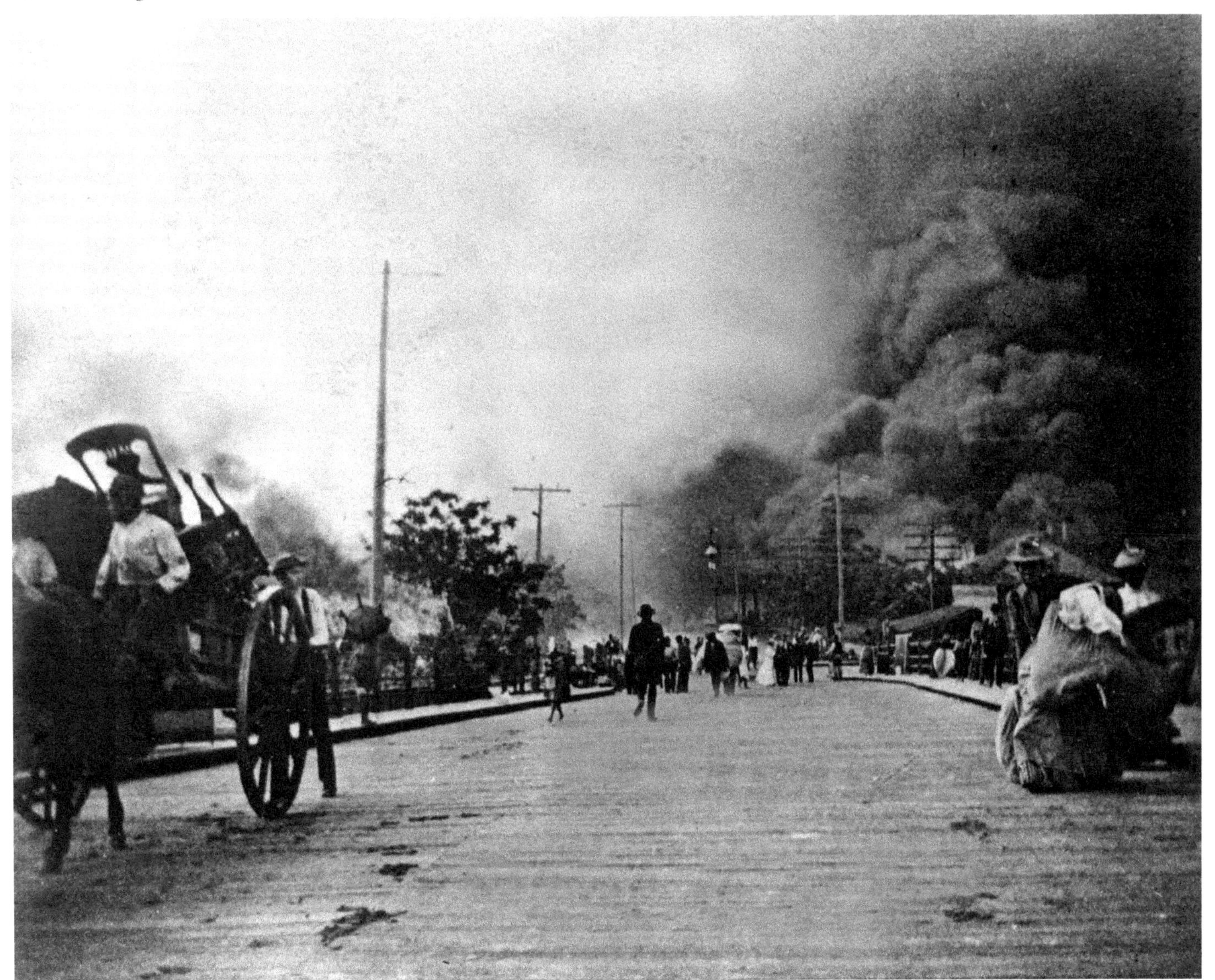

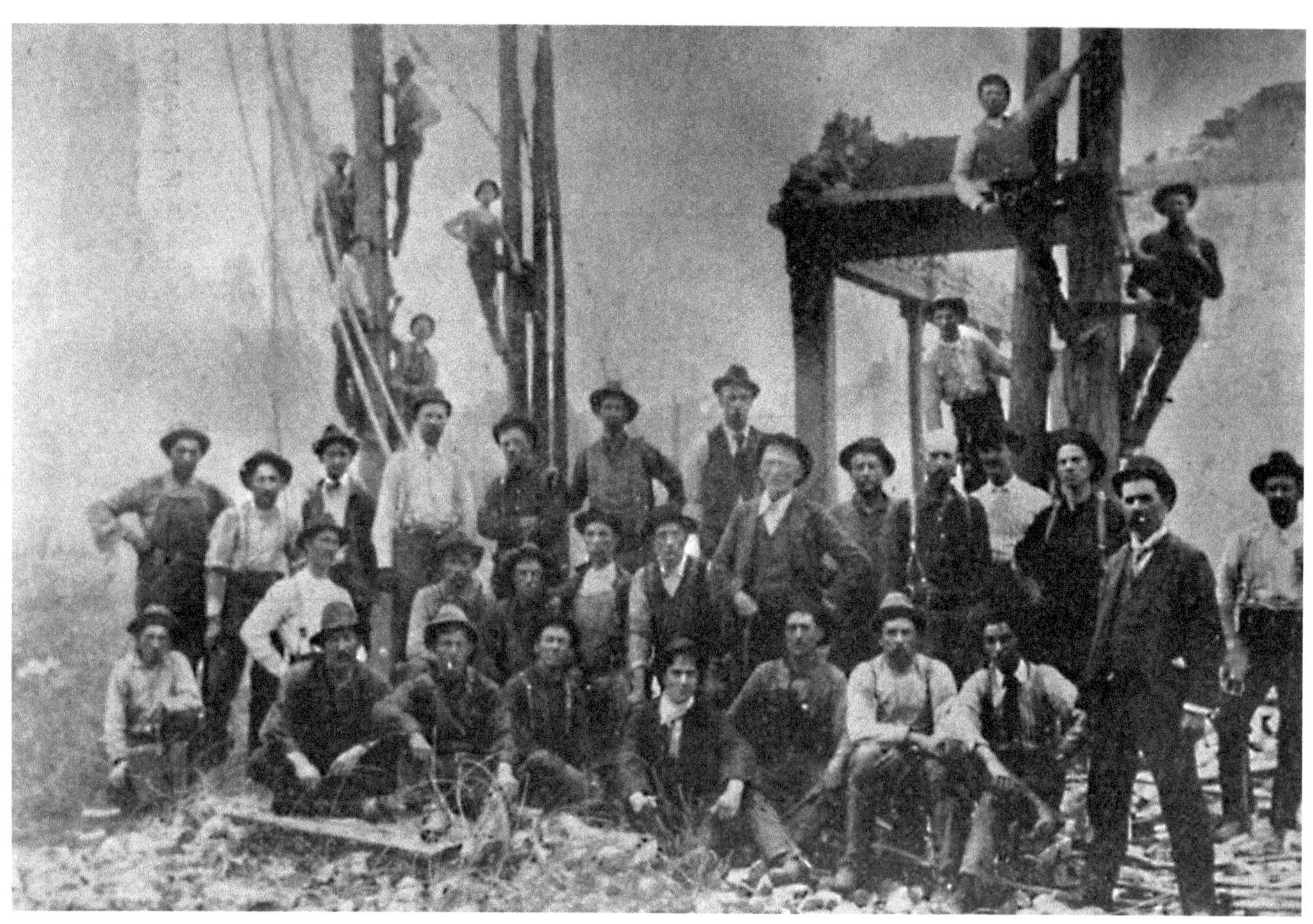

A group of Bell Telephone employees who formed an impromptu fire fighting unit during the Great Fire

The Women's Auxiliary Committee, shown here, was organized soon after the fire to assist women who expressed a need.

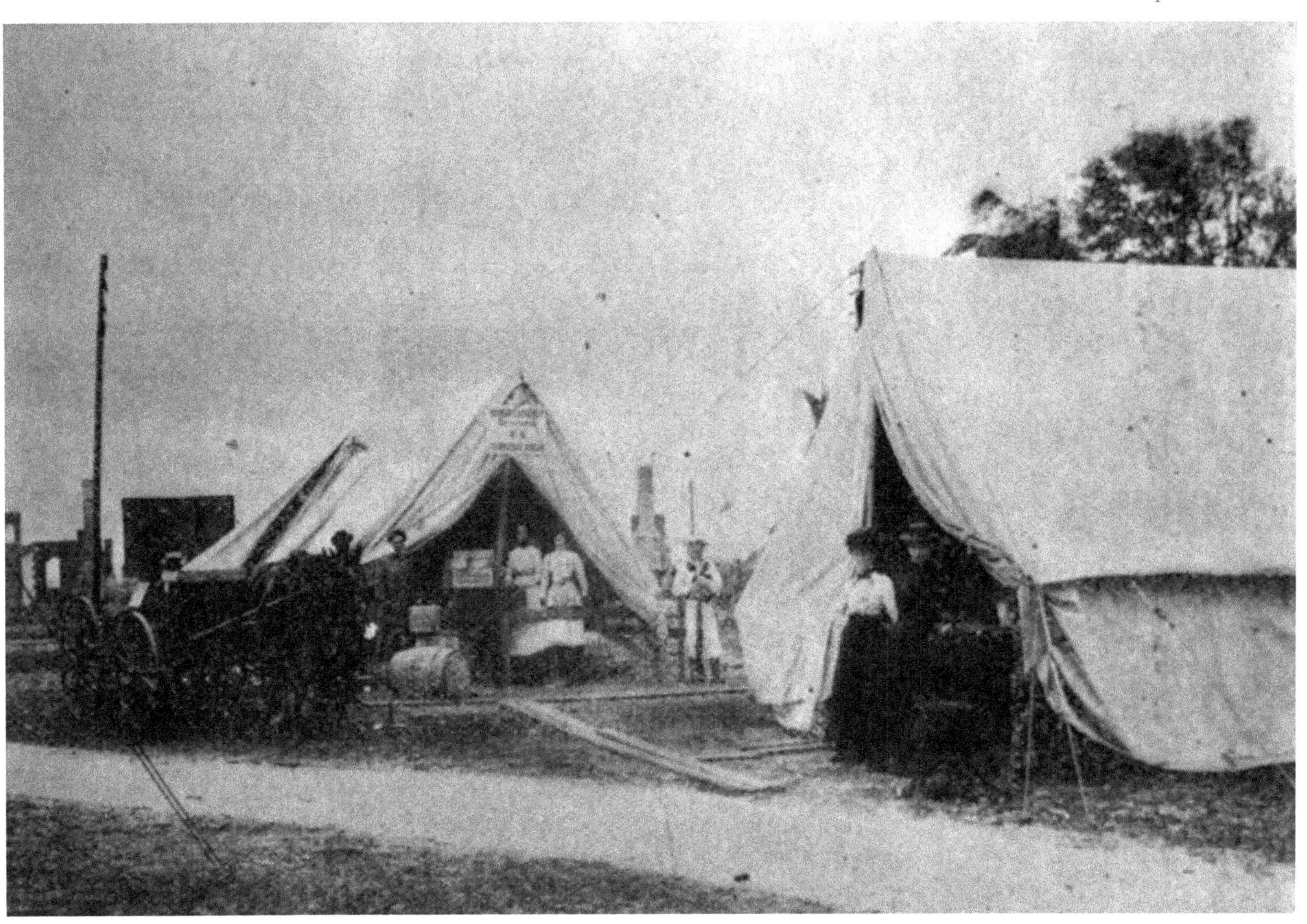

A skyline view, showing the New South city that Jacksonville had become by 1909, less than a decade after the Great Fire. The city's first "skyscraper," at left, the new 10-story Bisbee Building designed by Henry Klutho, was the first reinforced-concrete frame high-rise building in the state of Florida.

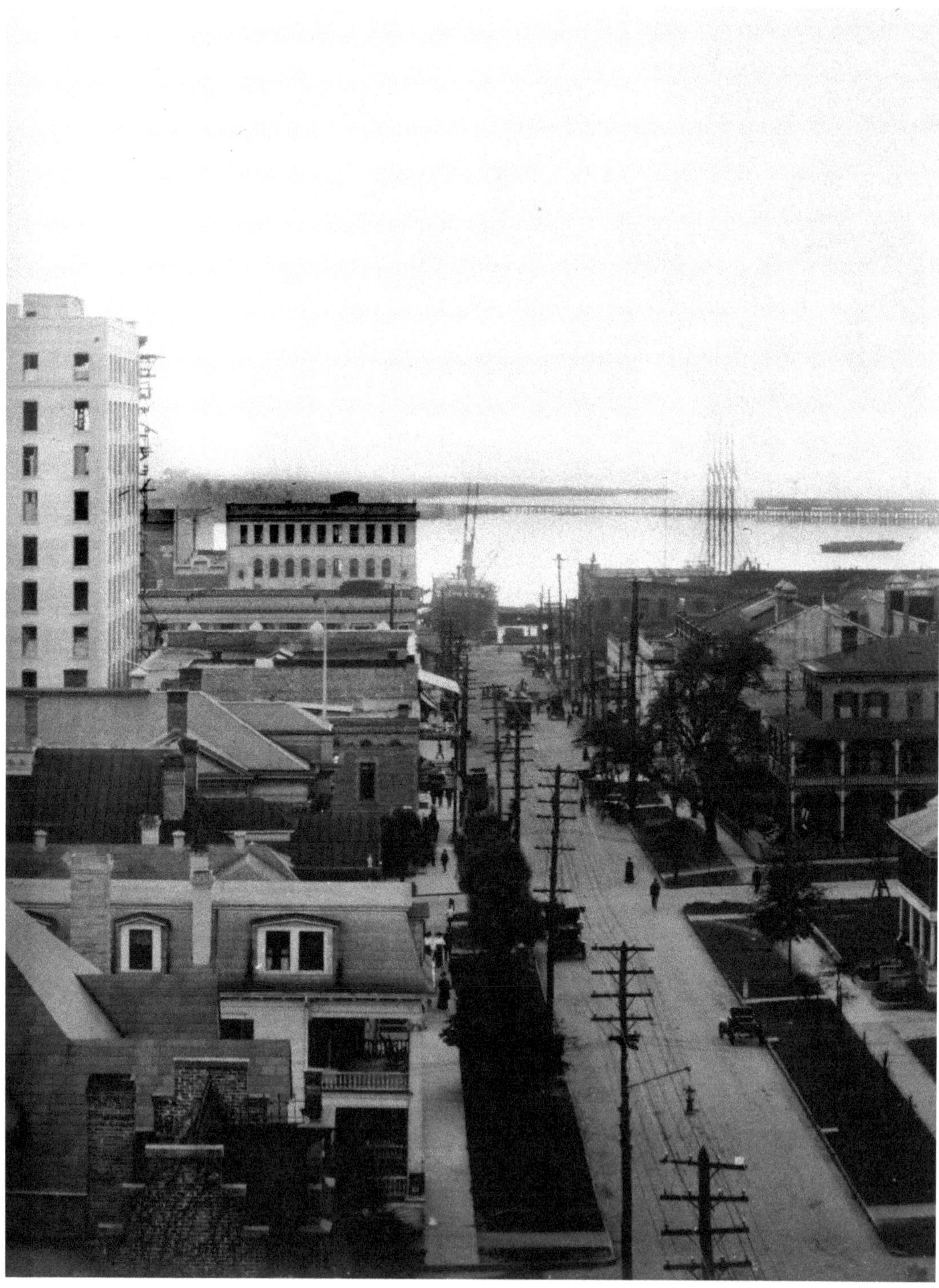

From Ashes to an Important New South City

(1902–1919)

The massive destruction of Jacksonville by the fire of May 1901 provided the people opportunity to create a completely new city. The more than 2,000 buildings consumed by the flames were replaced with new structures made of new materials and based on new designs. Steel-framed buildings went up and the first multistoried "skyscrapers" appeared. A young architect, Henry Klutho, who was strongly influenced by the "prairie style" of Frank Lloyd Wright, designed many government, commercial, and residential buildings. Klutho buildings are still in the downtown area and make up substantial portions of the historic districts of Springfield and Riverside today.

The rebuilding concentrated first on downtown Jacksonville. A new courthouse and city hall appeared a few years after the fire. With the assistance of funds donated by steel magnate Andrew Carnegie, the city built a new main library.

In the early twentieth century Jacksonville became the center of banking in Florida. Many of the commercial buildings in the city were the result of this burgeoning financial activity. Another new business came to town and stayed for nearly two decades—movie making. Until World War I, Jacksonville was known as the "winter land" of the film industry and at one time had more movie studios than any other city in the U.S. Actors making movies here included veterans of the theater and members of the famous theatrical family Lionel and Ethel Barrymore, and a neophyte from Georgia, Oliver Hardy, who would go on to become half of a famous comedy duo.

Adding to the economic vibrancy of the city was the rapidly growing port industry and the railroad business. The railroads, which had come to the city in the antebellum period, were prospering by the early twentieth century because of lines established by Henry Plant and later by Henry Flagler. Flagler also added to the panoply of hotels, with his establishments in the beaches area of Jacksonville, prompted by a reviving tourist industry.

Transportation by water was improved by way of ferries and steamboats, and on land by trolleys and the automobile, making possible new communities farther from the river and downtown. The opportunity for jobs and investment activities attracted newcomers. Others either settled here permanently or established winter homes. Having the most prominent and important impact on the city was the permanent winter residence of Alfred I. and Jessie Ball DuPont.

A fundamental way Jacksonville became a New South city was its conformity to the formalization of segregation. In 1901 the city government passed an ordinance mandating separation of the races on the trolley, the beginning of legislation that would soon result in the separation of the races in all areas of public life. African Americans protested, but after 1907 none would serve on the city council for sixty years.

As the majority of the city's population from the post–Civil War era to World War I, African Americans responded to segregation by being resourceful. Abraham Lincoln Lewis, for example, who began work as a boy with one of the city's lumber mills and worked his way up to entrepreneur, joined other ambitious black men to open the Afro American, the first insurance company established in the state of Florida.

The old Duval County Courthouse, shown here in 1912, was completed the year after the fire. Two years later it would be expanded by an annex. The courthouse building was demolished in 1960.

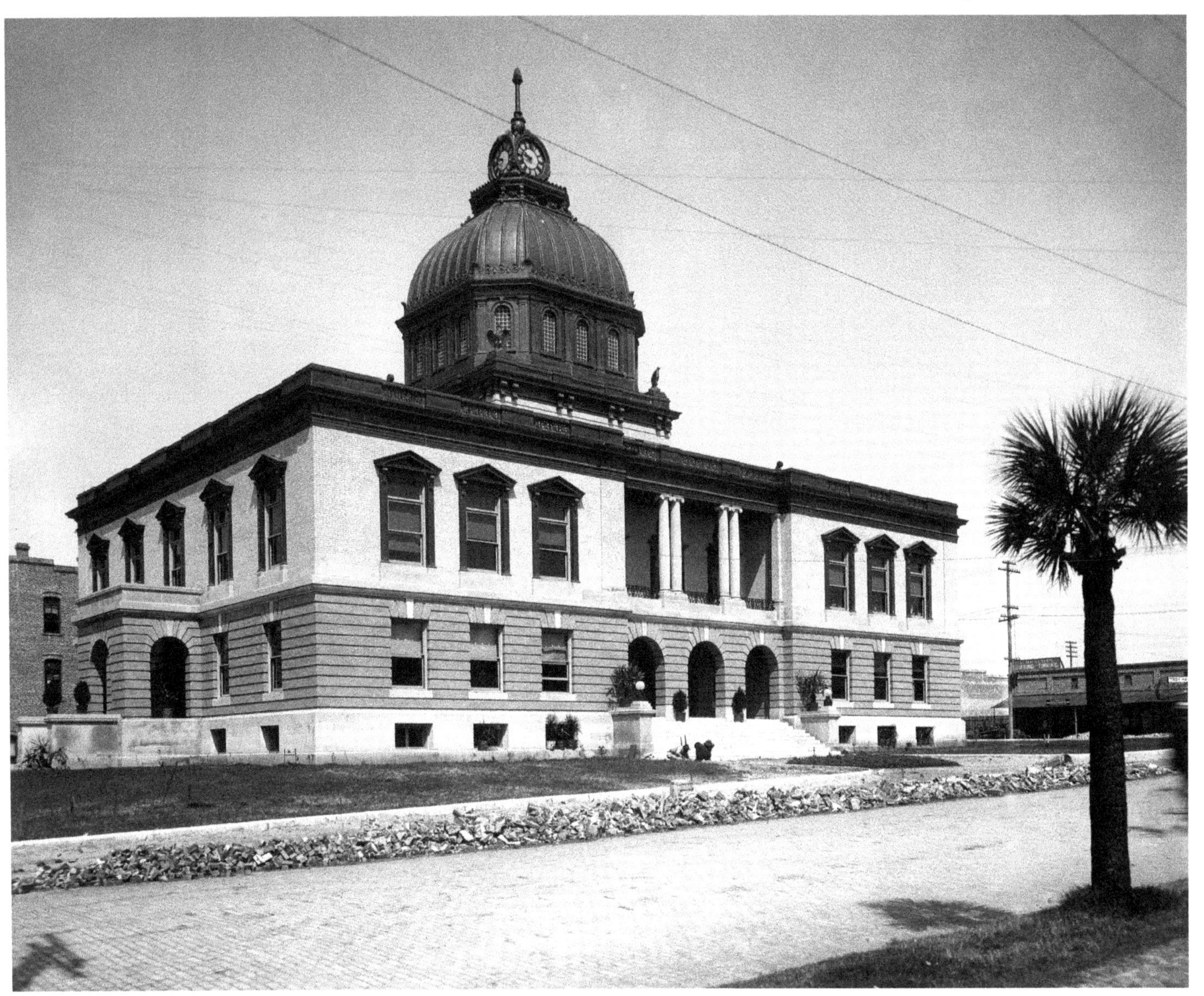

The city built its first major library building after the fire with the assistance of steel magnate Andrew Carnegie, who offered $50,000 if the city would provide a site and agree to allocate an annual $5,000 to the building's maintenance. The result, at the northeast corner of Ocean and Adams streets, is shown here. The library opened to the public in 1905.

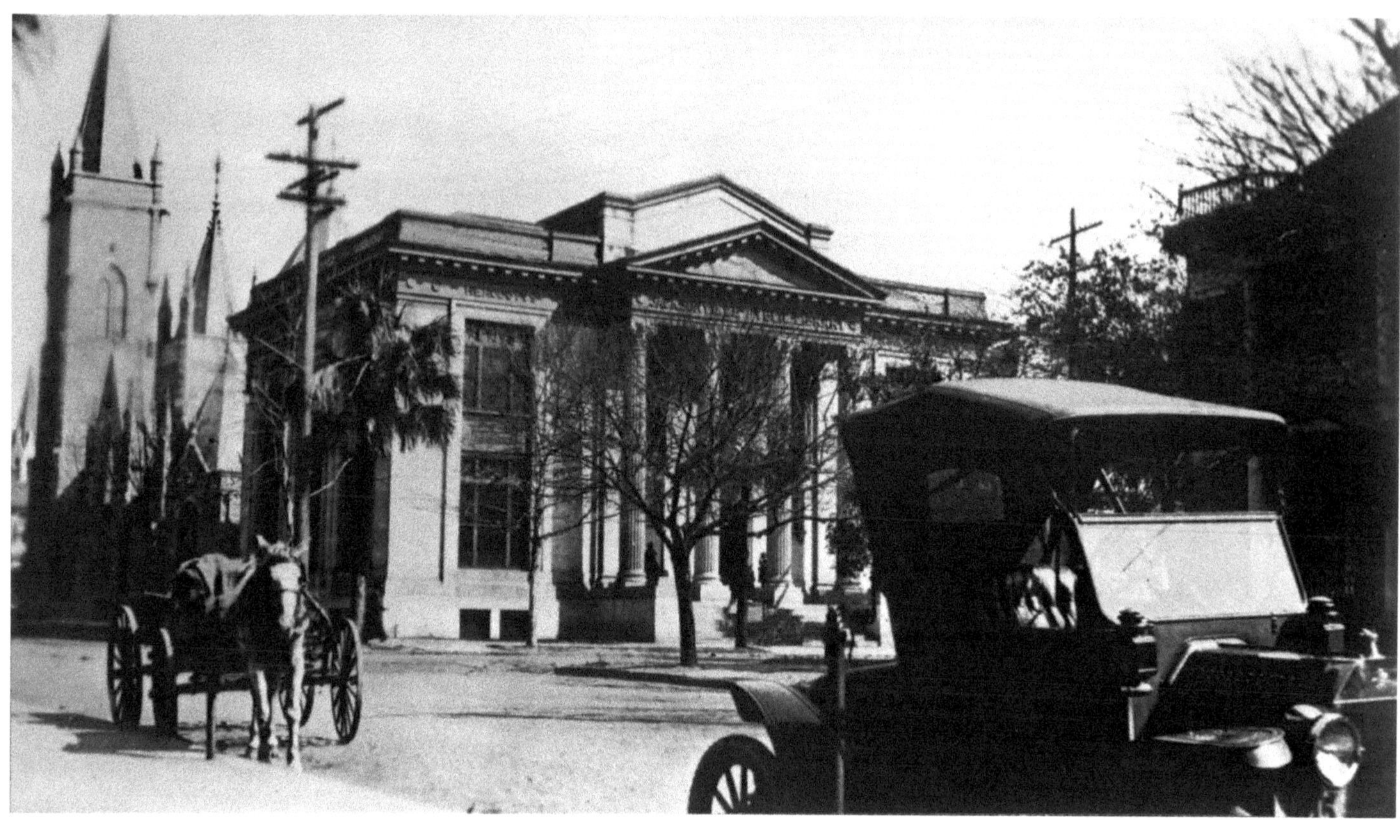

Shown here in front of the library are the first staff members.

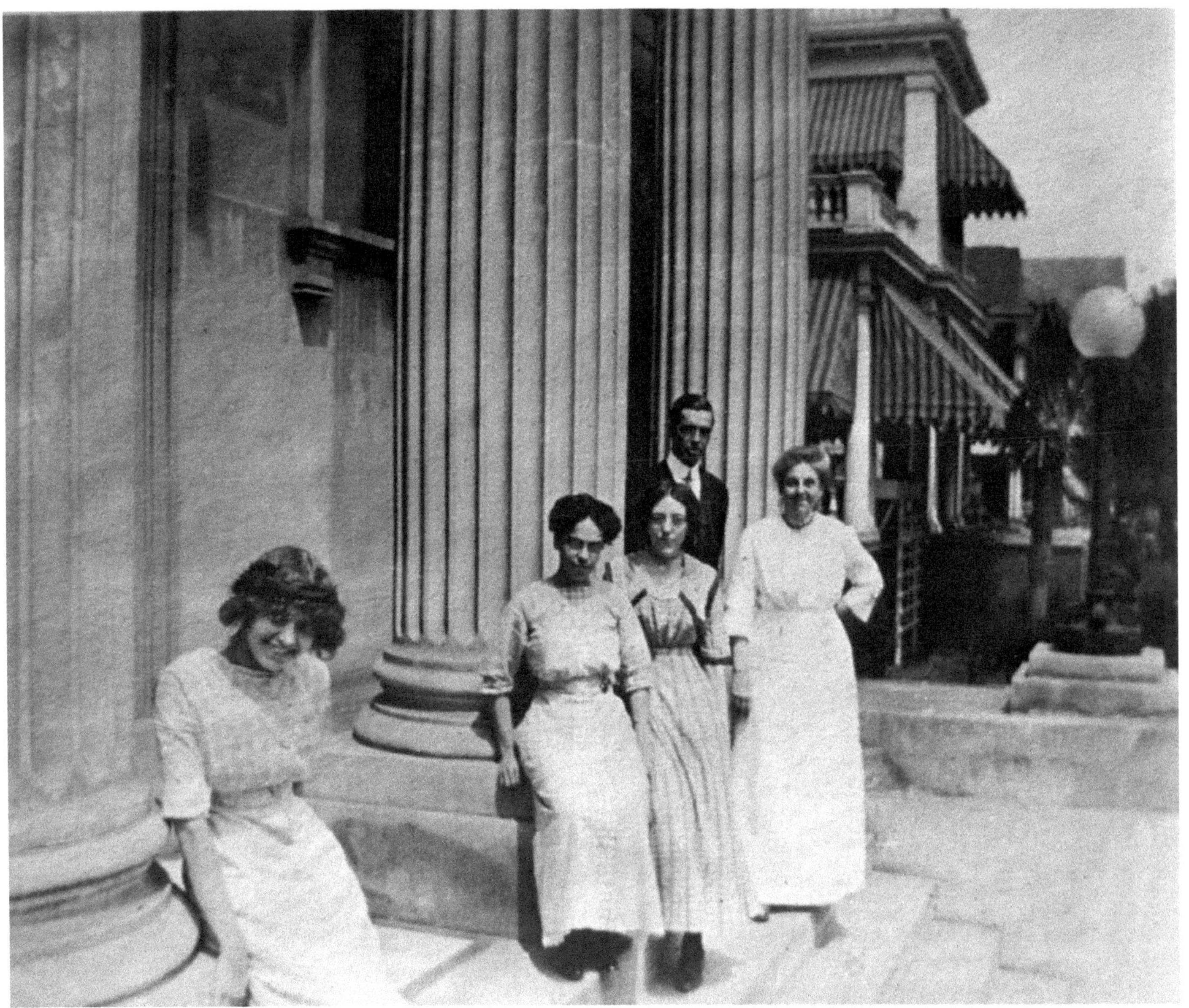

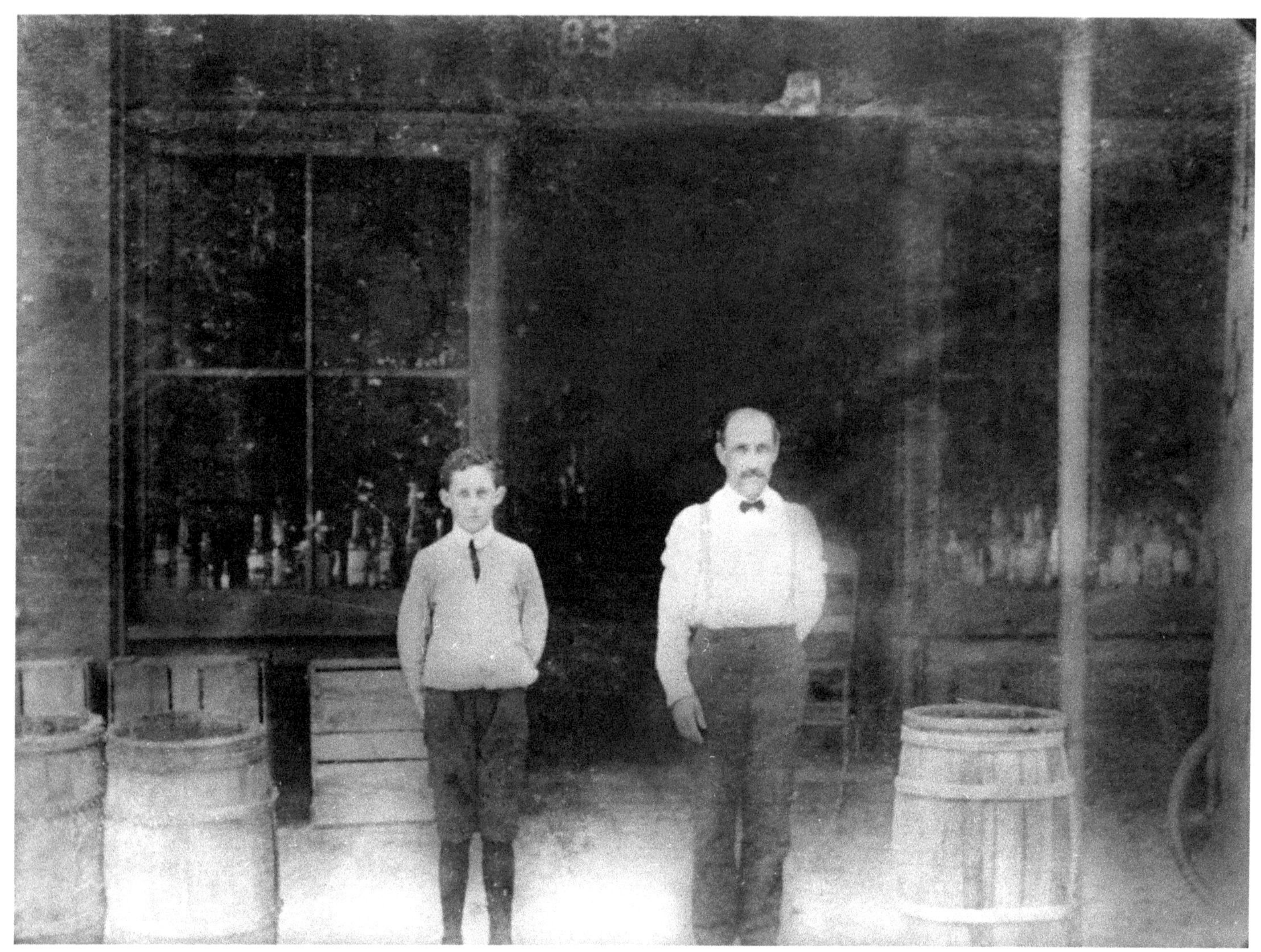

As Jacksonville's corporate structure developed, individual entrepreneurs like Harry Goldman, here with his son Abe in front of the family dry goods store, continued to be a key part of the business community. The Goldmans were a pioneer Jacksonville family.

Forsyth Street became the heart of Jacksonville's banking industry, and Jacksonville was the banking center of the state in the early 1900s. Here is a view of Forsyth Street looking north (named after General John Forsyth, U.S. Minister to Spain, who helped conduct the negotiations for the acquisition of Florida).

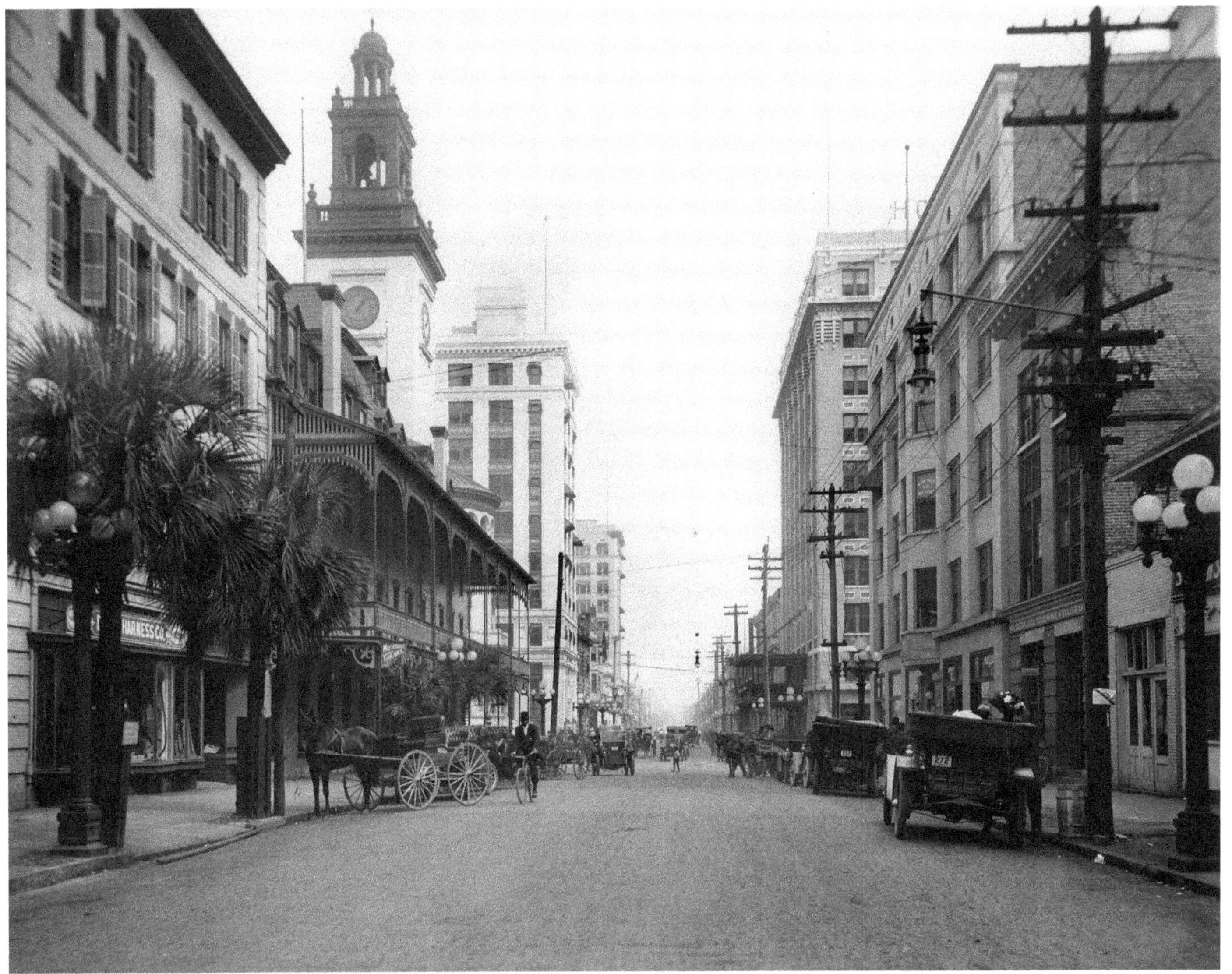

The Florida National Bank shown here next to the Bisbee Building in 1910 began in 1902 as the Mercantile Exchange Bank. Later it was purchased by the Florida Bank and Trust and became part of the Florida National Bank chain.

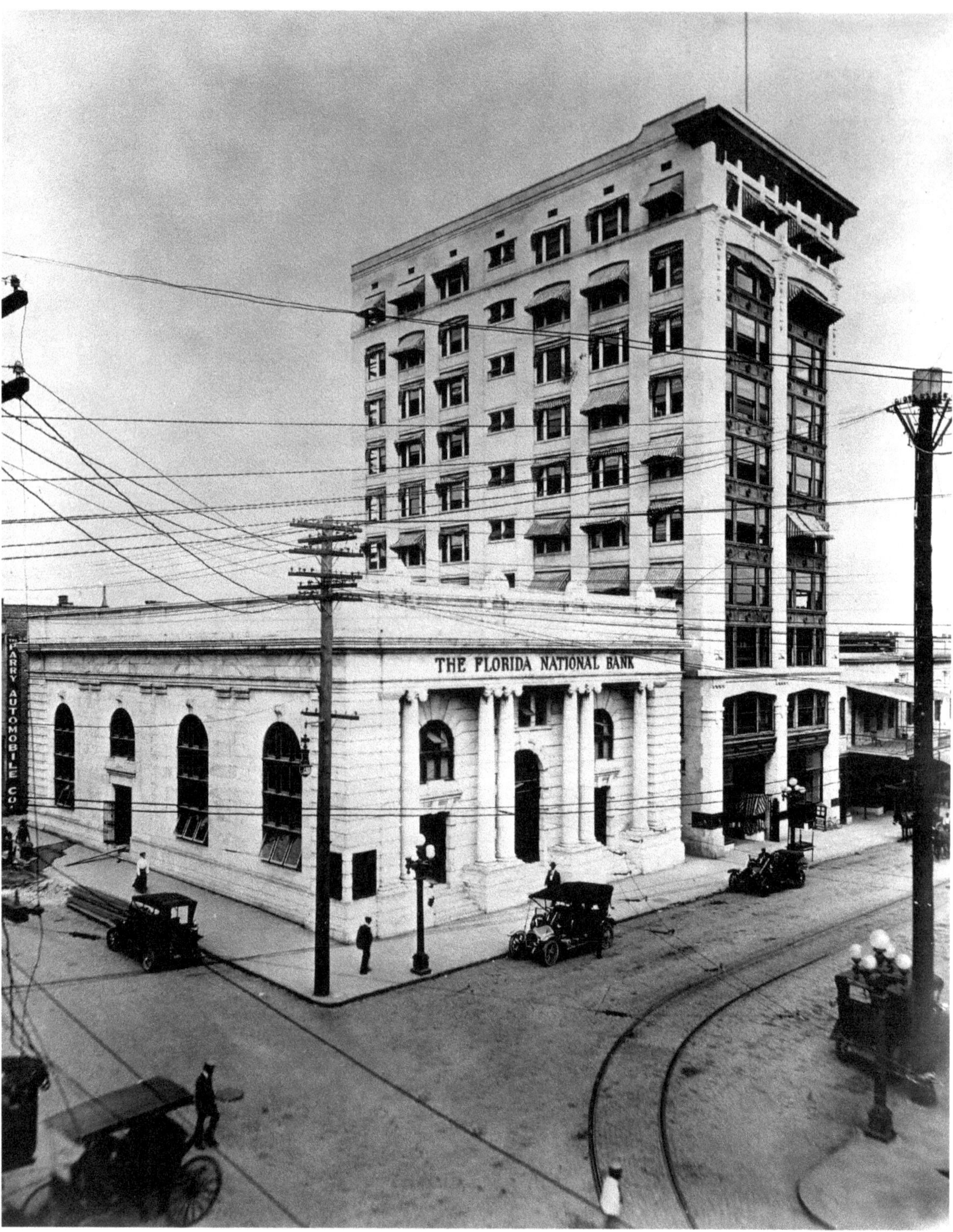

The Barnett Bank, organized in 1877, first opened in the Freedman's Bank Building at the southwest corner of Pine (Main) and Forsyth. Later the bank moved to the location shown here in 1910, at the northwest corner of Forsyth and Laura streets. The building was erected in 1898.

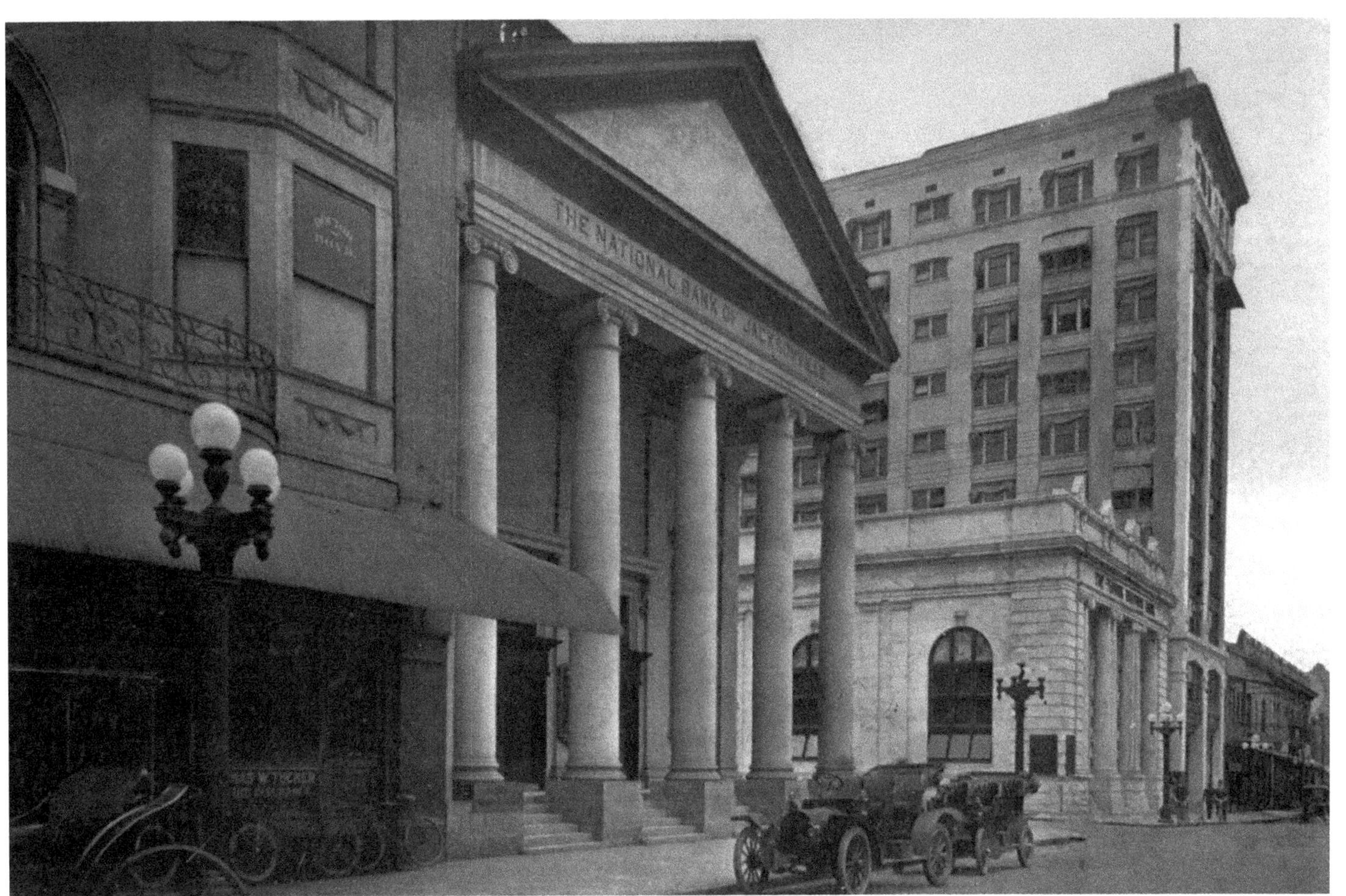

This building was constructed in 1904. In 1915 the Board of Trade Building became the Chamber of Commerce.

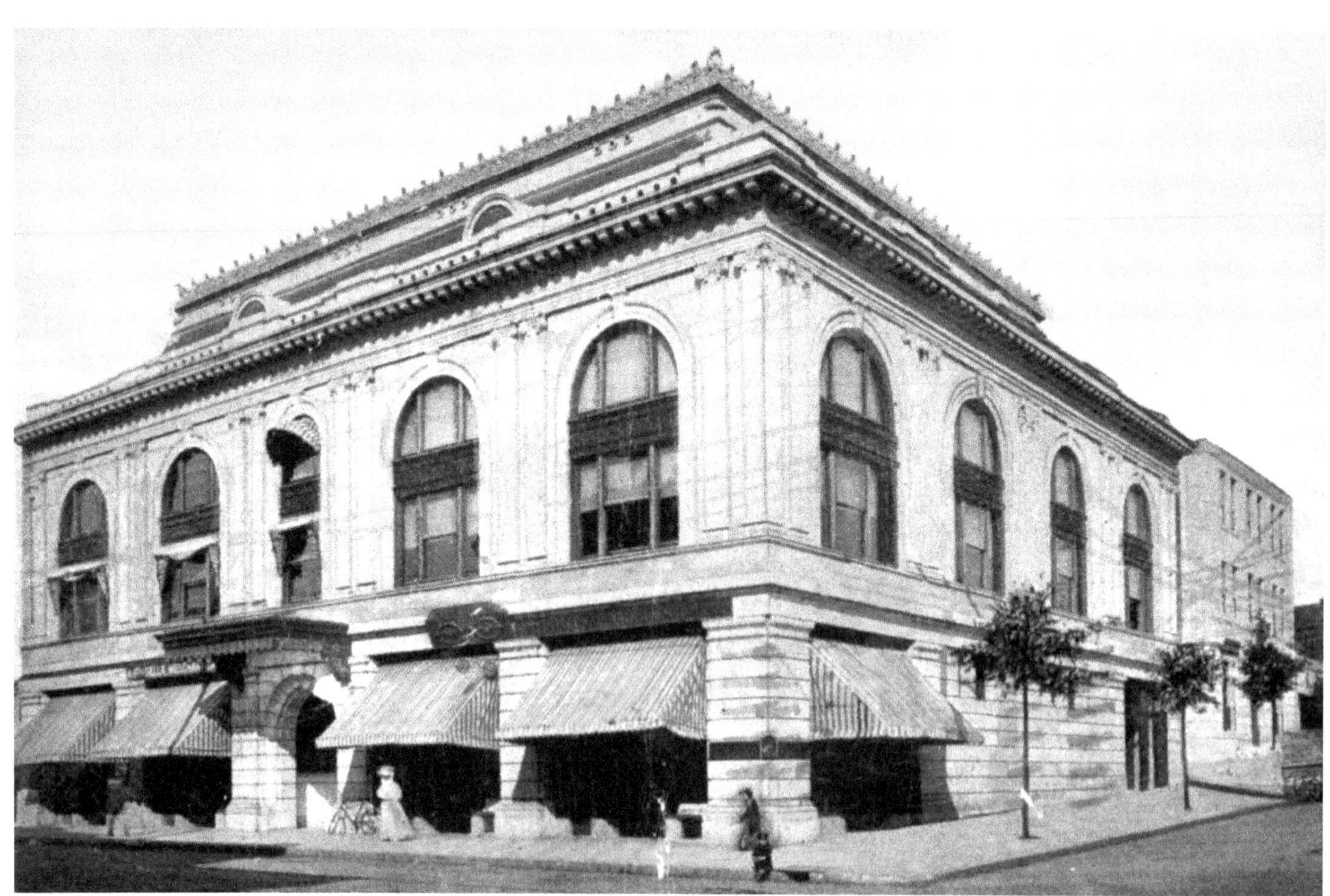

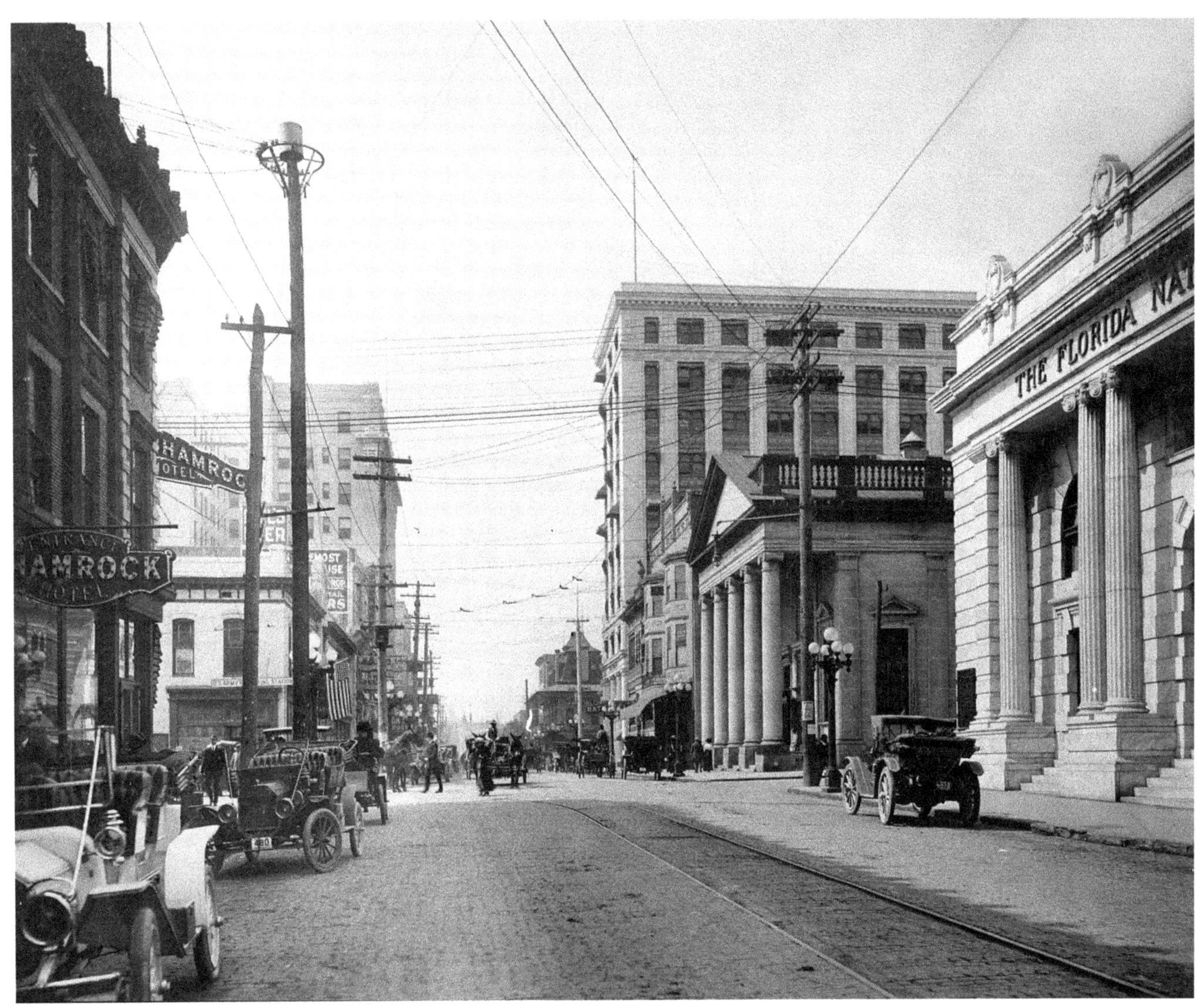

Forsyth Street looking north in 1912

One activity showing that recovery of the city was well under way was the yacht club, shown here in 1904. First organized in 1877, the Florida Yacht Club in Jacksonville is the city's oldest social organization. This building replaced the original club building destroyed in the 1901 fire.

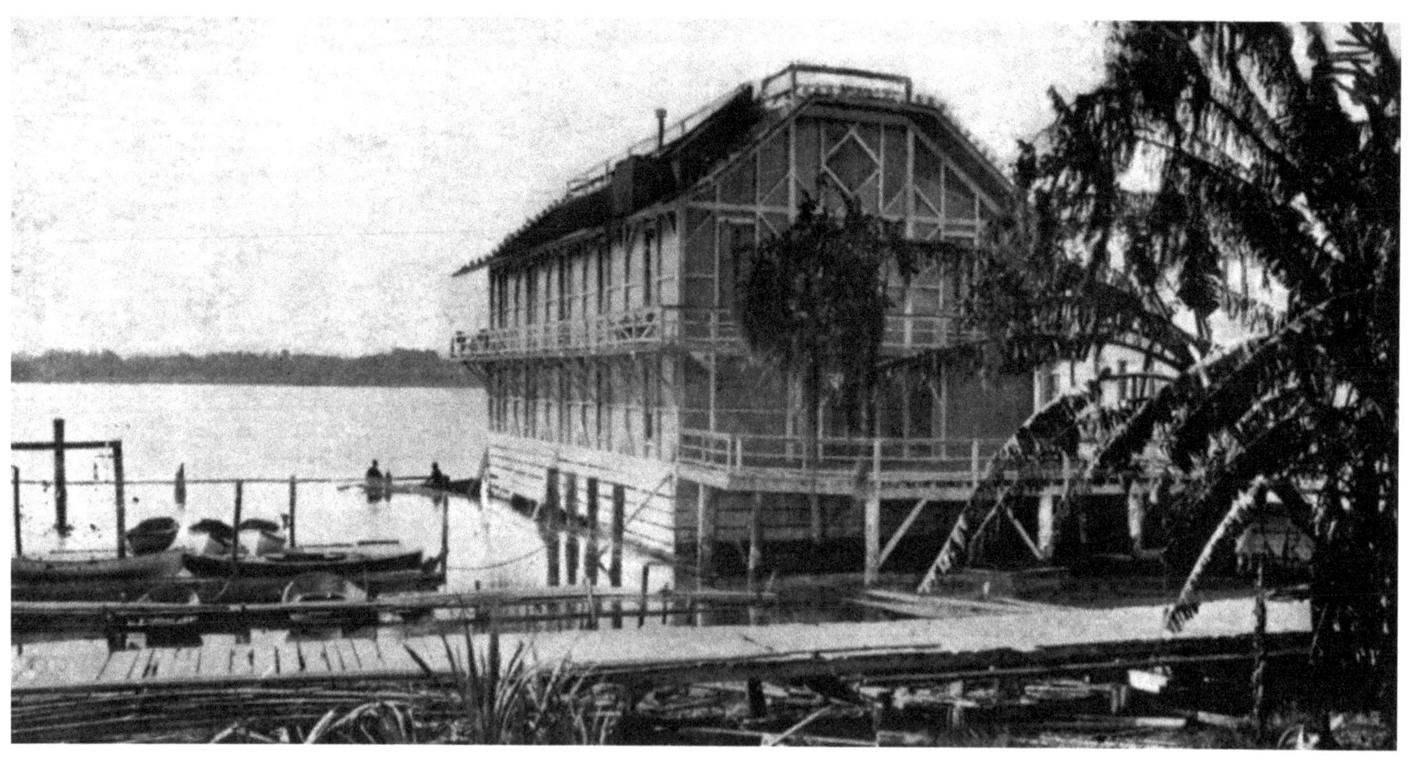

The lodge of the Benevolent and Protective Order of the Elks was first installed in 1891 and was the first Elks Lodge in Florida. The first club rooms were located at the southwest corner of Bay and Market streets. This building was demolished in 1925.

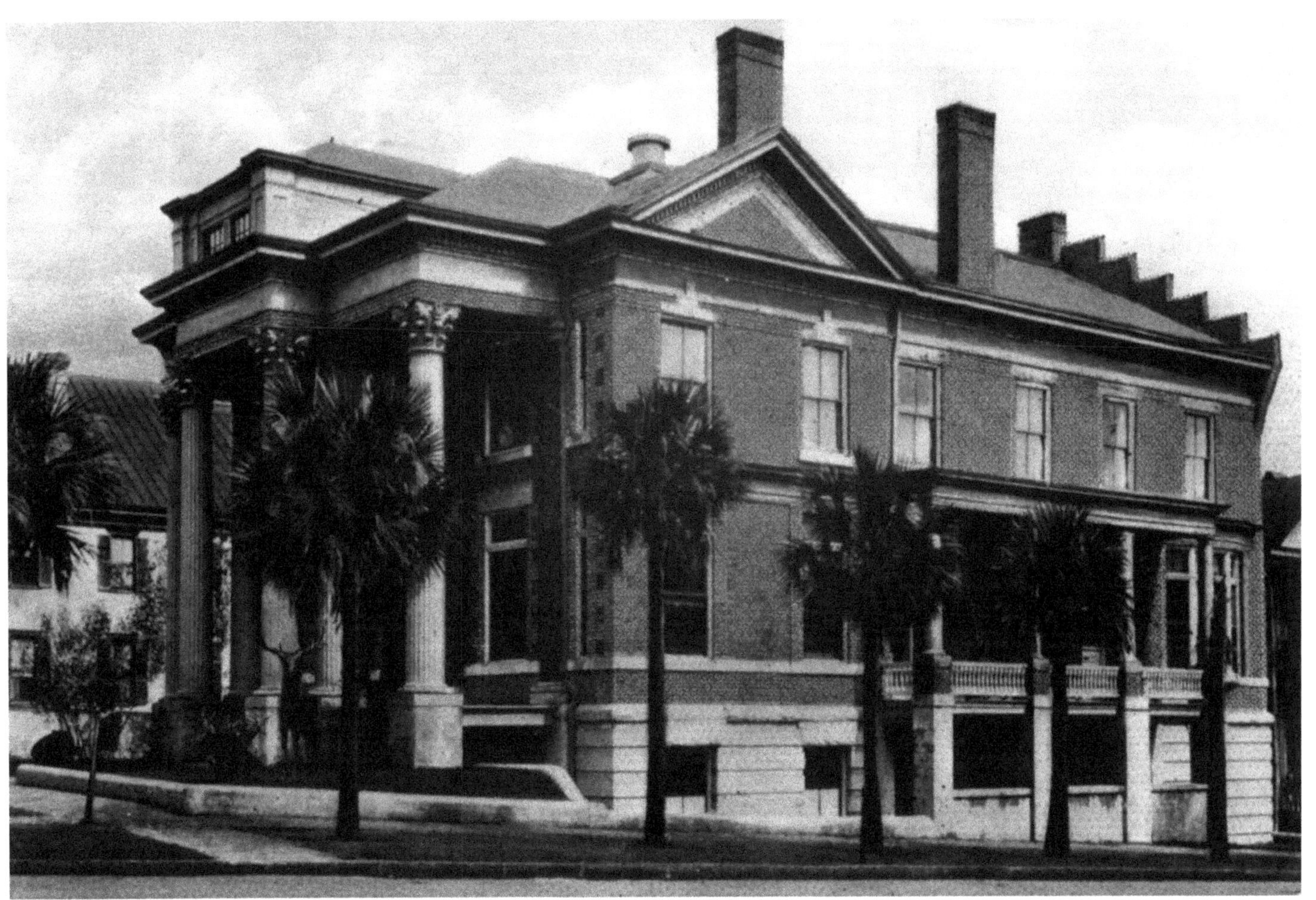

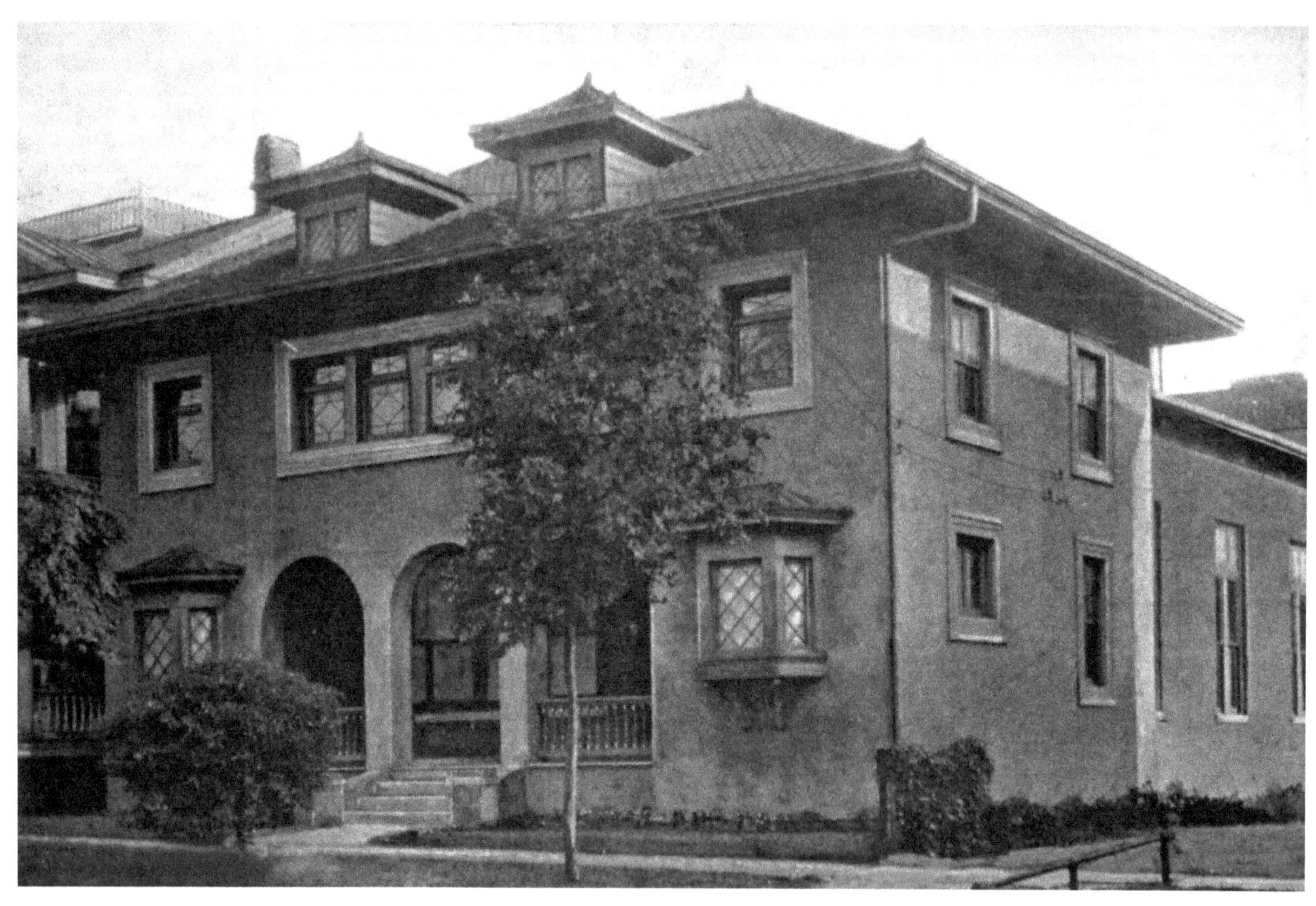

The Jacksonville Woman's Club was organized in the parlors of the Windsor Hotel in 1897. The club purchased a lot at East Duval Street in 1902 where this building was constructed. By the 1920s the Woman's Club had outgrown this structure and in 1927 relocated to its present residence on Riverside Avenue.

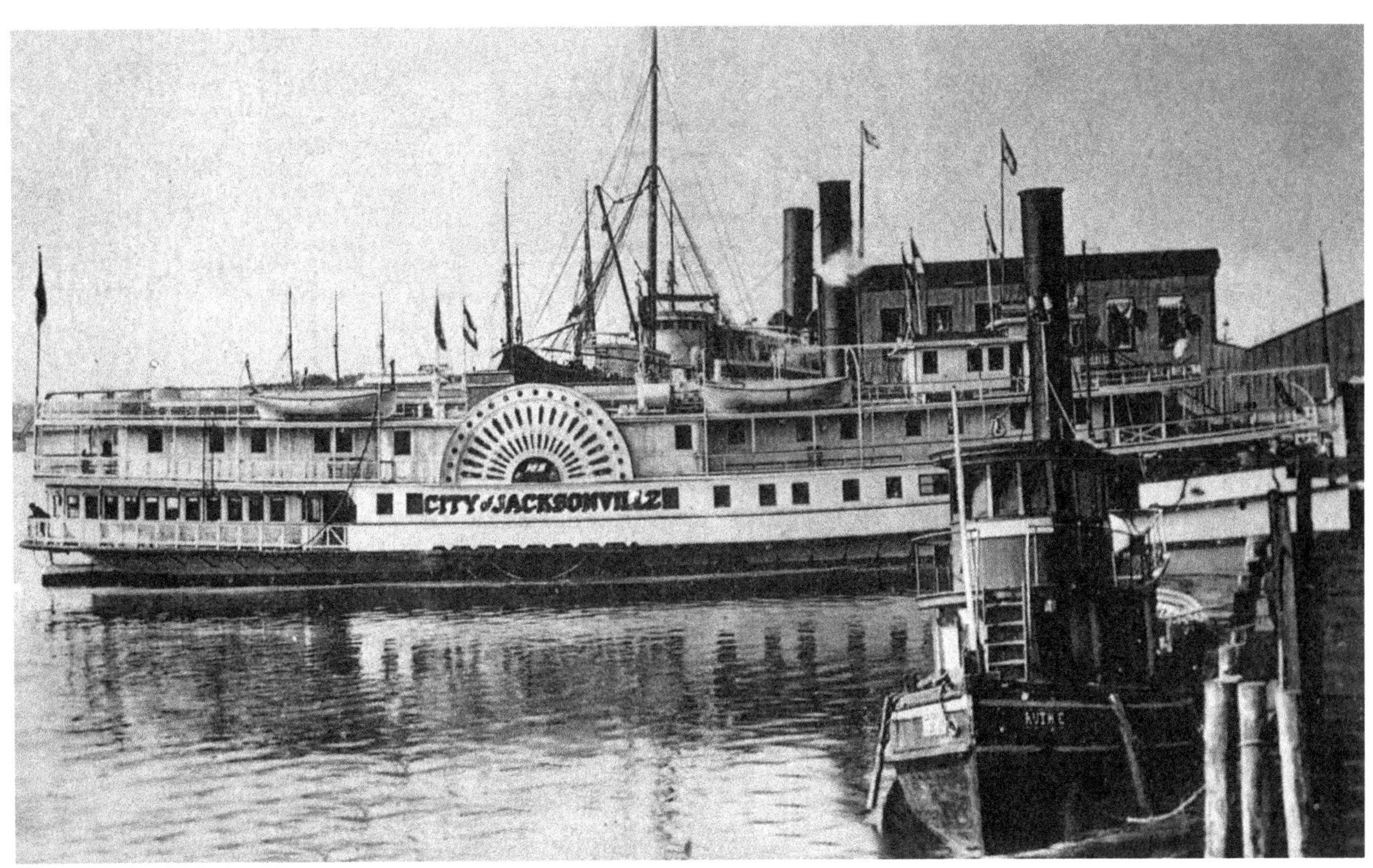

Steamboats like the *City of Jacksonville* and tugboats like the *Ruthie* pictured here were a common sight at the docks of the St. Johns River in the early 1900s. The tourist trade and commerce brought by these vessels were key to the robust economy.

The railroad industry flourished during the early twentieth century. The depot shown here in 1910 was completed in 1897, prompted by Henry Flagler, the owner of the Florida East Coast Railway. The Union Terminal replaced the depot in 1919.

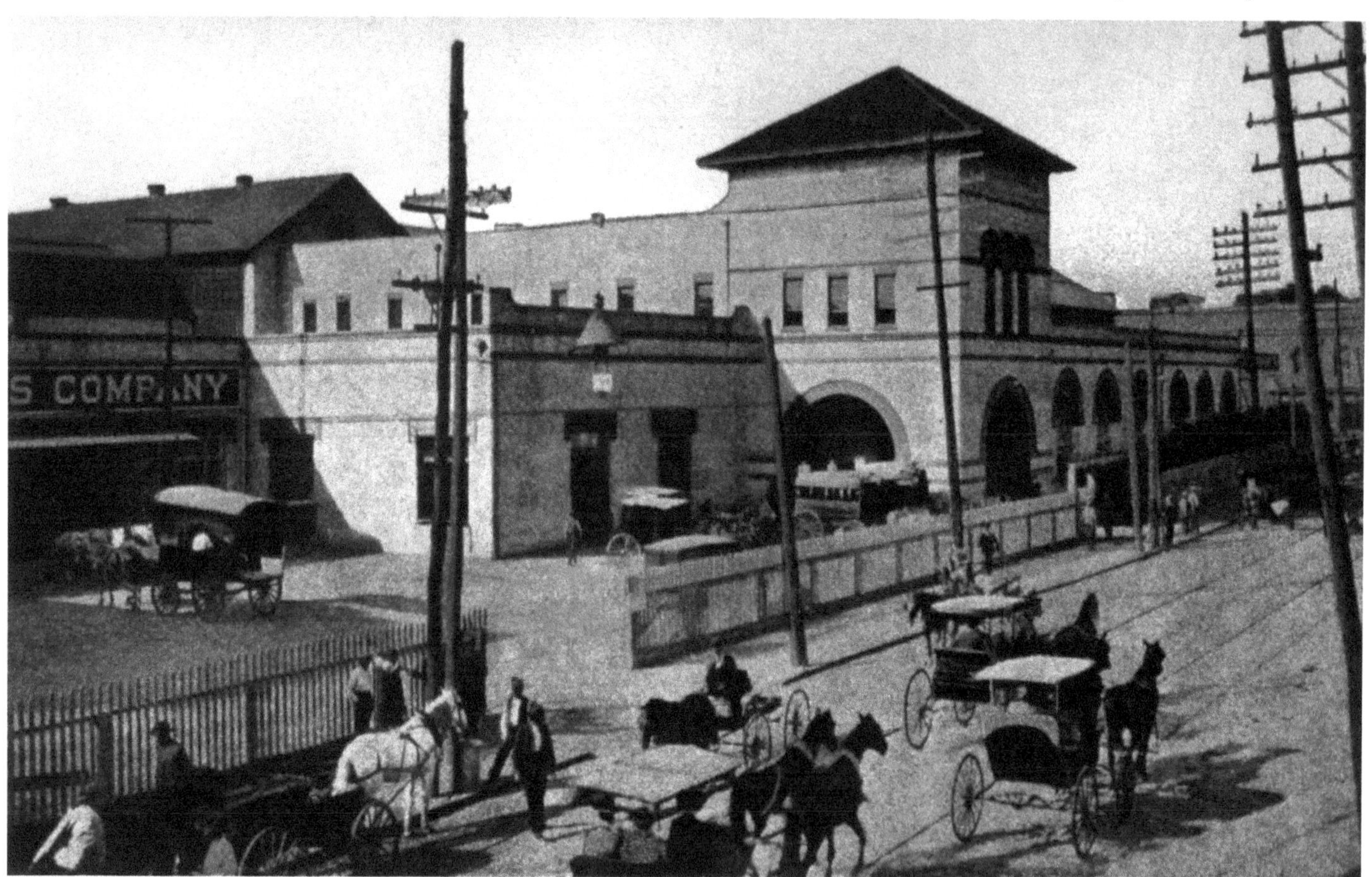

This view of Forsyth Street shows the trolley cars that operated until the 1930s. At the time of this photo, there were four main trolley companies in the city: the Jacksonville Company, the Duval Bridge Company, the South Jacksonville Municipal Railway, and the Ortega Company.

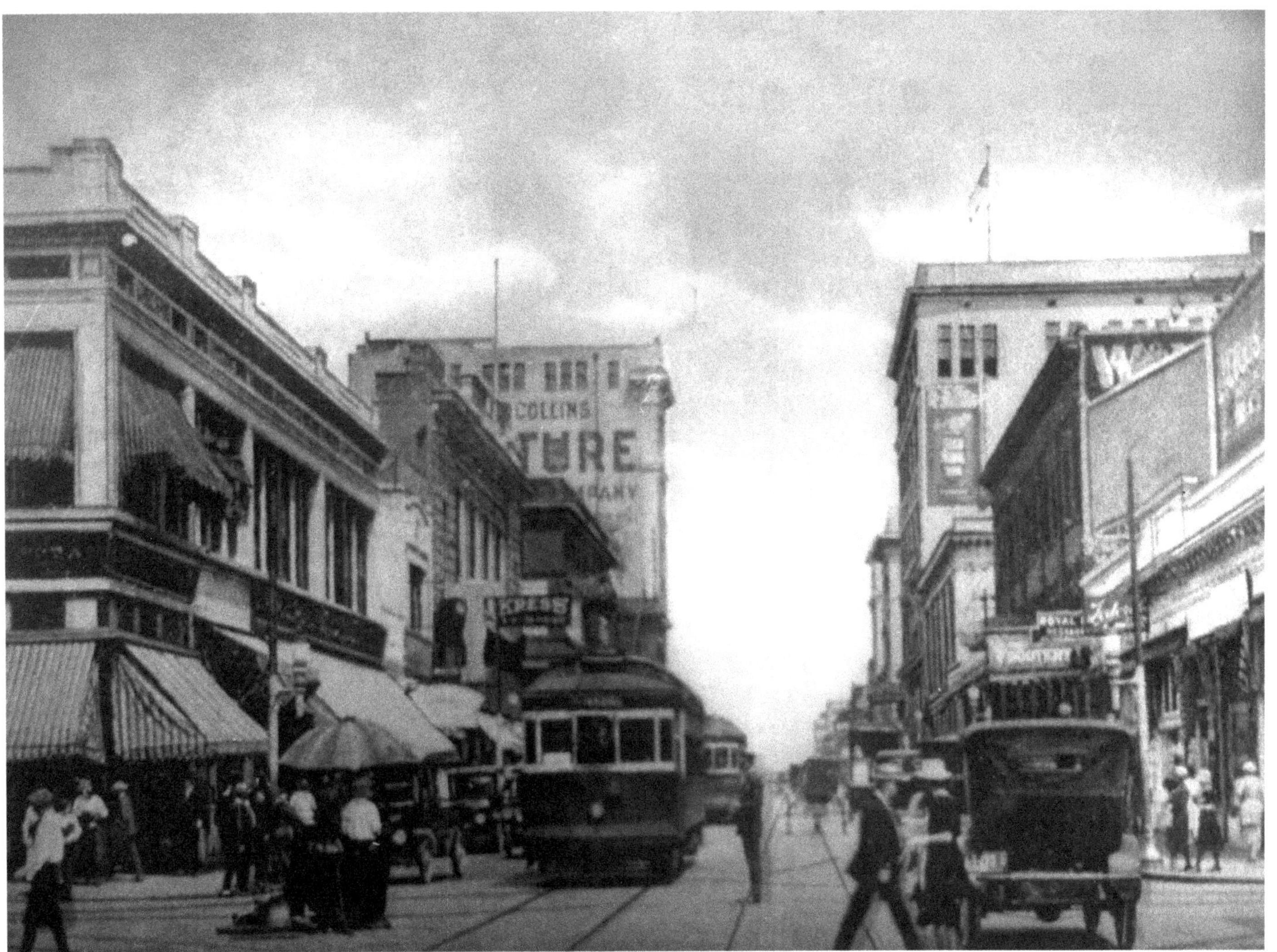

This scene of Bay Street looking north from Laura Street reveals a glimpse of Furchgotts Department Store. Also visible are the various modes of transportation—the trolley, bicycles, the ubiquitous horse-driven wagon, and automobiles, which were rapidly multiplying on the streets of Jacksonville.

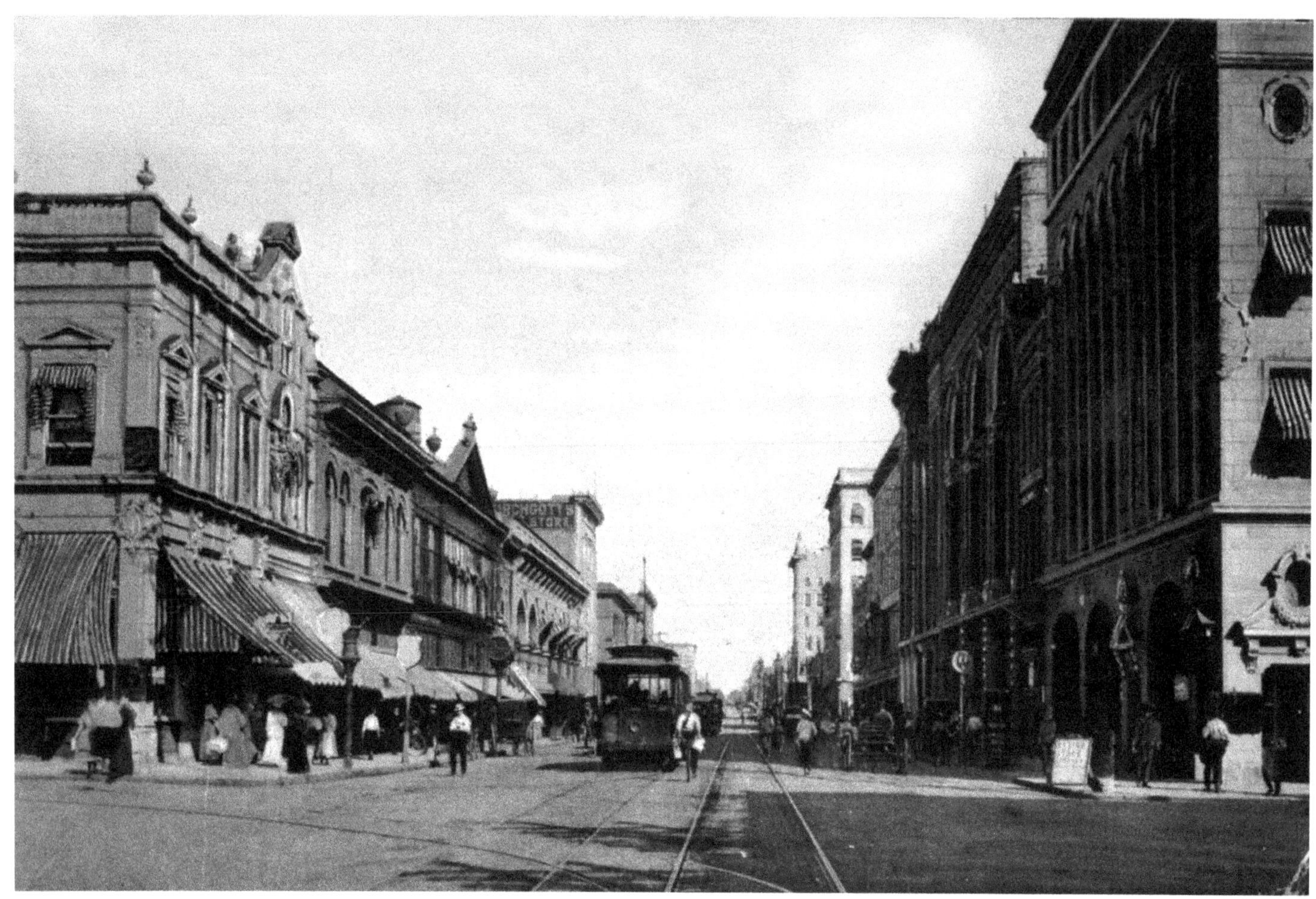

This view of West Bay Street looking southward provides a close-up of the trolleys and the Greenleaf and Crosby Clock at the northwest corner of Laura and Adams streets.

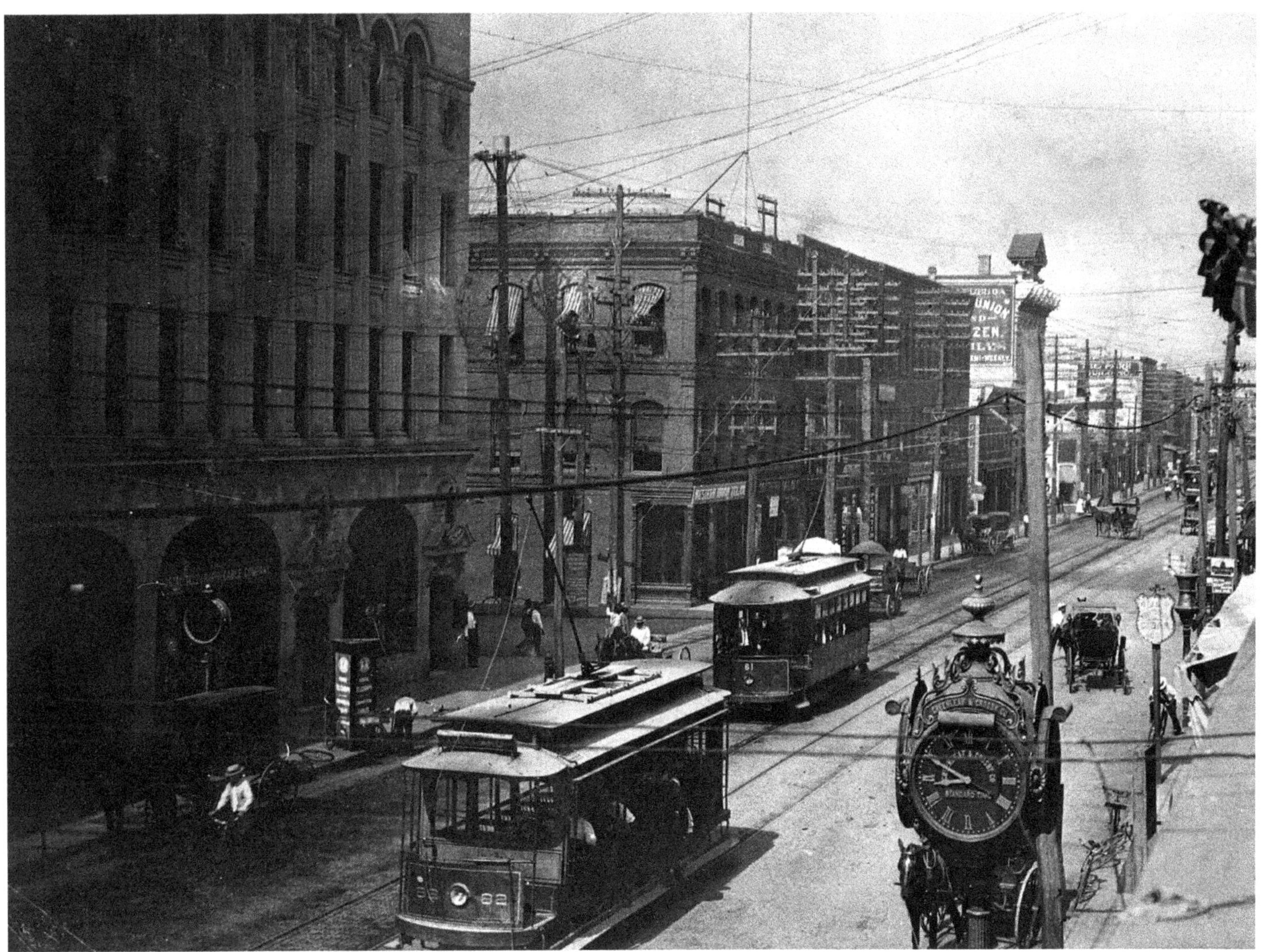

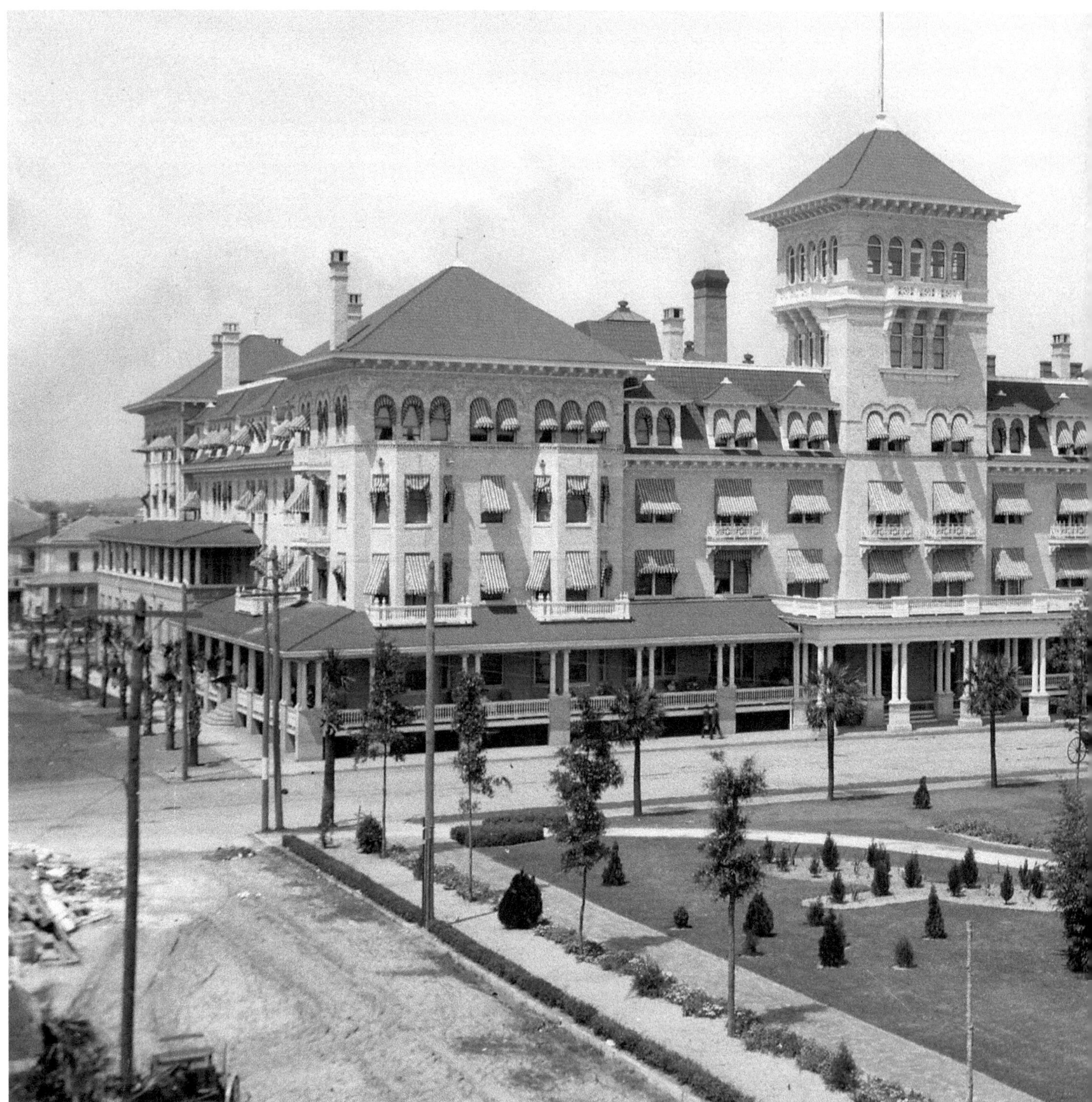

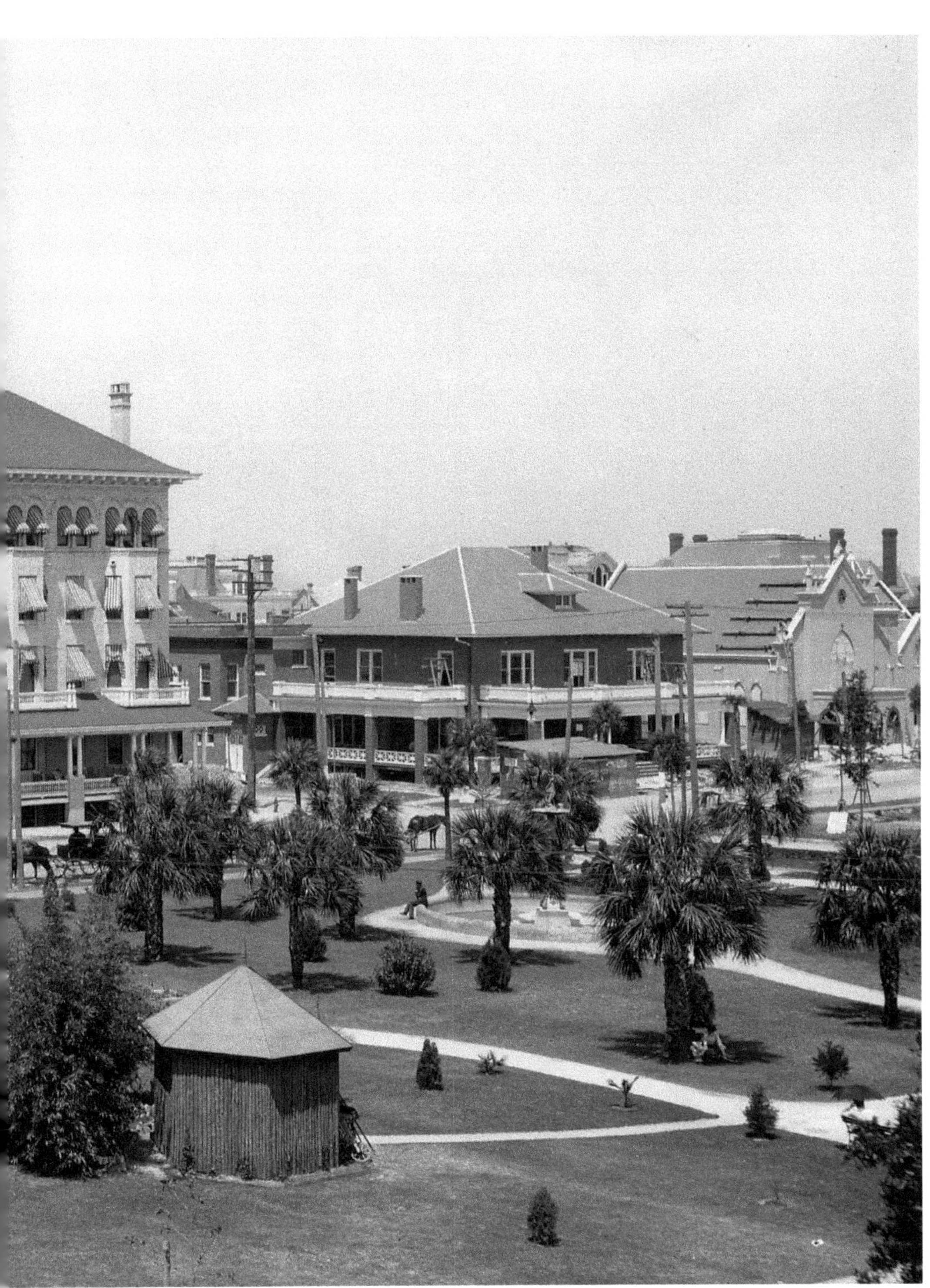

The Windsor Hotel (pictured here in 1903) began as a three-story wooden structure occupying the lot at the northwest corner of Hogan and Monroe streets in 1875. Shown here in 1902, the Windsor was the only large hotel destroyed by the 1901 fire and rebuilt. The new building was made of brick, stone, and steel, divided into sections by fire walls, and had accommodations for 500 guests.

The Duval Hotel, shown here in 1908, opened in 1893 at the northwest corner of Hogan and Forsyth streets and was one of the few buildings to survive the Great Fire. It partly rests on the most historic spot in Jacksonville—the site of the first house built in the city.

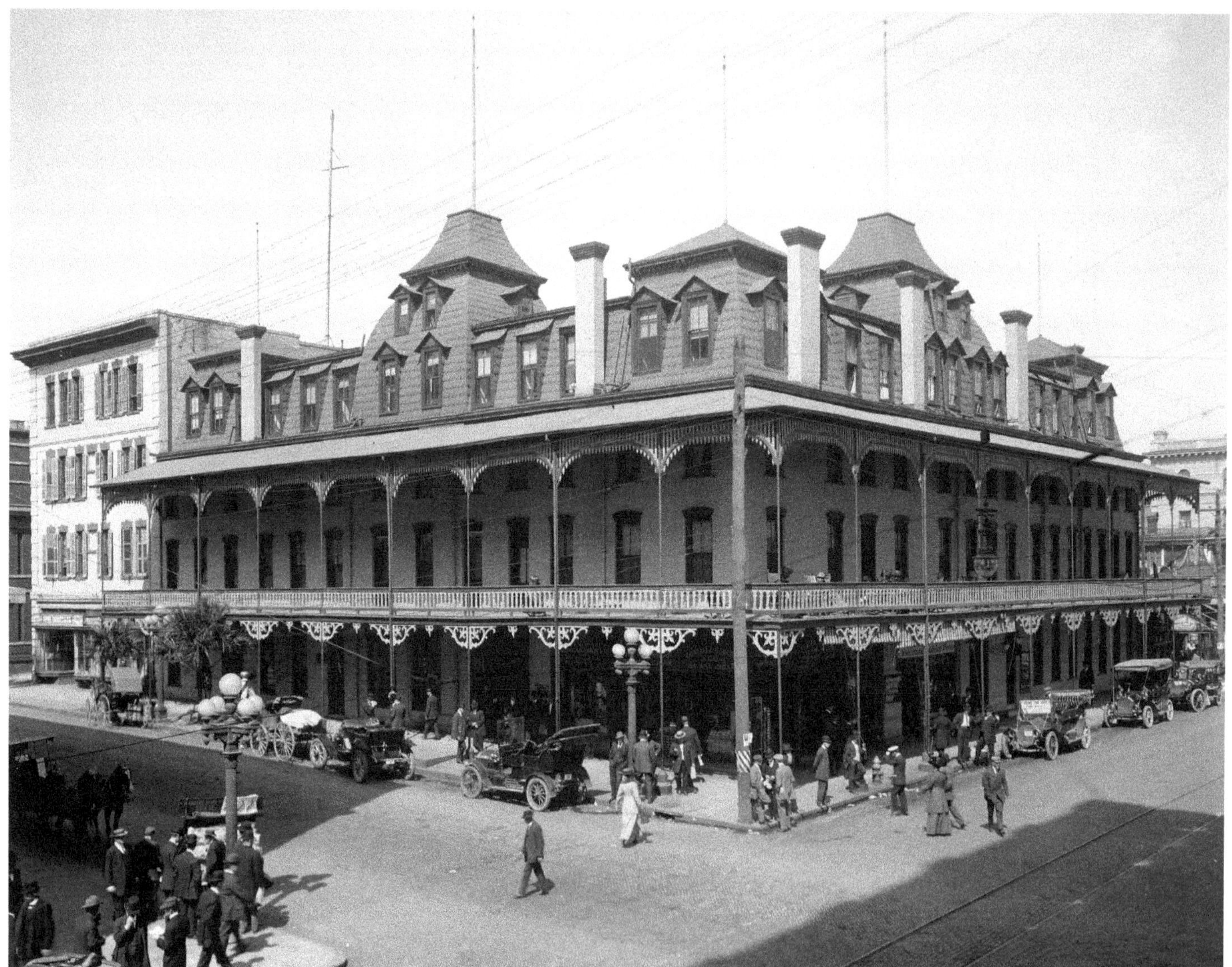

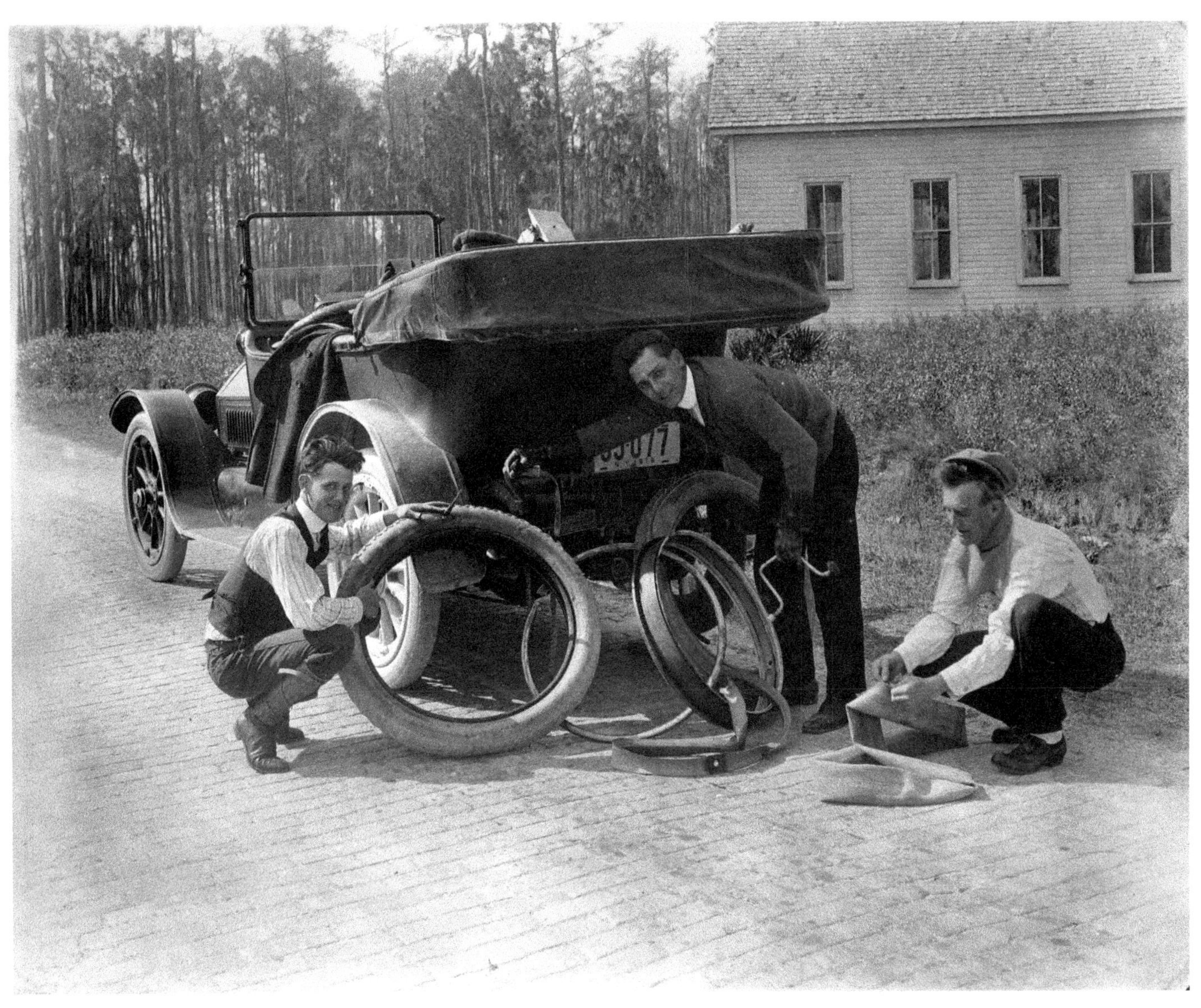

By the second decade of the twentieth century, automobiles were not only a means of transportation but also for some a hobby. The three men posing here in 1915 appear to be changing a flat.

People shown here are fishing off one of the city's piers in the early 1900s, a traditional leisure activity in Jacksonville.

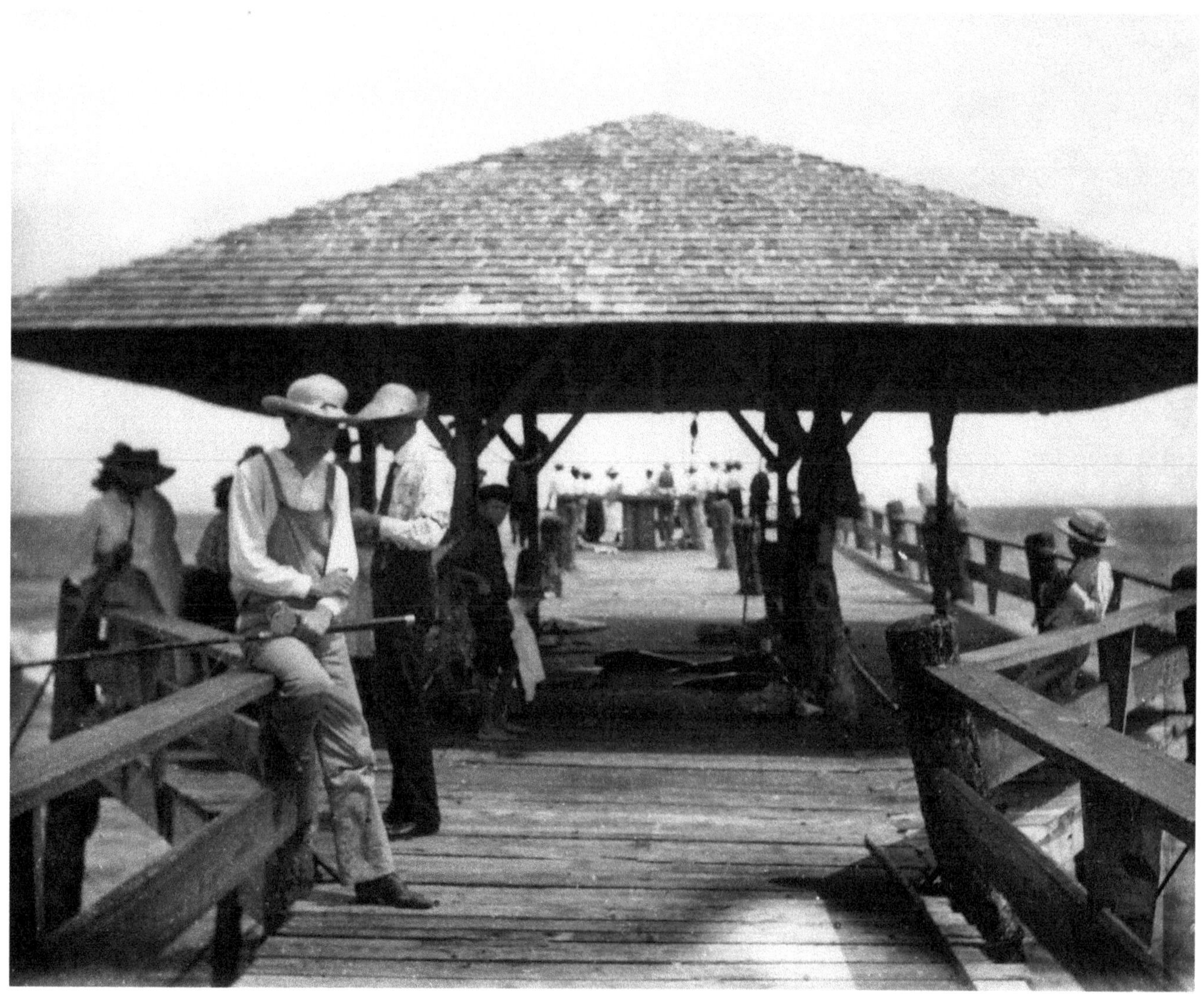

By the time this picture was taken, the city had a number of one-room schoolhouses like this one. This class portrait was taken in 1910.

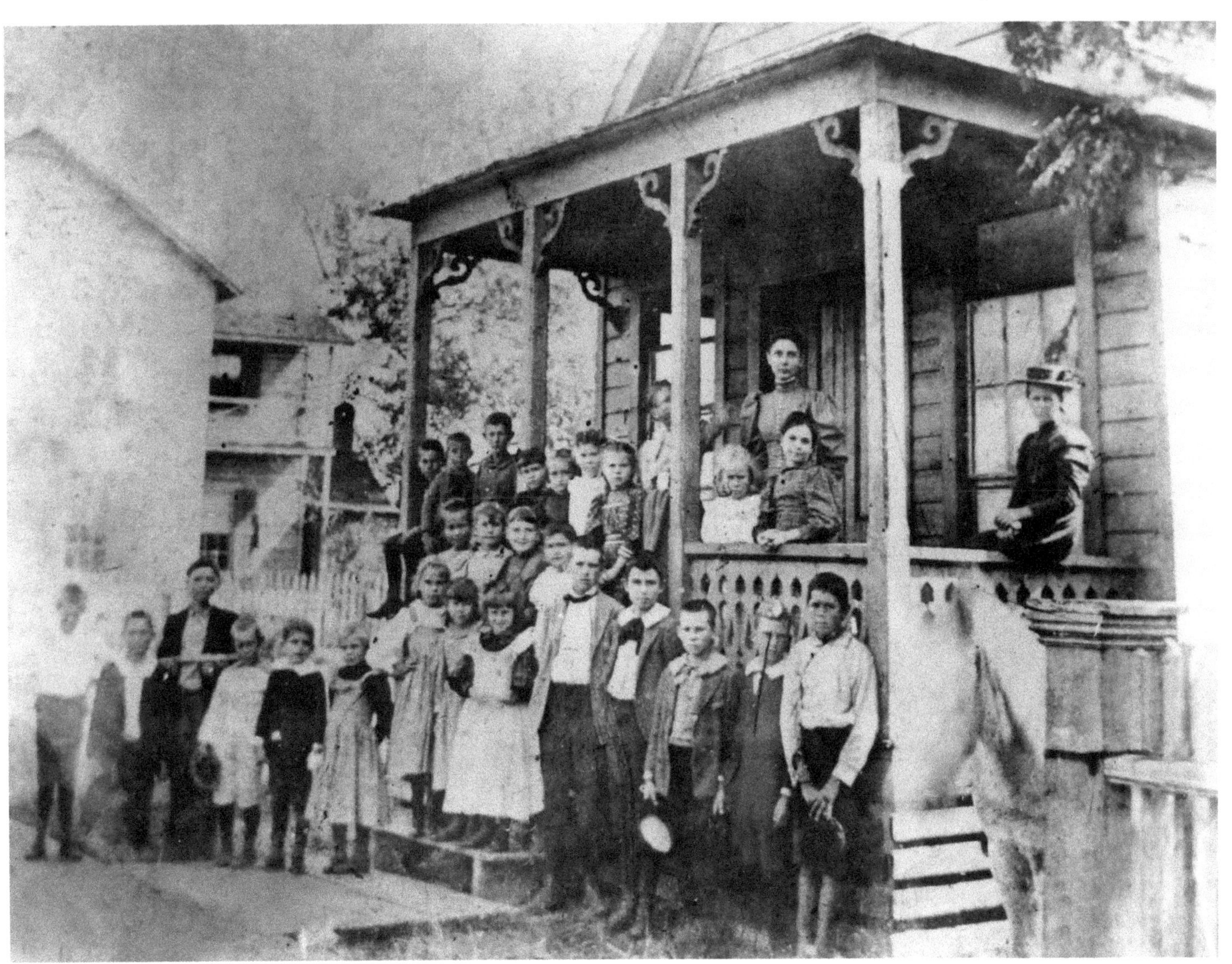

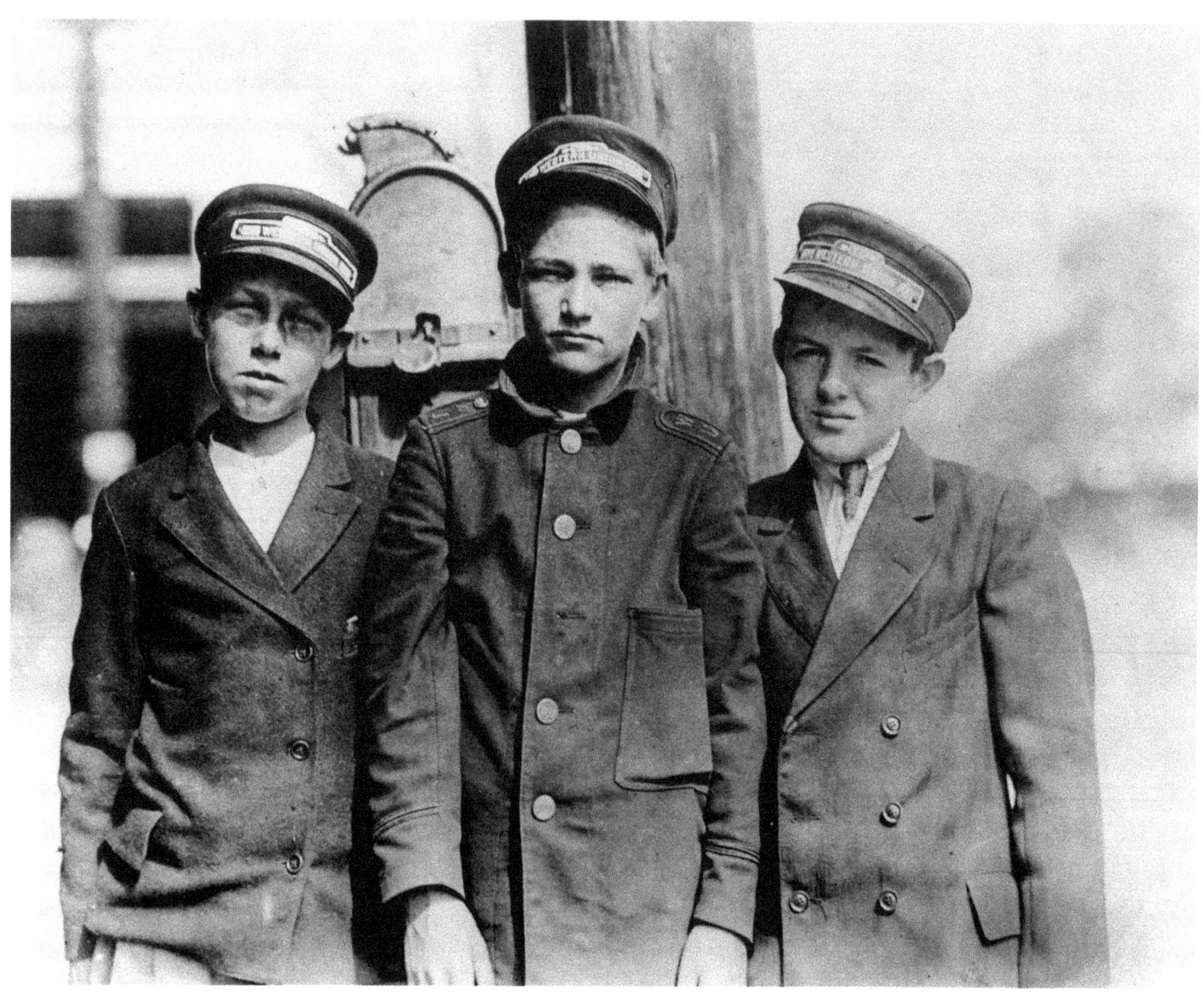

Children employed at various jobs, like these Western Union messenger boys, were also a common sight. When this picture was taken in 1913, the Western Union Telegraph Company was located at Bay and Laura streets.

The *Florida Times-Union*, originally the *Florida Union* in 1864, later became the *Florida Times-Union and Citizen.* In 1903 the paper adopted its current name. These young men are employed in the advertising department of the newspaper.

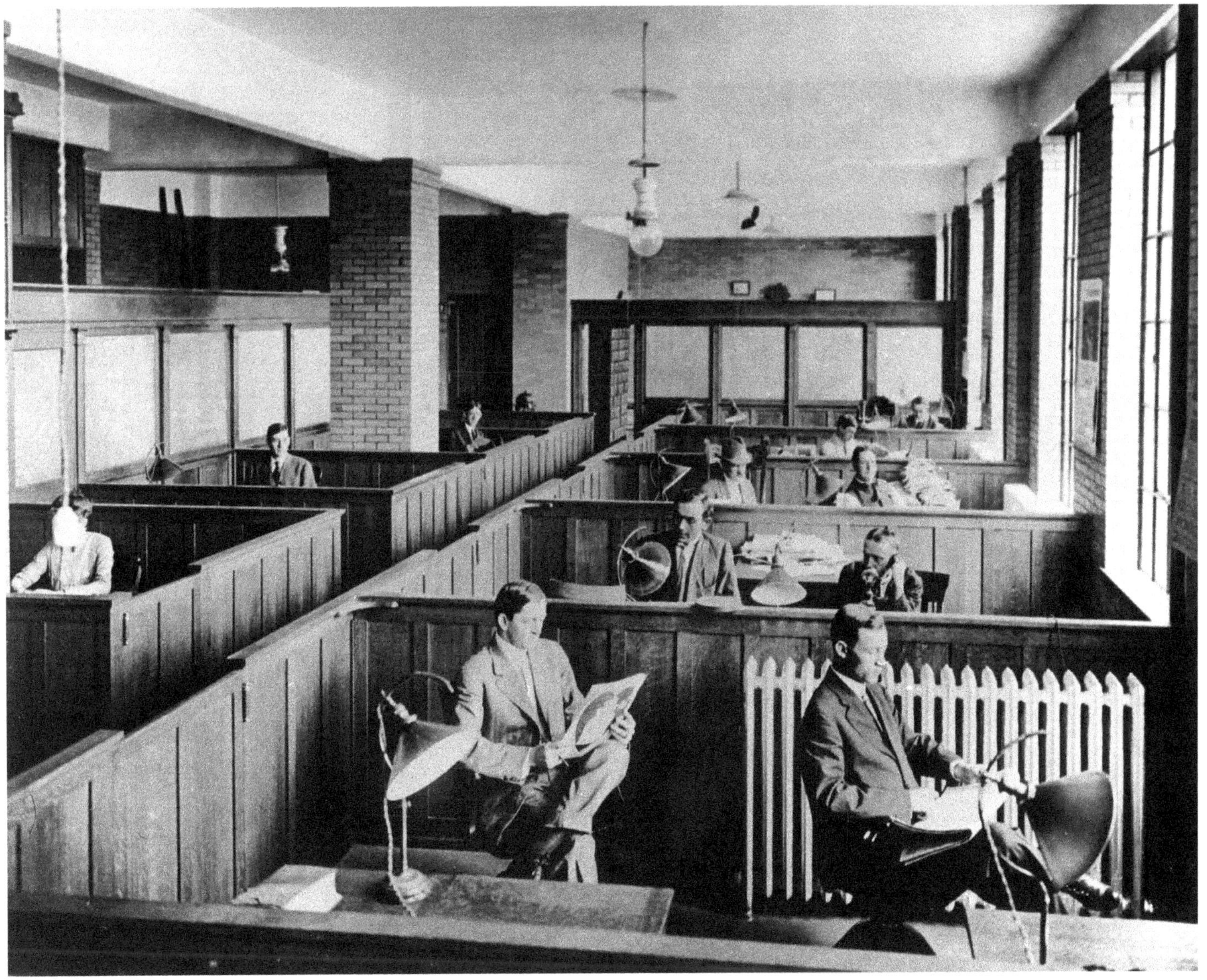

Florida Times-Union employees doing linotype in 1911

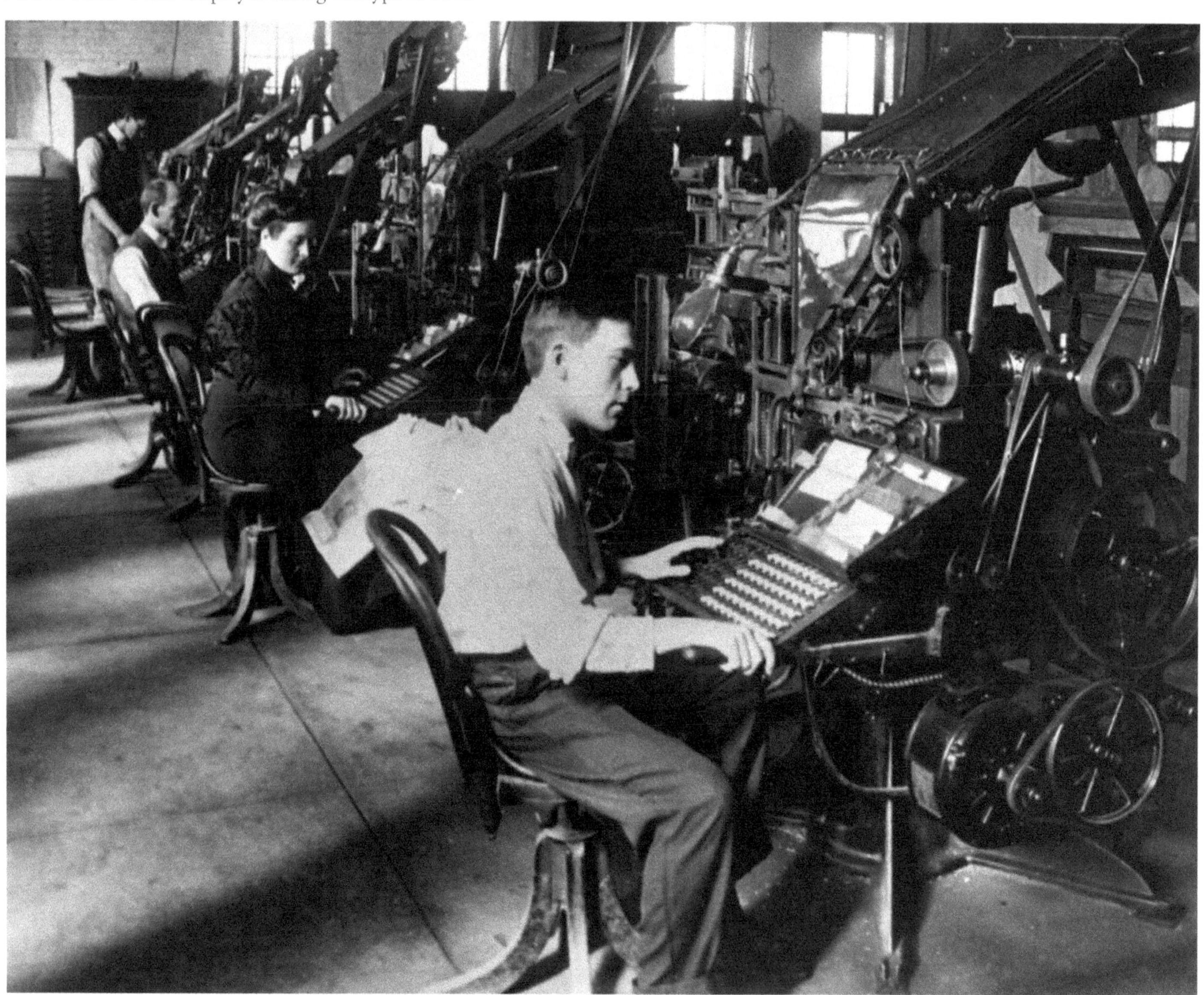

Women soon became the telephone operators, but here men are seen testing a telephone switchboard in 1914. According to early Jacksonville historian T. Frederick Davis, the first telephone in operation in Jacksonville (and perhaps Florida) was a "private line connecting the office of A. M. Beck at Bay and Pine (Main) Streets with Inland Navigation Company at the foot of Laura Street."

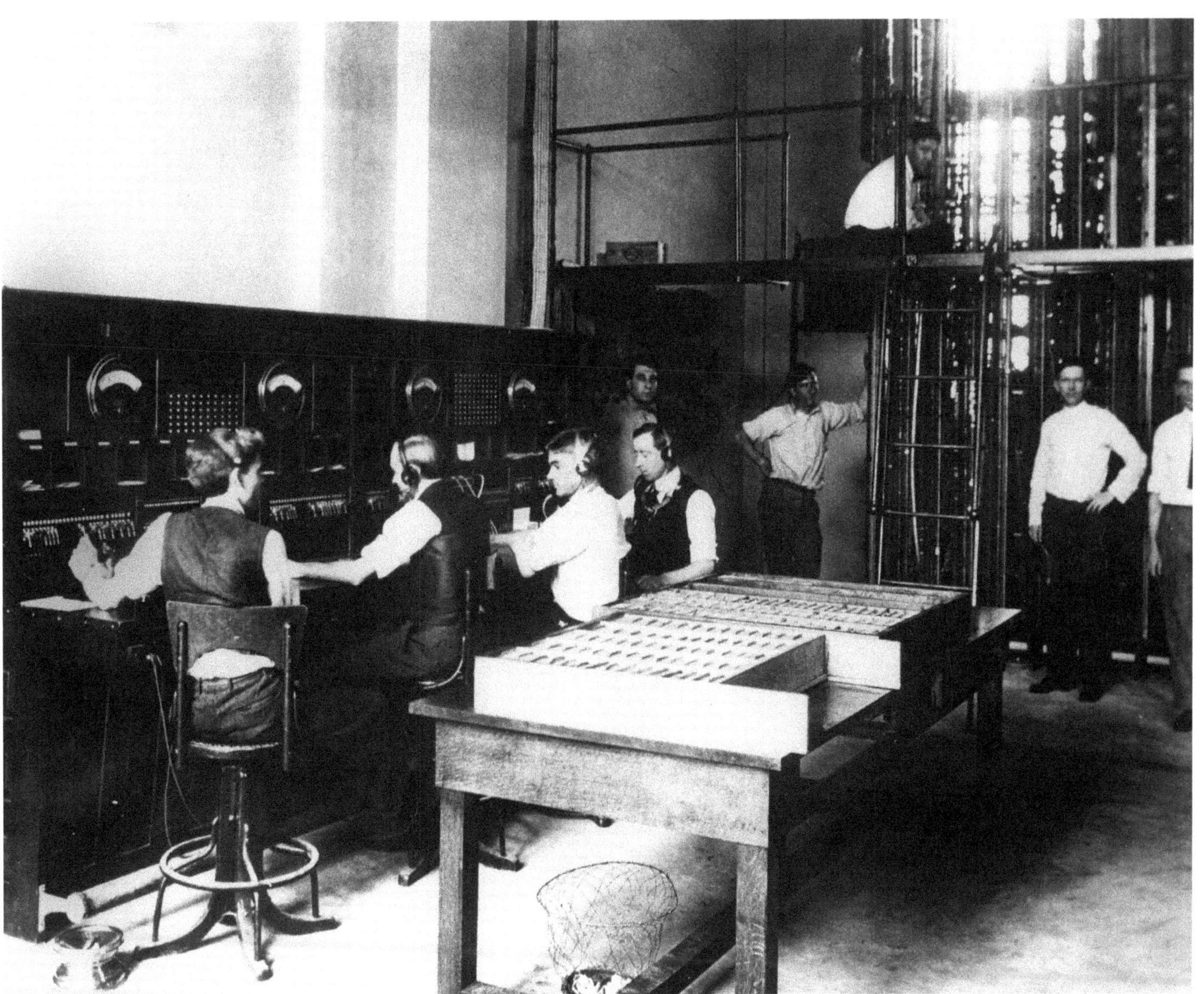

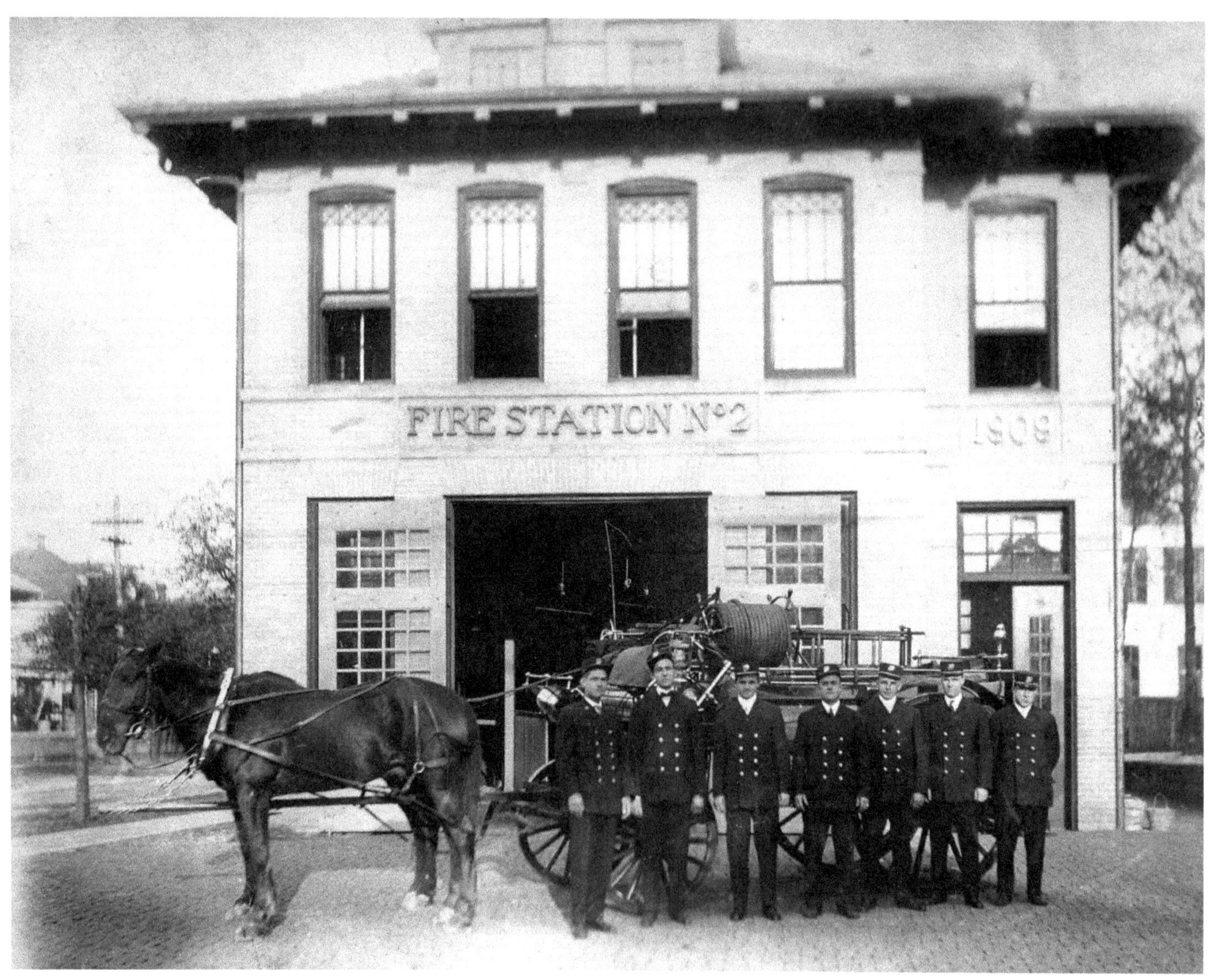

The city government first authorized funds for a fire department in 1886. Fire Department No. 2 was first located at the west side of Main Street between Church and Ashley streets. In 1898 it was moved to the west side of Main Street between State and Orange. After the fire the station was rebuilt on the same site, and by 1915, when this photo of firemen and their horse-driven wagon was taken, the department was stationed on the southeast corner of 4th and Main streets in Springfield.

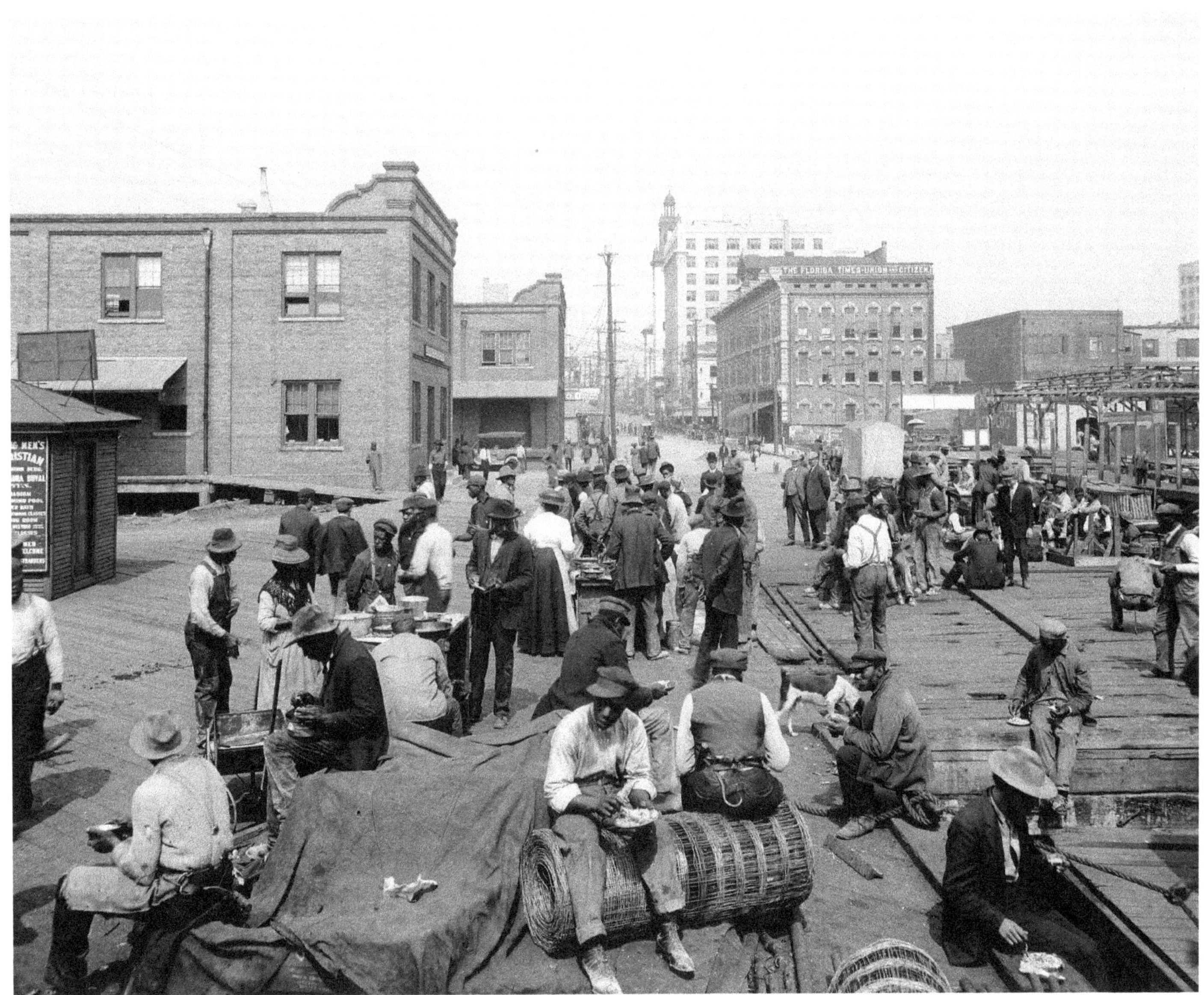

African American men were chief among the workers along the city's docks. This 1912 picture shows dockworkers at their dinner (lunch) hour.

The Gibbs Gas Engine Company, shown here in 1911, was among the many businesses located on the docks by the early twentieth century.

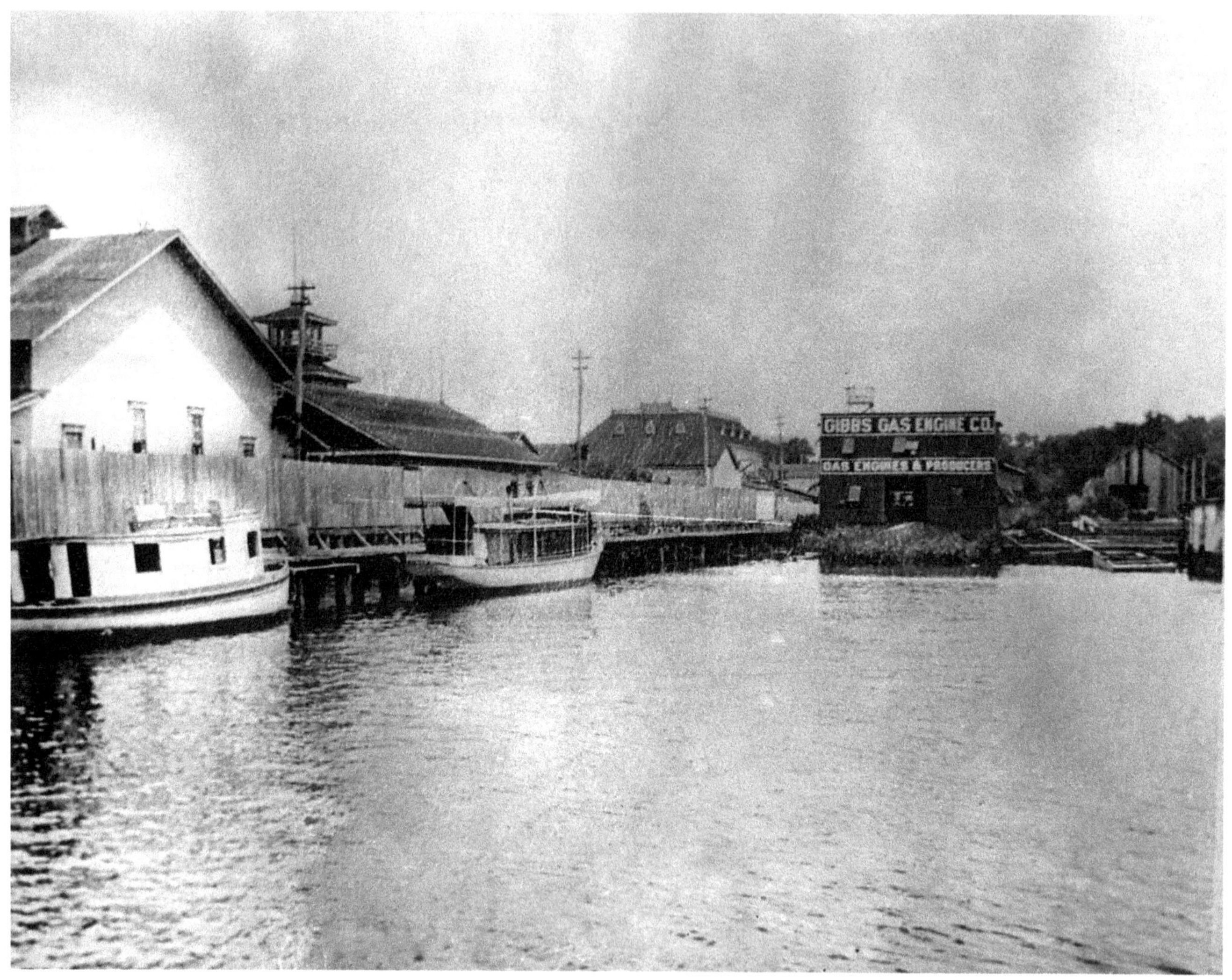

Because of the yellow fever and other epidemics in the nineteenth century, the city had learned the value of providing residents with an adequate water supply. These men are laying water pipes. Also visible is the Palms Hotel.

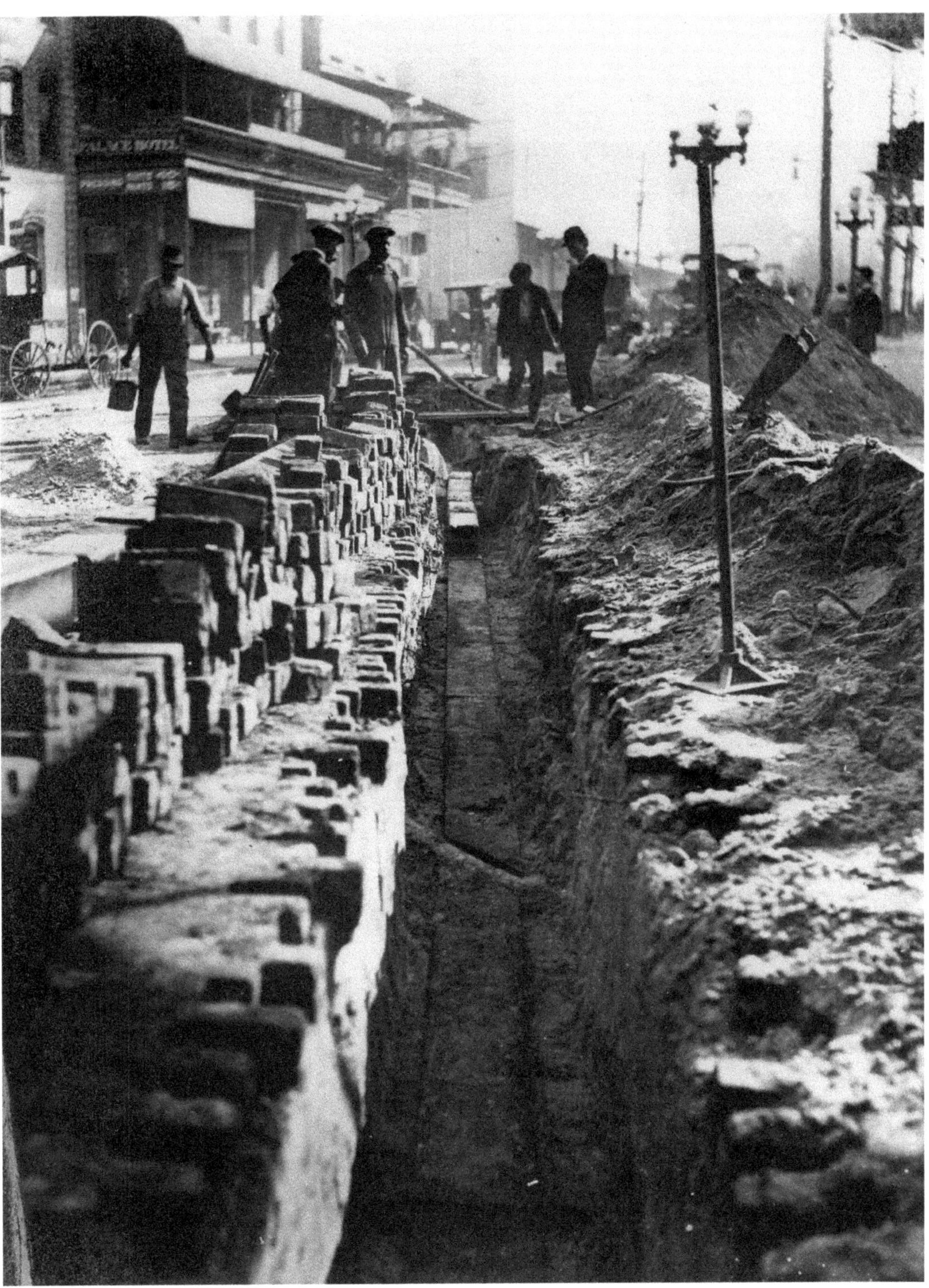

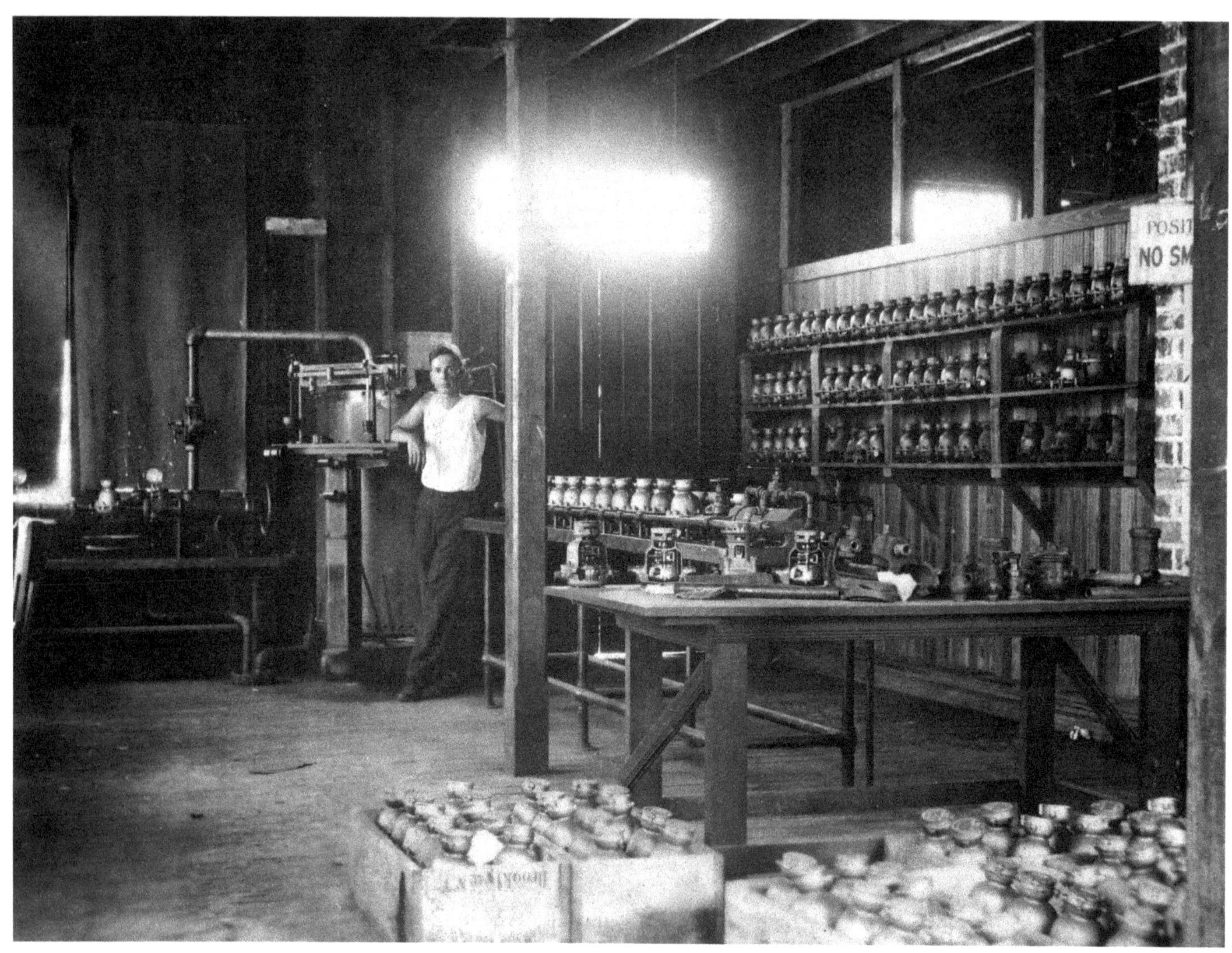

An employee in the Water Department's meter shop in 1914

This festive scene is a view of Forsyth Street in 1914. The flags of both the U.S. and the Confederacy are shown proudly waving.

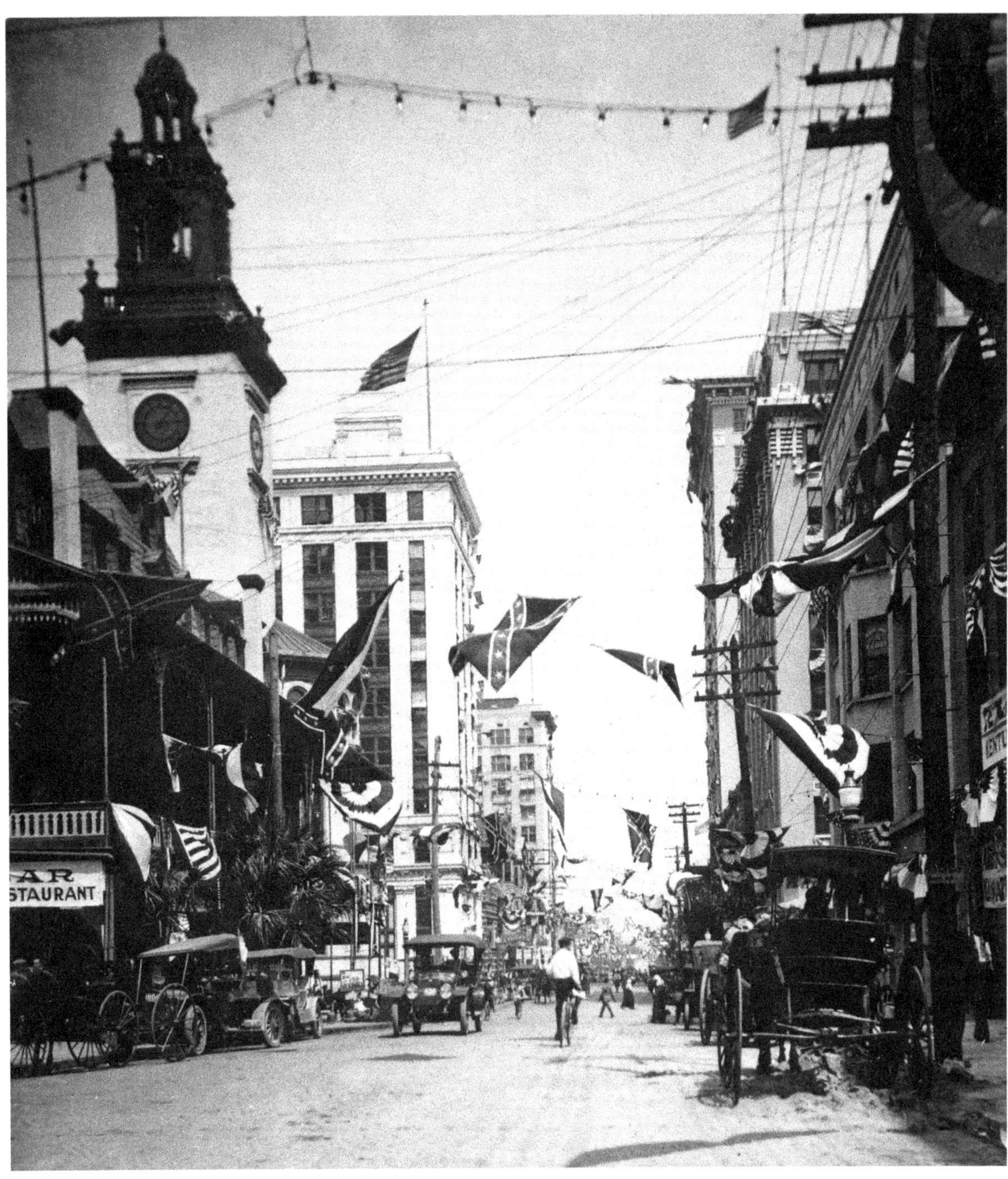

In this view of Forsyth Street, at the intersection of Hogan, the Windsor Hotel is visible at left.

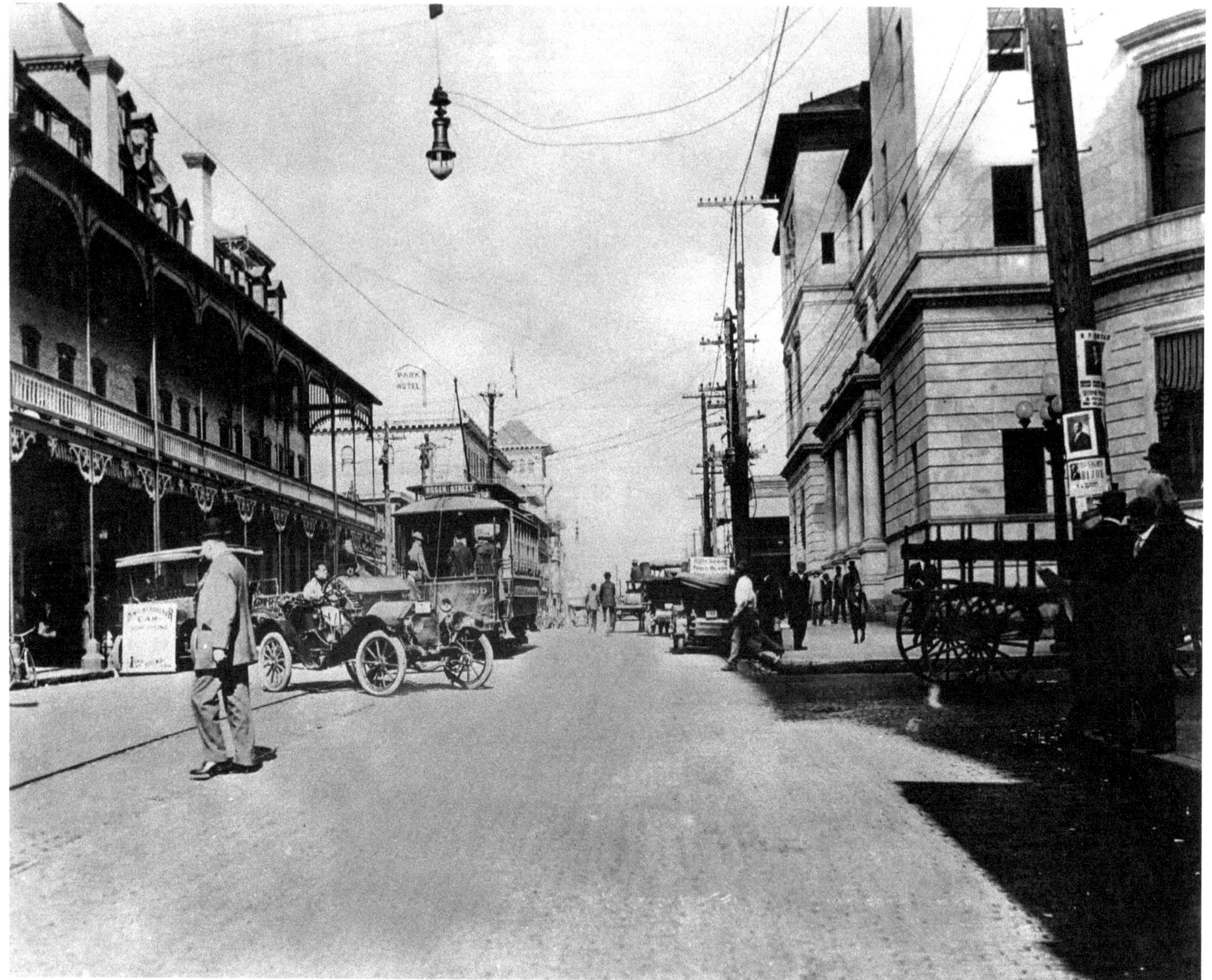

This view of Forsyth Street at the intersection of Hogan Street reveals movie theaters, which were becoming part of the cityscape. The Metropolis and Imperial Theatres are partly visible at opposite sides.

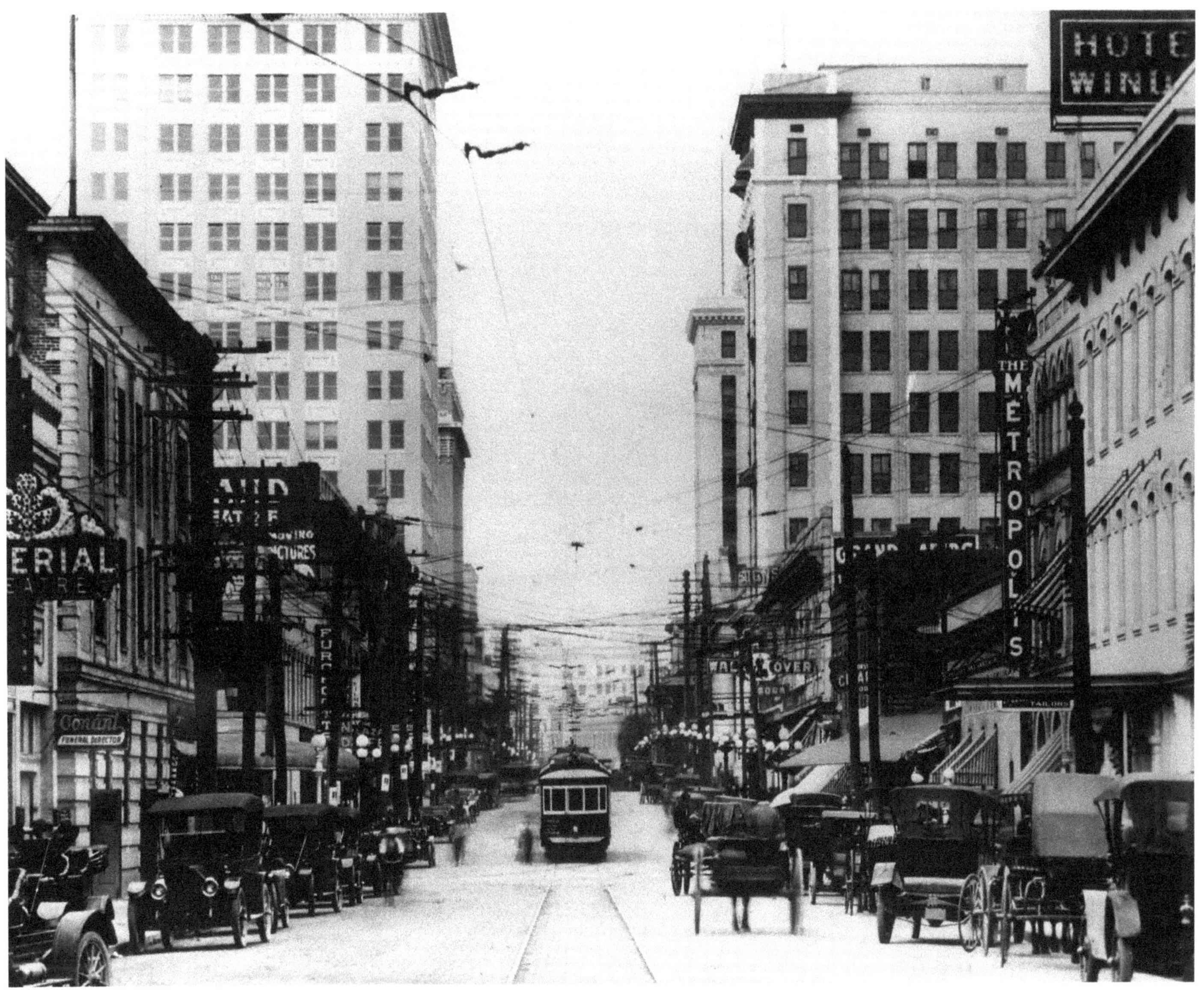

The shipbuilding industry that began in Jacksonville in the 1800s was given a boost by the Great War. Besides constructing new vessels for the war, local shippers benefited from the ongoing repair work. Ships awaiting repair are shown here in 1918.

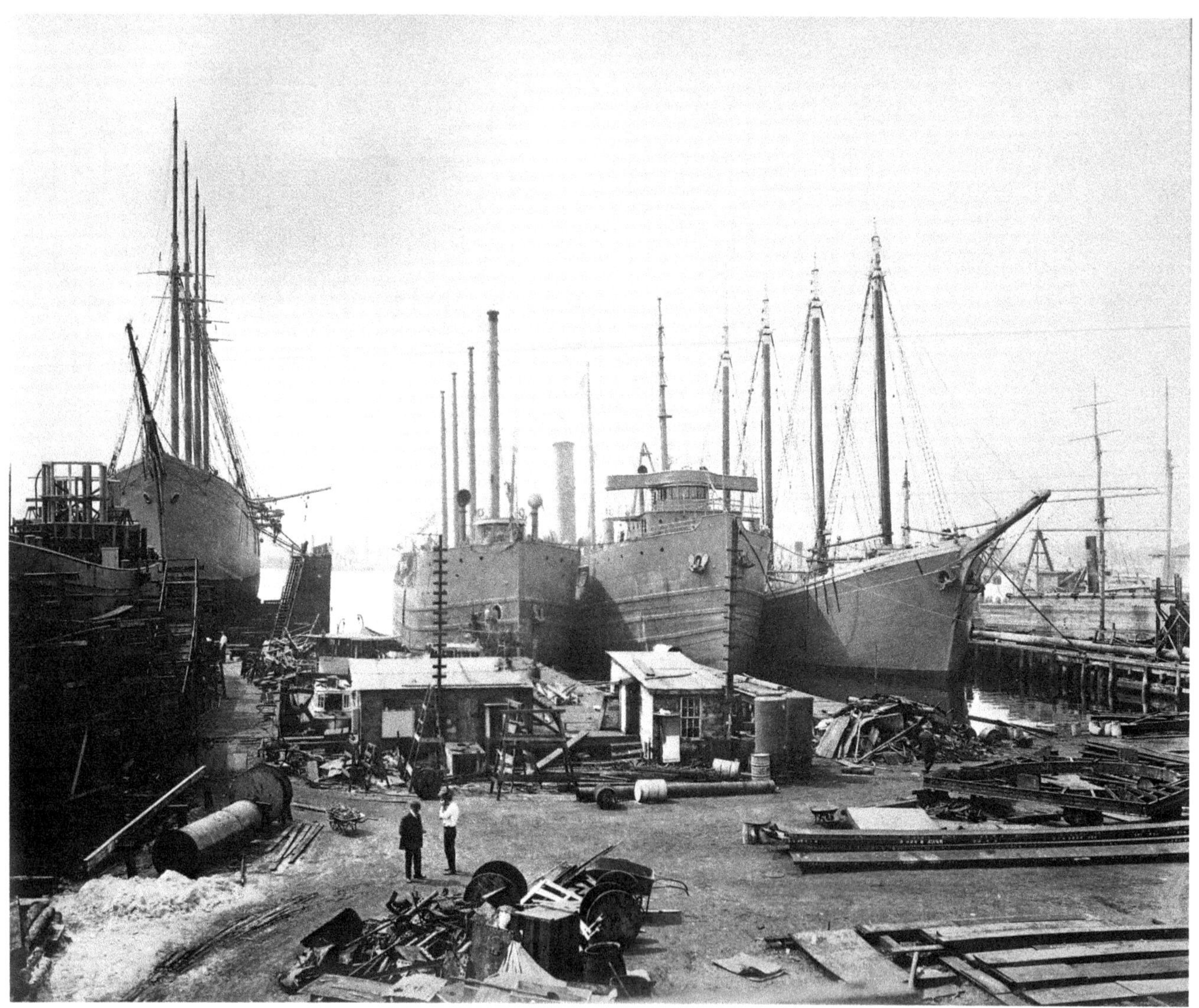

Ship repairs under way in 1918

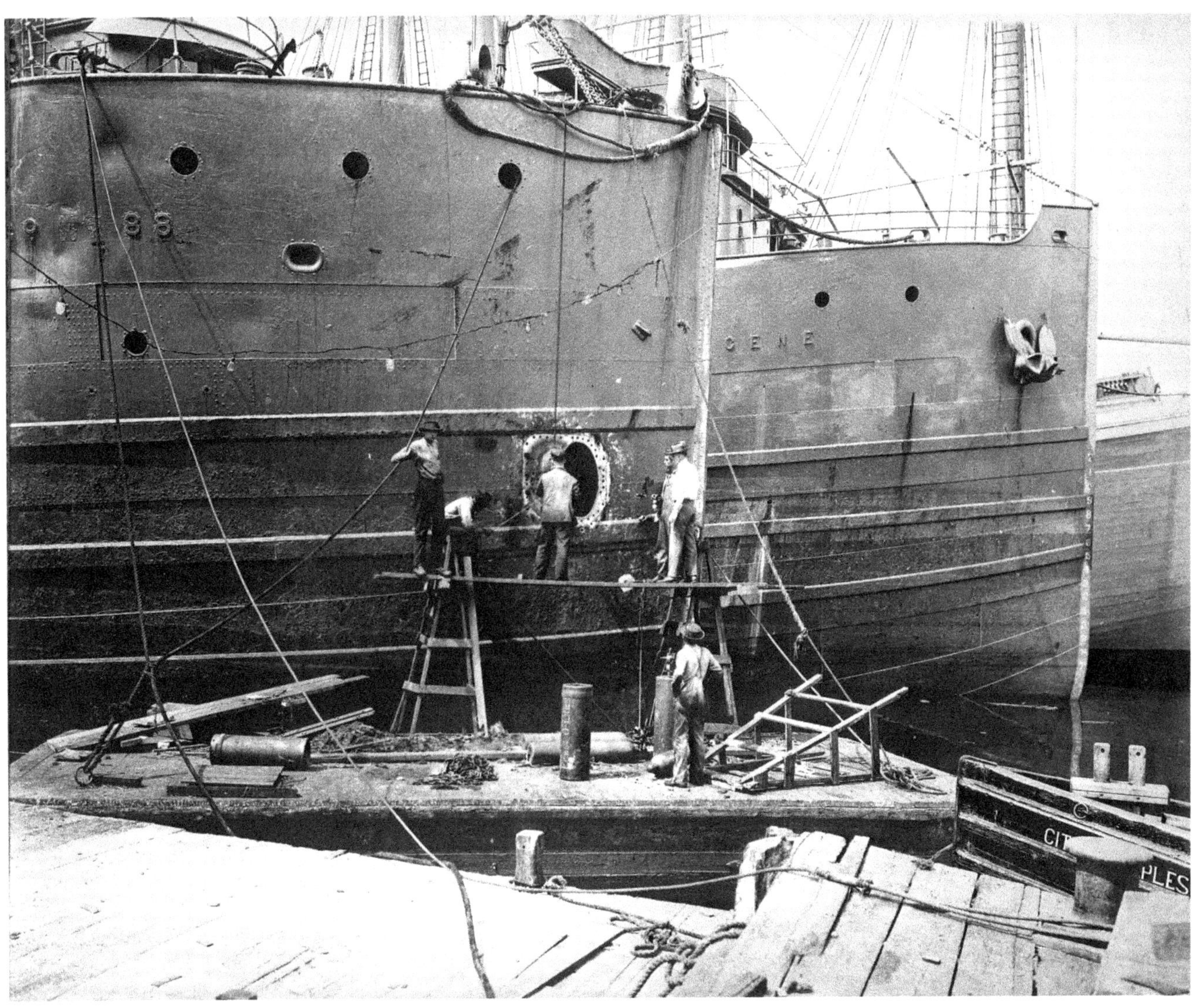

As early as 1907, the Florida legislature authorized the establishment of a permanent state military camp. The camp was completed in 1909 to be used as a Florida National Guard base. Later it was taken over and expanded by the federal government and reopened in 1917 as camp James E. Johnston (for the Confederate general who before the Civil War was quartermaster of the U.S. Army). After World War I the camp was renamed J. Clifford Foster.

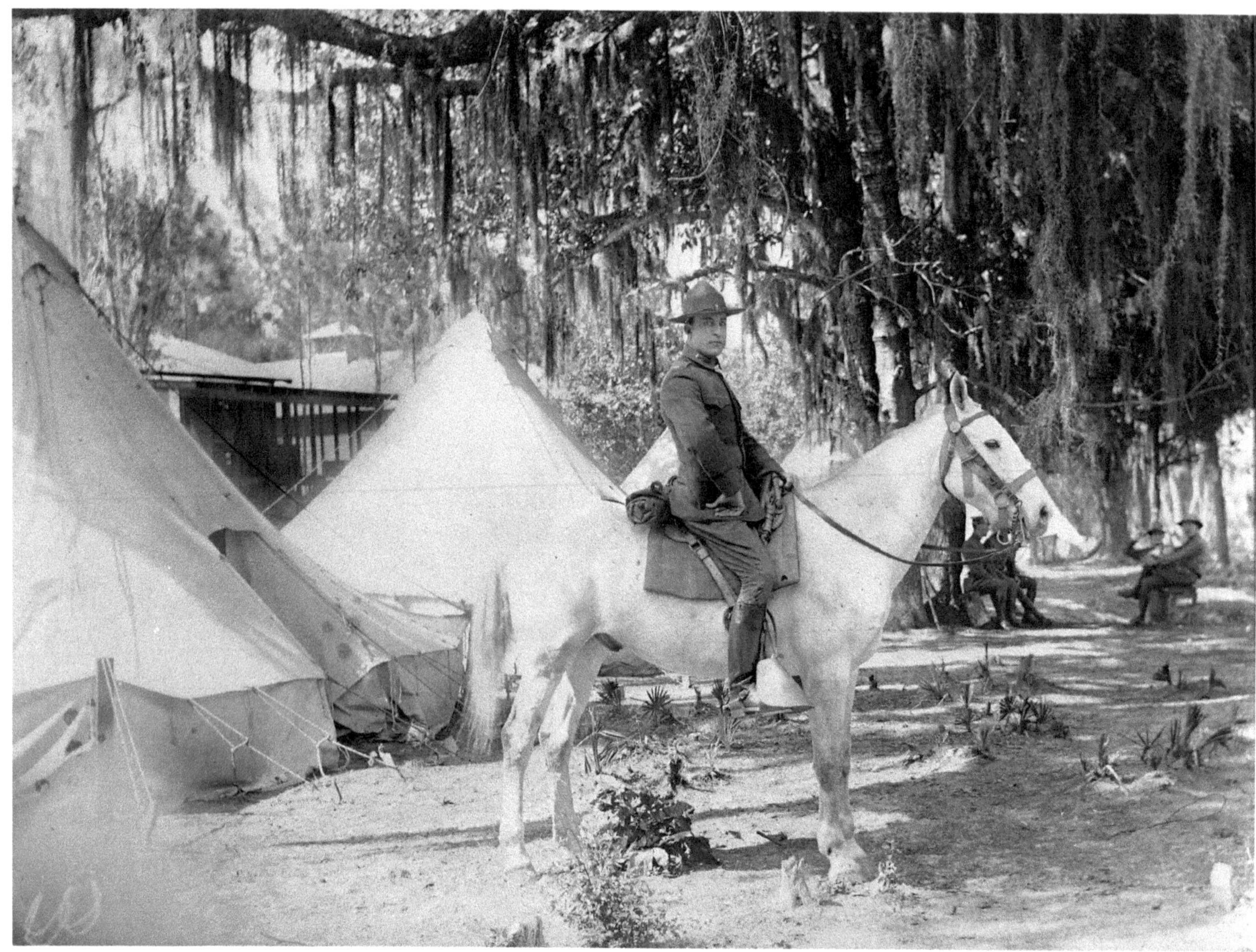

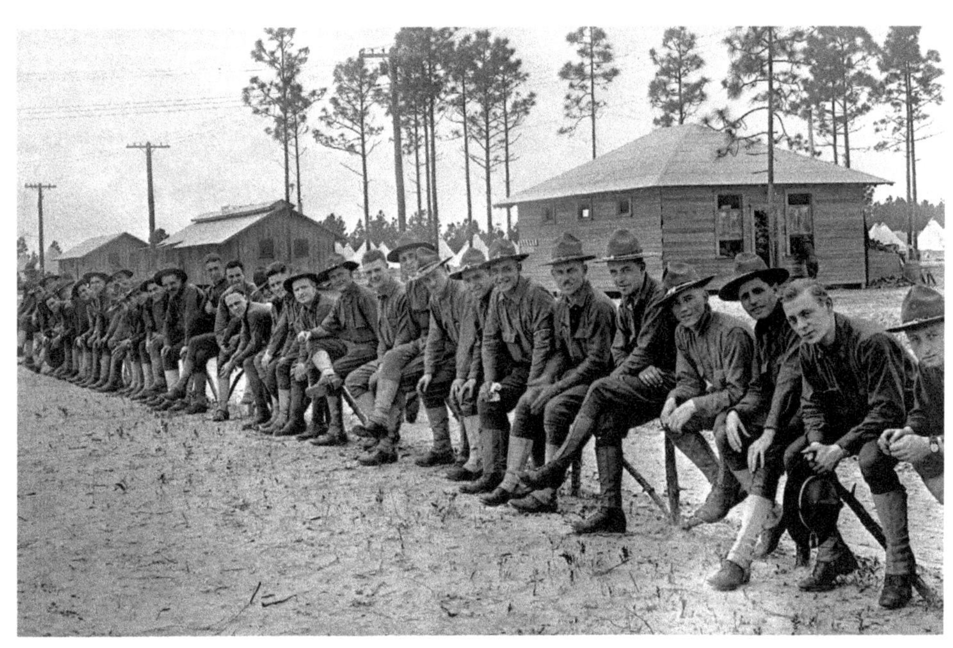

World War I–era soldiers at Camp Johnston

Camp Johnston soldiers at an outdoor mess

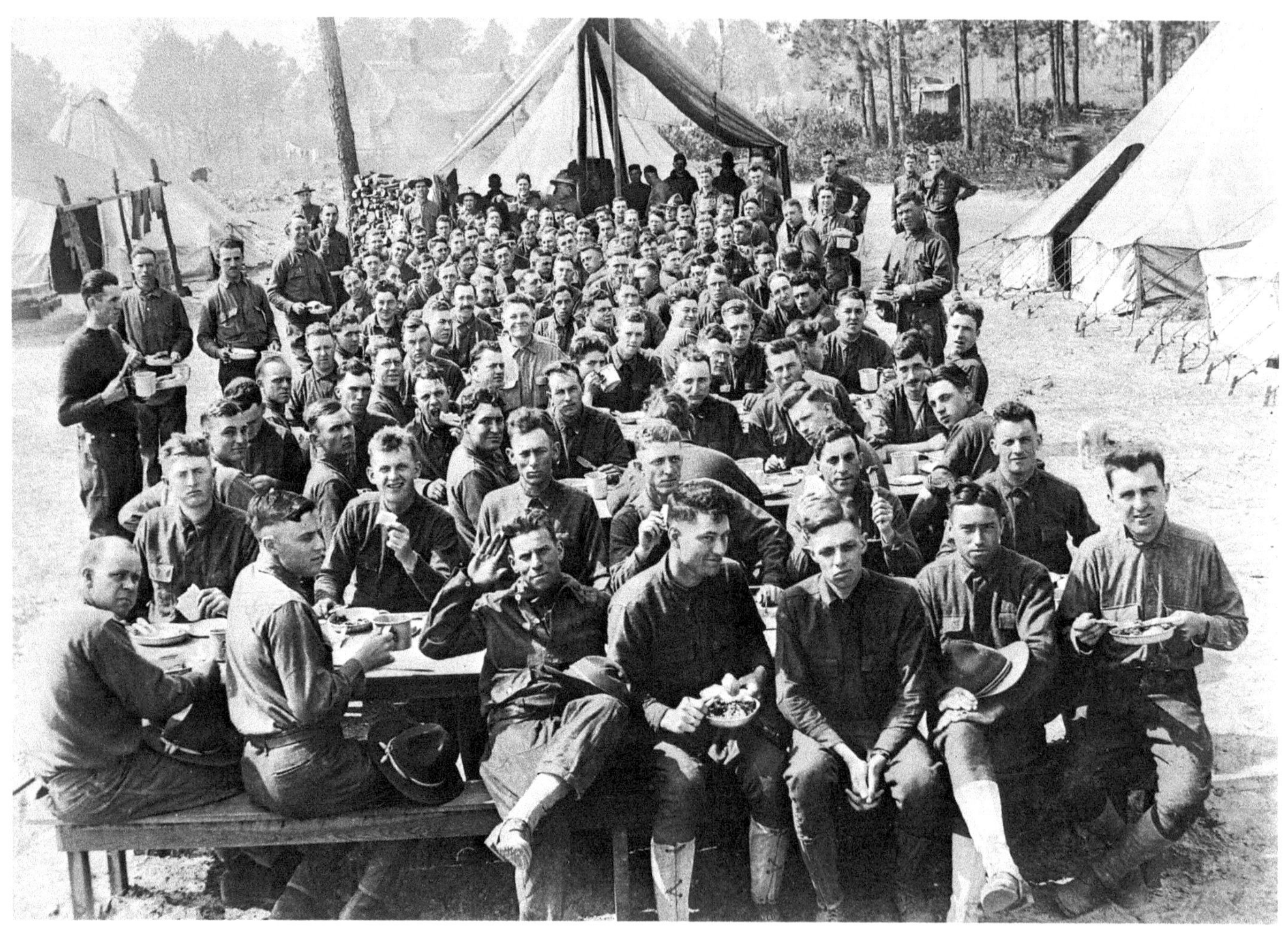

Camp Johnston cooks take time out to pose for the camera.

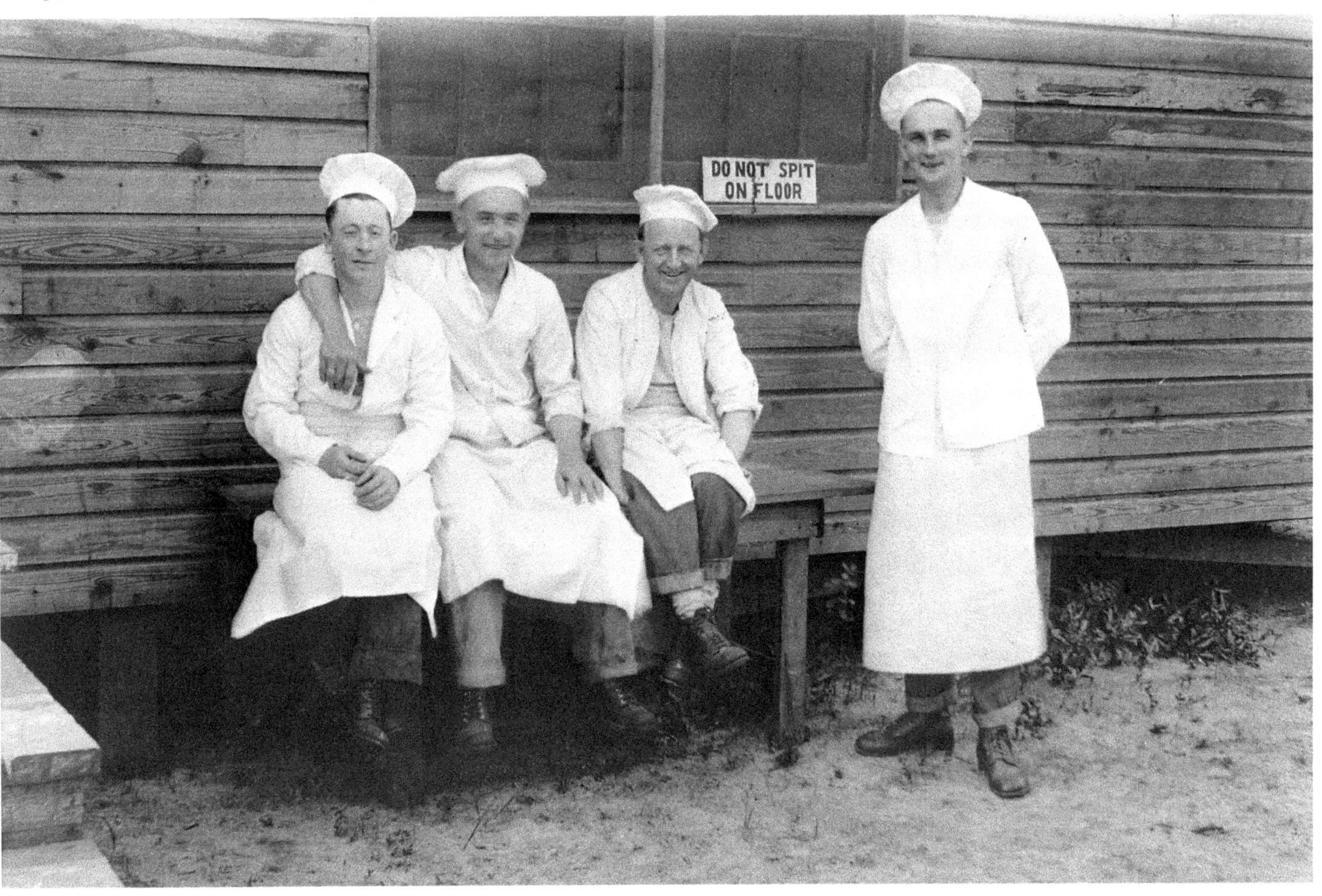

The Jacksonville waterfront and skyline in 1923, from the docks to development northward

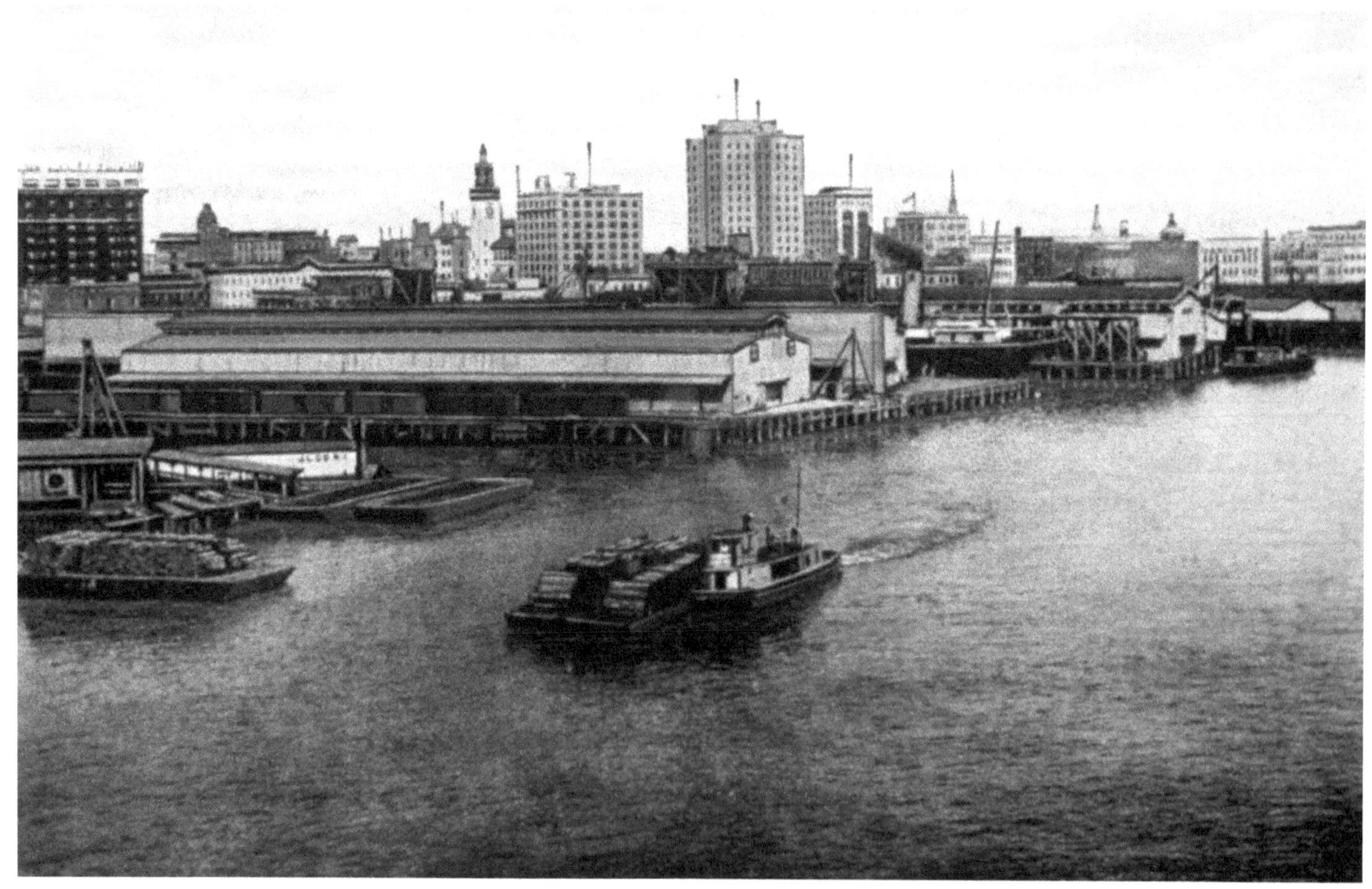

From the Roaring Twenties to the Era of the Great Depression

(1920–1939)

The 1920s began on a high note. President Calvin Coolidge proclaimed that the "business of America is business," and Jacksonville did its part. The urban landscape revealed the growing importance of the corporate component of the city's economy. The business district of downtown Jacksonville continued to blossom. Bank and other commercial buildings enlarged the cityscape.

Railroads remained among the most significant corporations. By the 1920s, Henry Flagler's Atlantic Seaboard was the most important. The city continued to be the hub of railroad activity, with lines flowing east and west, north and south. To accommodate railroad traffic and the many passengers, Union Station, built by Flagler's company, opened in 1920. The port and shipbuilding industries continued to thrive.

During the decade of the jazz age, Florida contributed another avenue to the pursuit of wealth—real estate. Jacksonville felt the impact with the development of new suburban areas, particularly Riverside. It was during this period that construction began on the homes and other structures designed by Klutho and others. These various economic activities influenced the rising affluence of the city during the twenties. Meantime, community life evolved generally with the growing number of educational, cultural, and other civic resources, as well as recreational activities.

The party came crashing down with the beginning of the Great Depression of 1929. Jacksonville residents, like the rest of the nation, experienced the long-term impact of the collapse of the nation's economy. With the assistance of New Deal programs and determination in face of adversity, which Jacksonvillians had demonstrated after the Great Fire and earlier challenges, the city clung to survival until World War II brought a sea change to the economy.

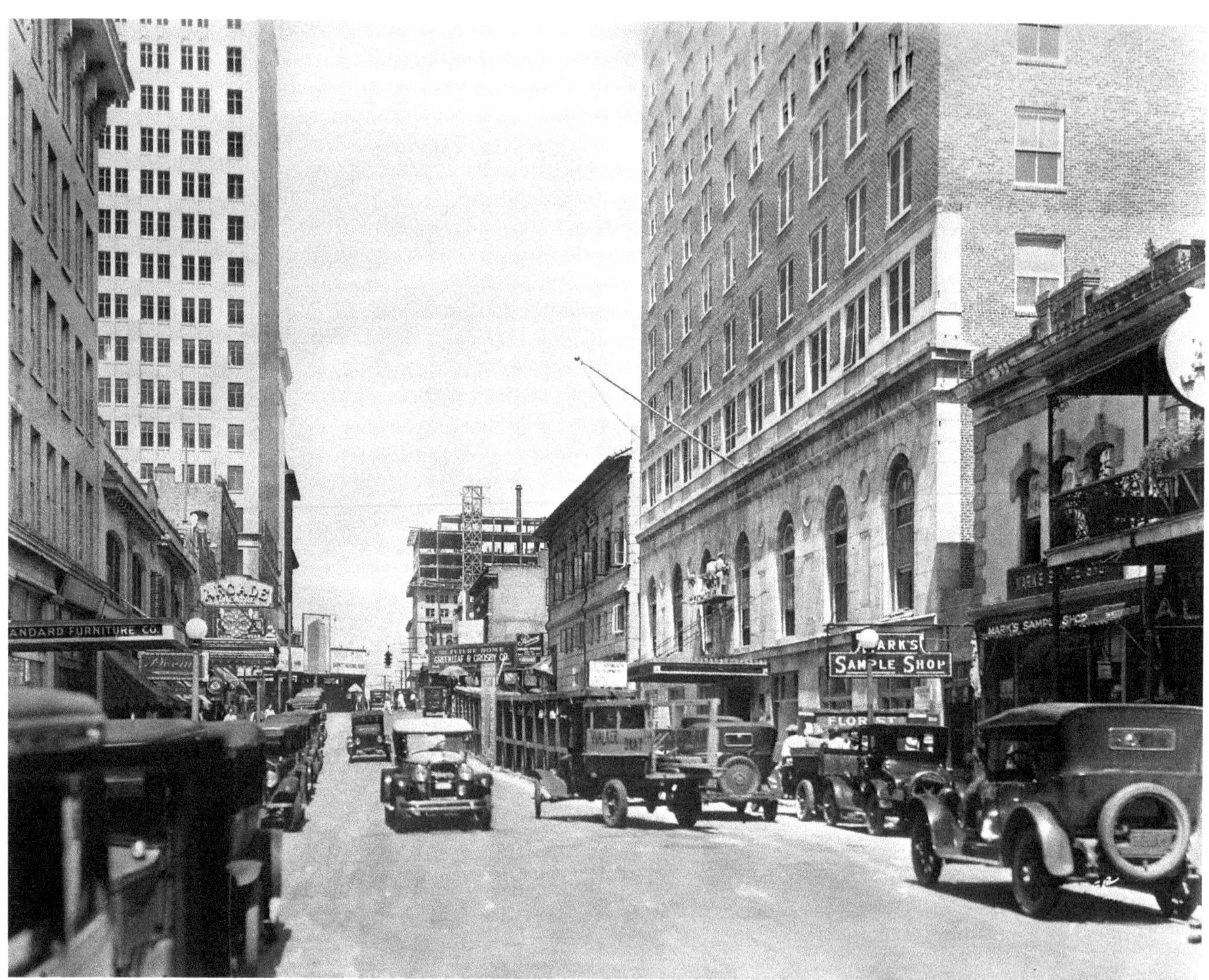

The expansion of the business district to Adams Street is shown here. Automobiles have replaced horse-driven wagons and trolleys as the vehicle of choice.

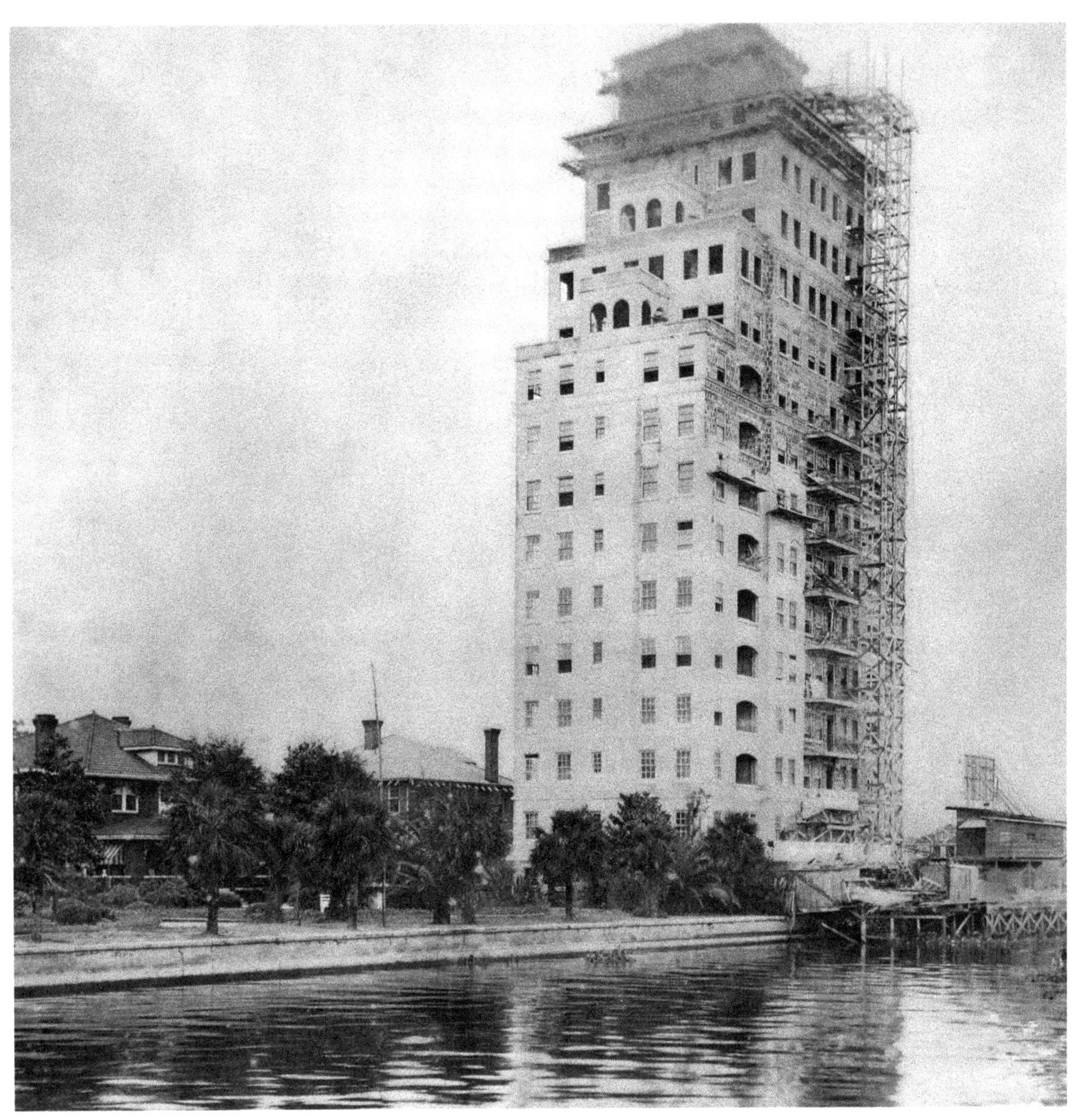

The Park Lane Apartments, shown here under construction, represented a new kind of real estate and the influence of the Florida land boom of the 1920s.

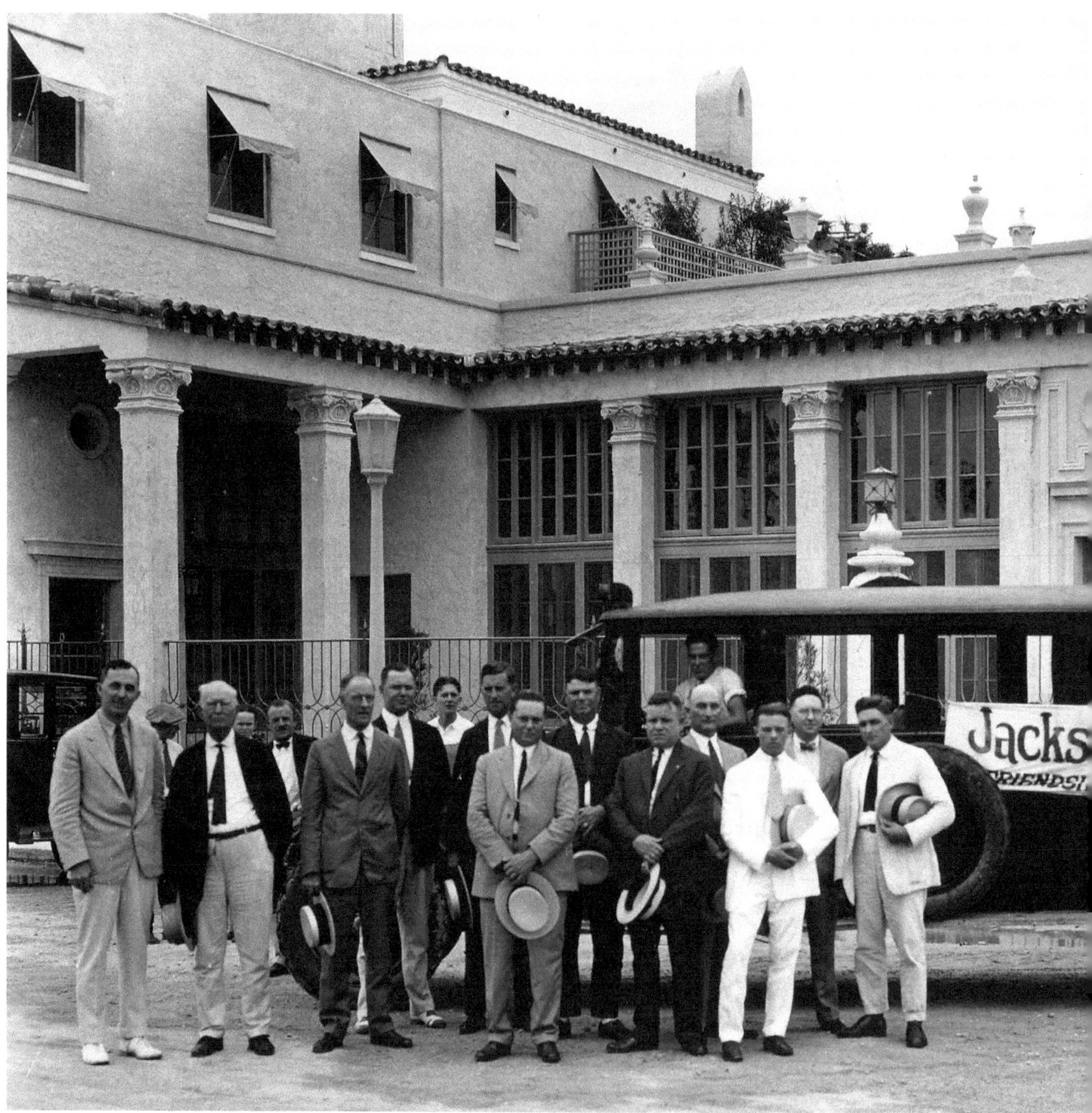
Jacks

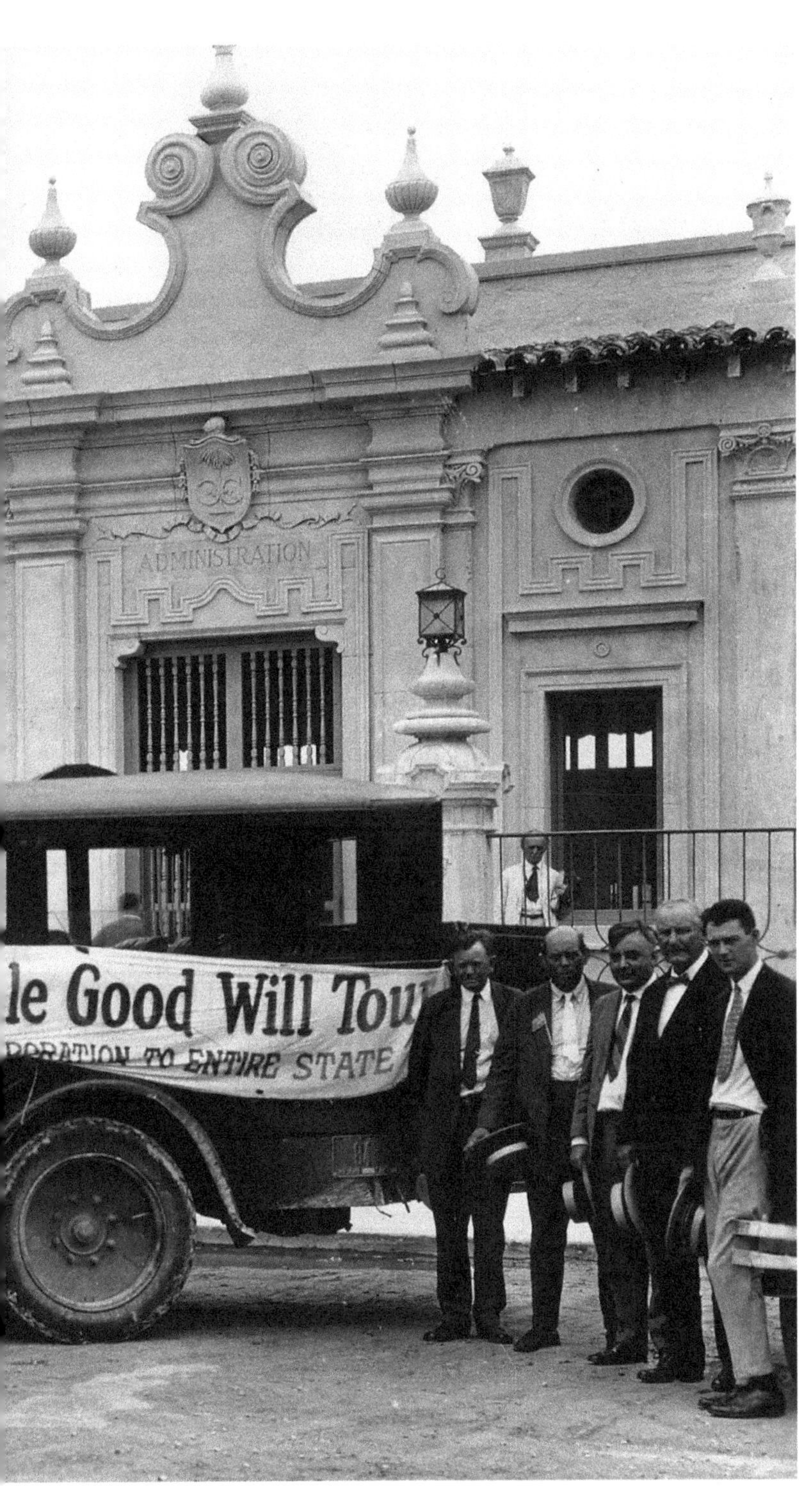

This good will tour of Jacksonville businessmen before the Great Depression illustrates that times were good and expectations of greater prosperity high.

The Atlantic Coast Line Railroad owned this building, which housed a number of other businesses.

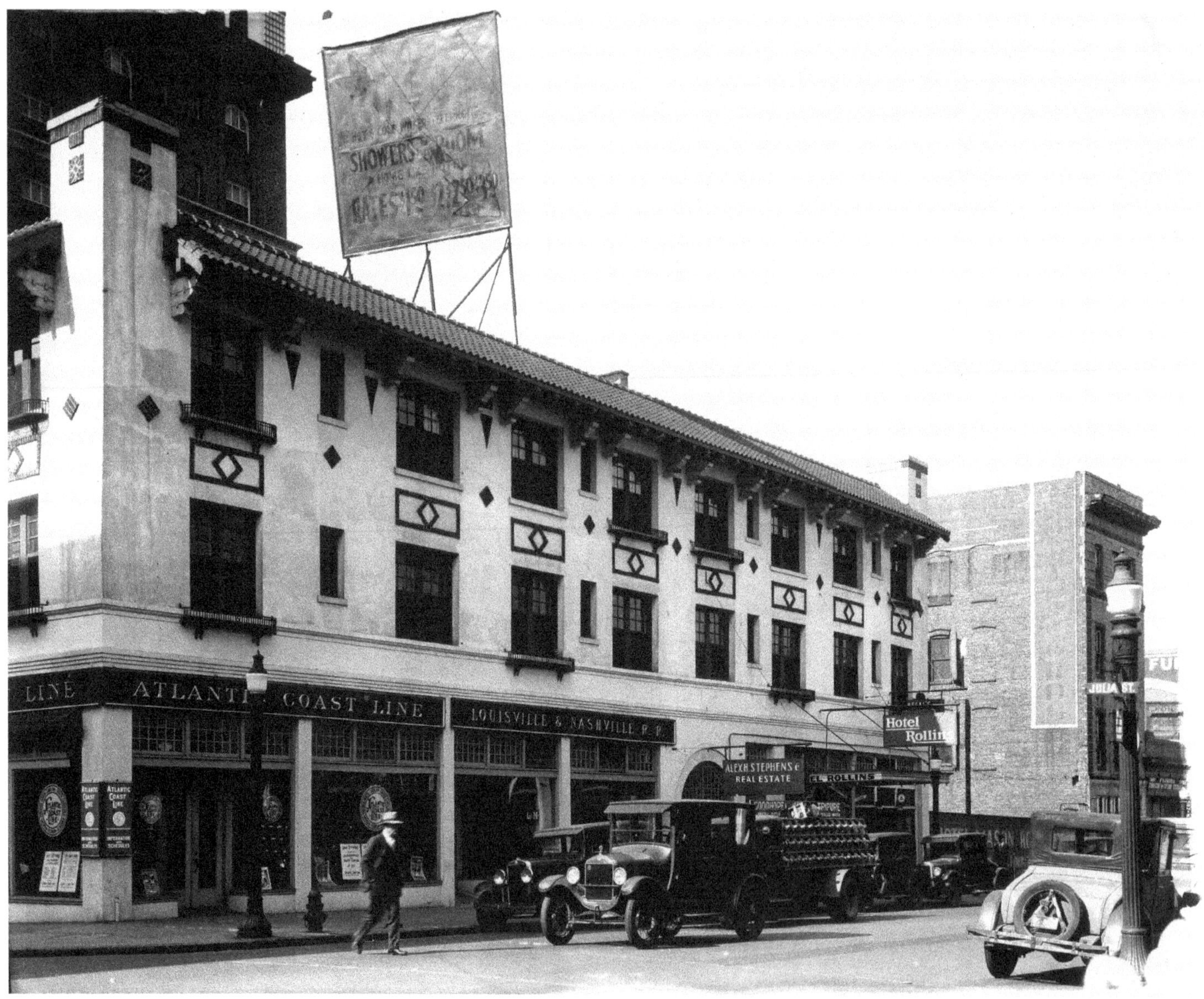

In 1920 the new Union Station built by Henry Flagler opened for business.

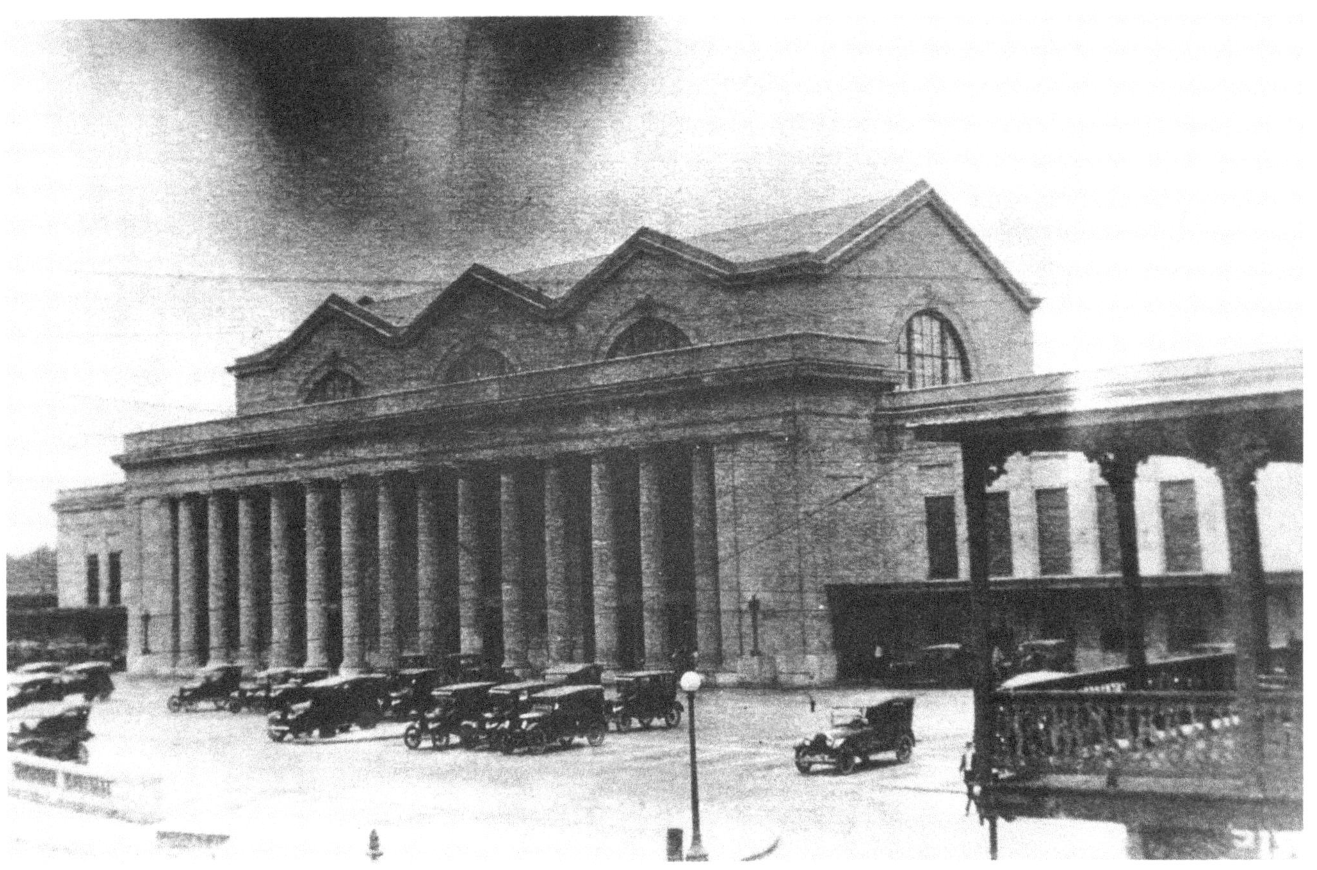

A Union Station side street

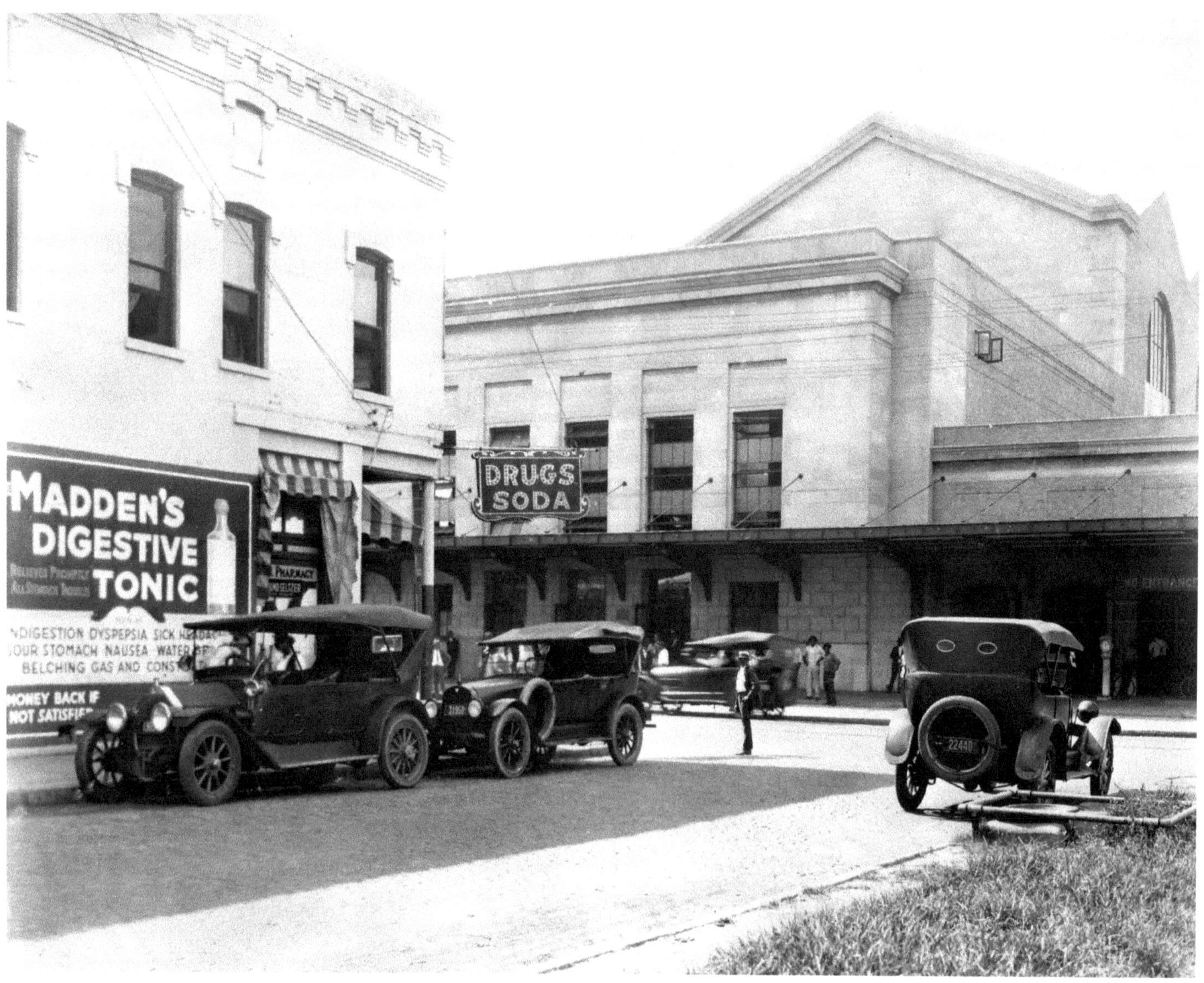

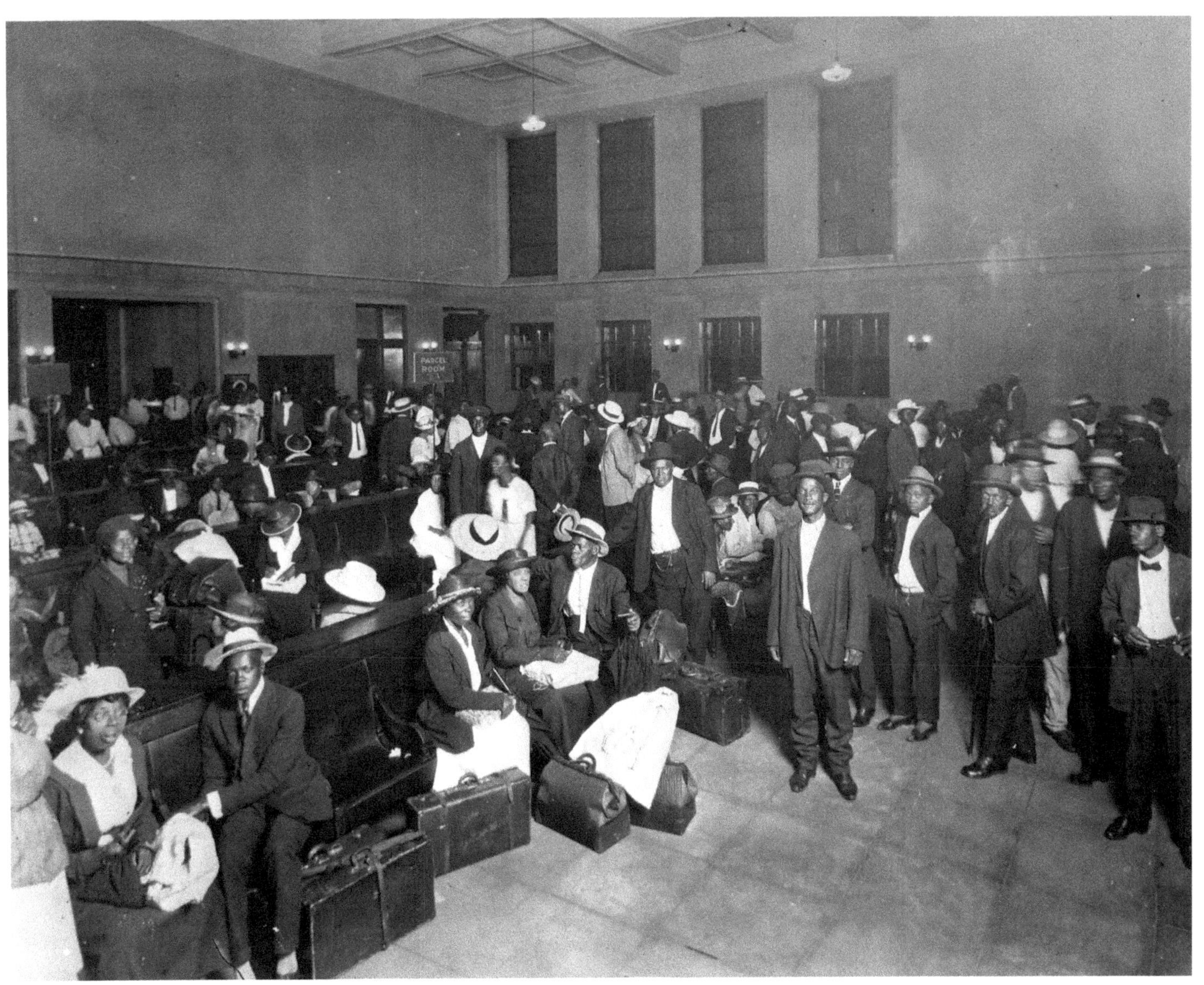

African Americans in the "Colored Waiting Room" of the Union Station train depot.

People arrive at and depart Union Station by car and trolley, as the numbers of automobiles in the station parking lot climb.

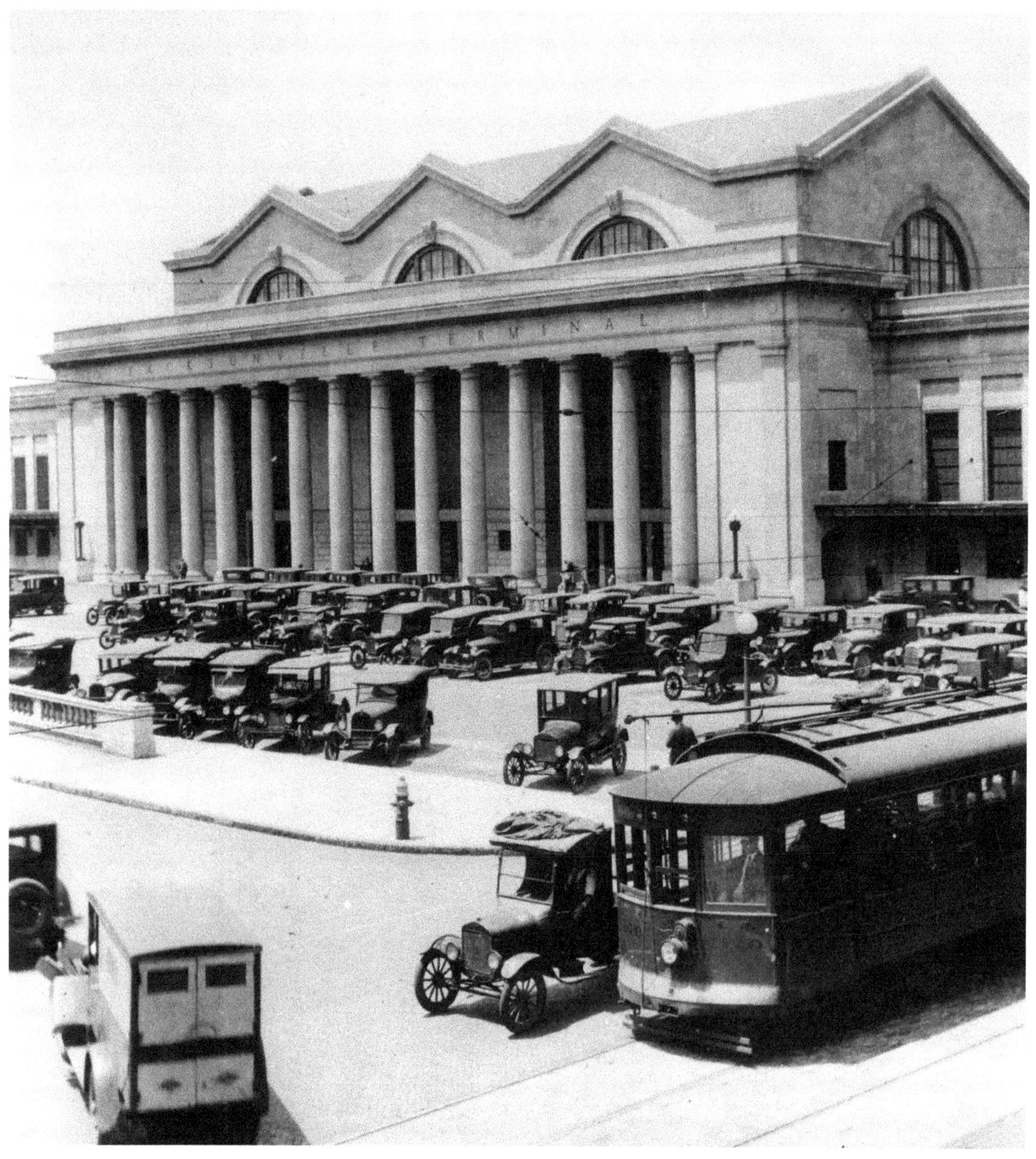

To accommodate the growing railroad lines, the city built its first main bridge across the St. Johns River. Before the bridge, railway cars were ferried on barges.

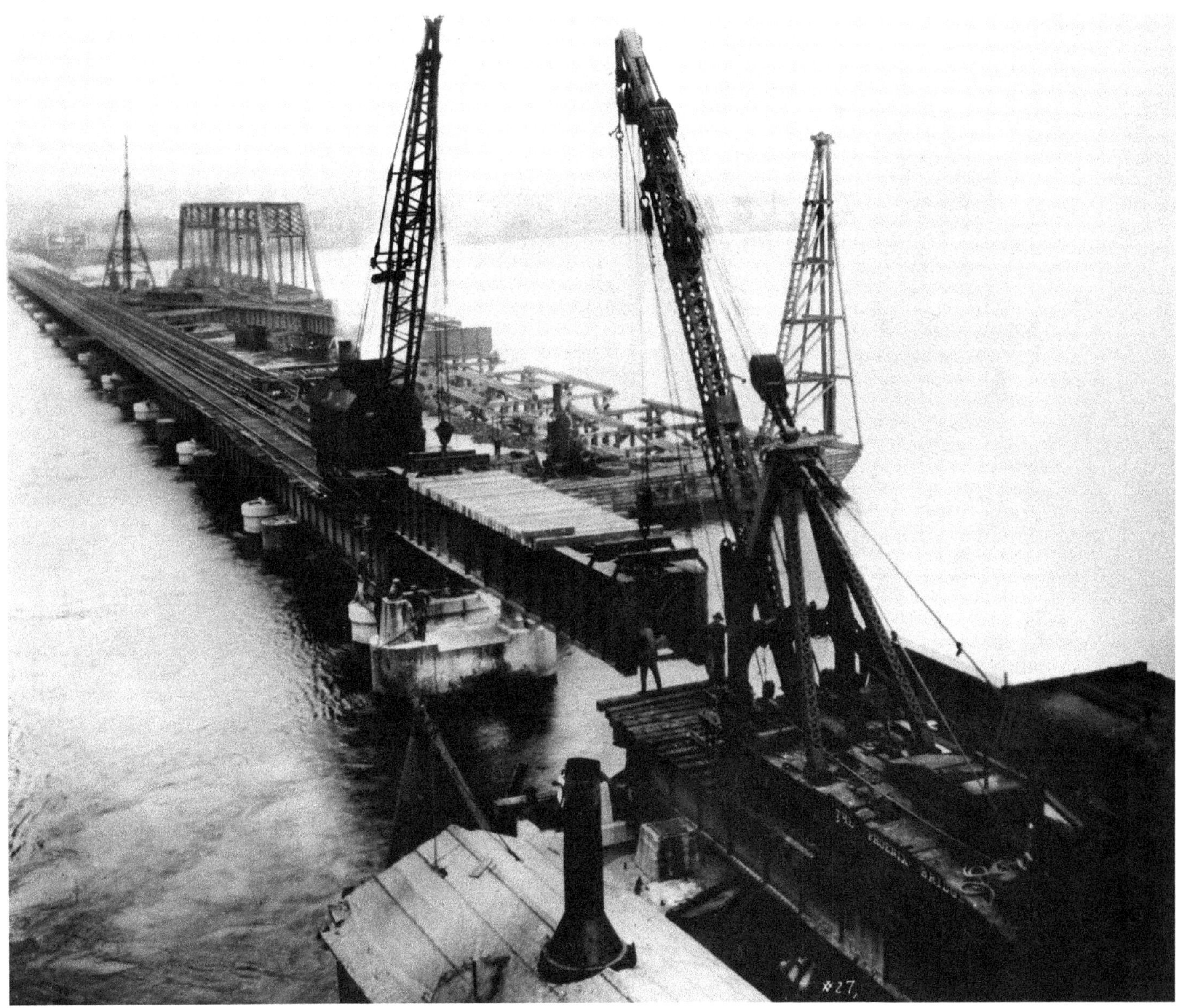

Advances in technology are reflected in the city's Municipal Engineering building on north Main Street, pictured here in 1922. Renovated in 1983, it is one of few historic buildings still standing on Main Street.

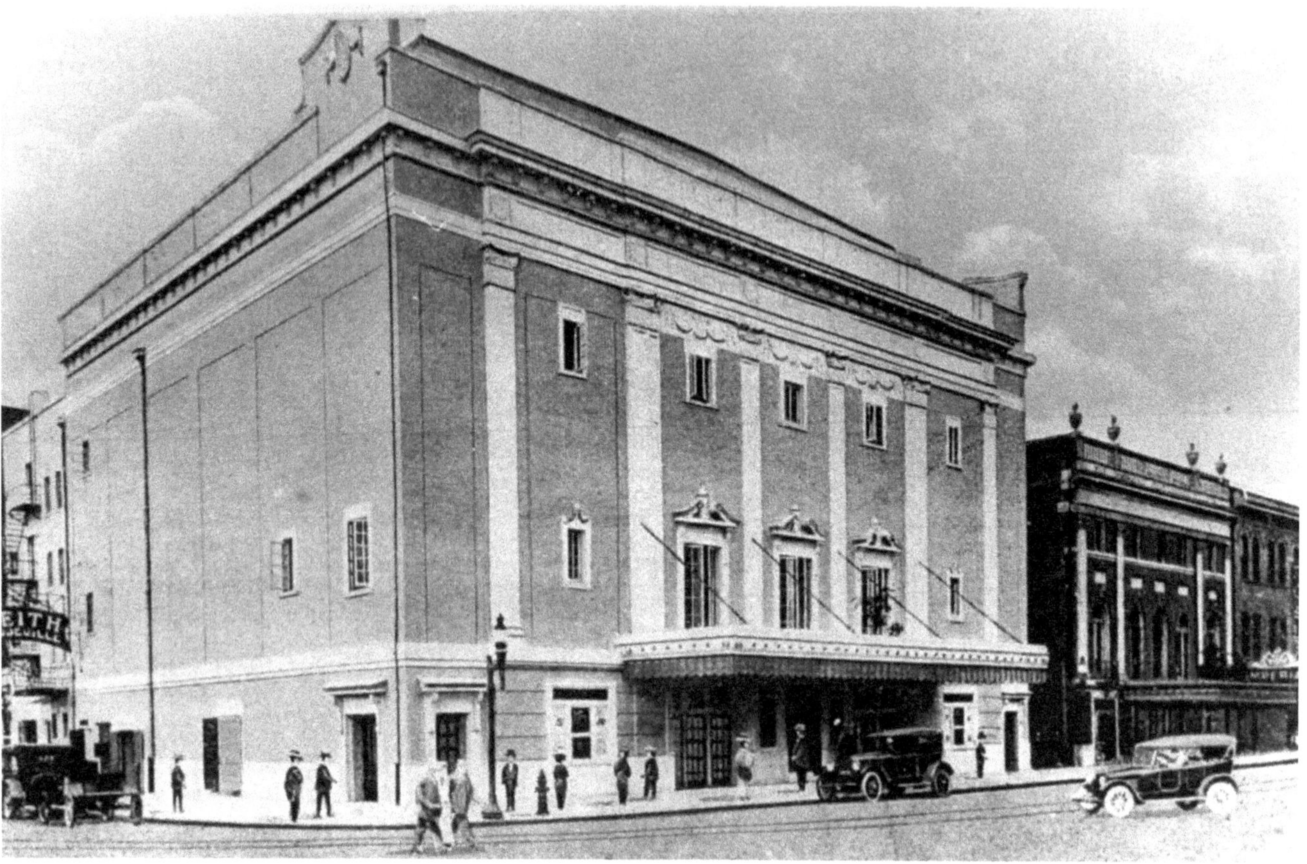

Car races had become the rage by the jazz age. This photo shows celebrity race-car driver Sig Haughdahl in his Fiat with his personal mechanic Jimmy Chai in 1921. In the early 1900s automobile races began at Atlantic Beach.

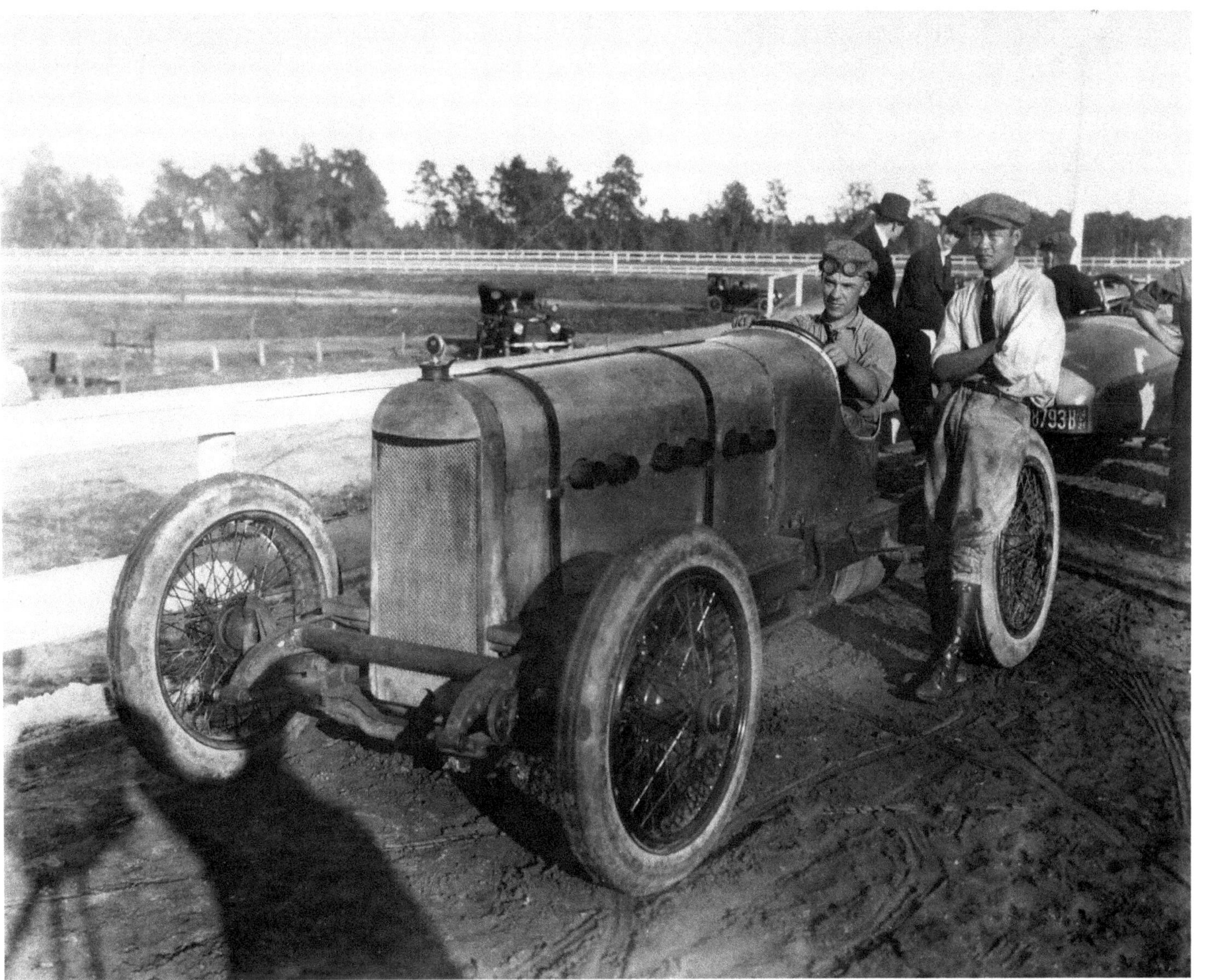

Line-up for an auto race at the Jacksonville Fairgrounds in 1922

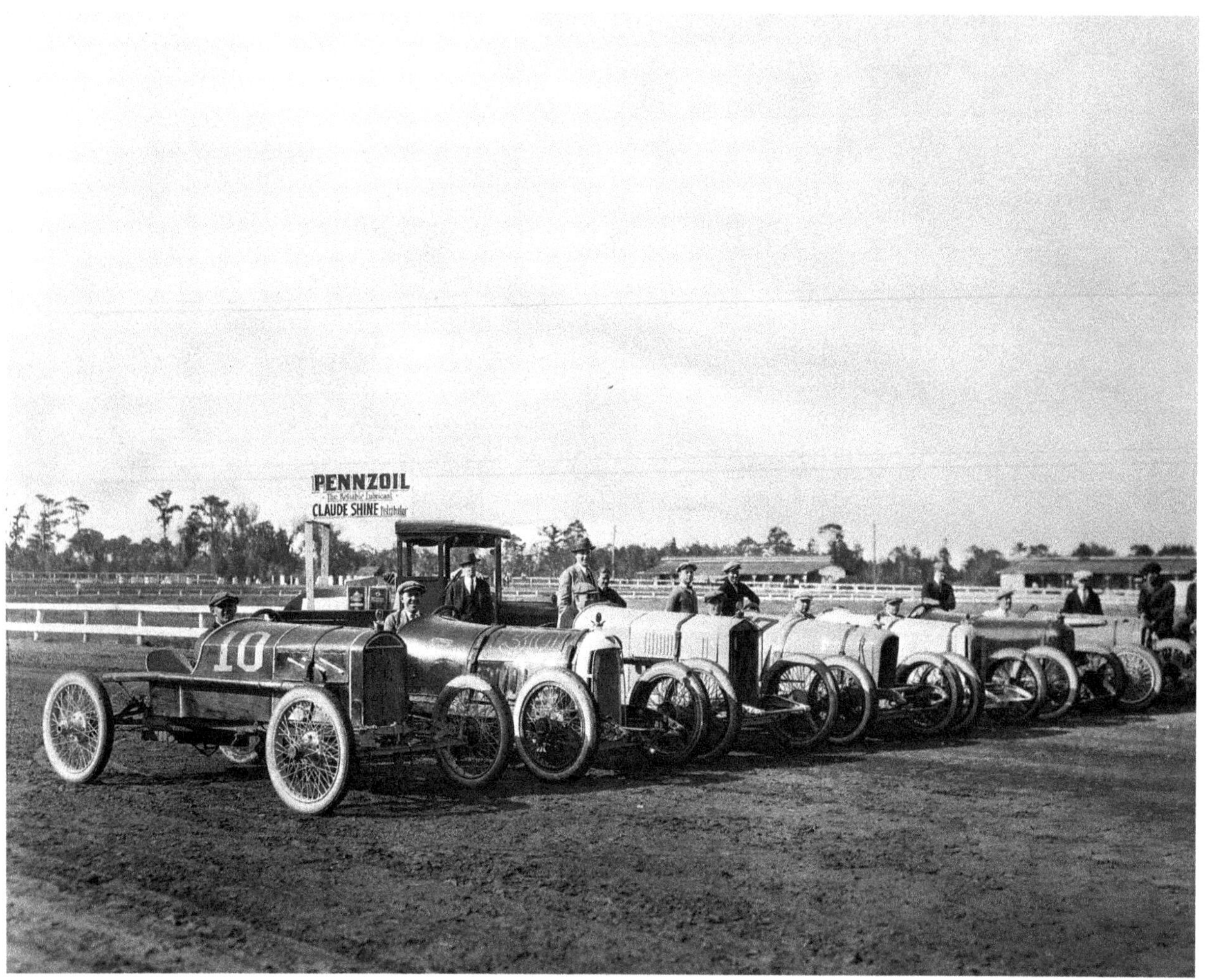

While Henry Ford's cars were being marketed to the common man, a demand for luxury cars rose. Here mechanics and other employees, likely of the Claude Nolan Cadillac Company, pose for a group shot. This company was founded in 1907 and is the oldest car dealership in the city.

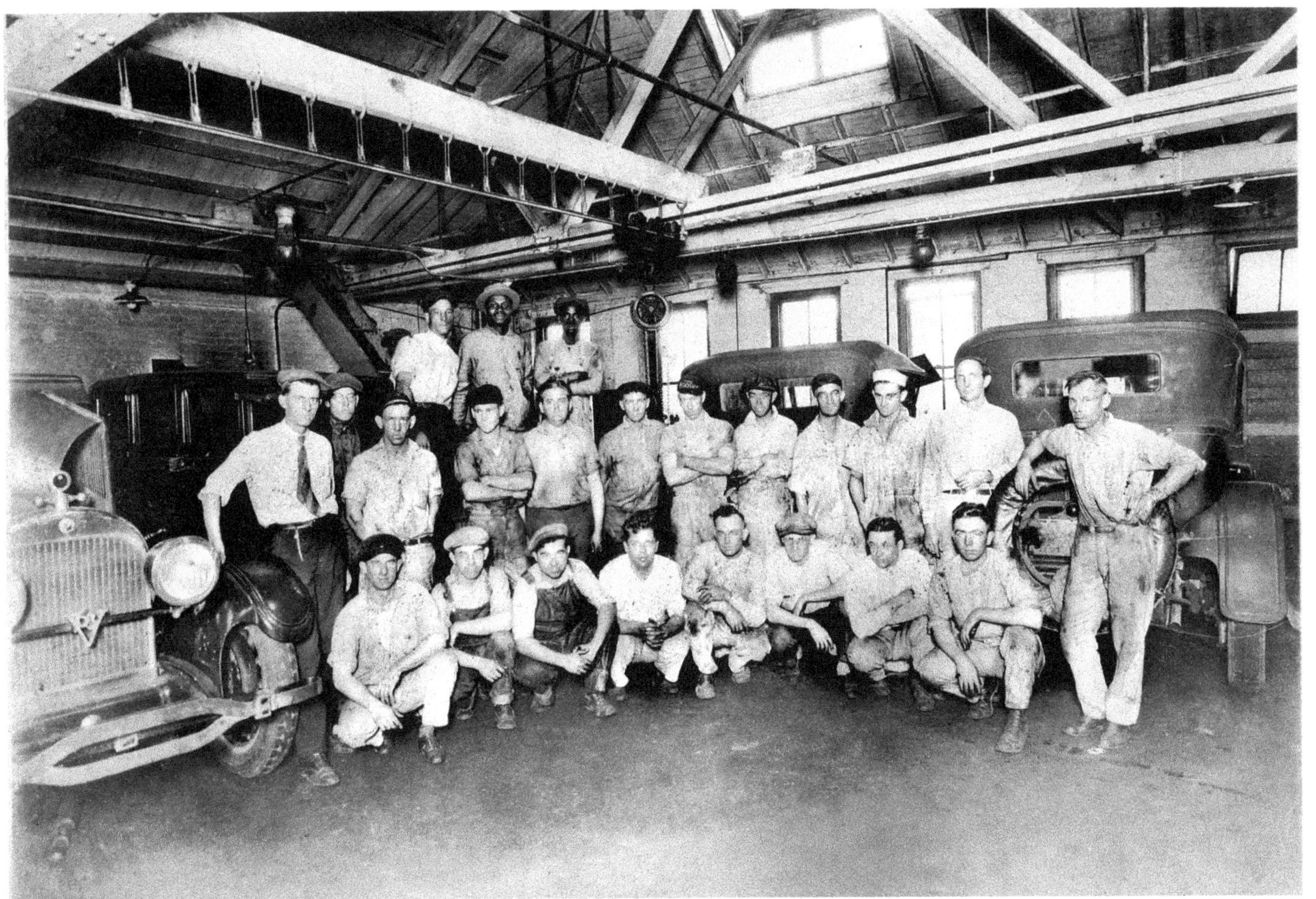

The greatest celebrity of the 1920s, the Lone Eagle Charles Lindbergh is shown here with his *Spirit of St. Louis* on a stop in Jacksonville during the nationwide tour following his famous transatlantic flight.

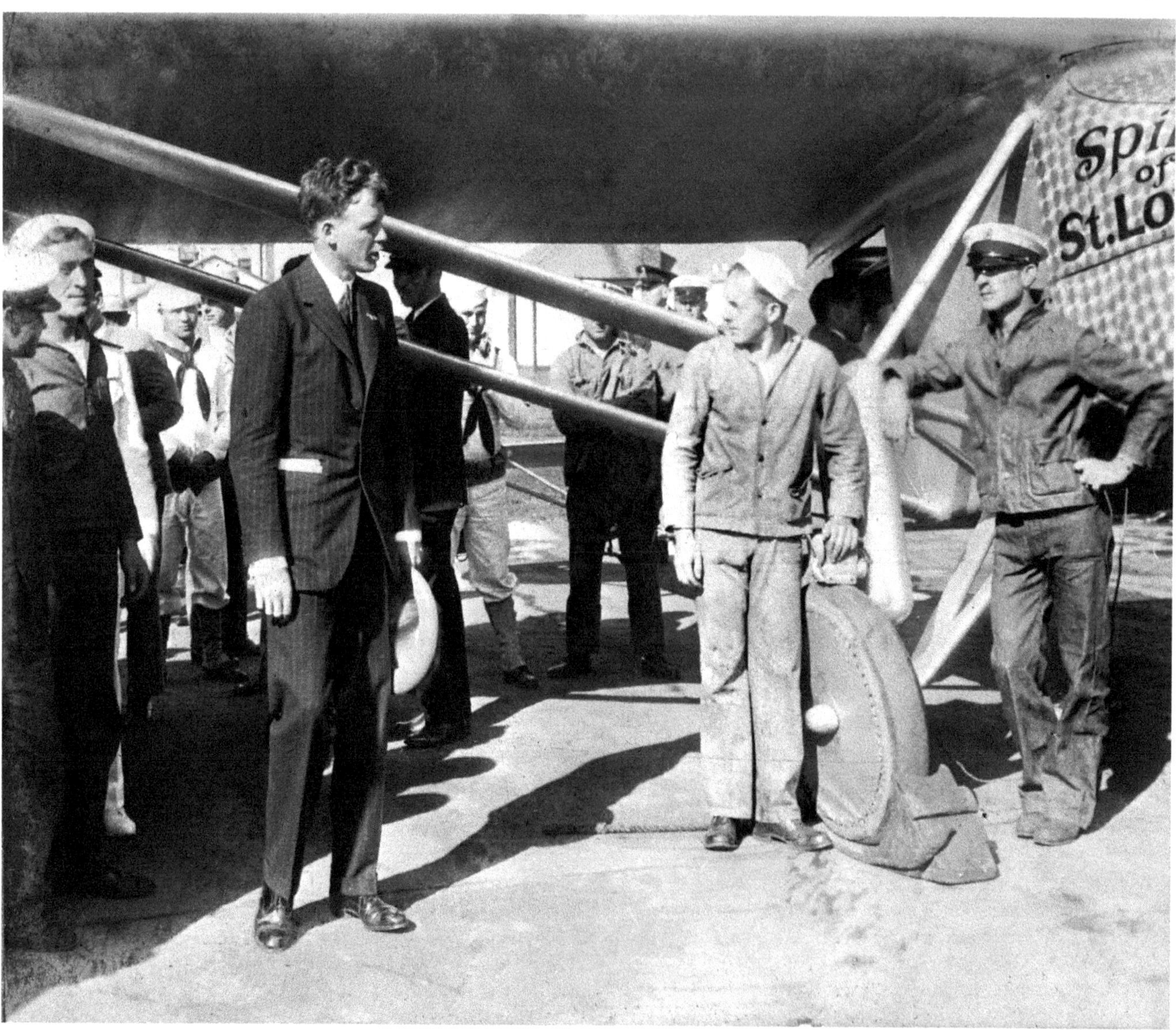

These young women seem not to have a care in the world as they pose for the camera on the wings of an airplane on the beach. By this time airplanes were no longer a novelty. Many people had seen the stunts of barnstorming pilots, and some had flown.

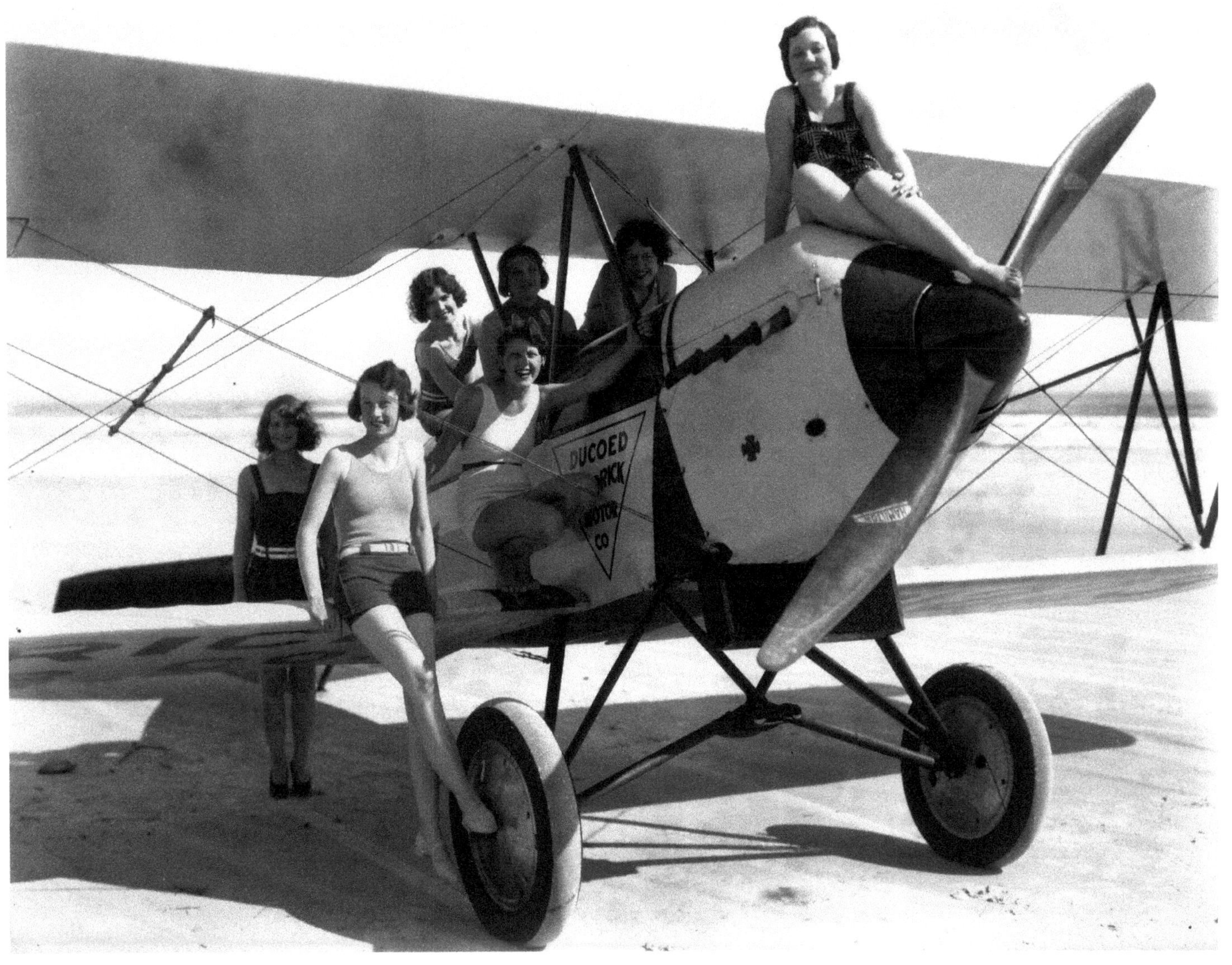

Members of the Woodmen of the World Life Insurance Society pose at Mayport in 1930. Little of the Depression that began the preceding year is in evidence.

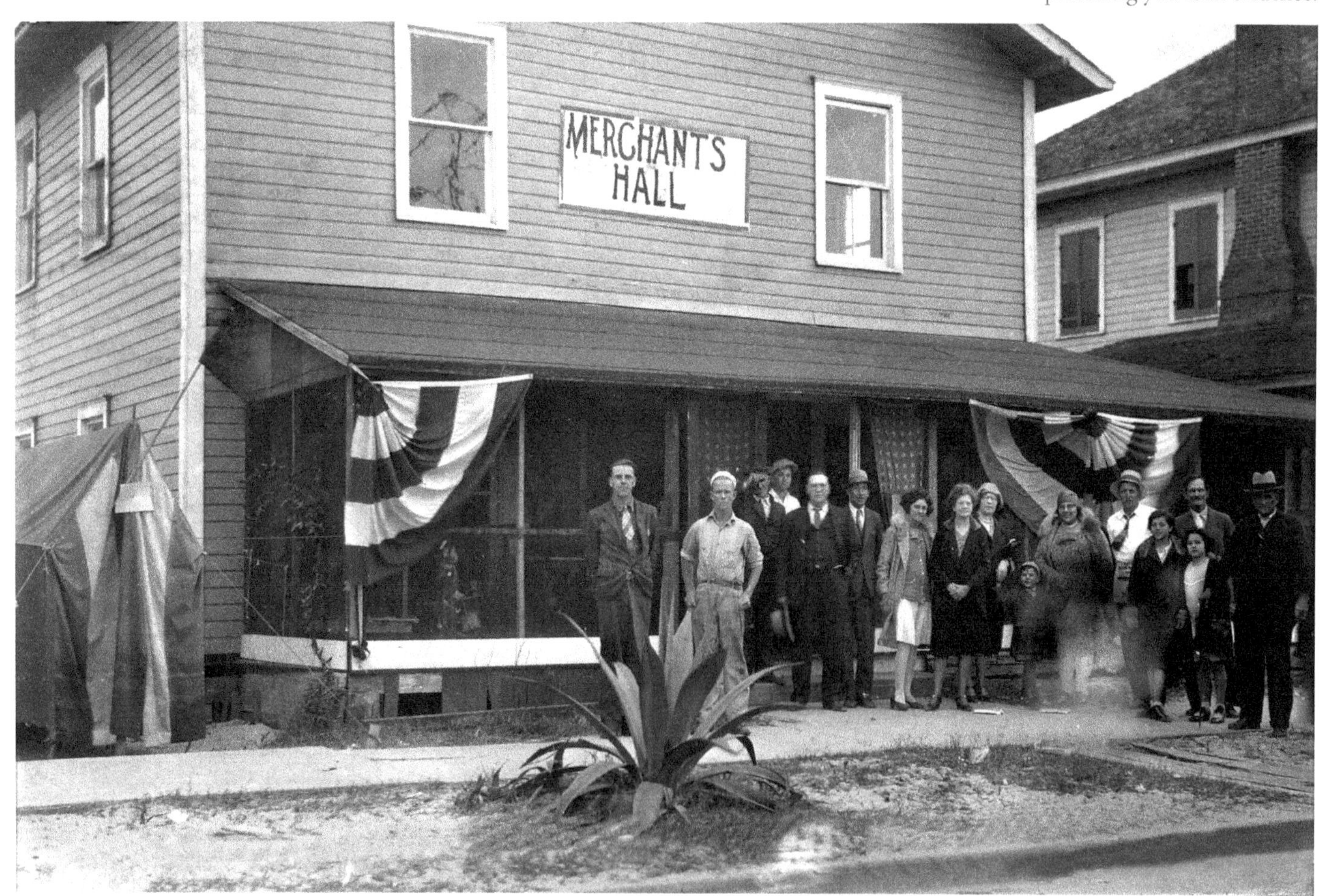

Golf courses, abundant on the Florida landscape today, had begun in earnest by the 1920s. These men are playing at the Municipal Golf Course, built for $112,000, which opened November 8, 1928. A fee of 50¢ a day, which included a locker, shower, and a towel, was required.

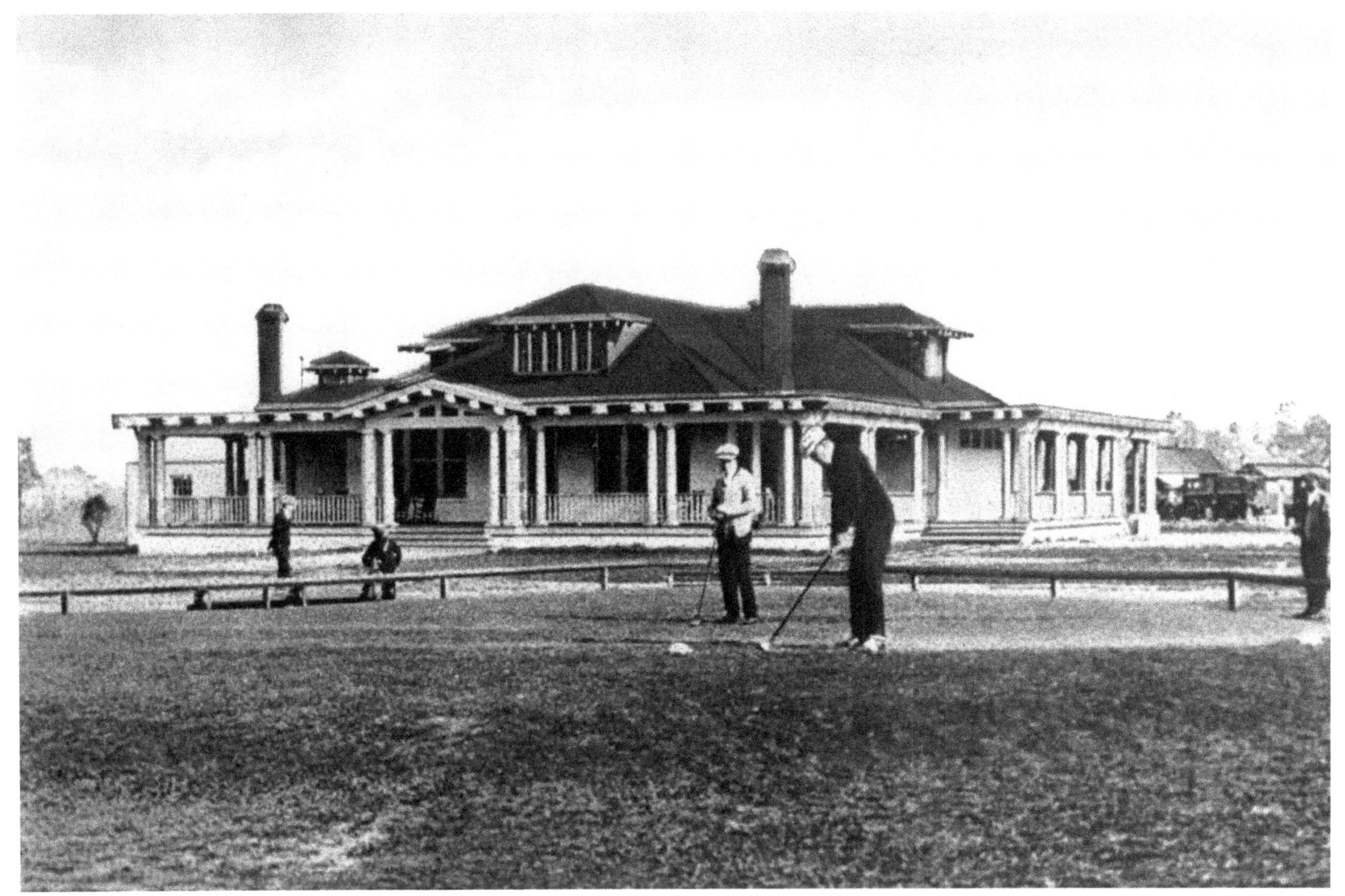

Officers of the U.S. Army, Lieutenant Colonel J. H. Spengler and Major Fred H. Davis are shown at Camp J. Clifford R. Foster (former Camp Johnston). Major Davis served as the state attorney general from 1927 to 1931.

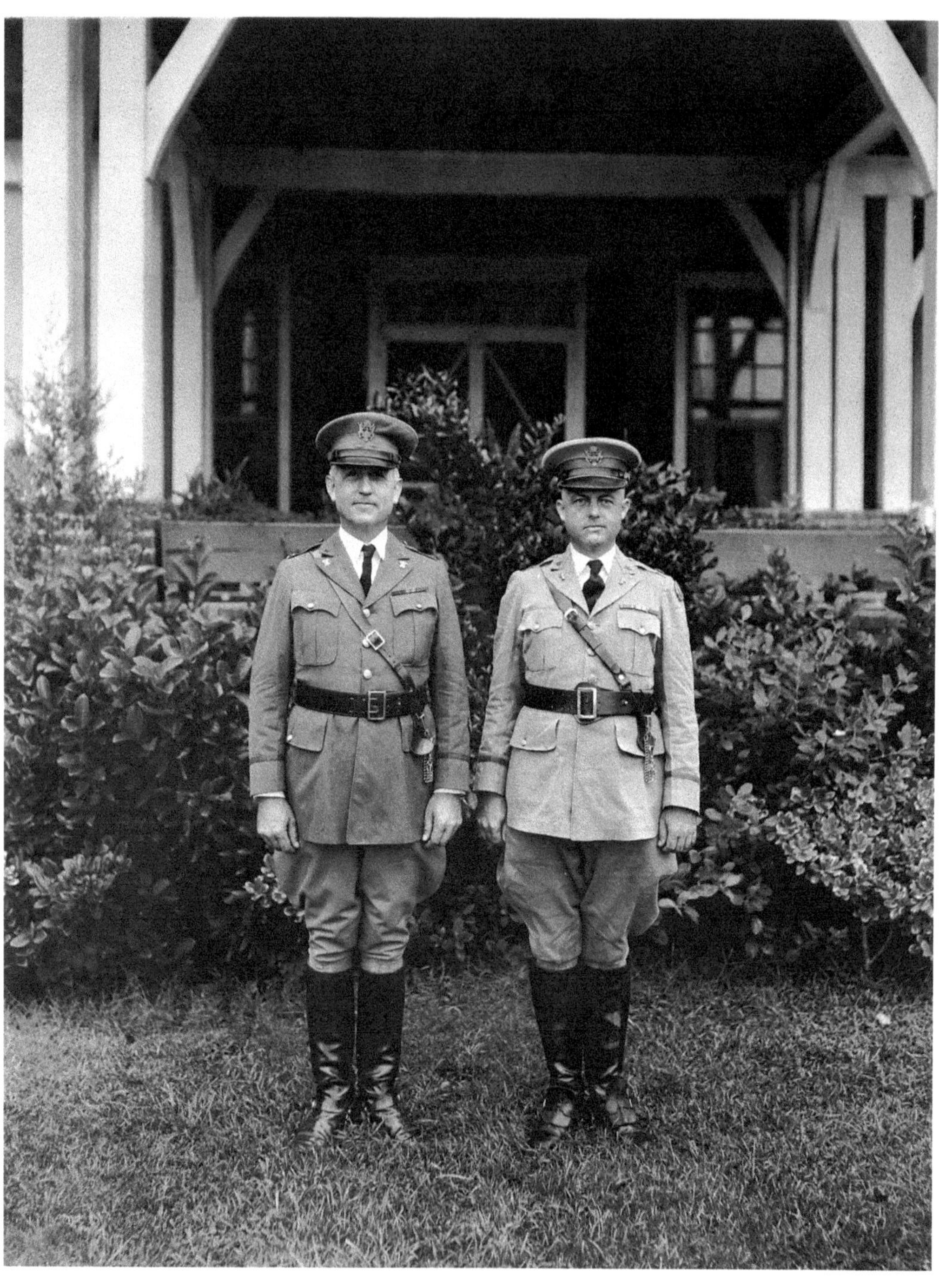

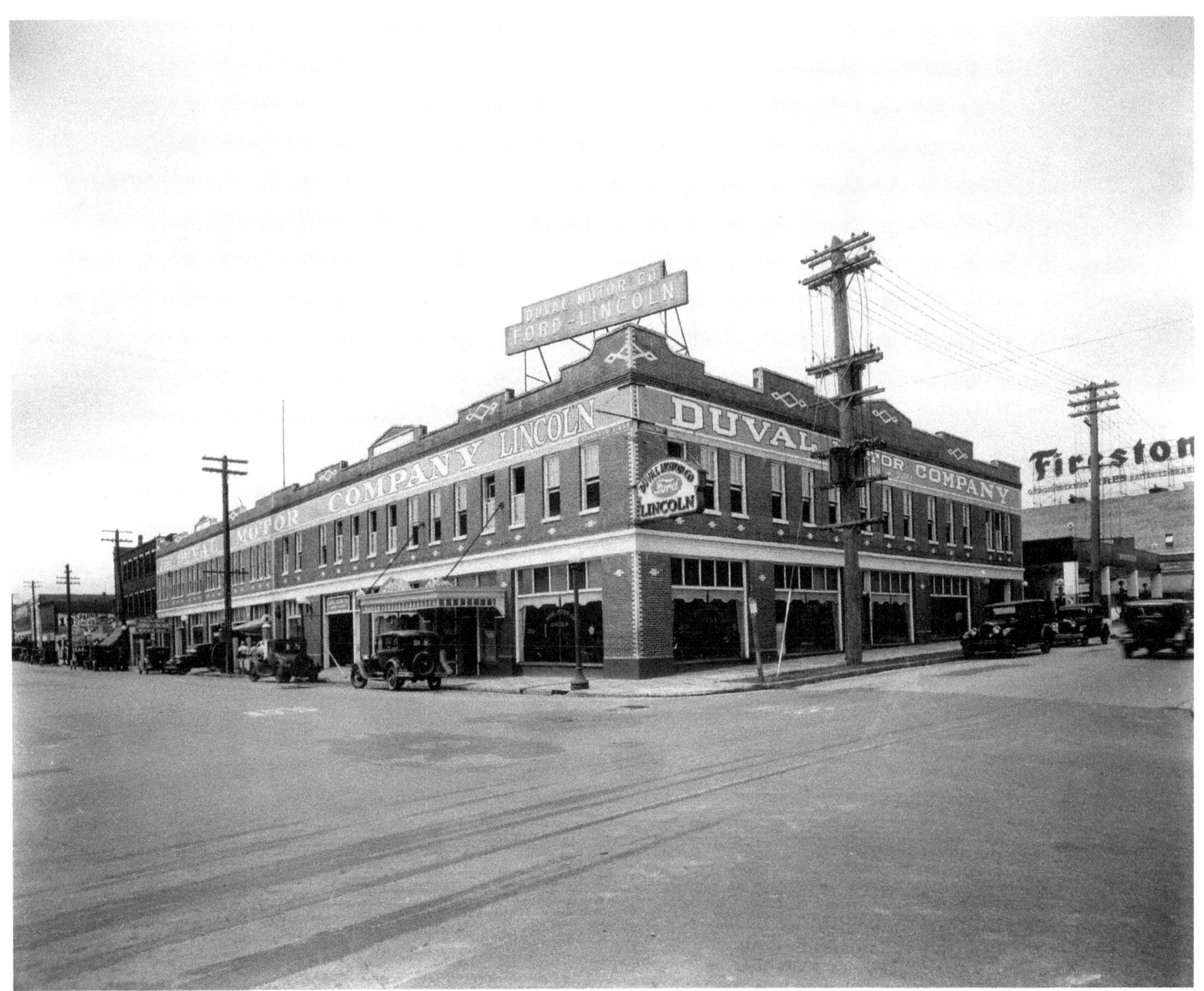

The Duval Motor Company on West Forsyth Street near Lee Street, one of the city's automobile dealerships, is shown here in 1930. Despite the hard times, Jacksonville business faces forward, confident of renewed prosperity.

The newly elected president, Franklin Delano Roosevelt, pays Jacksonville a visit in 1933.

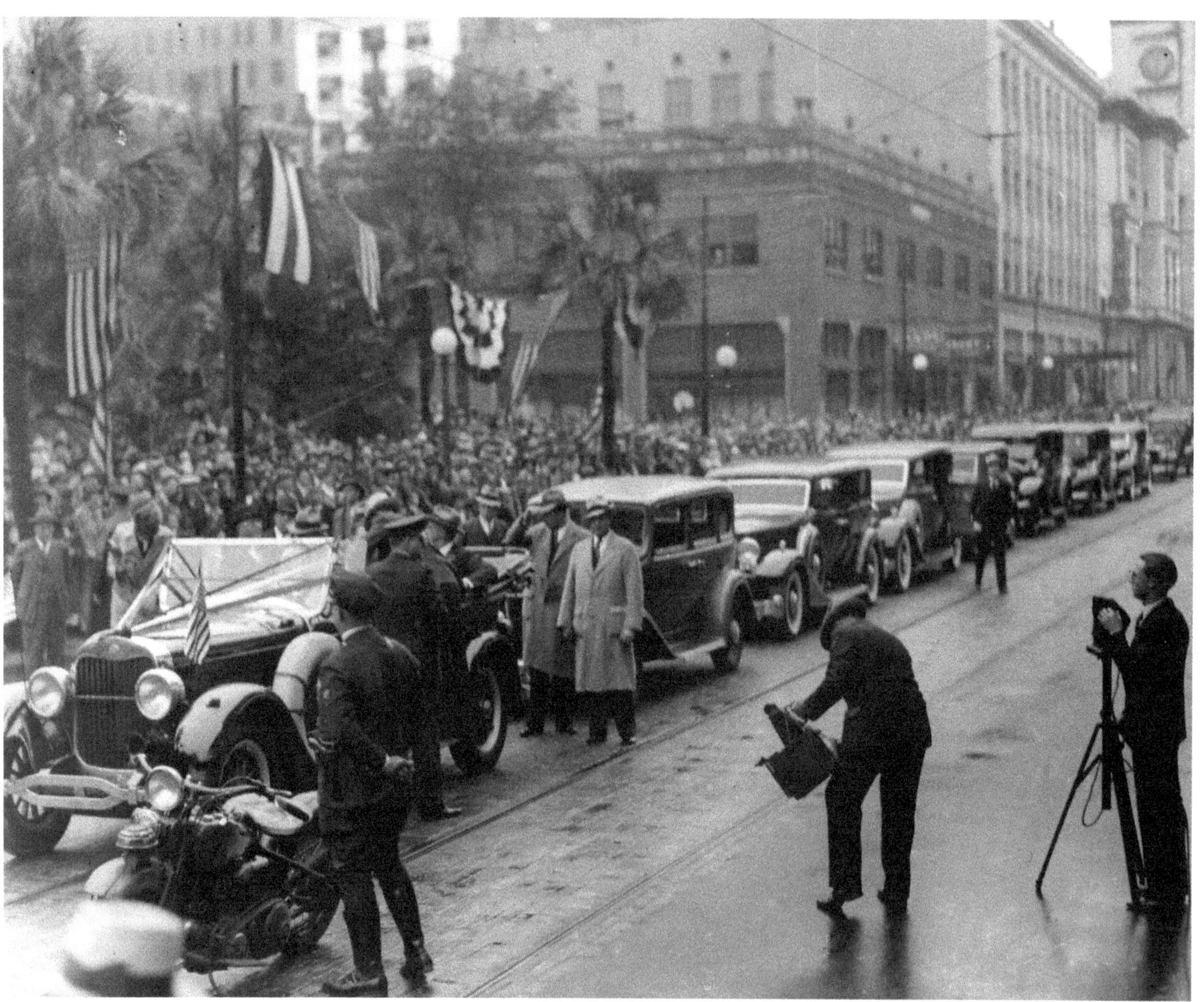

These men are beneficiaries of the New Deal programs initiated by President Roosevelt. As enlistees in the Federal Emergency Relief Administration, they are employed here laying track for airport construction.

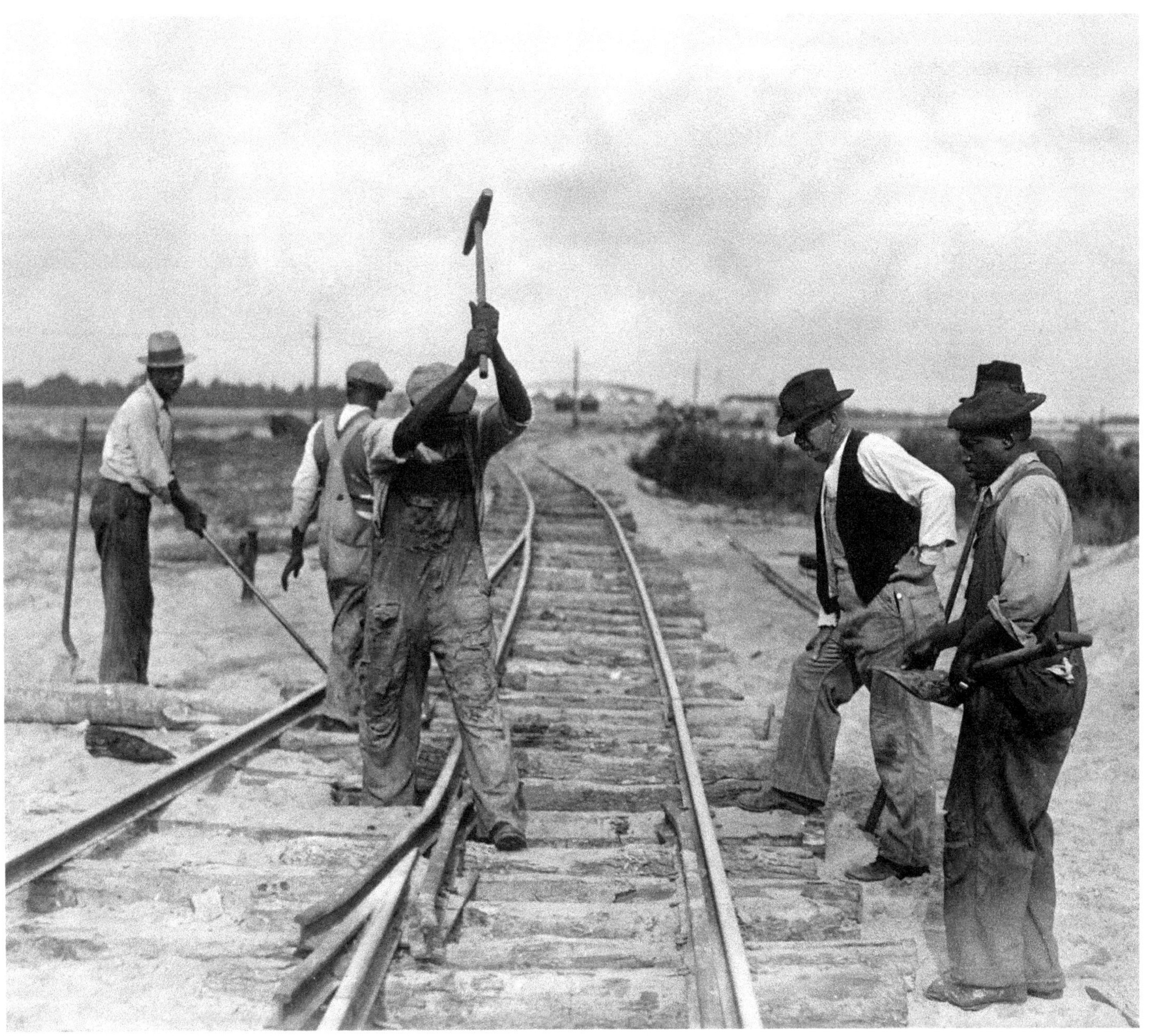

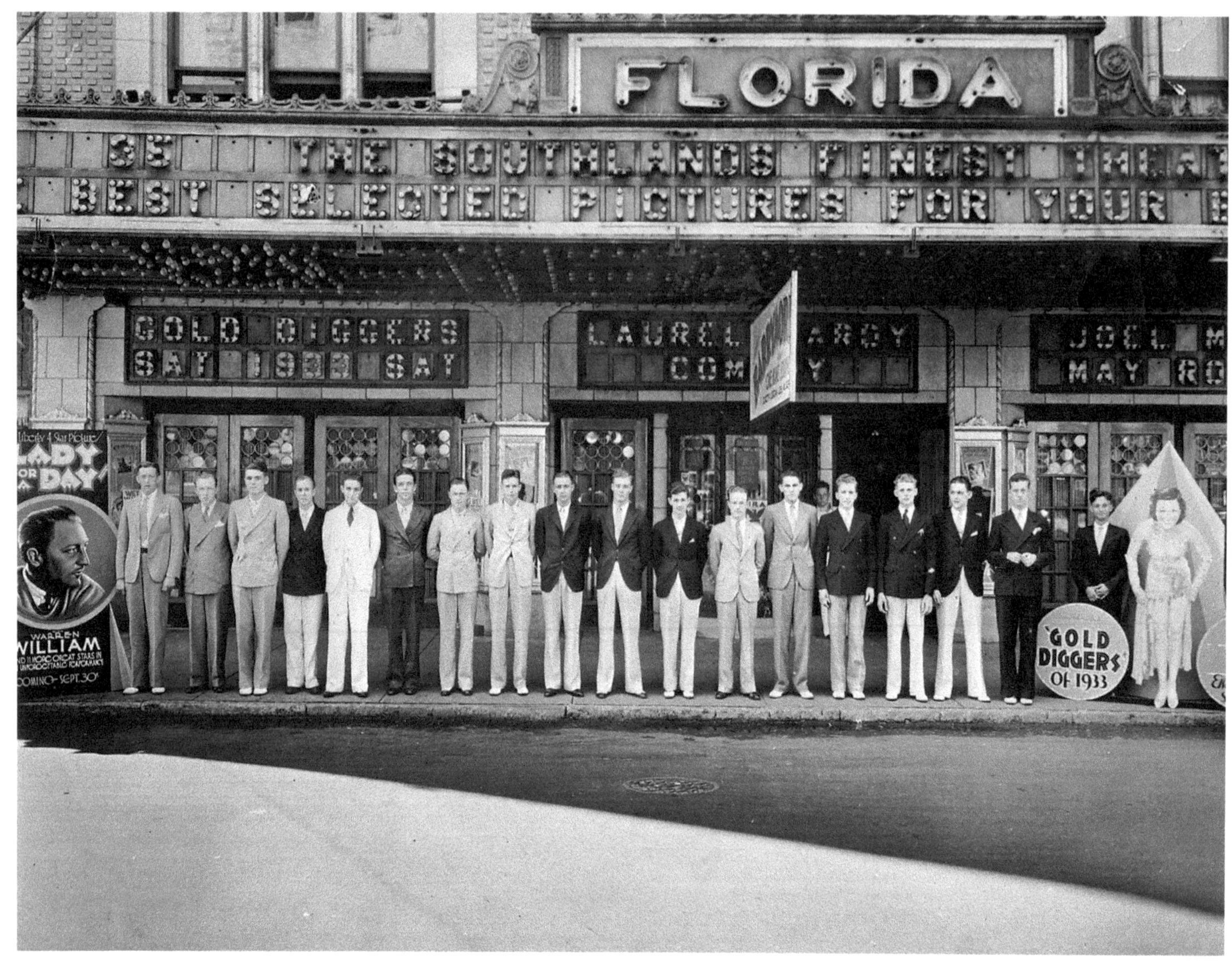

In spite of the Depression, the show goes on. Employees pose in front of Jacksonville's newest movie palace, the Florida Theatre, which opened in 1933. Today this theater is one of the city's main historic landmarks and continues to serve the public.

The Mason Hotel, 11 stories tall, was constructed of steel, granite, and brick. Built for George M. Mason for $1 million, the hotel opened to the public in 1913 with 250 guest rooms. Located on Bay Street, it afforded a view of the St. Johns River from penthouse apartments and became one of Jacksonville's most popular hotels. It was later called the Mayflower.

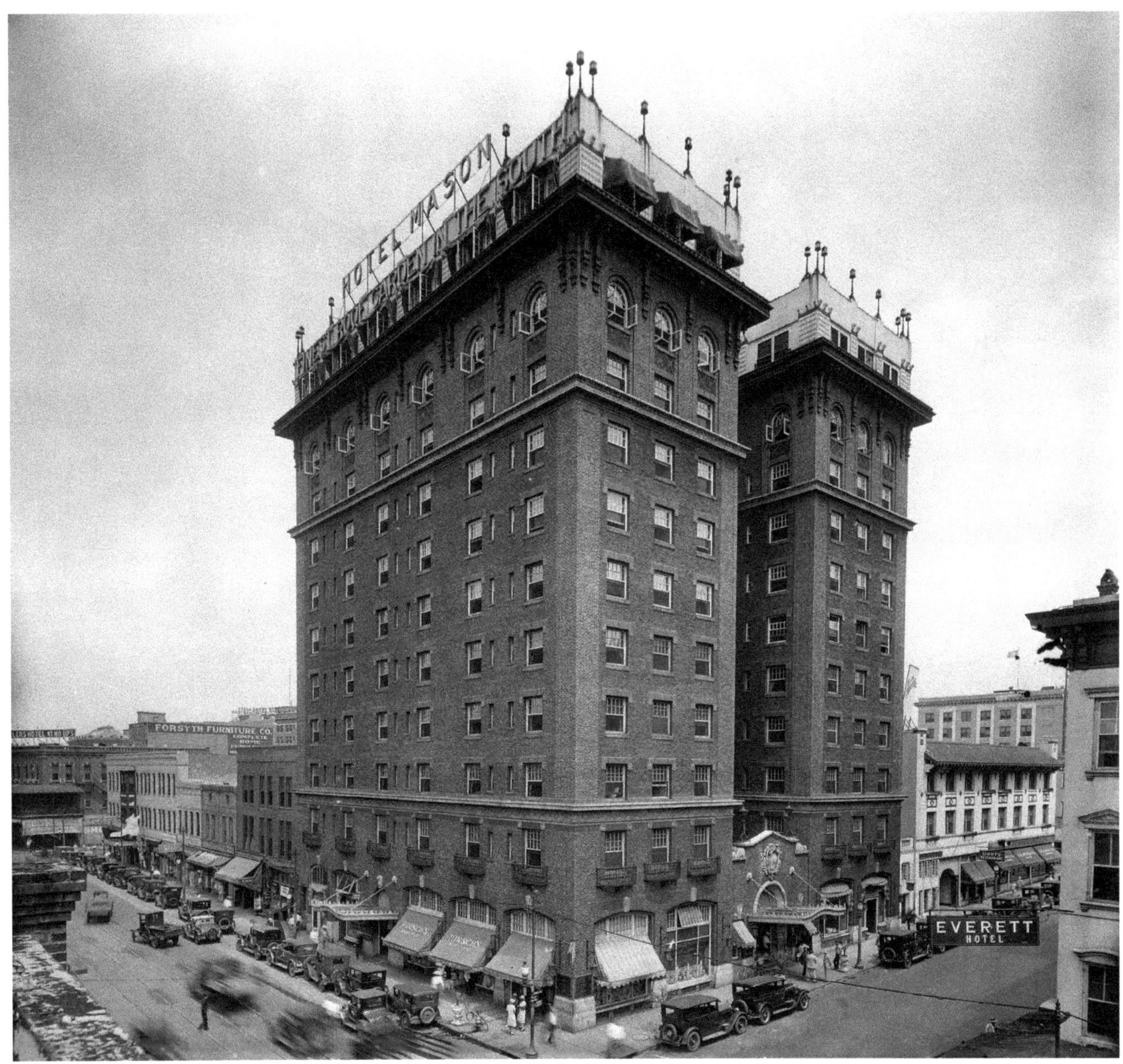

A Smith, Richardson & Conroy delivery truck in 1933

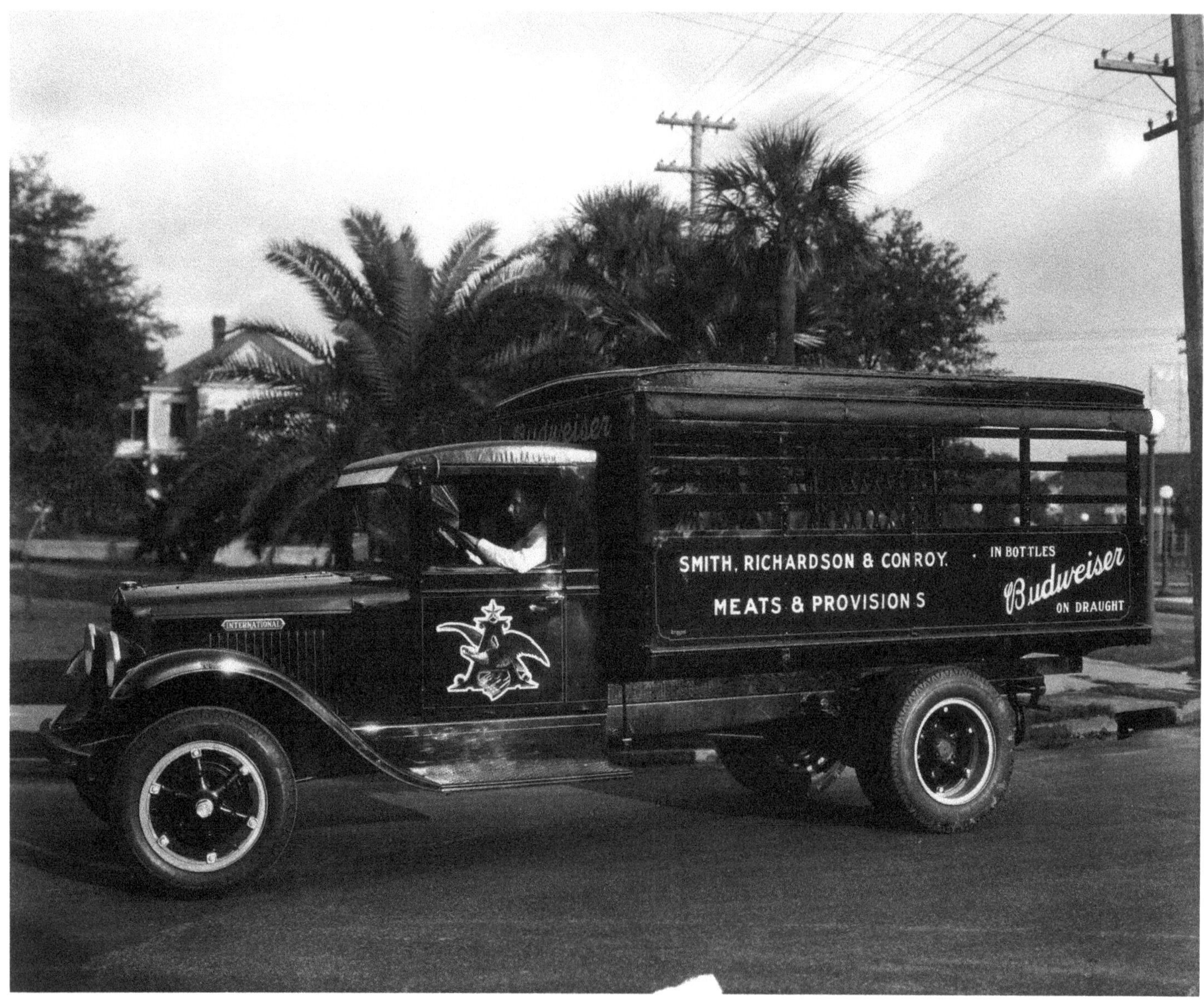

Men with safety inspection vehicles stand in front of the L. S. Teague auto repair shop in 1936.

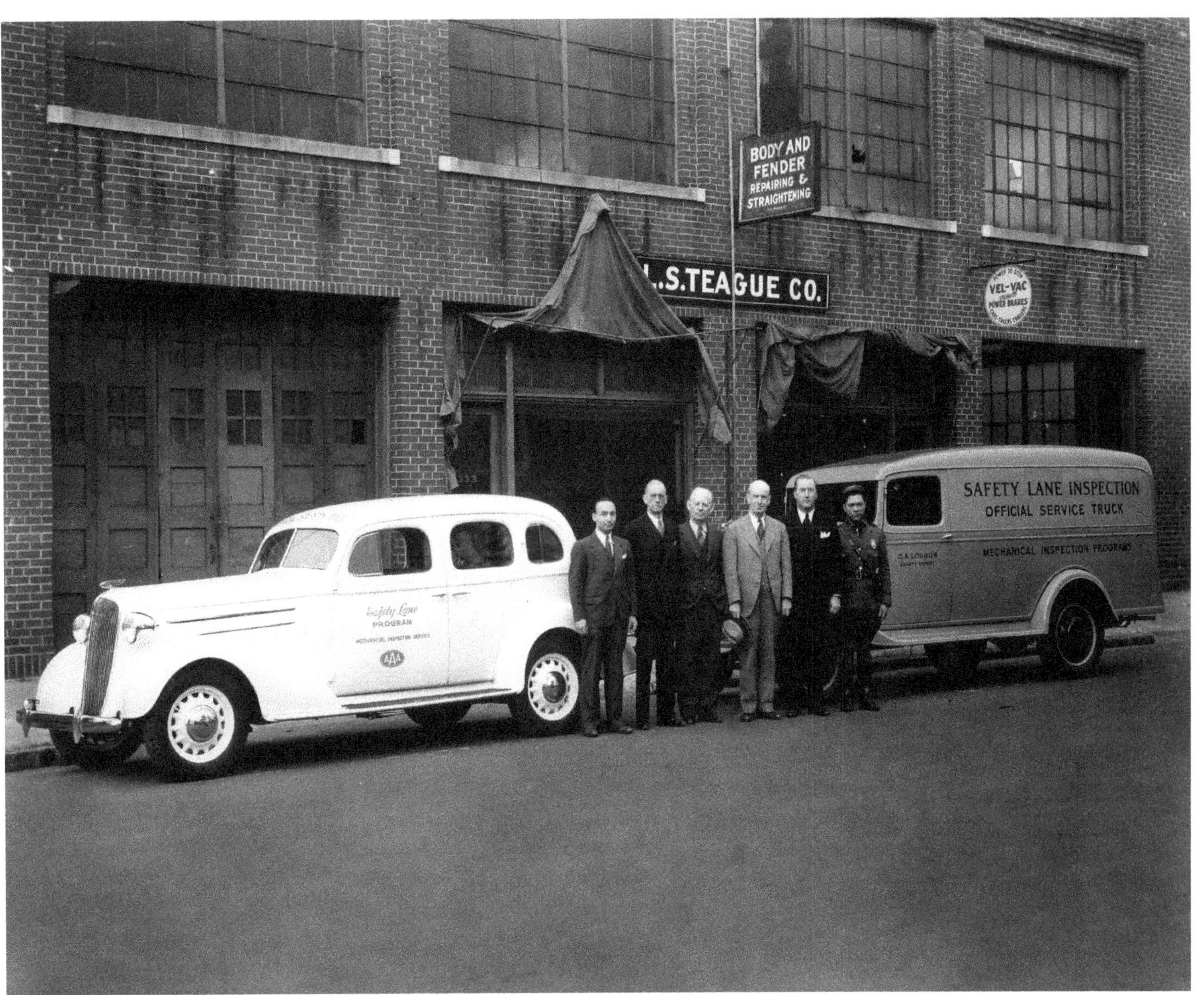

The Arcade Theatre on Adams Street was another popular movie house in the 1930s. The French Novelty and Modern Luggage shops, which added to downtown commerce, are also visible.

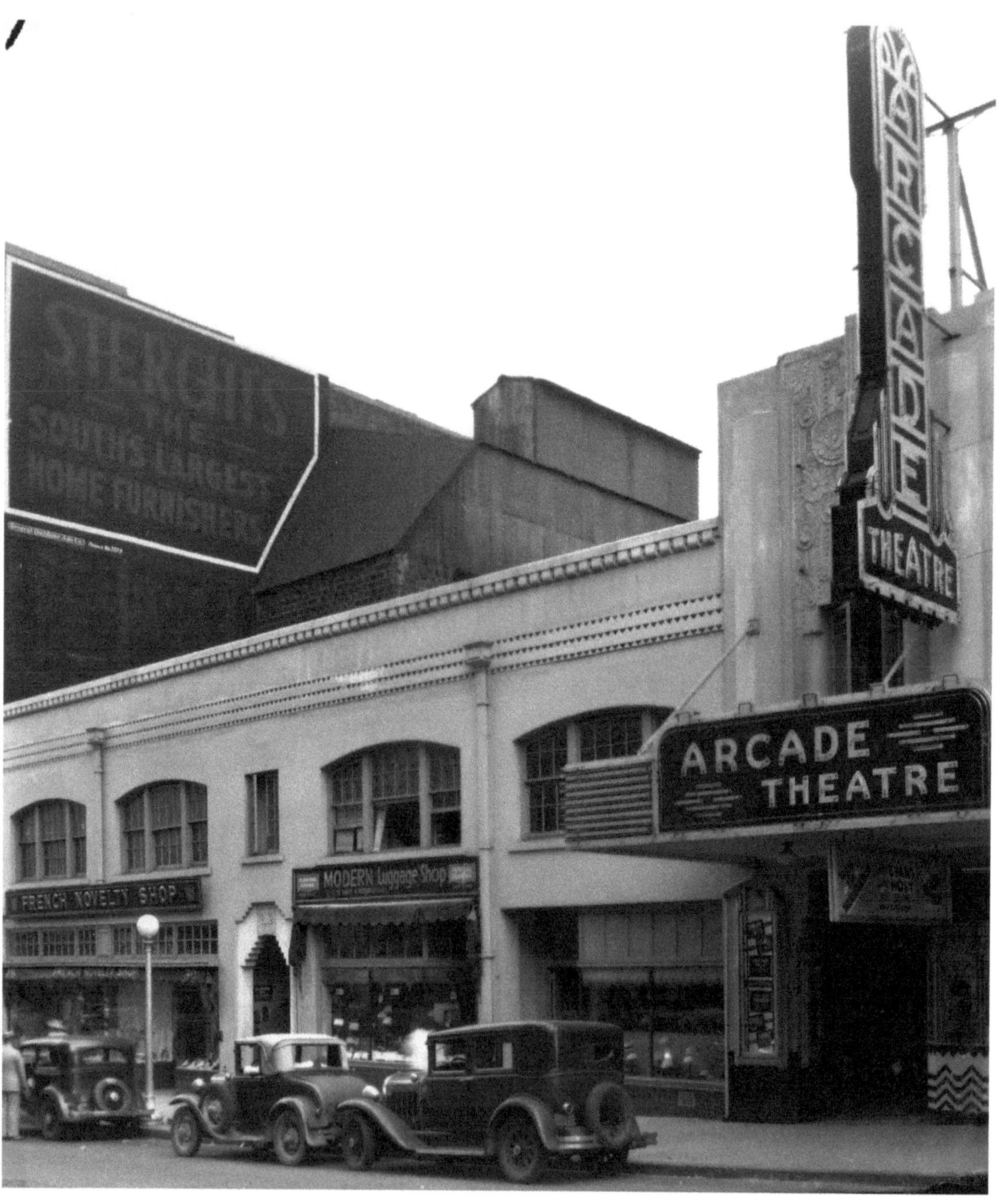

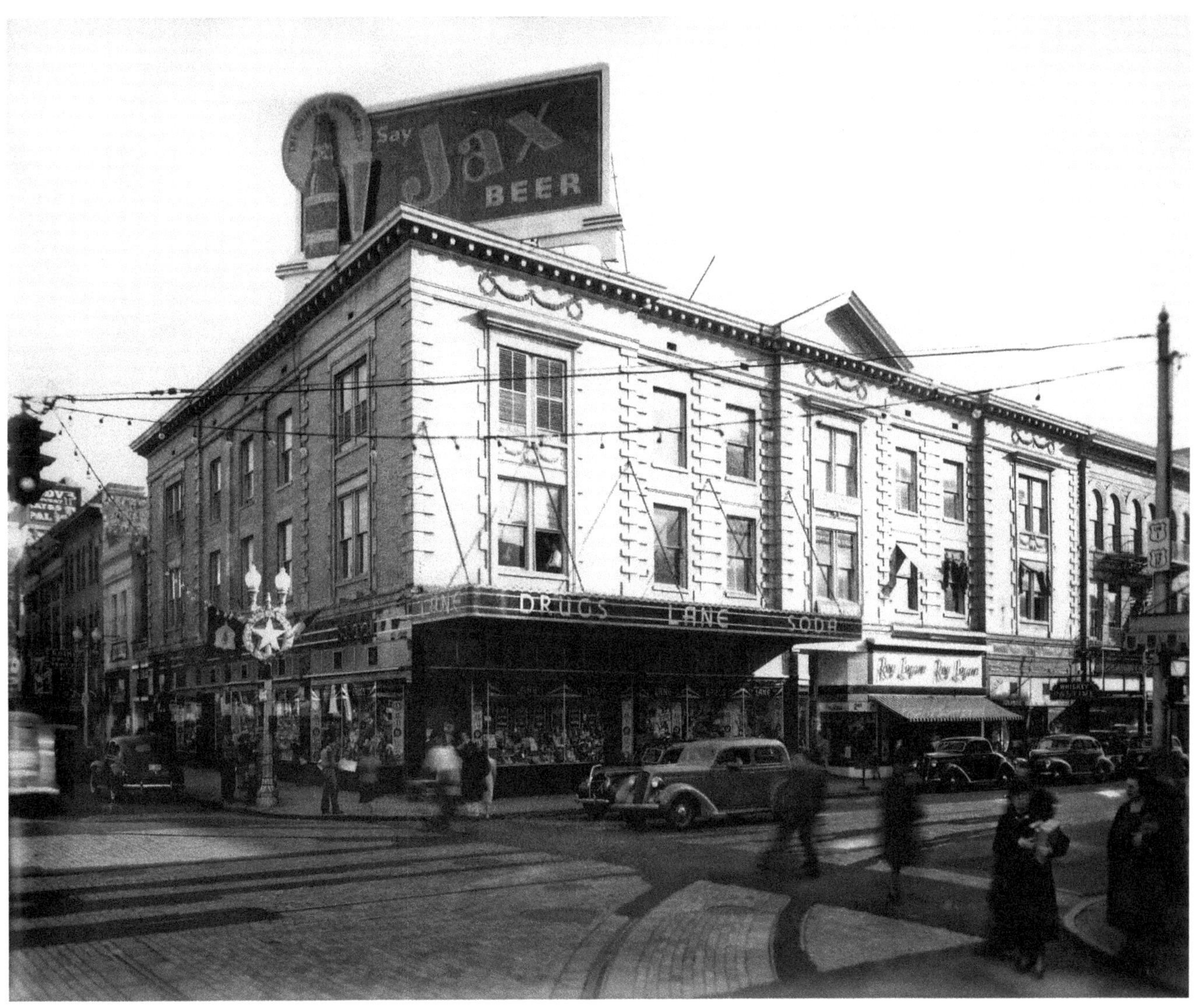

The commercial establishments shown here in 1939 include the Lane Drugstore and the Rainbow Grill on Forsyth Street.

Women employees at a crab-processing plant remove meat from the shells in 1939.

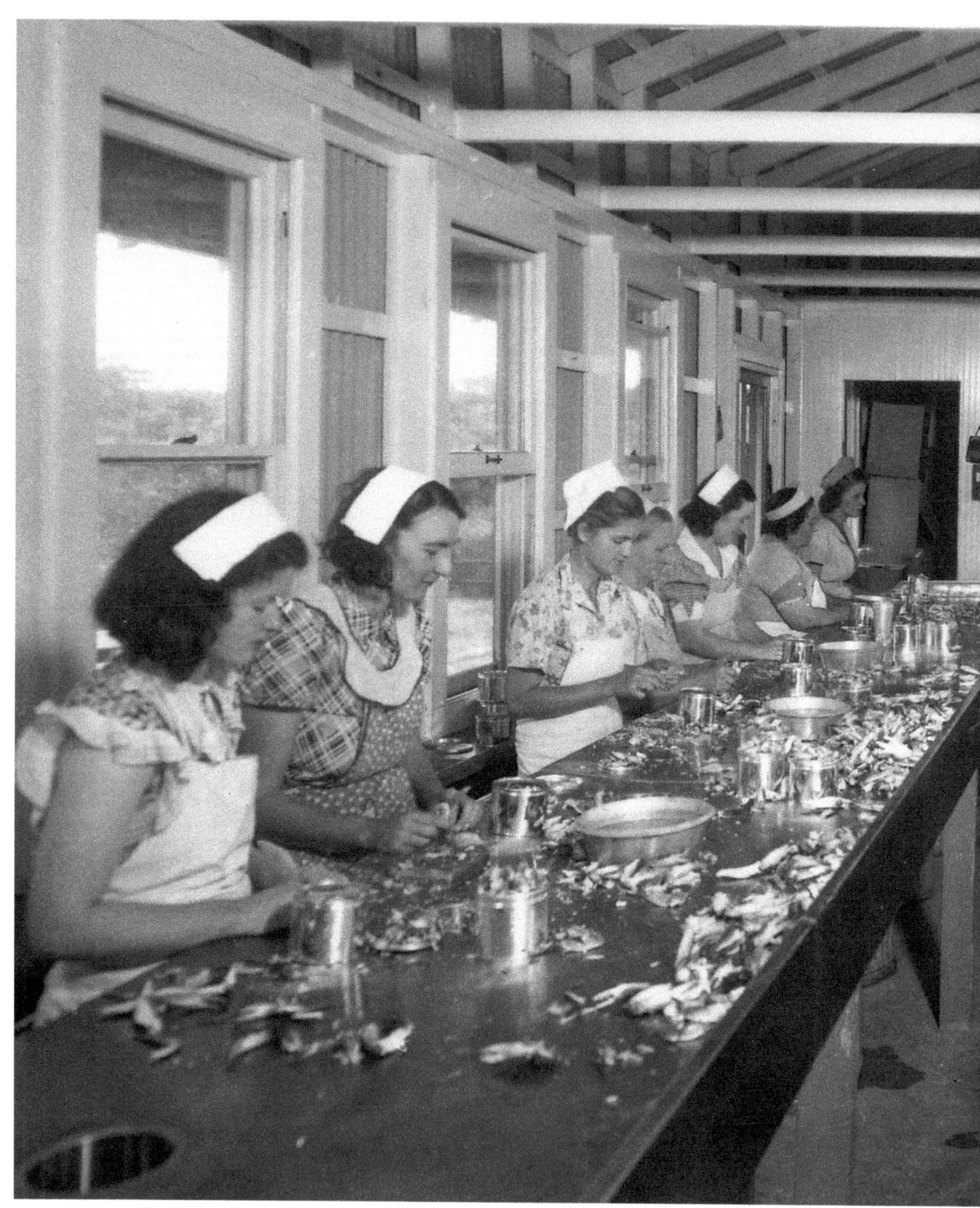

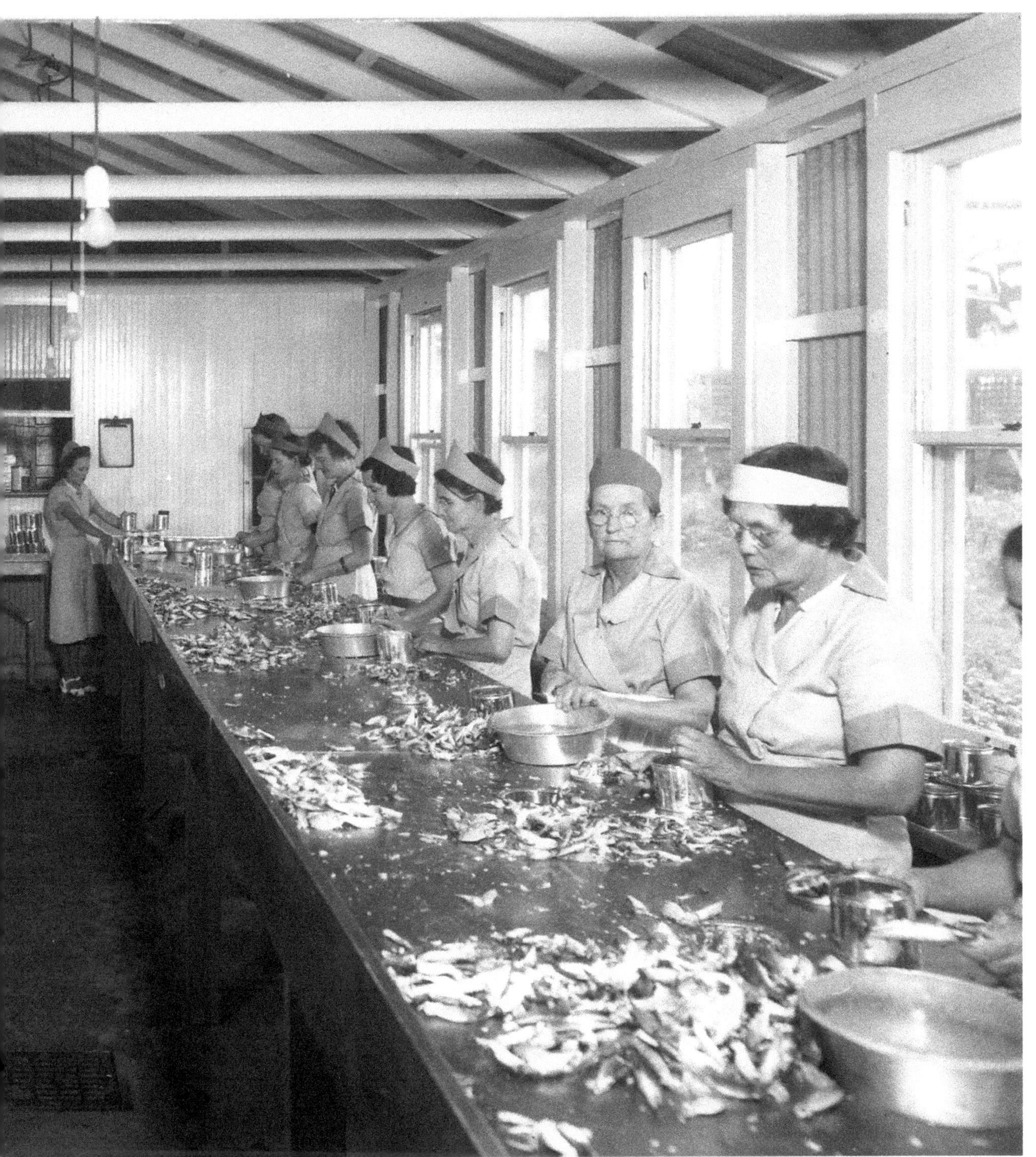

Founded in 1875 as the first secondary school for whites in Jacksonville, Duval High School is shown here in 1936. The original school building was constructed in 1877 and used until destroyed in the Great Fire of 1901. After assuming temporary quarters in the LaVilla Grammar School, the school moved to the new building completed in 1908. This building was used until the 1970s, when it was converted into an apartment complex called Duval-Stevens Apartments.

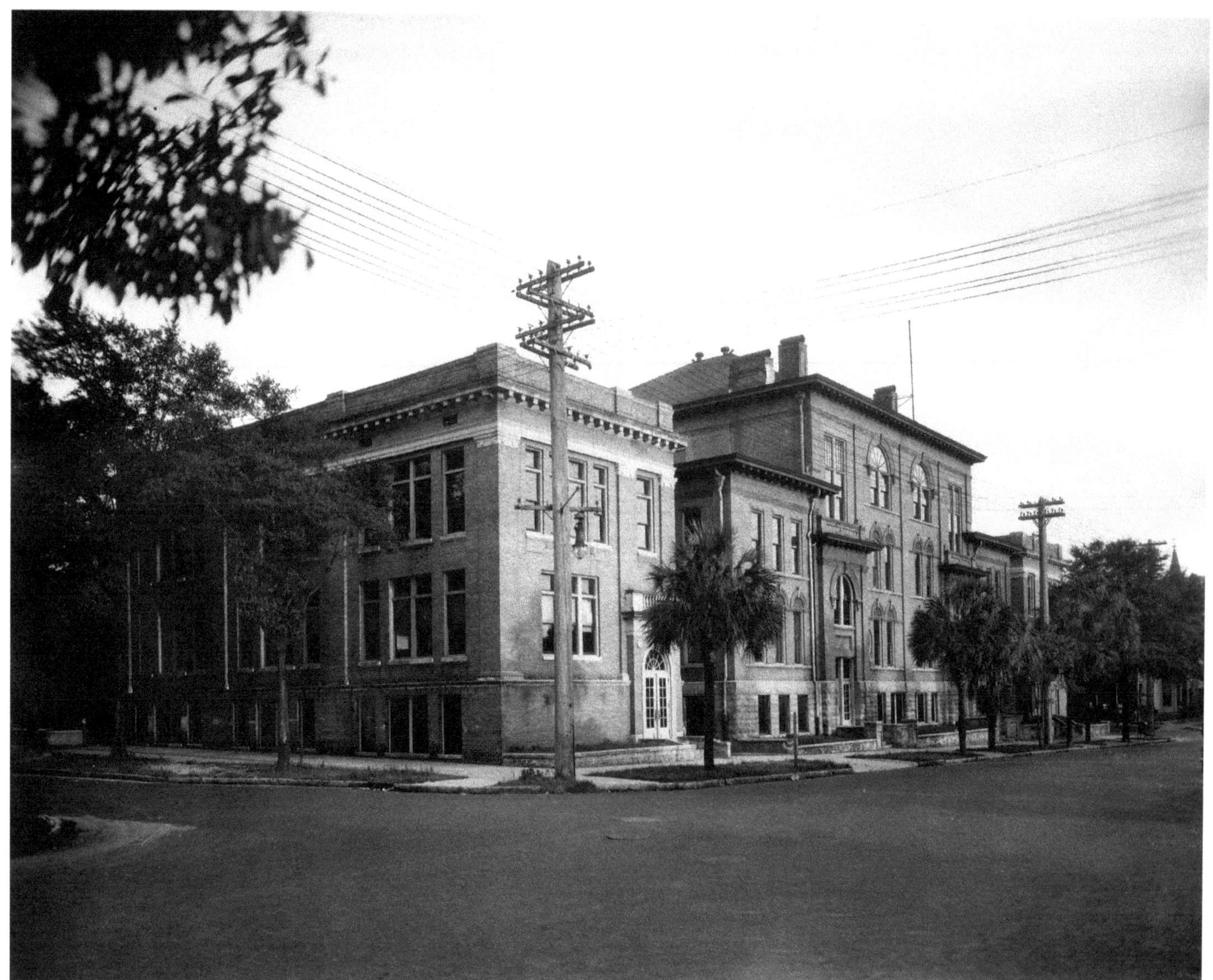

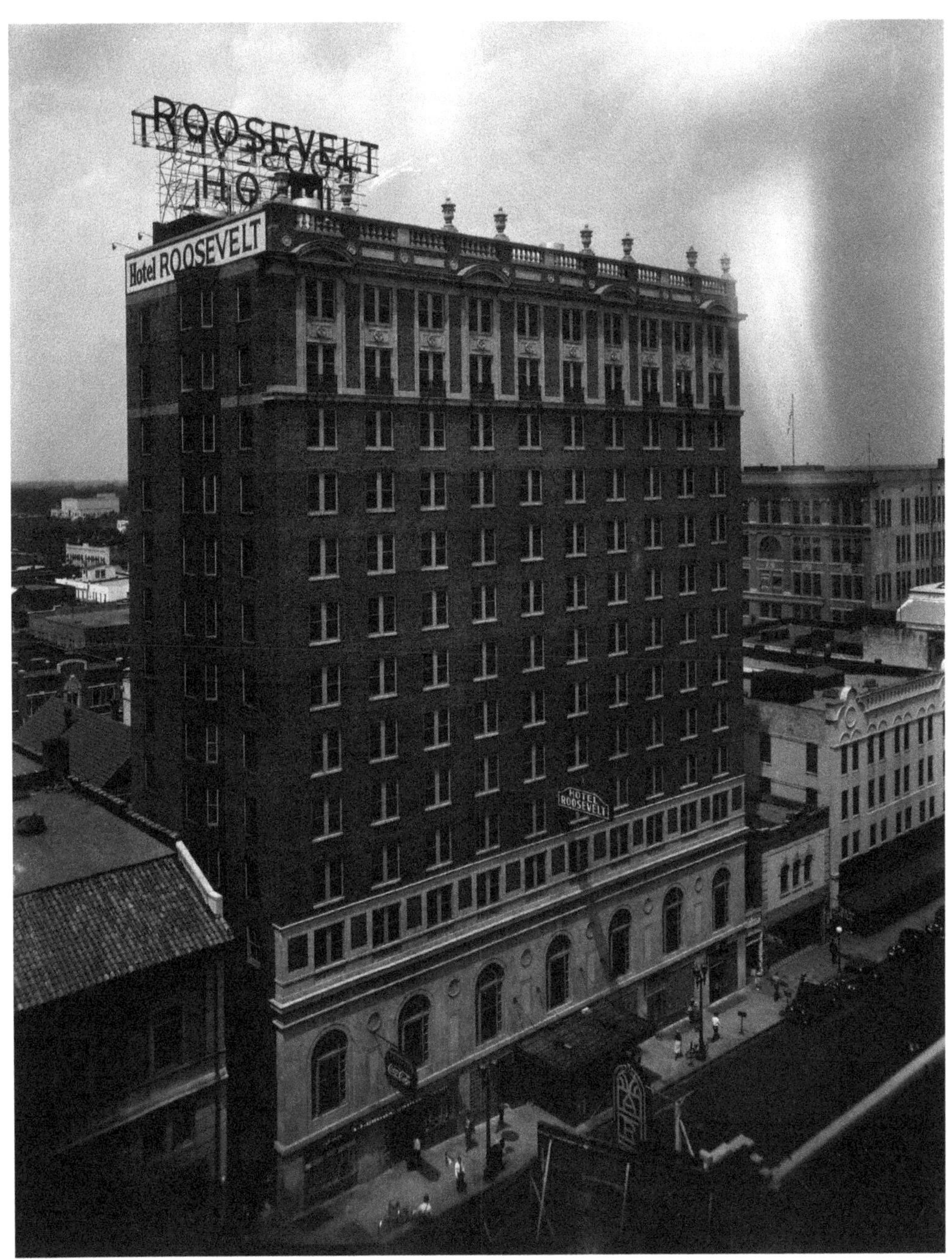

Shown here in 1937, the Roosevelt Hotel, formerly the Carling Hotel, was built in the mid-1920s on West Adams Street. When it opened in 1926 it was advertised as having the "latest equipment in the rooms." After being vacant for a number of years, the building was renovated into condominiums.

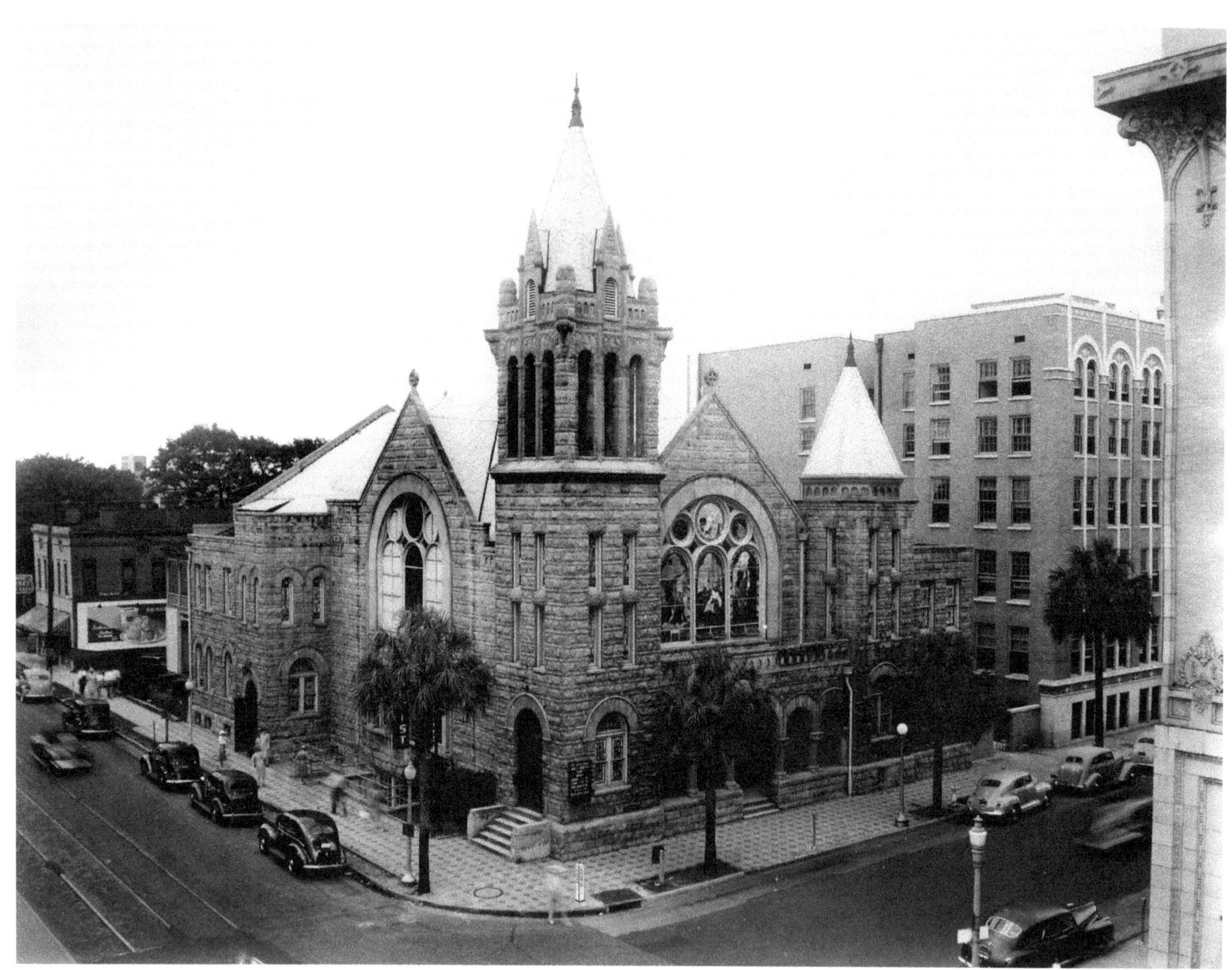

A Baptist Church formed in Jacksonville in 1838. This structure, built after the Great Fire, is shown here at the corner of Hogan and Church streets in 1935.

The Riverside Presbyterian church building, pictured here in 1939, was built in 1927. The original building, known as the "Little Brown Church," was demolished on this site in 1925.

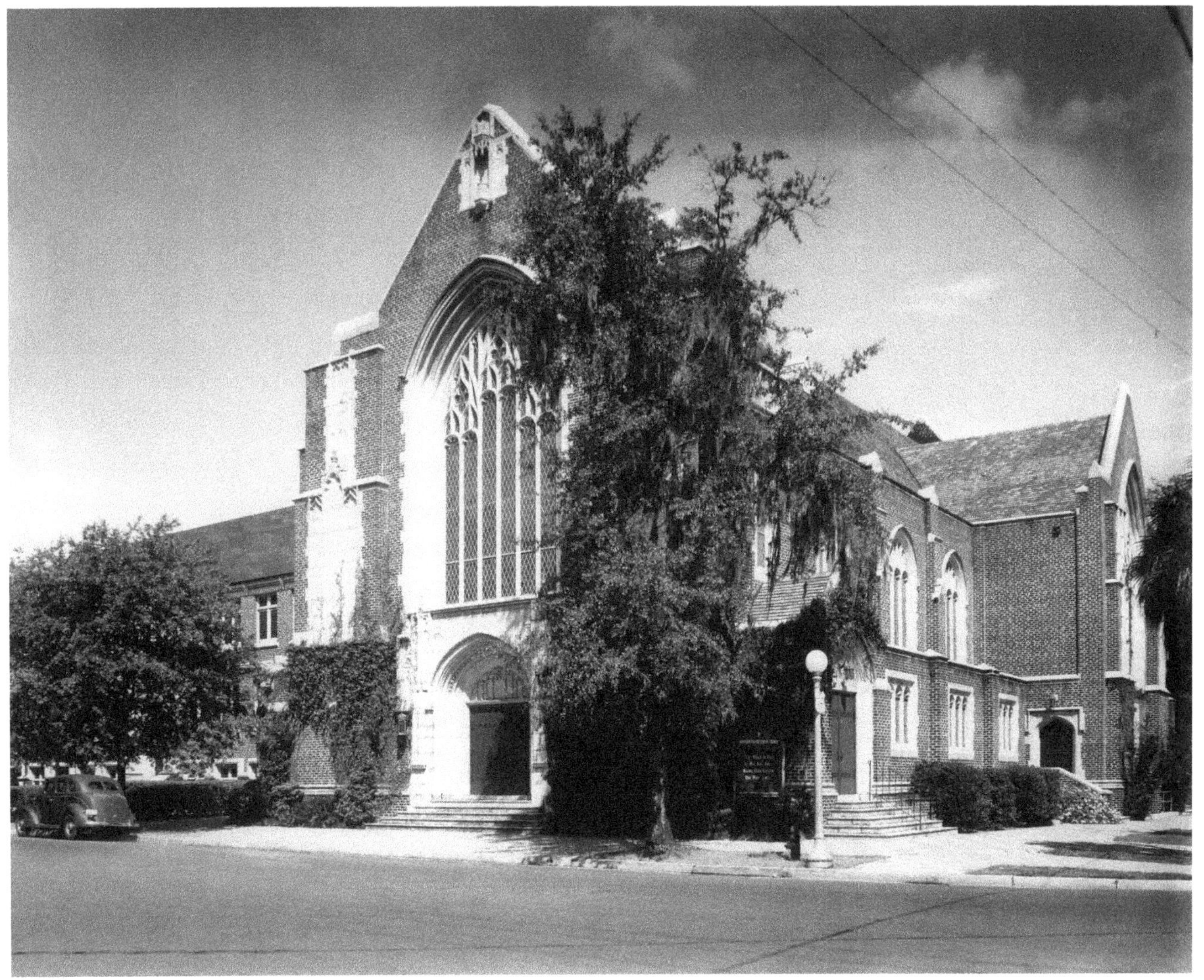

Boy Scouts in a circus parade in downtown Jacksonville in 1939

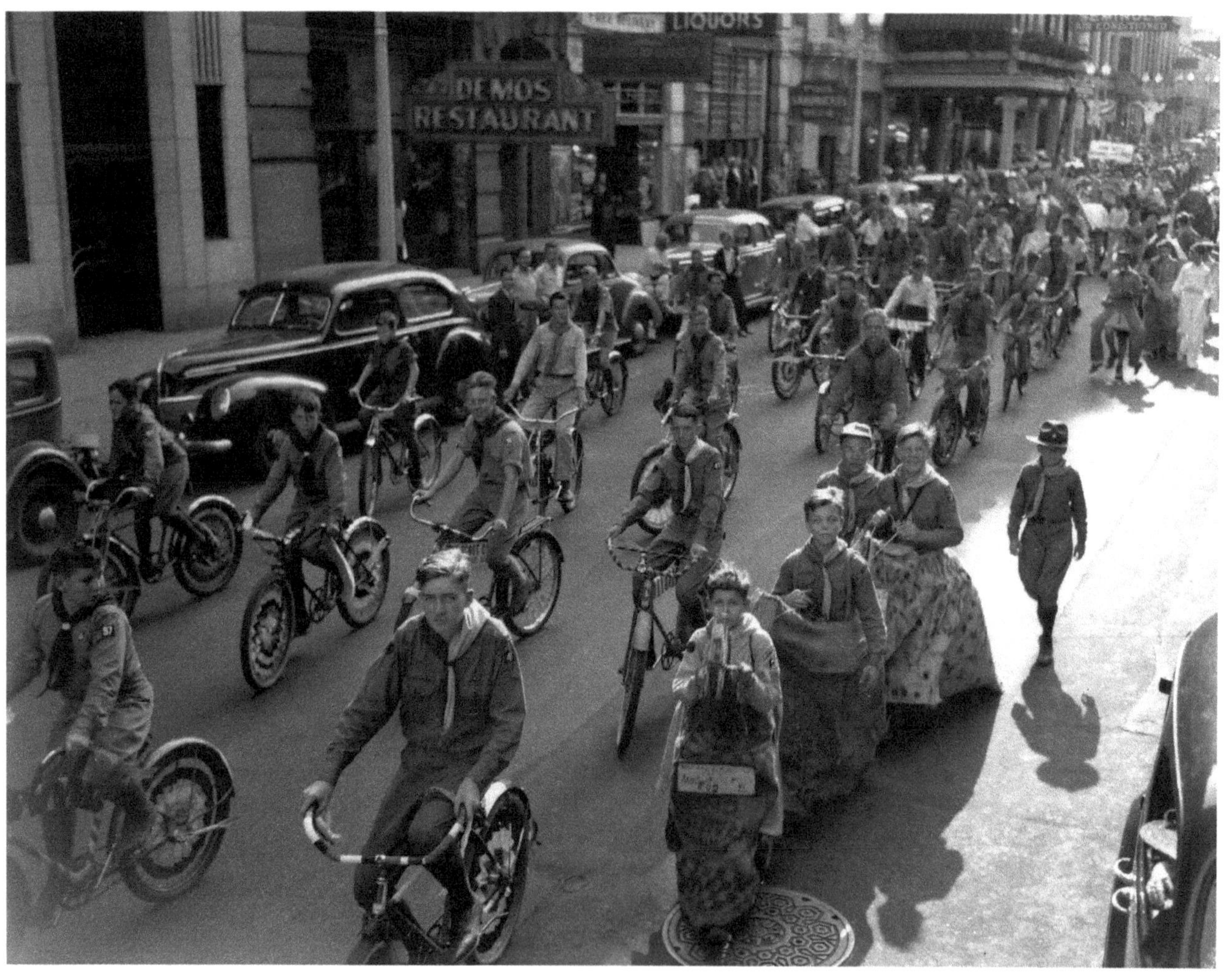

A student at the private school Bolles takes an eye test. Bolles School was founded in 1933 as a military academy. In 1961 it became a boys' prep school. Ten years later it became coeducational.

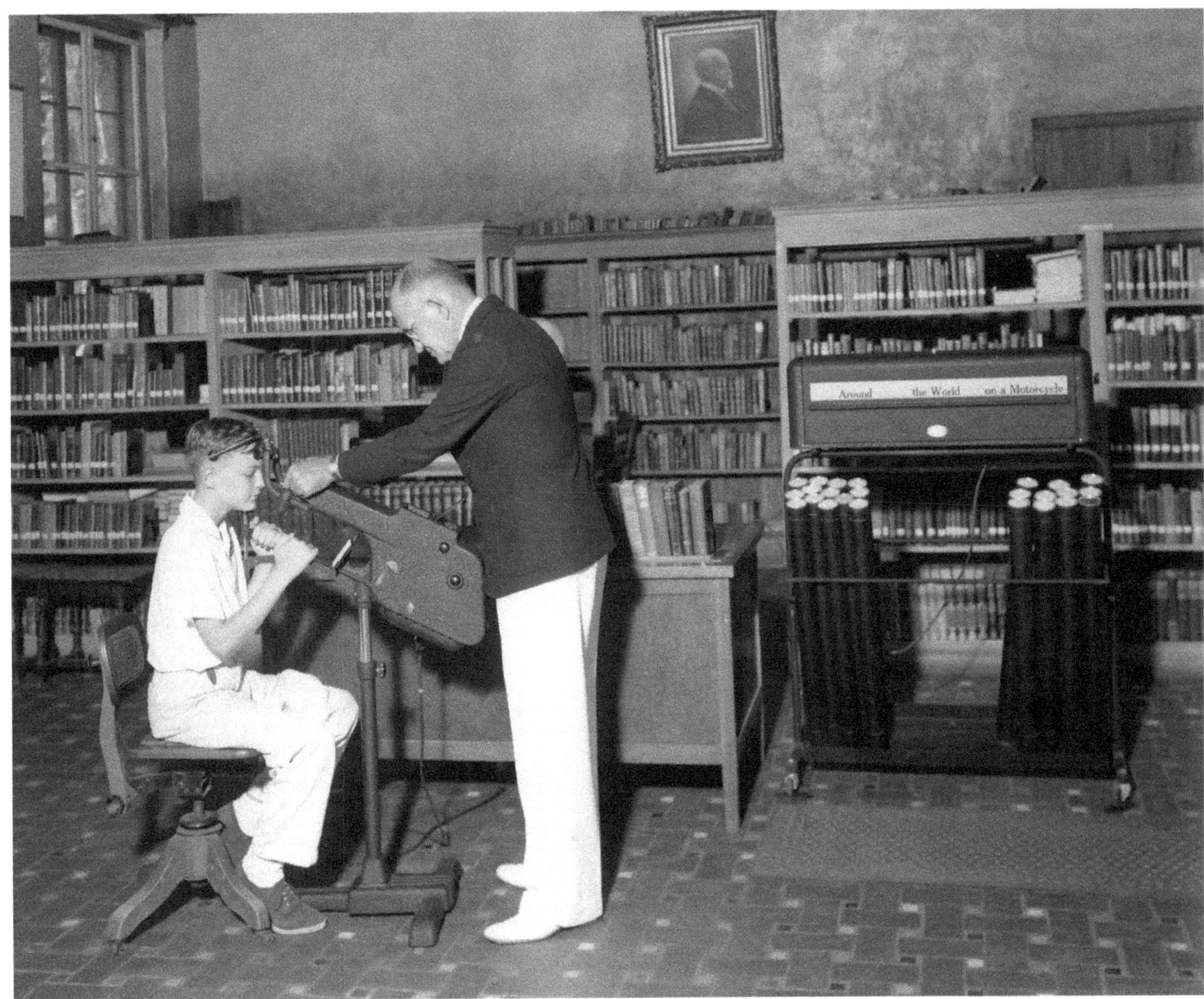

With new roads and automobiles more abundant, the beaches area of Jacksonville had become a leading destination for many by the 1930s, and the Casa Marina, shown here in 1938, had become a popular dining spot. Opened in 1925 and billed as the "only modern fire-proof hotel at the World's finest beach," it remains open as the last of the early-twentieth-century major resort hotels.

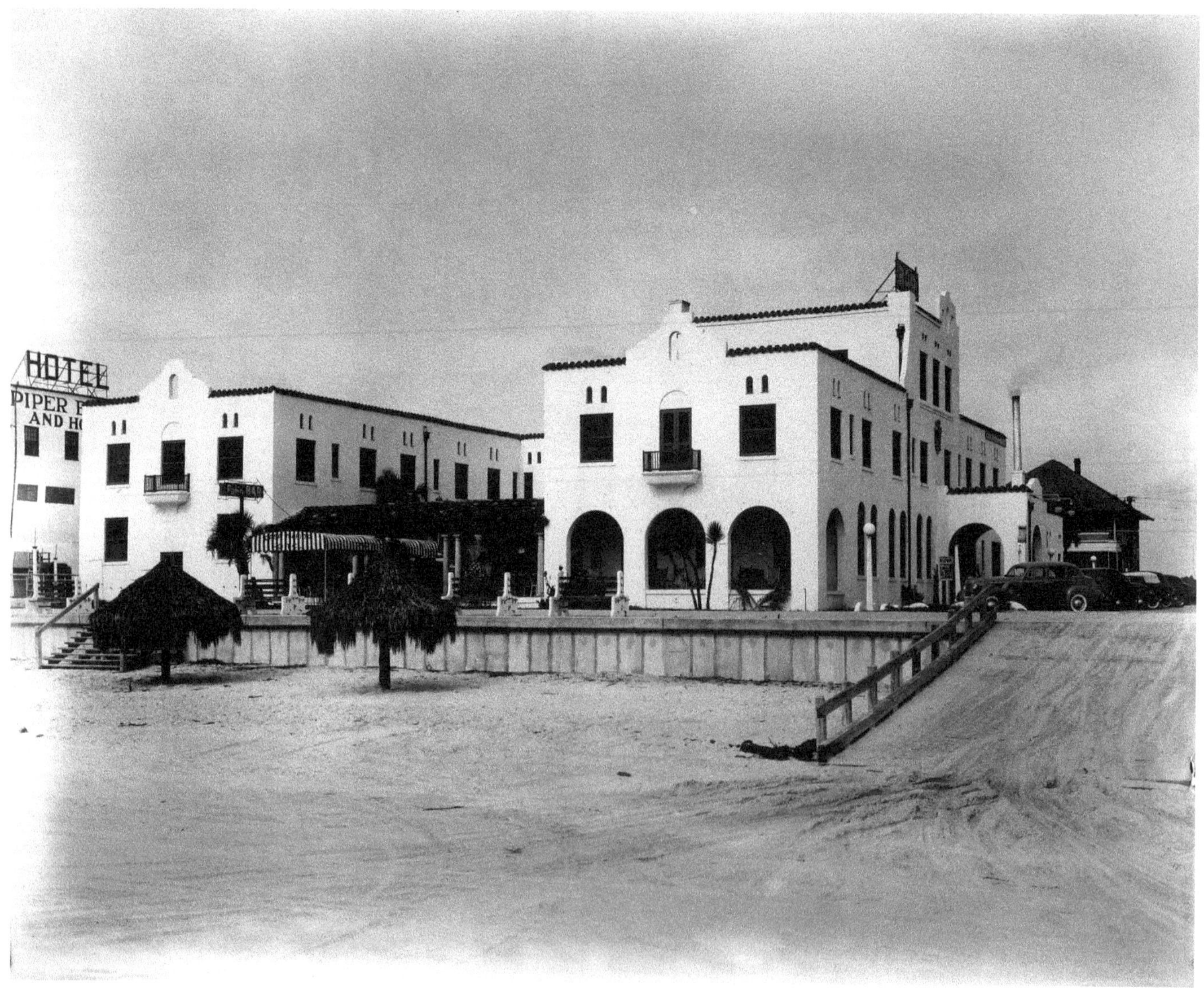

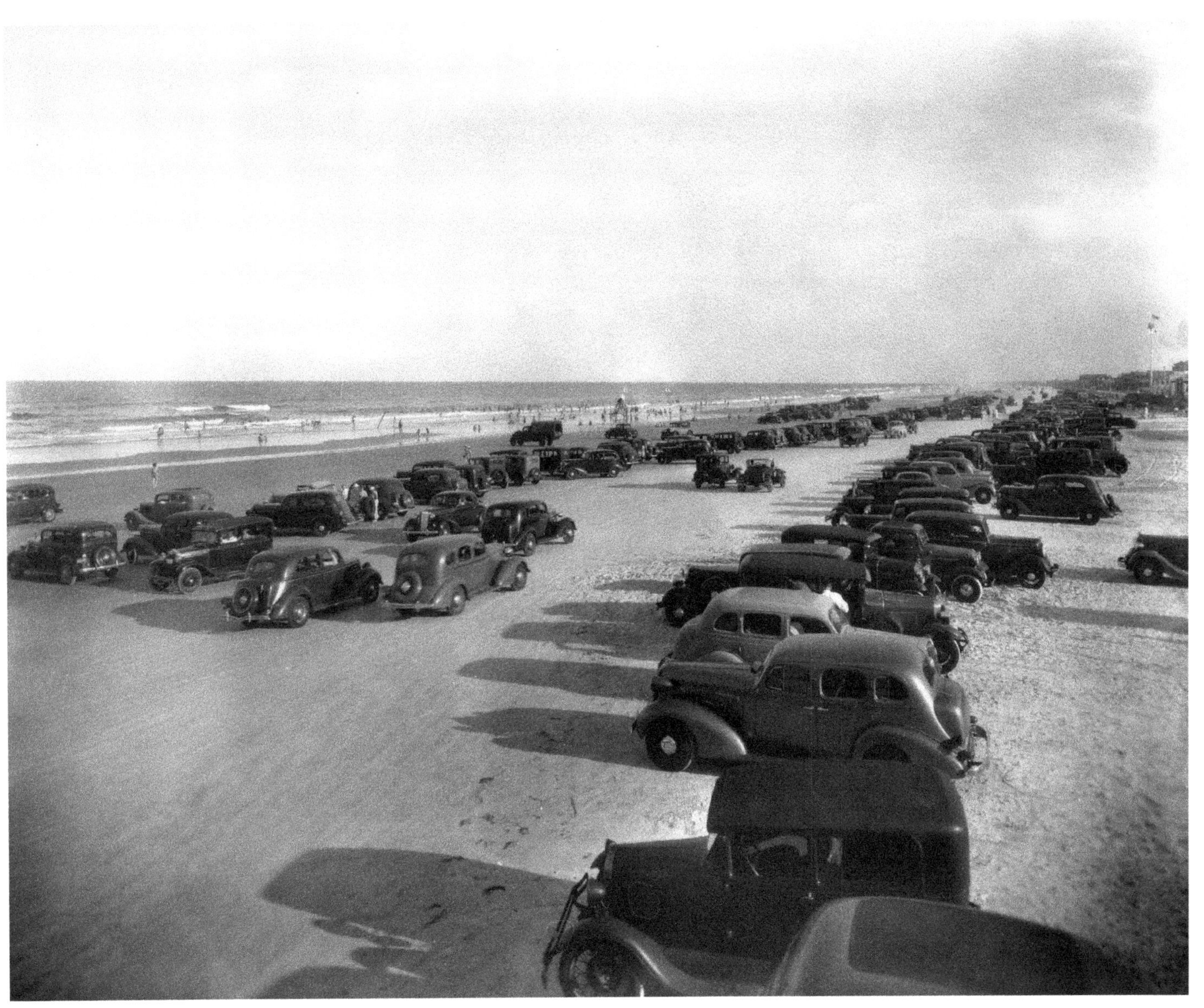

Automobiles on the beaches of Florida became a commonplace part of the landscape. Shown here is a day at the beach in 1936.

People on the beach in the 1930s

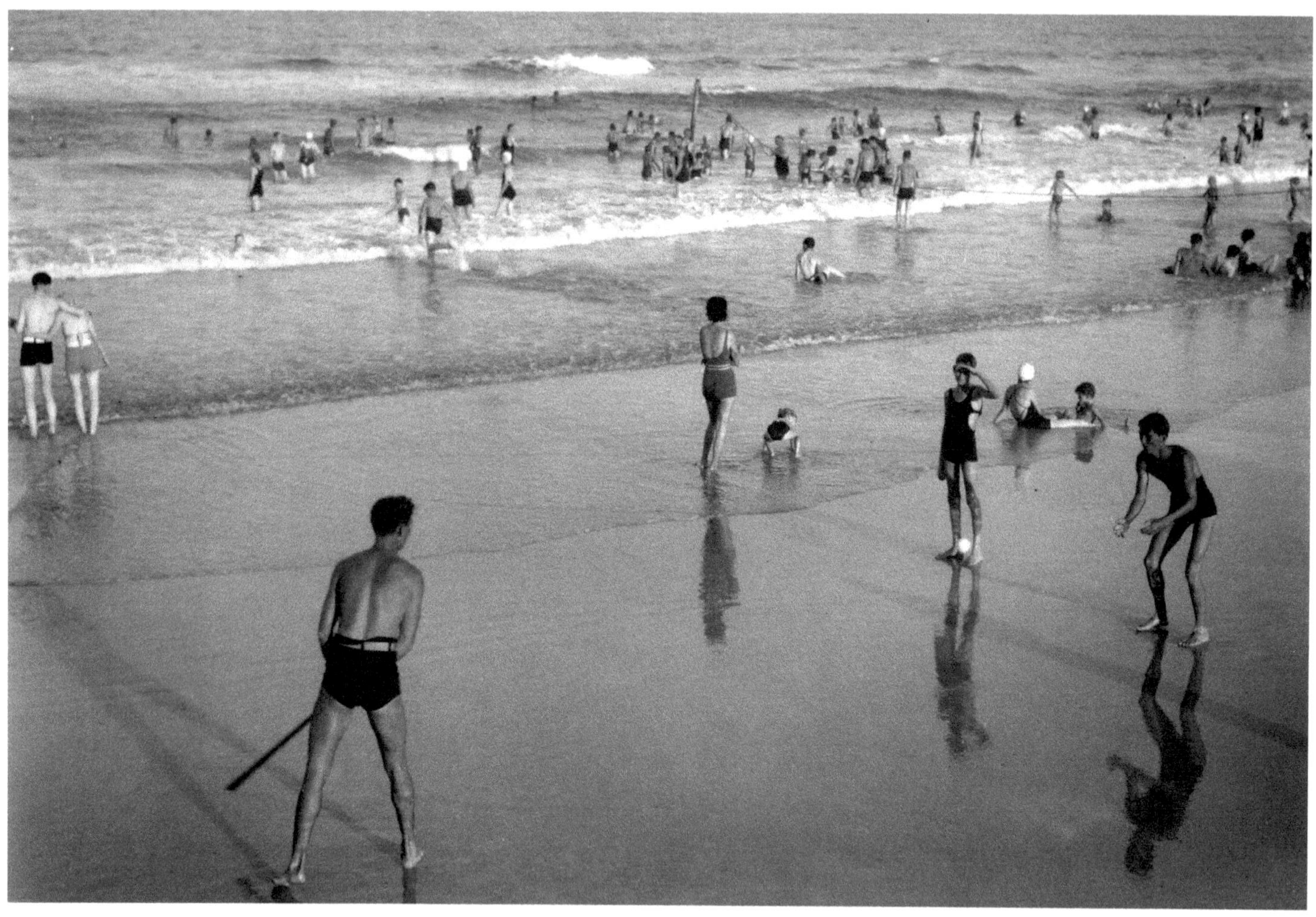

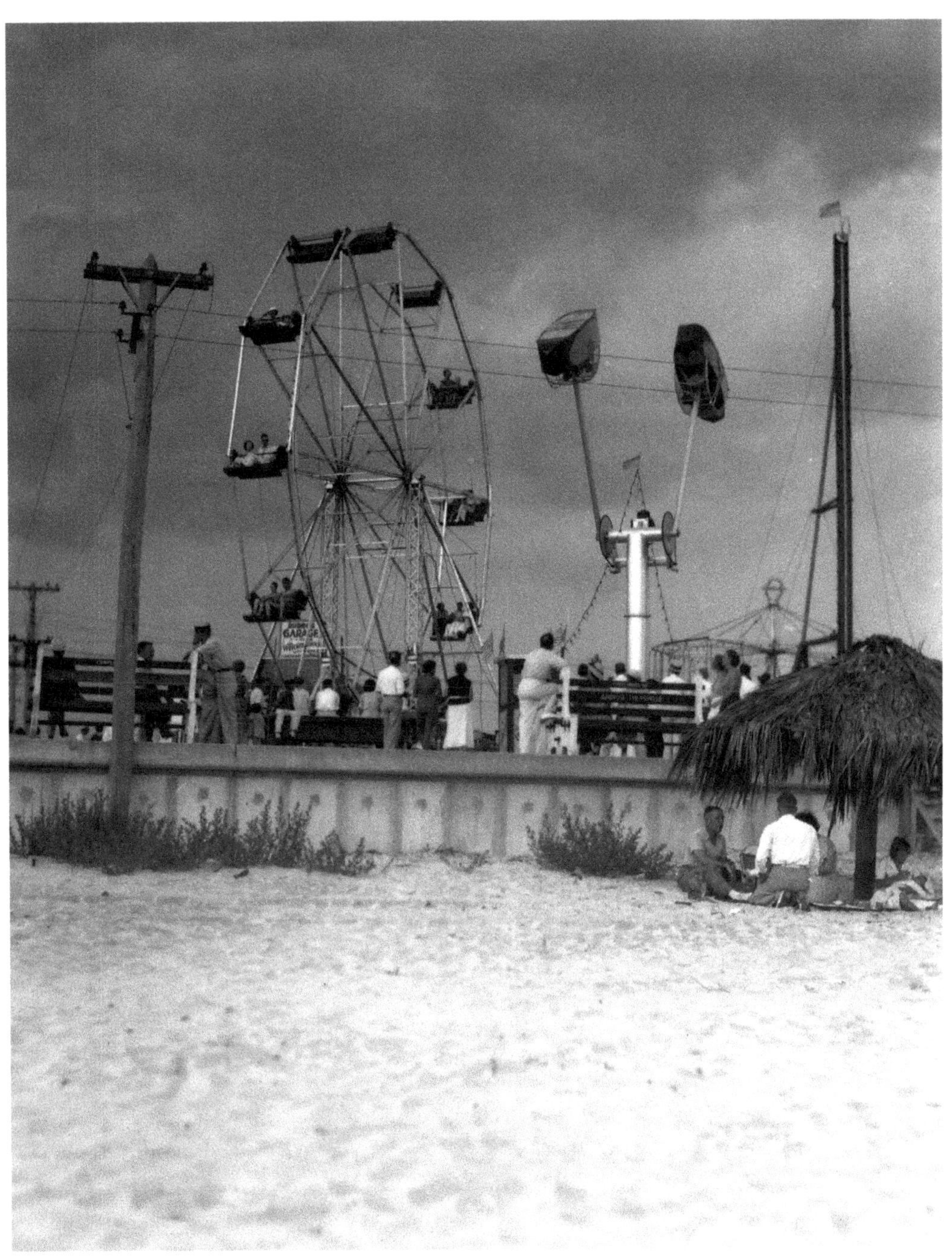

A Ferris wheel and other carnival rides at the beach in the 1930s

People fishing from the pier in the 1930s

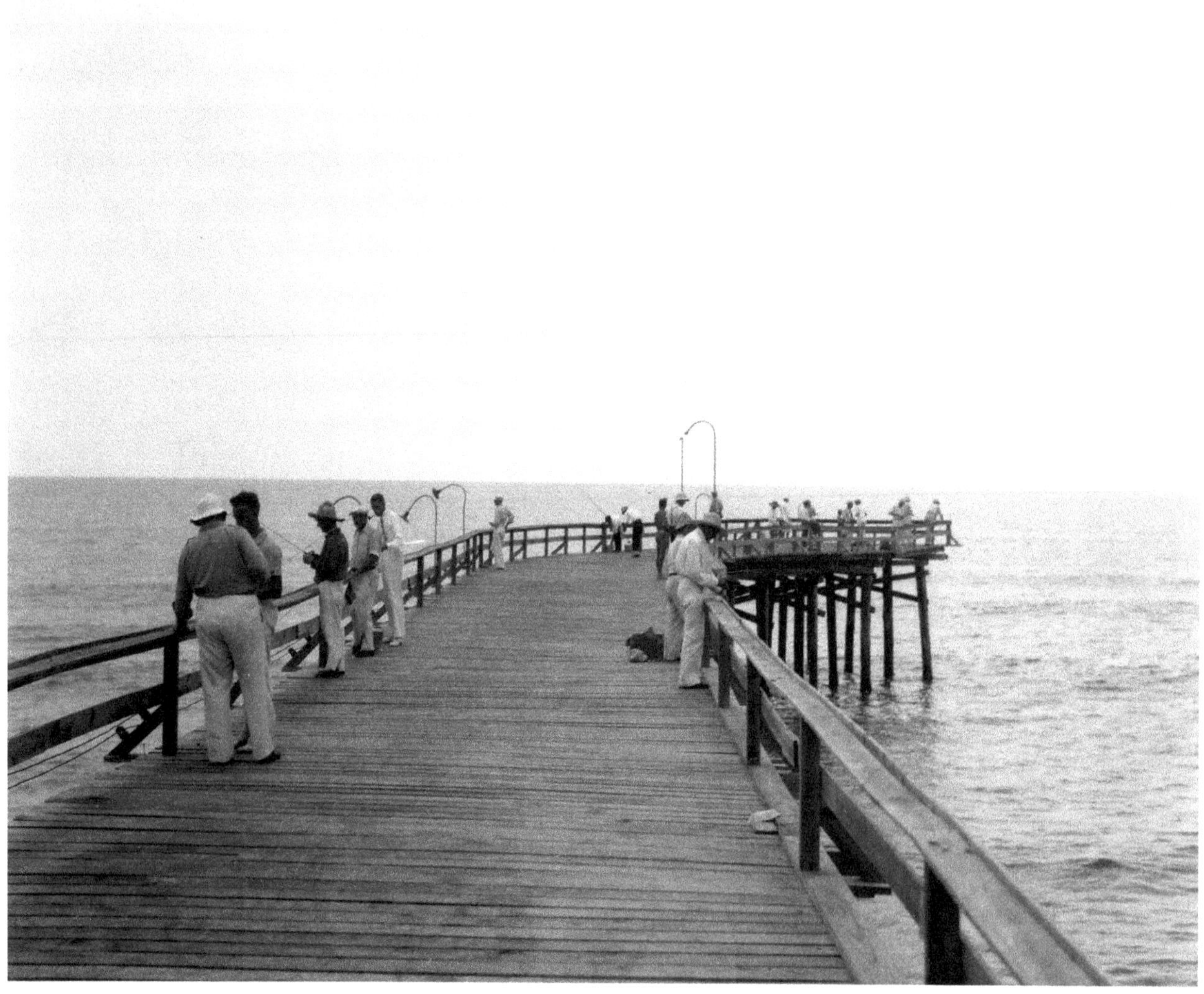

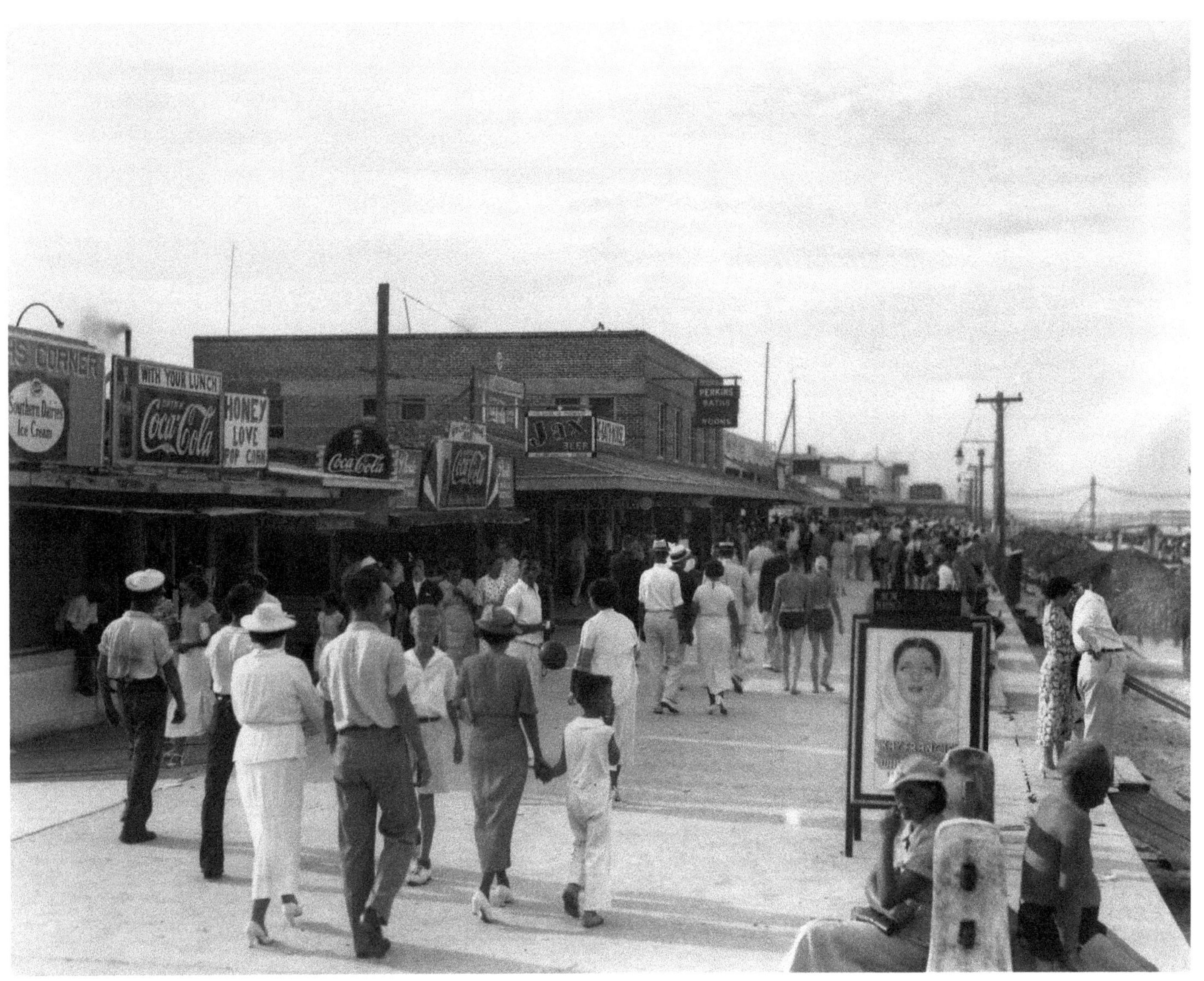

Amusement and shopping at the beach in the 1930s

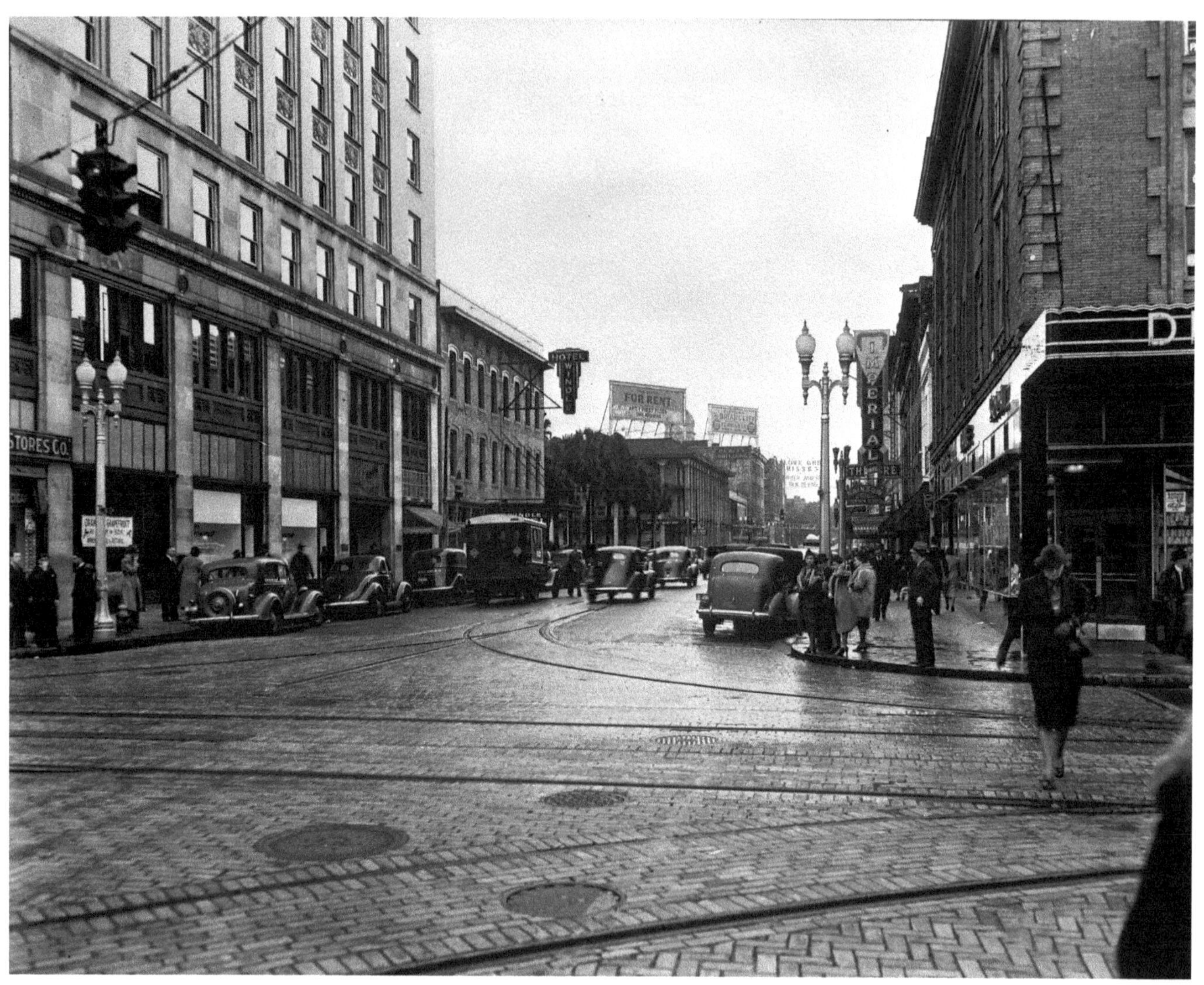

This view of Adams Street in 1938 suggests a dreary Depression-era day. On the national scene by this time, a partial recovery was under way.

The growth of major department stores in the twenties is illustrated by the Levy Building shown here. This structure, located on West Adams Street, was built in 1927.

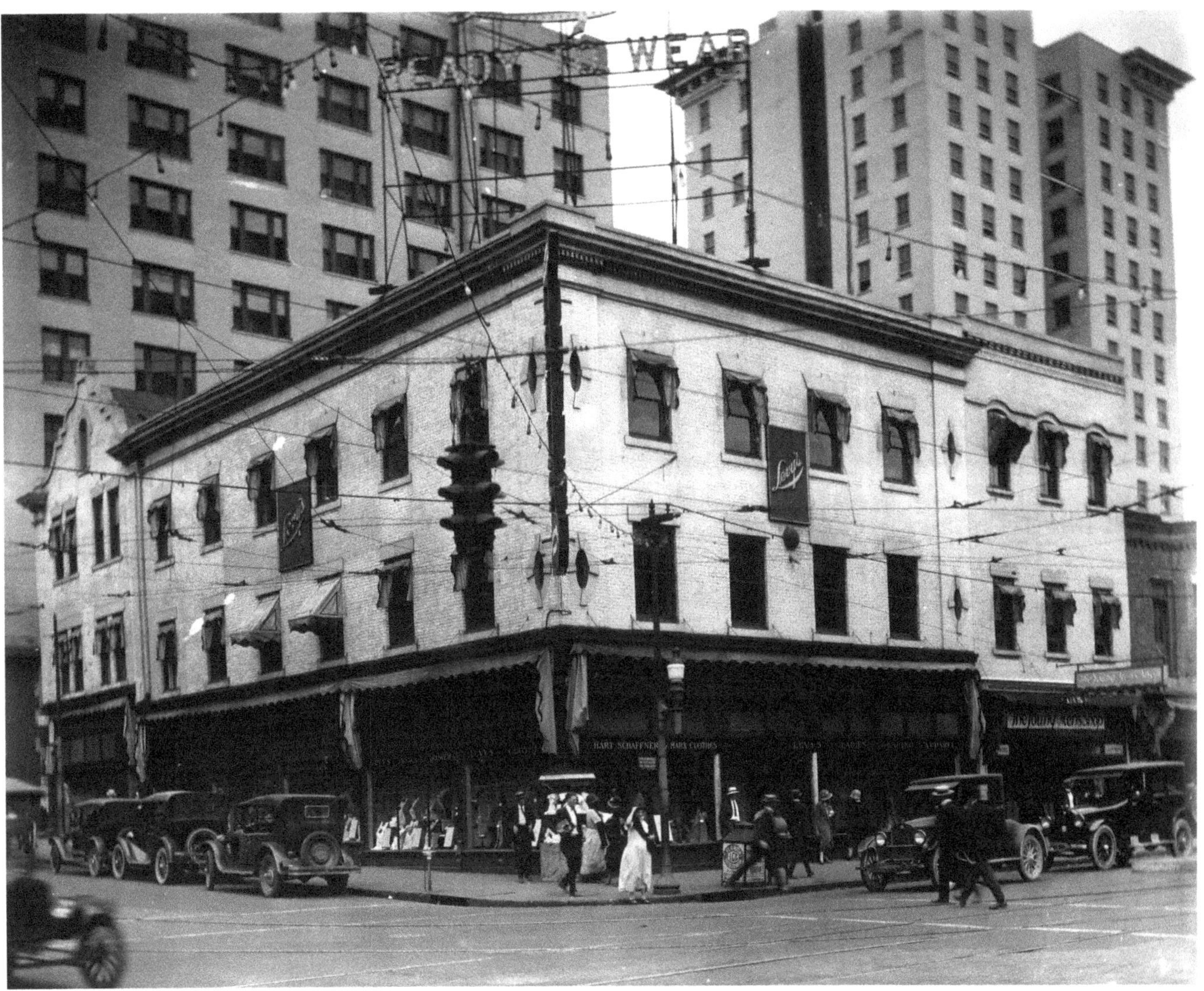

President Roosevelt inspects personnel at the new Naval Air Station in the 1940s.

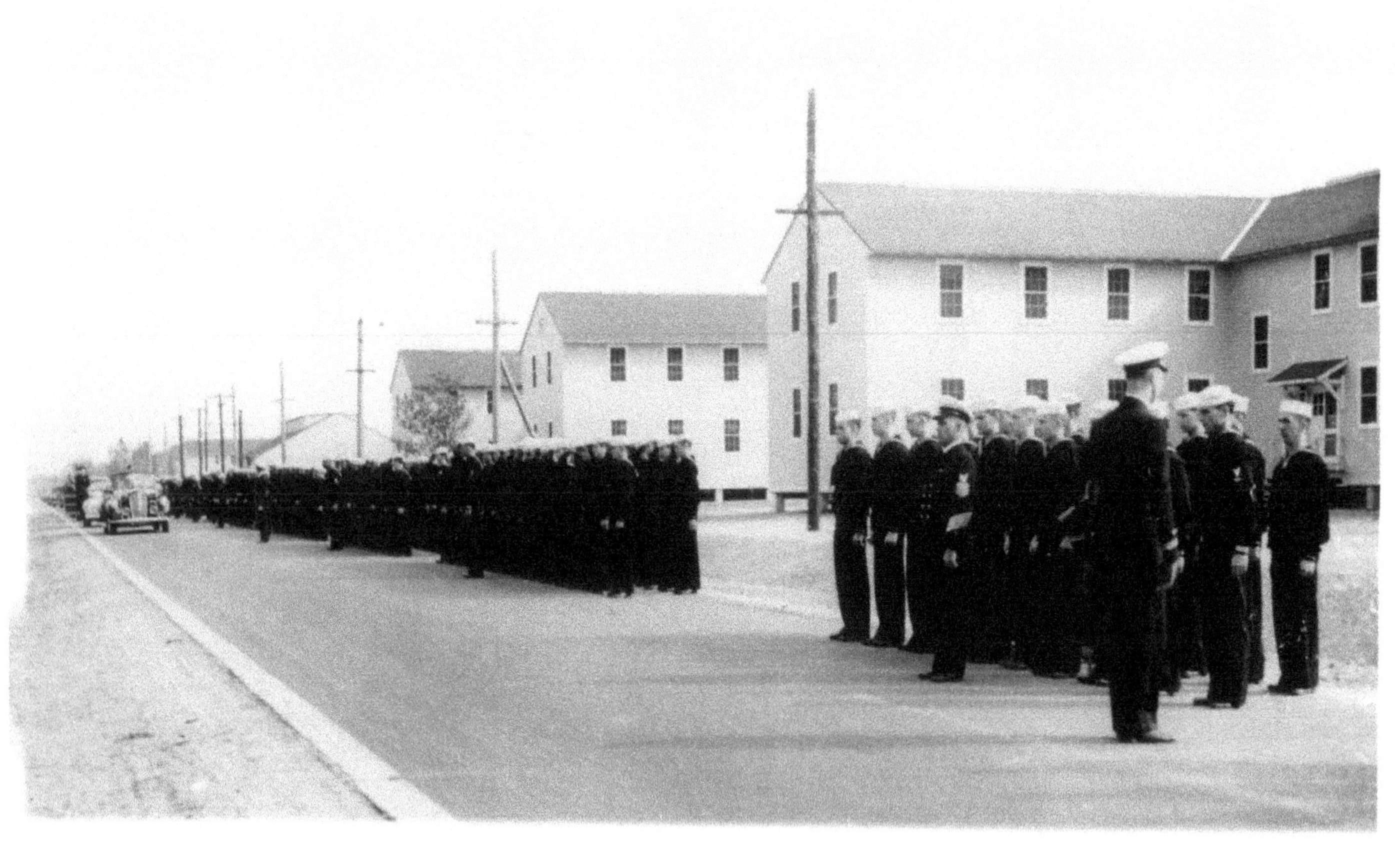

From World War II to the Sixties

(1940–1960s)

Soon after the U.S. entered World War II, a new entity came to town—the Naval Air Station—and became a permanent part of the community. Again, the river played a role. Following the Japanese attack on Pearl Harbor, the United States government scrambled to build up the navy and to construct bases for the new vehicles of warfare, airplanes. Jacksonville city leaders lobbied hard for and were successful in getting a naval base. City officials initiated a special bond campaign to generate funds to purchase land for the navy. The Naval Air Station provided not only an important military installation for the country, but a boost to the local economy.

Another boost to the city's economy came by way of the shipbuilding industry. This industry provided employment for men, as well as women. Work in this sector and other war industries increased the trend of women working outside the home. Many returned to traditional roles as wives and mothers at the conclusion of the war, but those who needed the work continued, if possible, or found jobs in other areas.

The return to normalcy after the Second World War coincided with a new rise in economic growth. By the 1950s, owing to the G.I. Bill and growing employment and other economic opportunities, many in Jacksonville joined the ranks of the American middle class with houses in the suburbs, family automobiles, and new products, particularly televisions, as permanent fixtures in the home.

The 1950s were not only a time of prosperity and traditional family values, but also they mark the beginning of the civil rights movement, which would transform the nation, particularly the South. After the 1954 *Brown* v. *Board of Education* Supreme Court decision that removed support for segregation, civil rights activists began to mobilize to bring about racial justice. This campaign did not become visible in Jacksonville until the 1960s. Nevertheless, it did result in the beginning of desegregation in the city and the inclusion of African Americans in the decision-making process.

In 1967 African Americans and for the first time ever women were elected to the Jacksonville city council. The following year the city took the controversial move of combining county and city governments, resulting in a more efficient government and use of the city's resources. This consolidation put Jacksonville on the path to a new wave of city building that continues today.

On the eve of U.S. entry to the war, life was calm and normal in the city. The economy seemed to be recovering. This view of Forsyth Street in 1940 shows the new stores Thom McAn, Butler's Shoes, F. W. Woolworth, as well as the Arcade Theatre and the Florida National Bank.

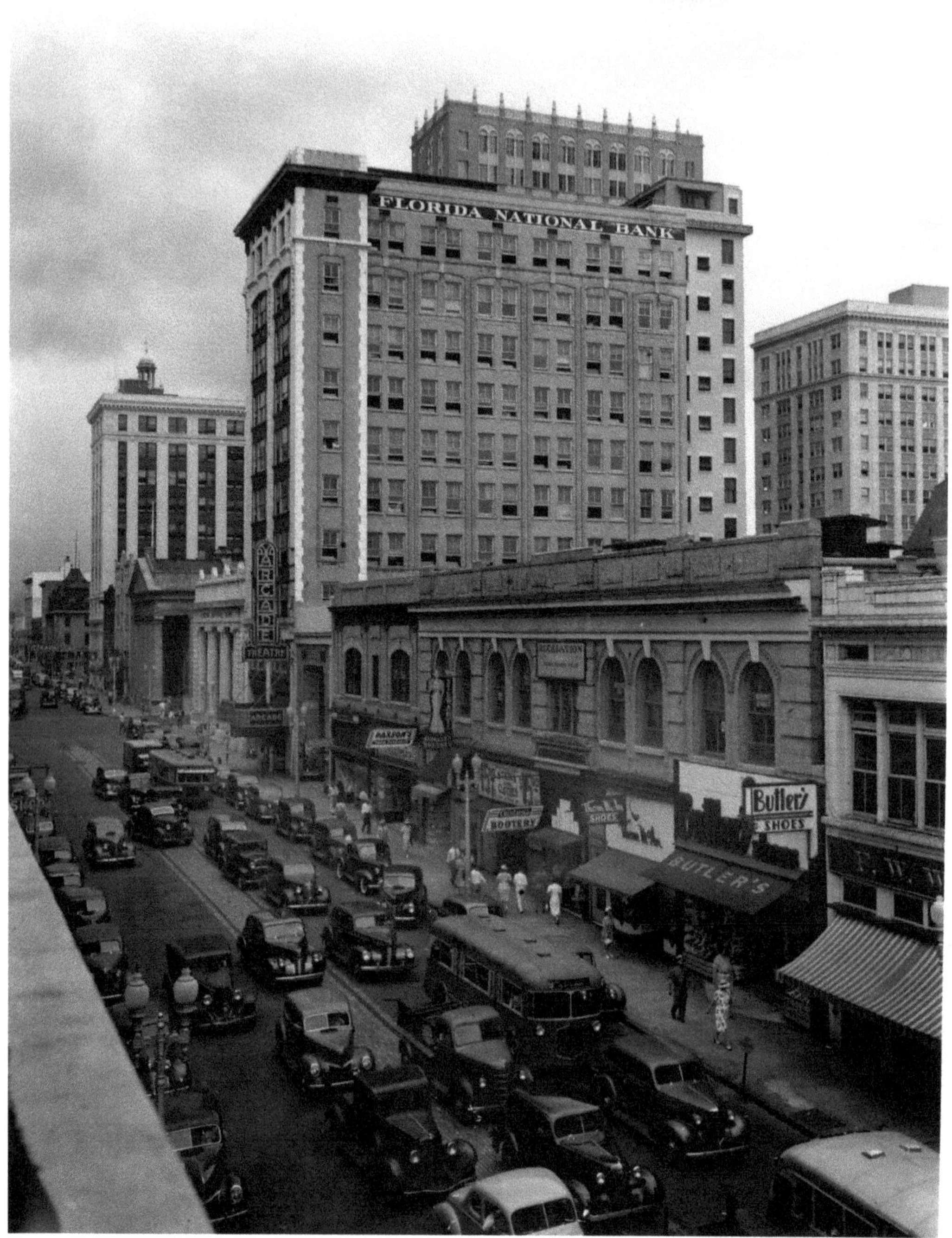

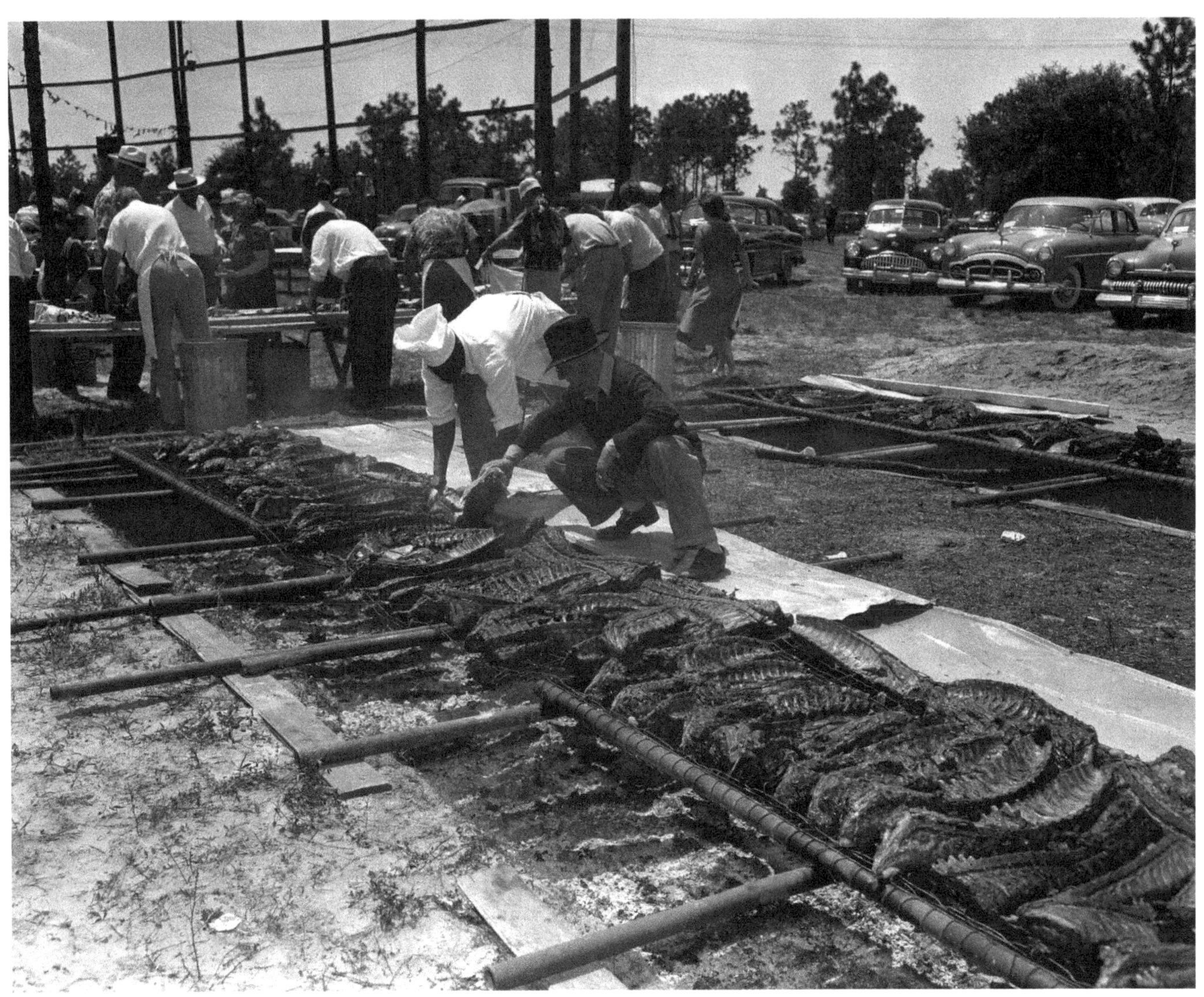

Here men prepare ribs for the Main Street Bridge barbecue.

The Epping Forest mansion of Alfred I. and Jessie Ball DuPont

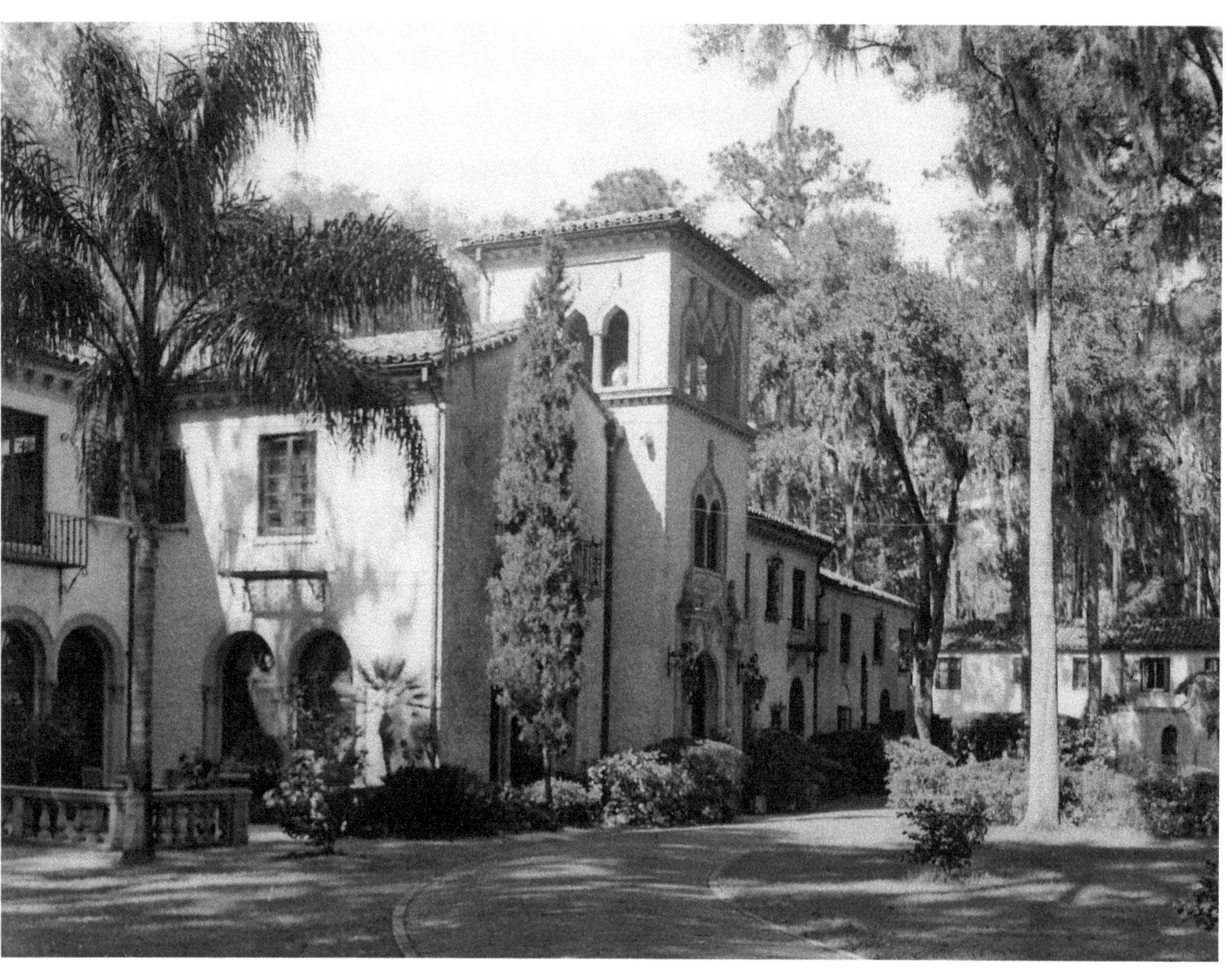

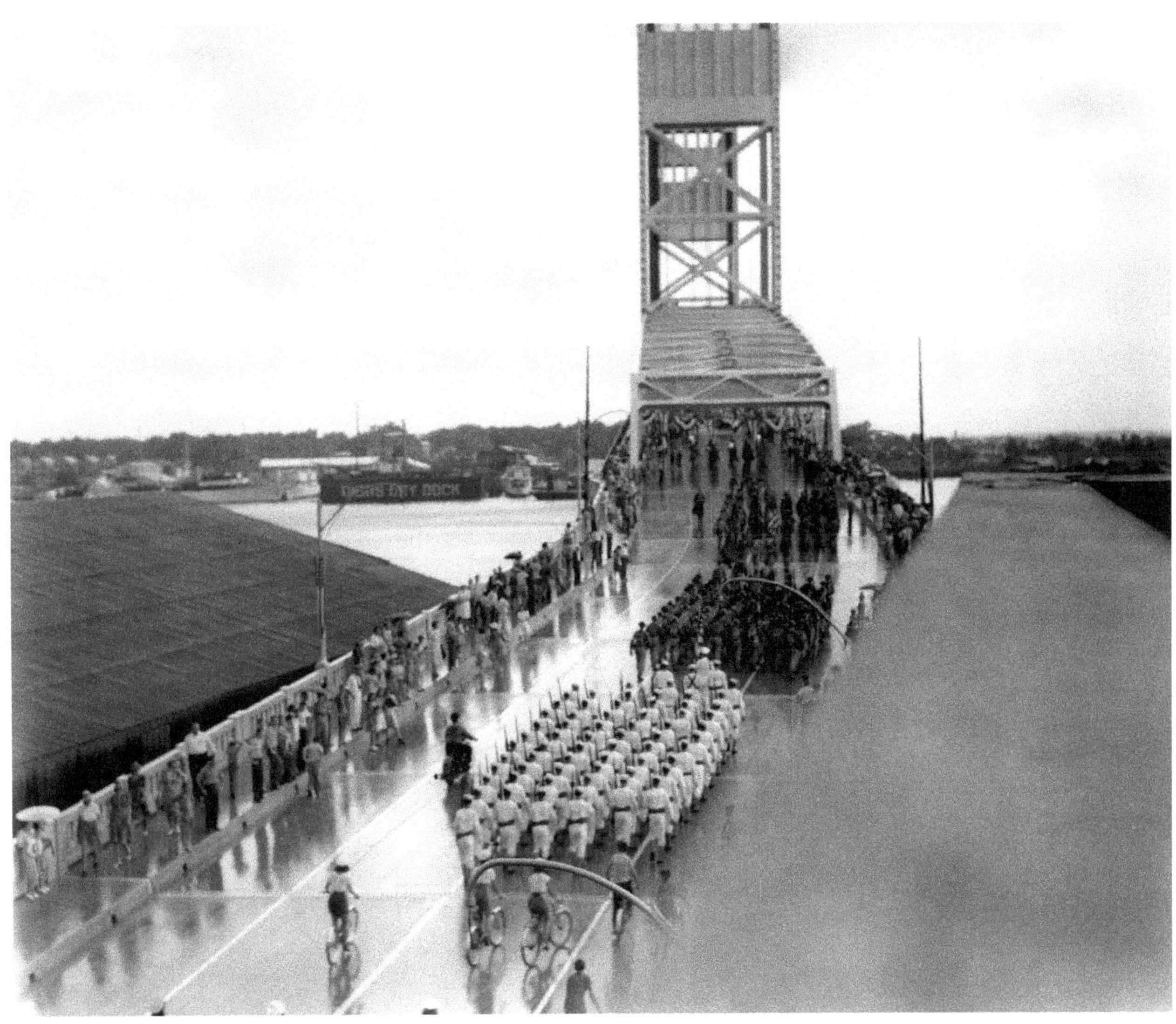

By the twentieth century, bridges connected the parts of the city separated by the St. Johns River. Here the new Main Street Bridge opens in 1941.

The J. C. Penney Store on Hogan Street is shown here. This store, as well as Sears and Woolworth, would be targets of civil rights activists in 1960.

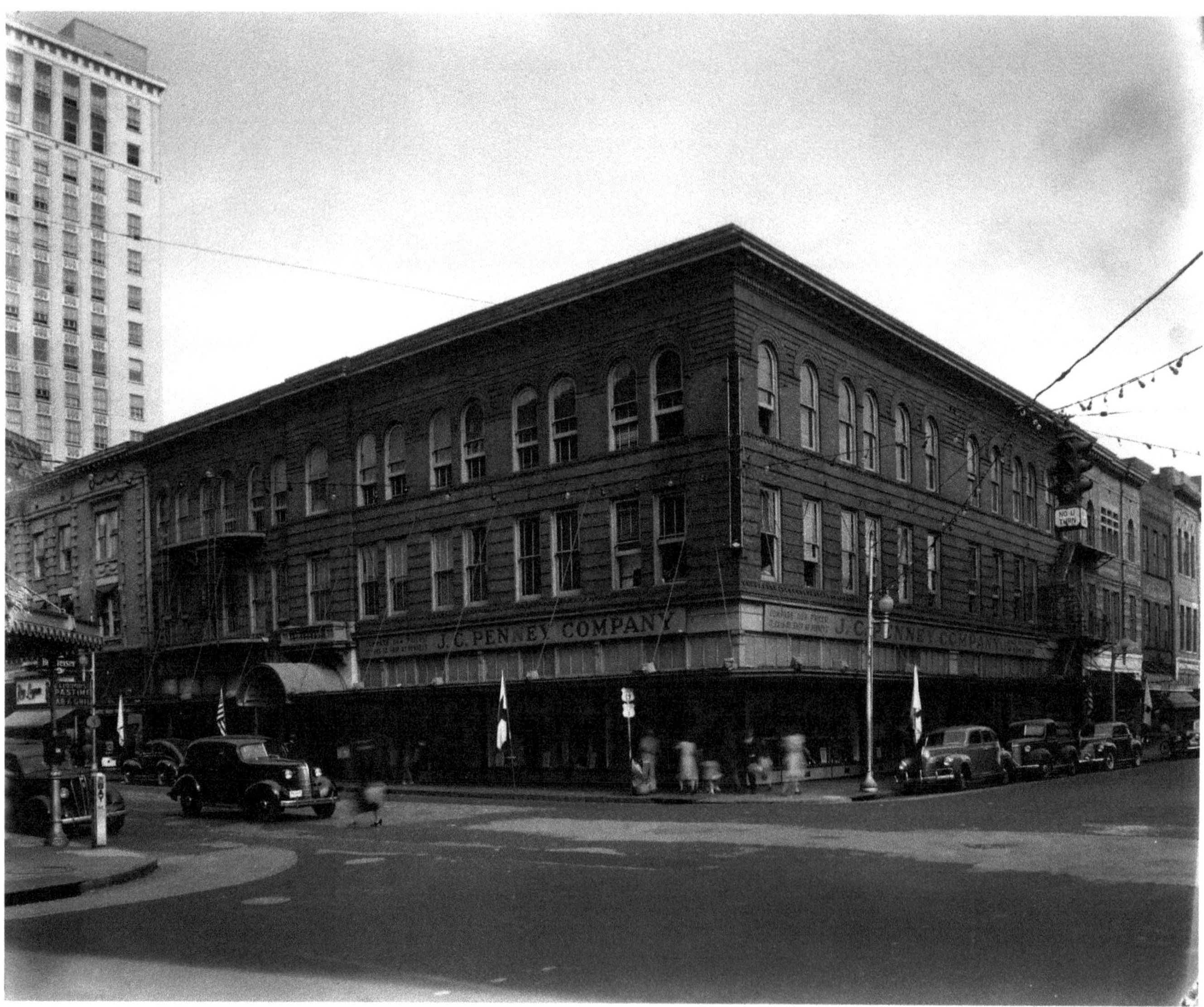

Although the city has not experienced another devastating fire like the 1901 disaster, smaller fires always threaten structures and people. Pictured here is the aftermath of a fire at the Clyde-Mallory Railroad Lines in 1941.

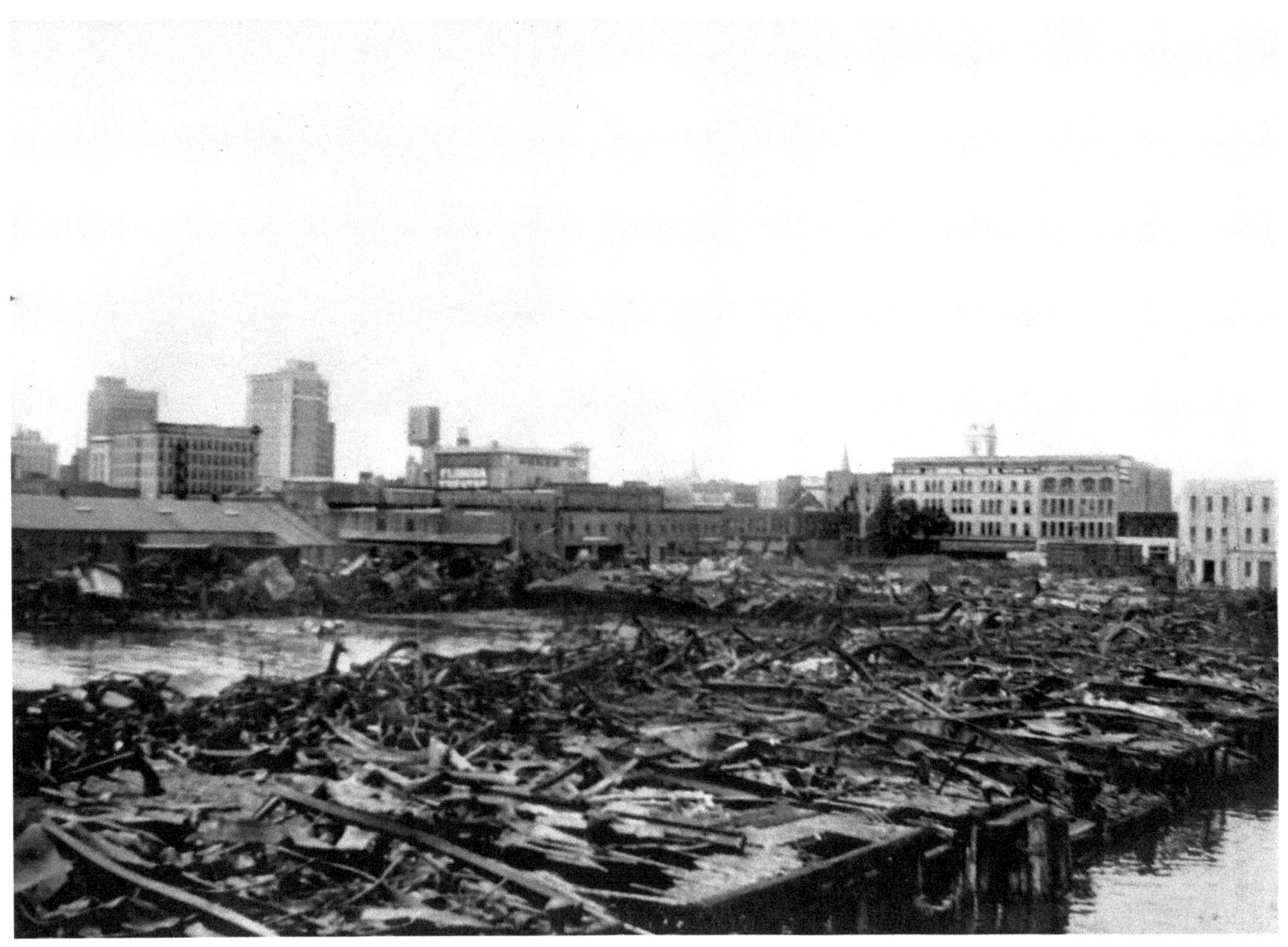

The Imperial Theatre on Forsyth Street in 1941

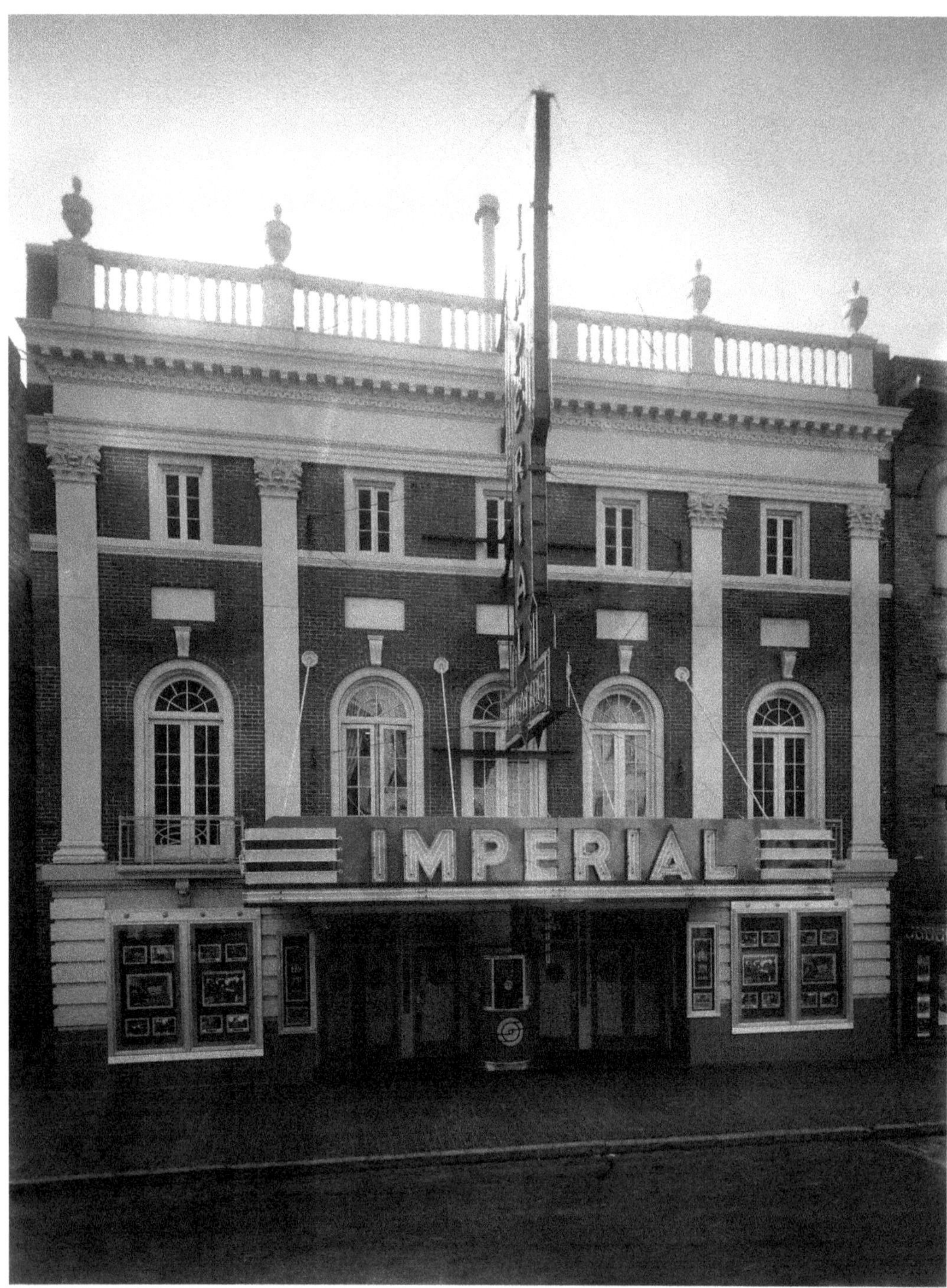

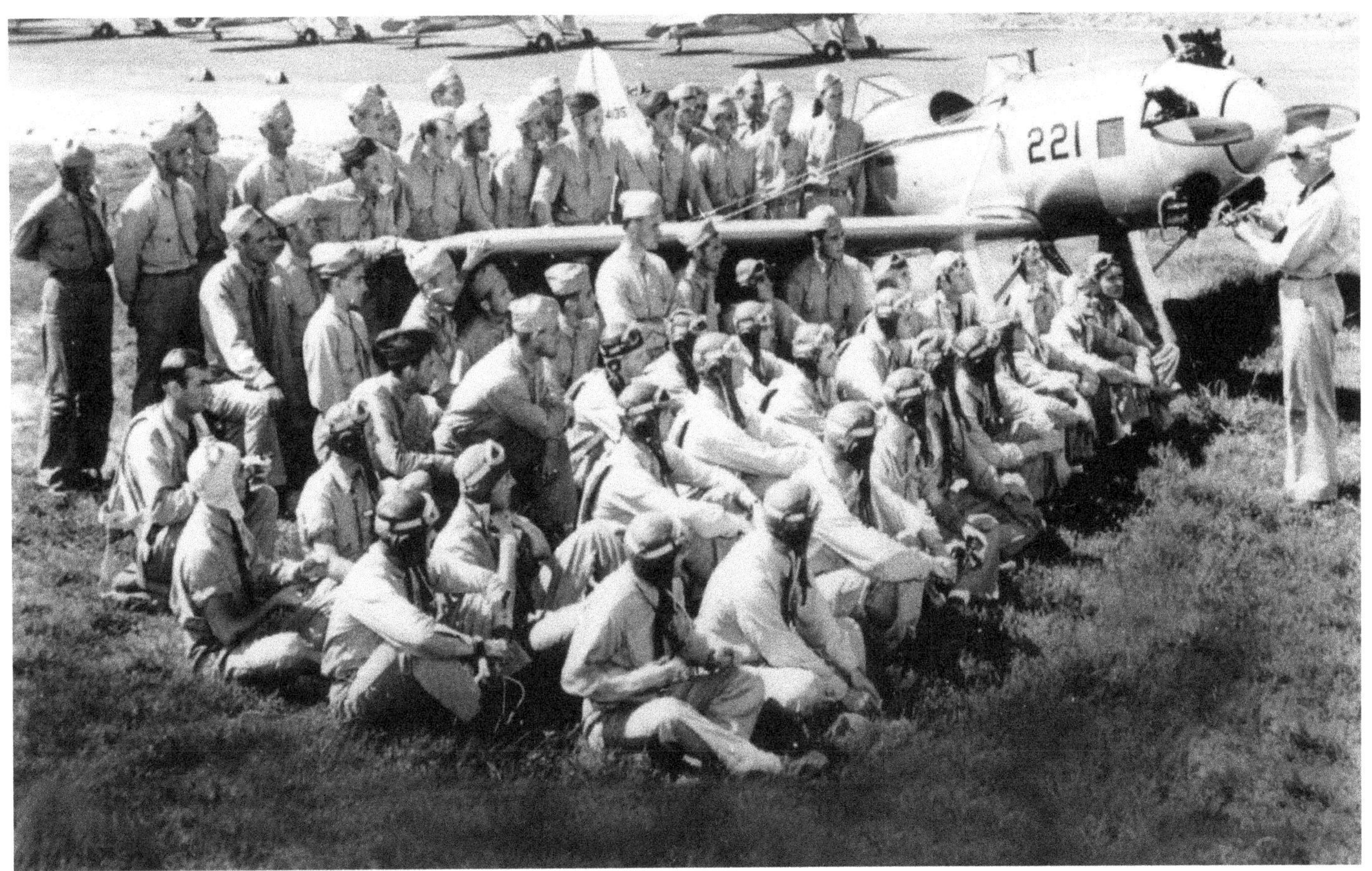

Many young men were trained as pilots, including the brother of future president John F. Kennedy, Joseph P. Kennedy, Jr., at the Naval Air Station in Jacksonville. This photo shows an instructor and students of the VN-11A primary training squadron (ca. 1941).

The races continued to be separated in all areas of life in Jacksonville after the war. This is a picture of Brewster Hospital's children's ward. Brewster Hospital, located on Jefferson Street, was created for African Americans in the early twentieth century when only the county hospital accepted black patients. In the 1980s and 1990s it served as hospice space for Memorial Hospital. The building was demolished in 2006.

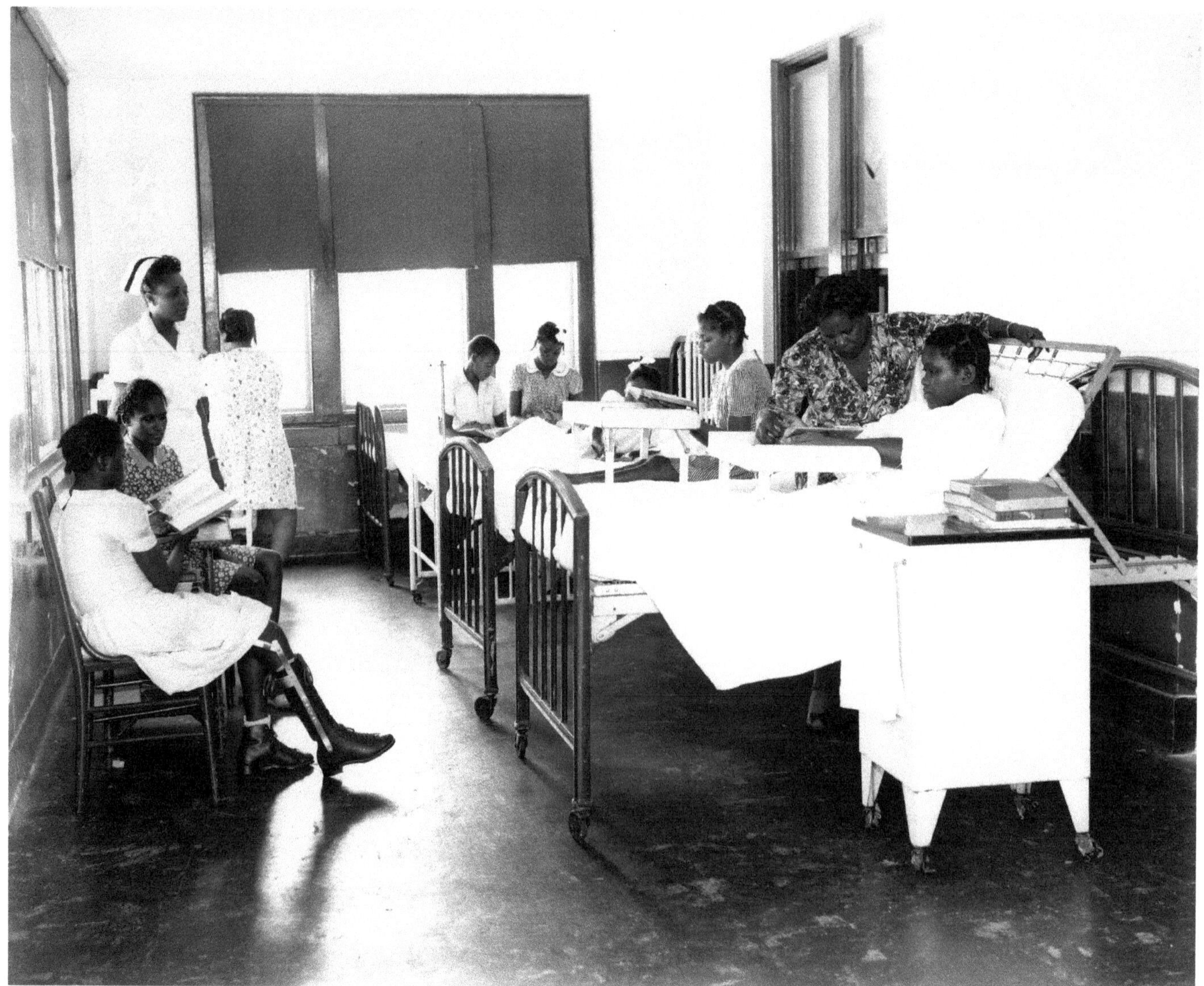

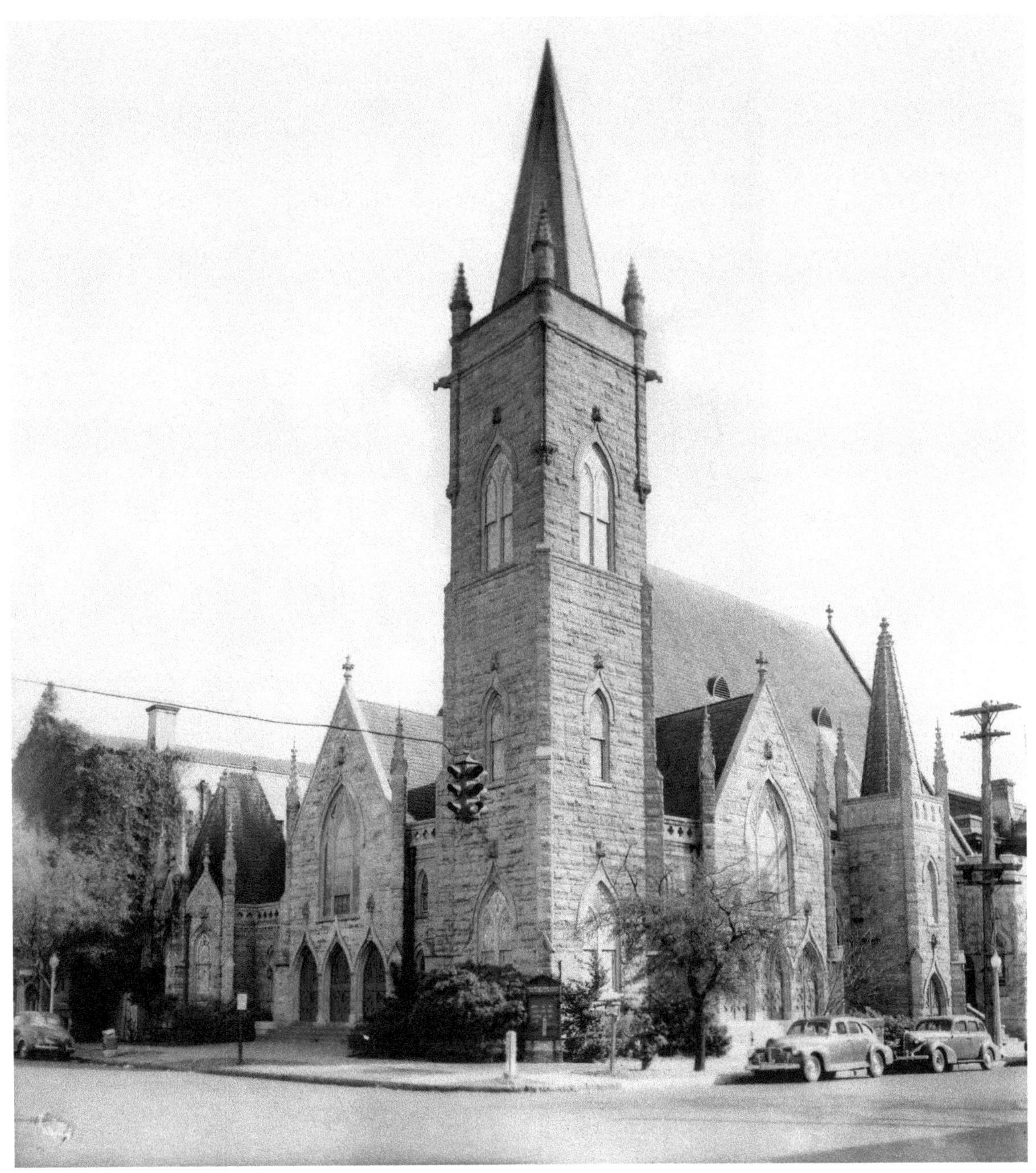

First Presbyterian Church in 1946

The Young Men's Christian Association building is pictured here in 1946. The first YMCA was established in Jacksonville in 1870.

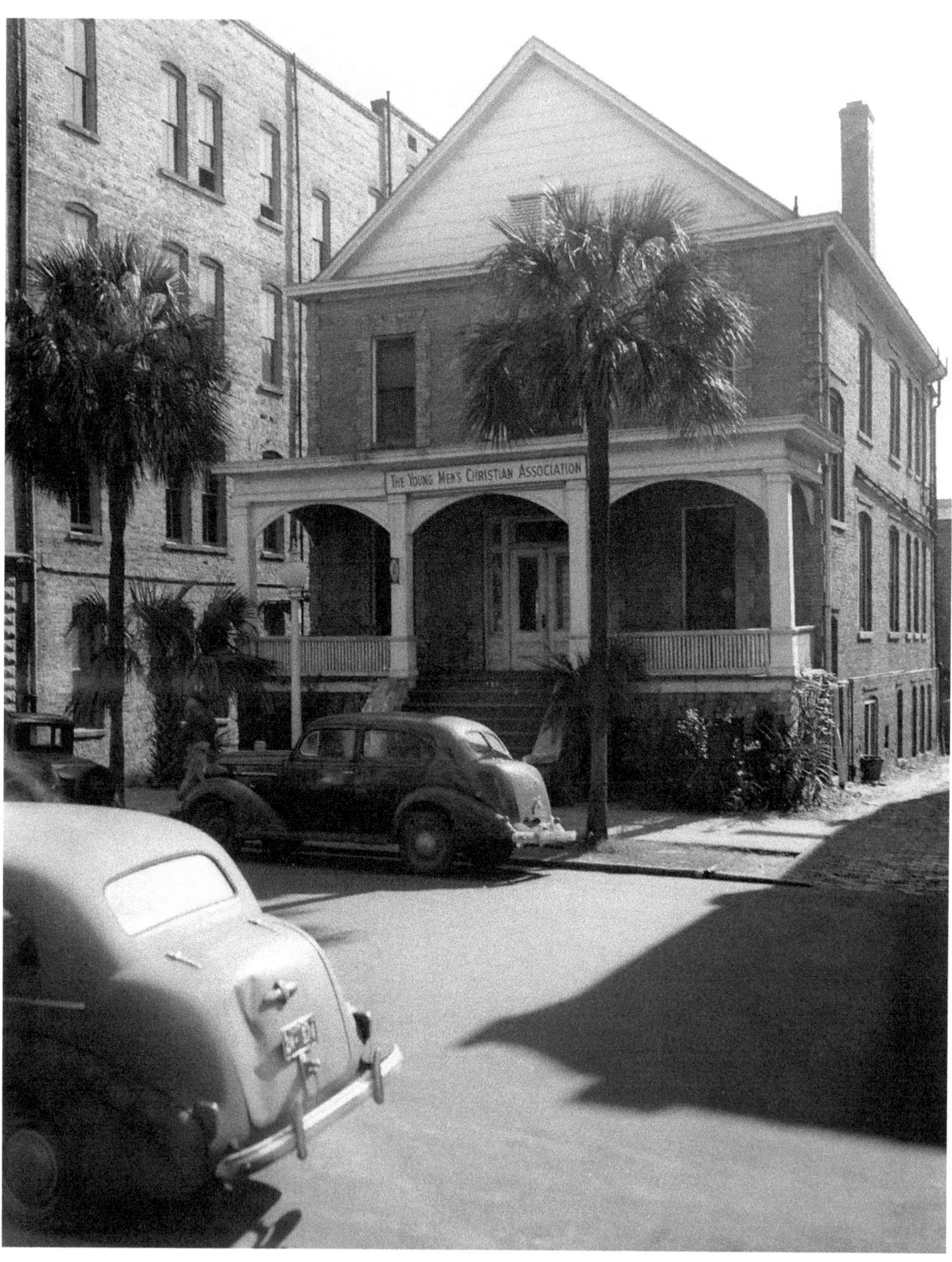

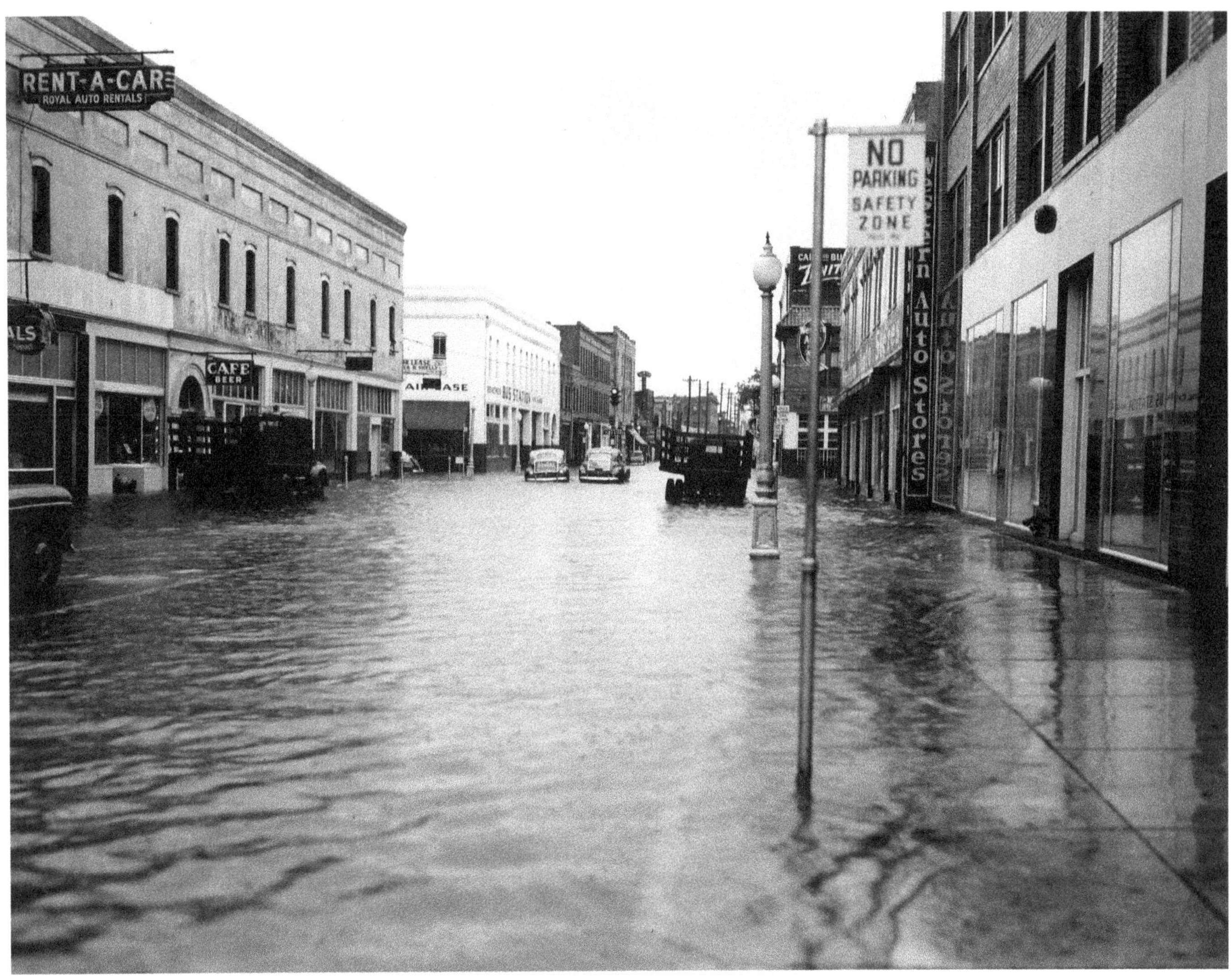

As this photo of Adams Street shows, the city, particularly streets near the river and other bodies of water, continued to be plagued by flooding.

In the postwar era the railroads continued to be a major part of the Jacksonville economy. These men shown here in 1945 are machinists for the Seaboard Air Line Railway Company.

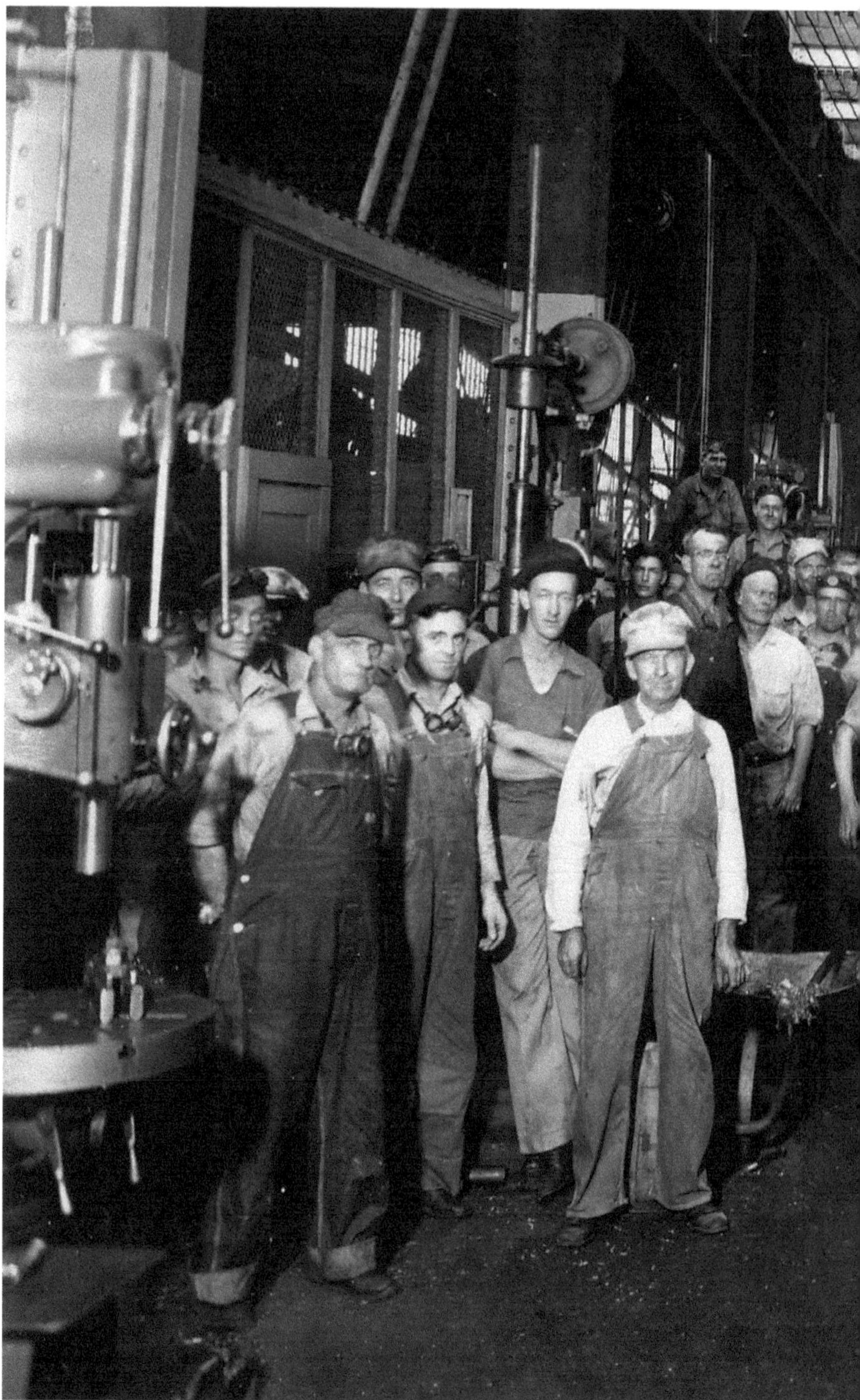

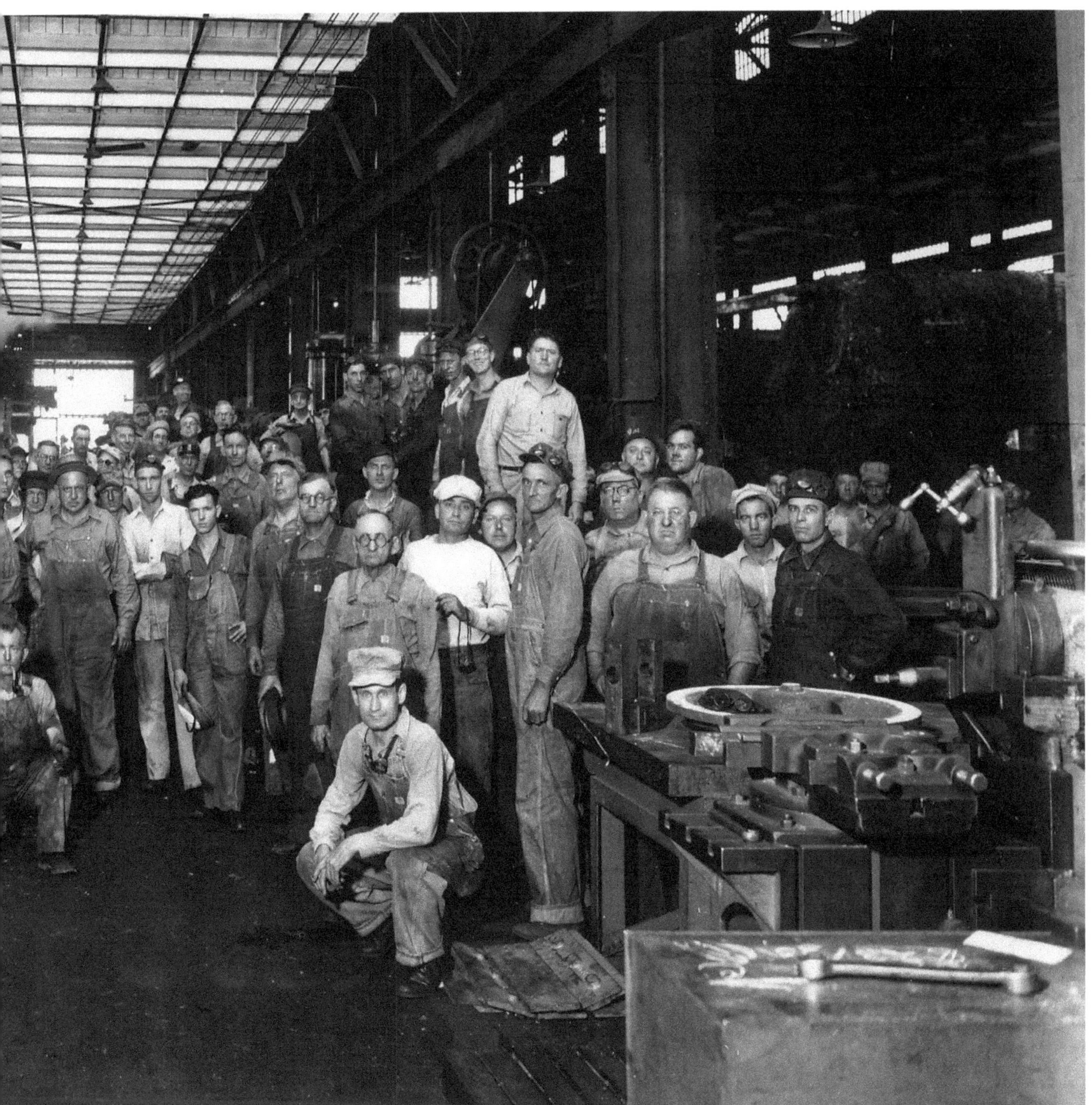

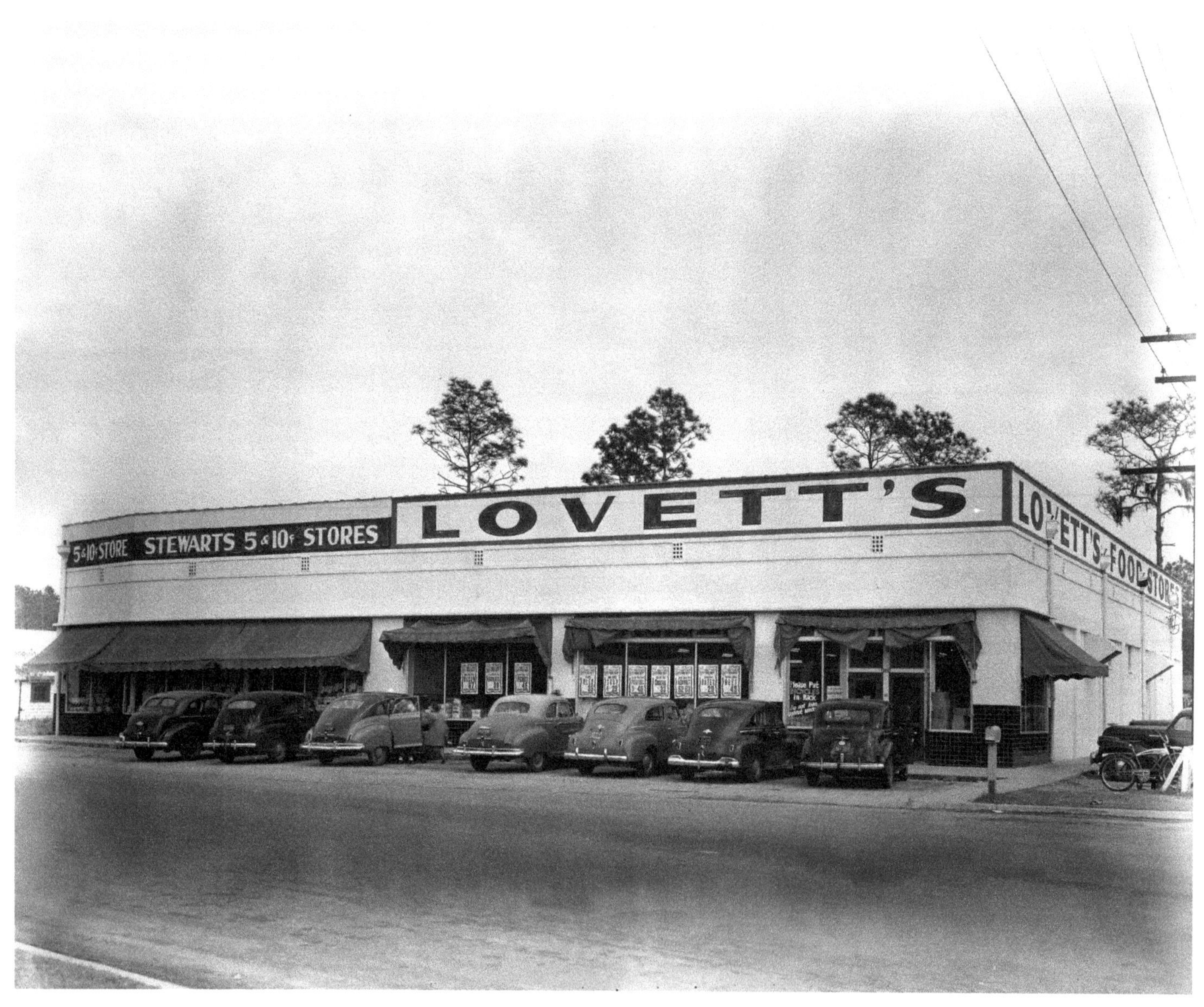

Lovett's Supermarket illustrates the growing presence of a new kind of food store, the supermarket, which arose during the late 1940s and 1950s. There were a number of Lovett's stores in the city.

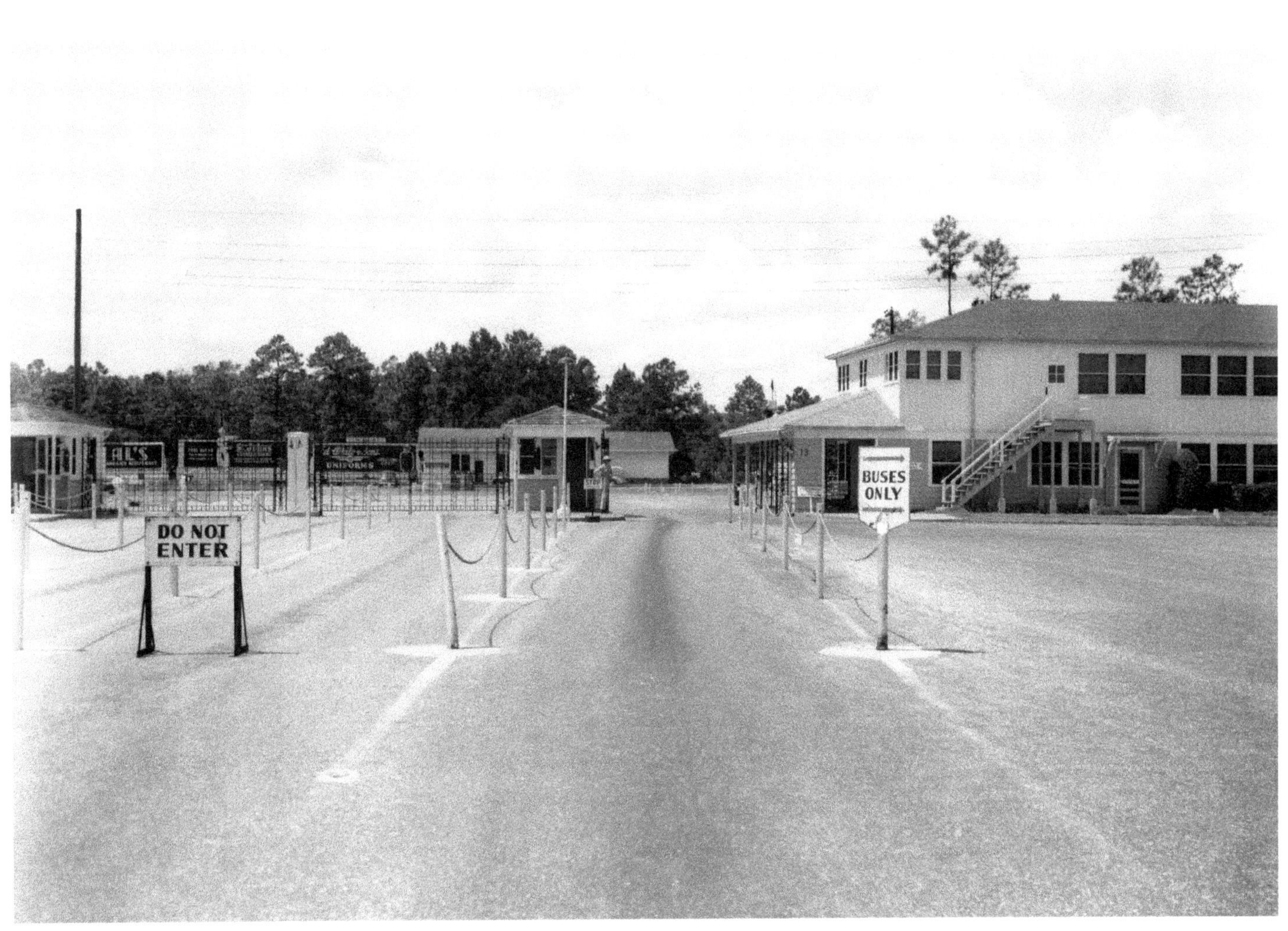

By 1947, when this photo was taken, the Naval Air Station (NAS) had become a permanent part of the city.

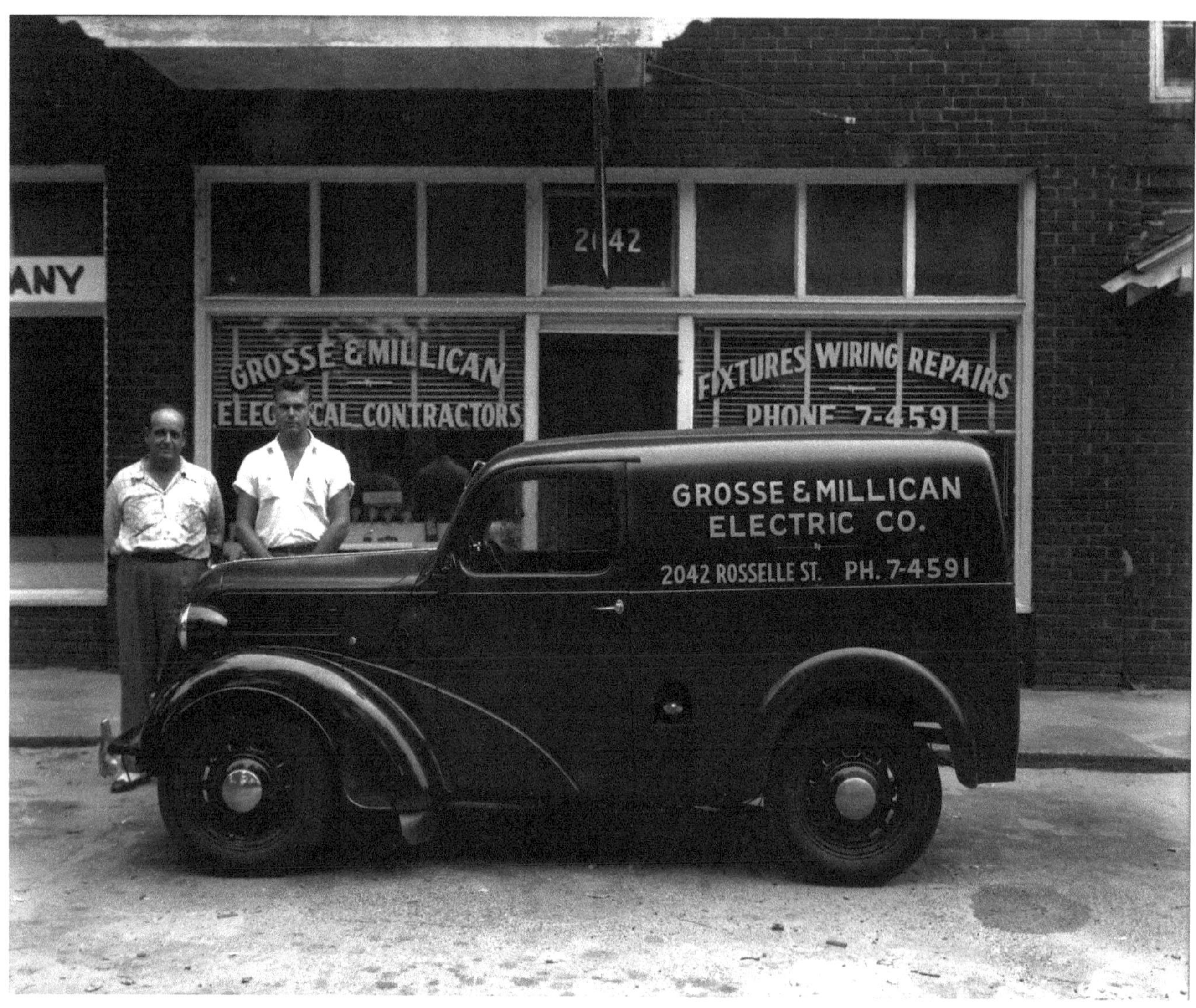

Smaller businesses continued to proliferate in the postwar years. Here two men stand beside a truck in front of the Grosse and Millican Electric Company.

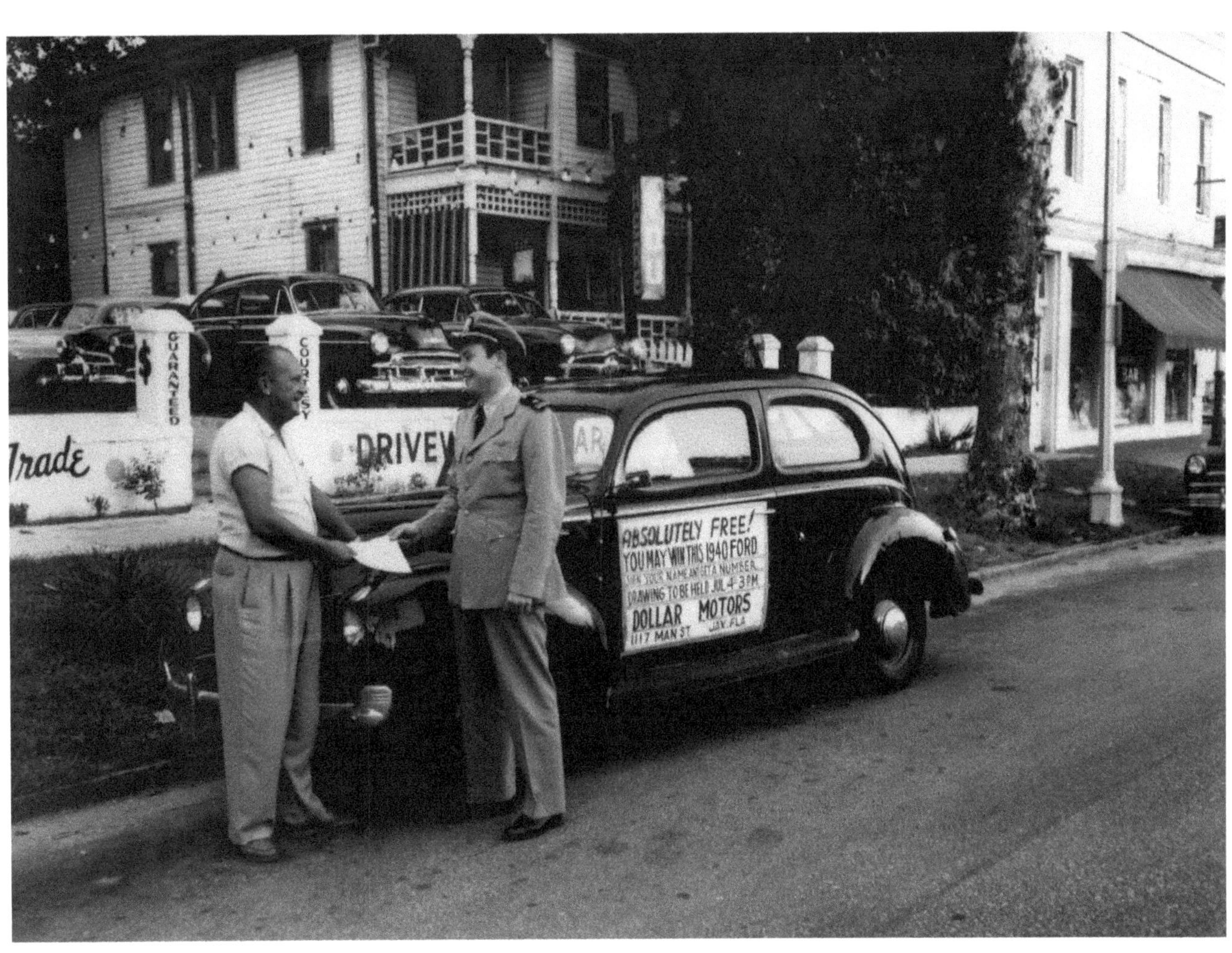

This soldier has apparently won the car parked behind him from Dollar Motors, a used-car dealership.

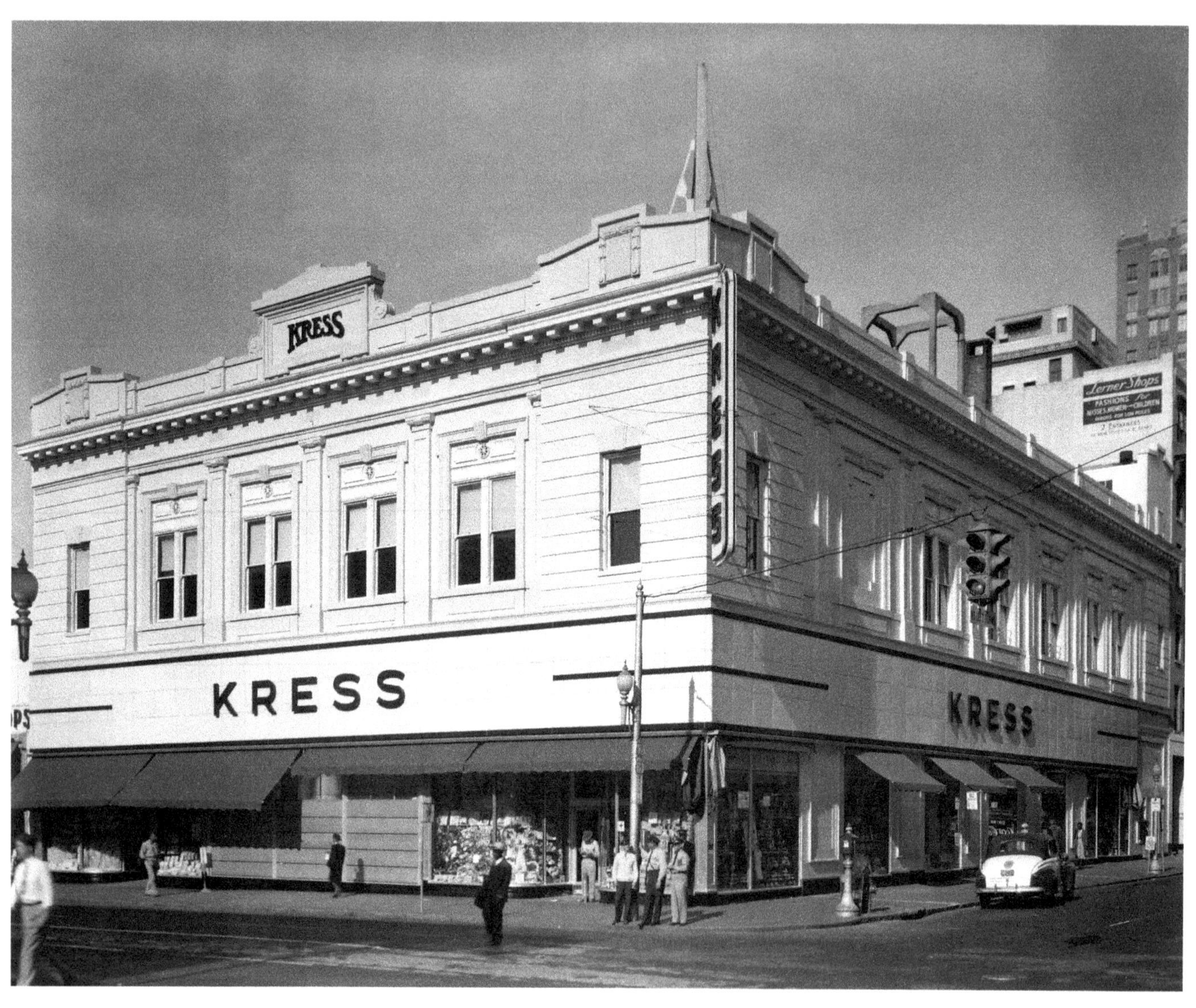

The Kress five-and-dime was a leading example of discount stores, which grew in number in the postwar years.

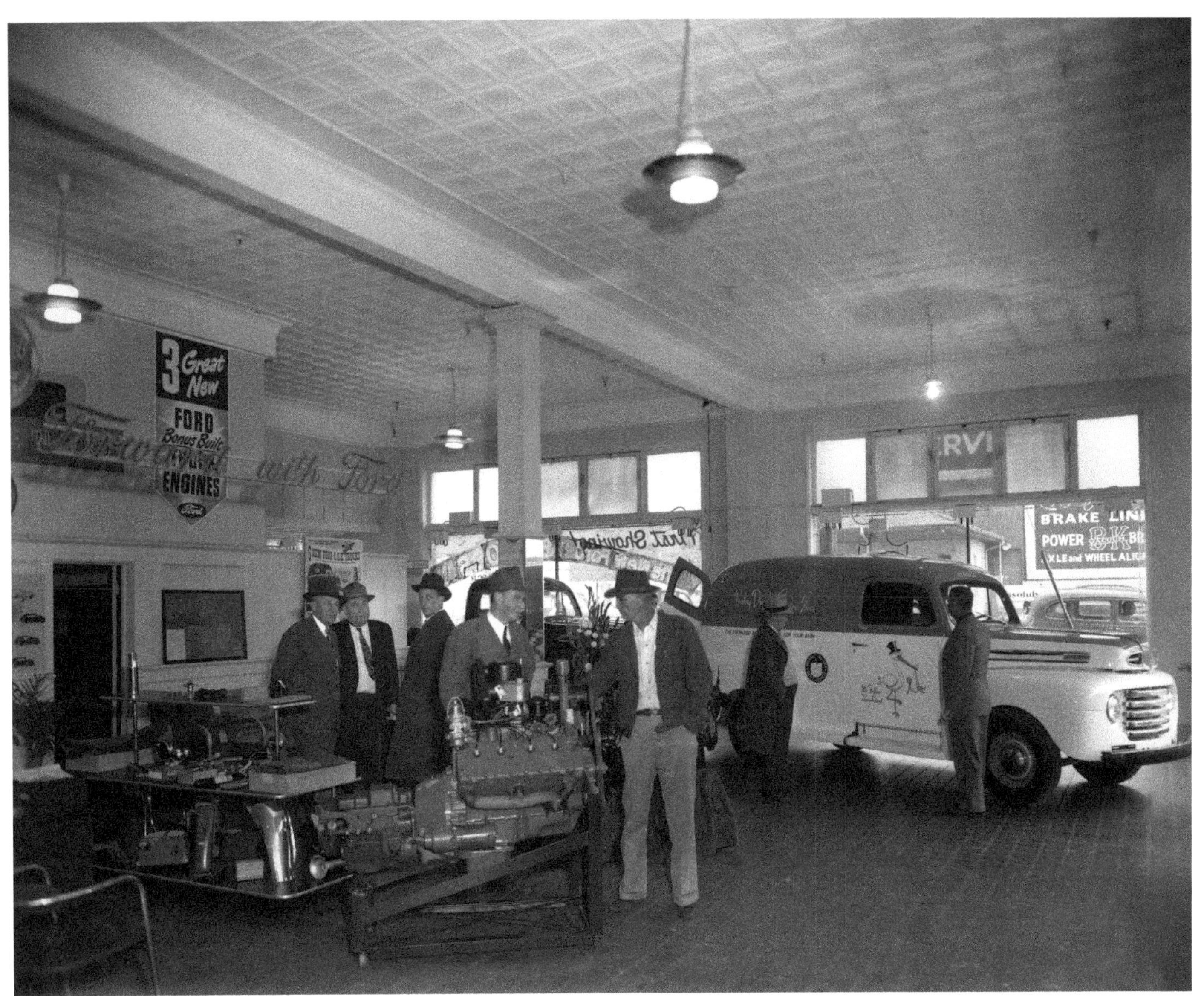

Automobiles continued to proliferate around the city. Shown here are men on the floor of the showroom at the Duval Motor Company in 1948.

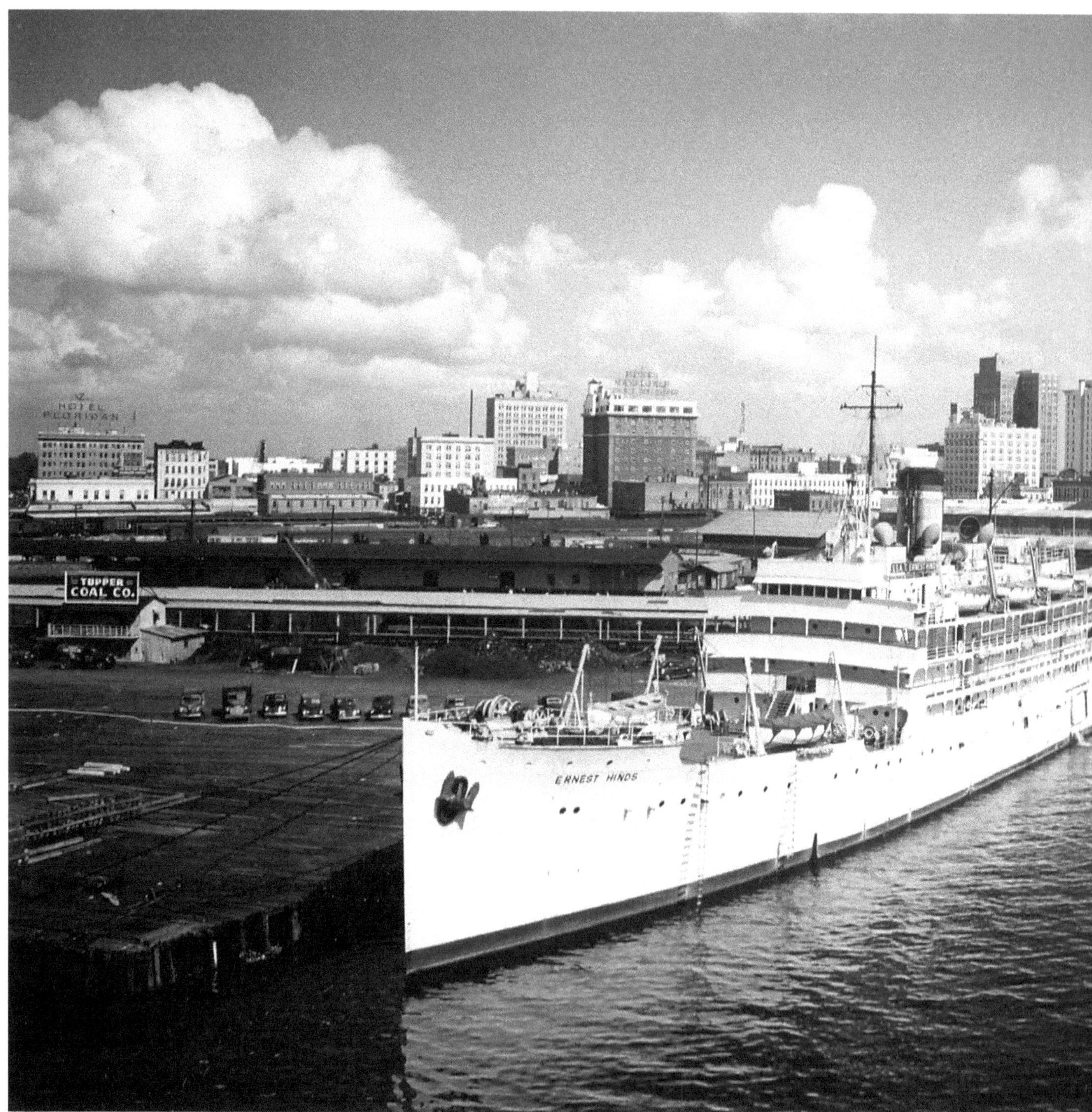
HOTEL
FLORIDAN
TUPPER
COAL CO.
ERNEST HINDS

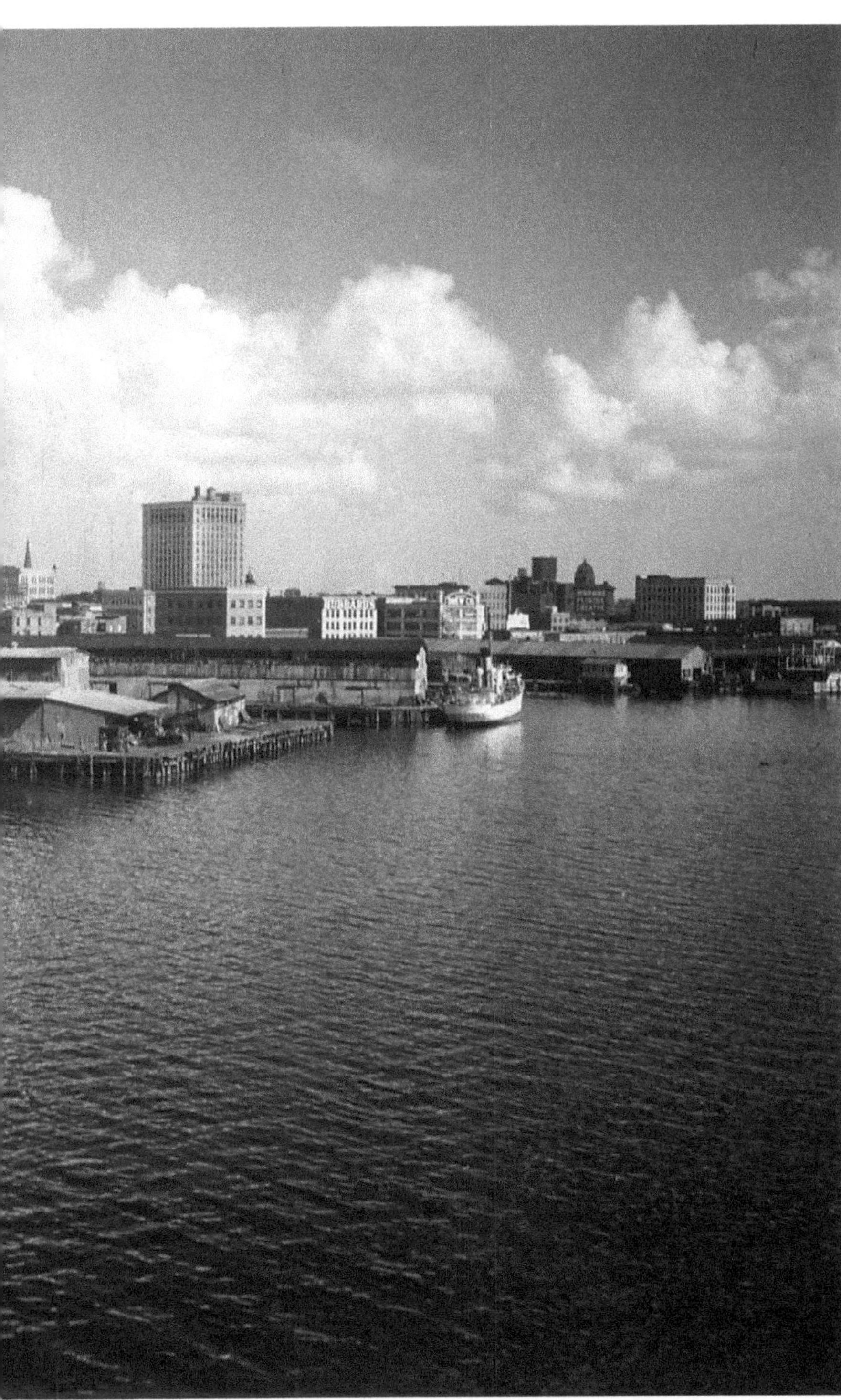

The docks continued to be an important aspect of the urban landscape. This is a view of Jacksonville dockside, in 1946.

The service attendant became a staple during the 1940s. An attendant is shown here at the airport service station in 1949.

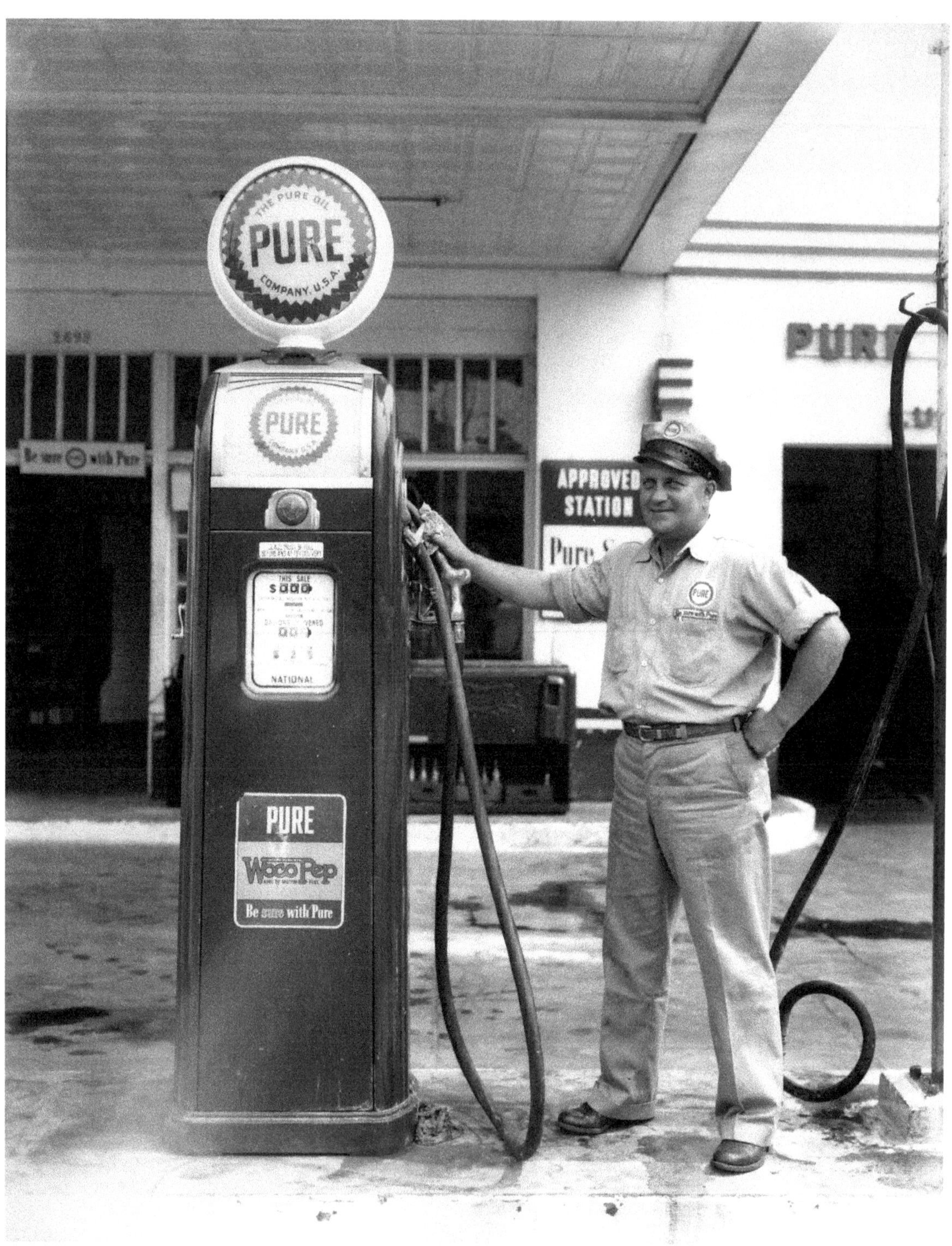

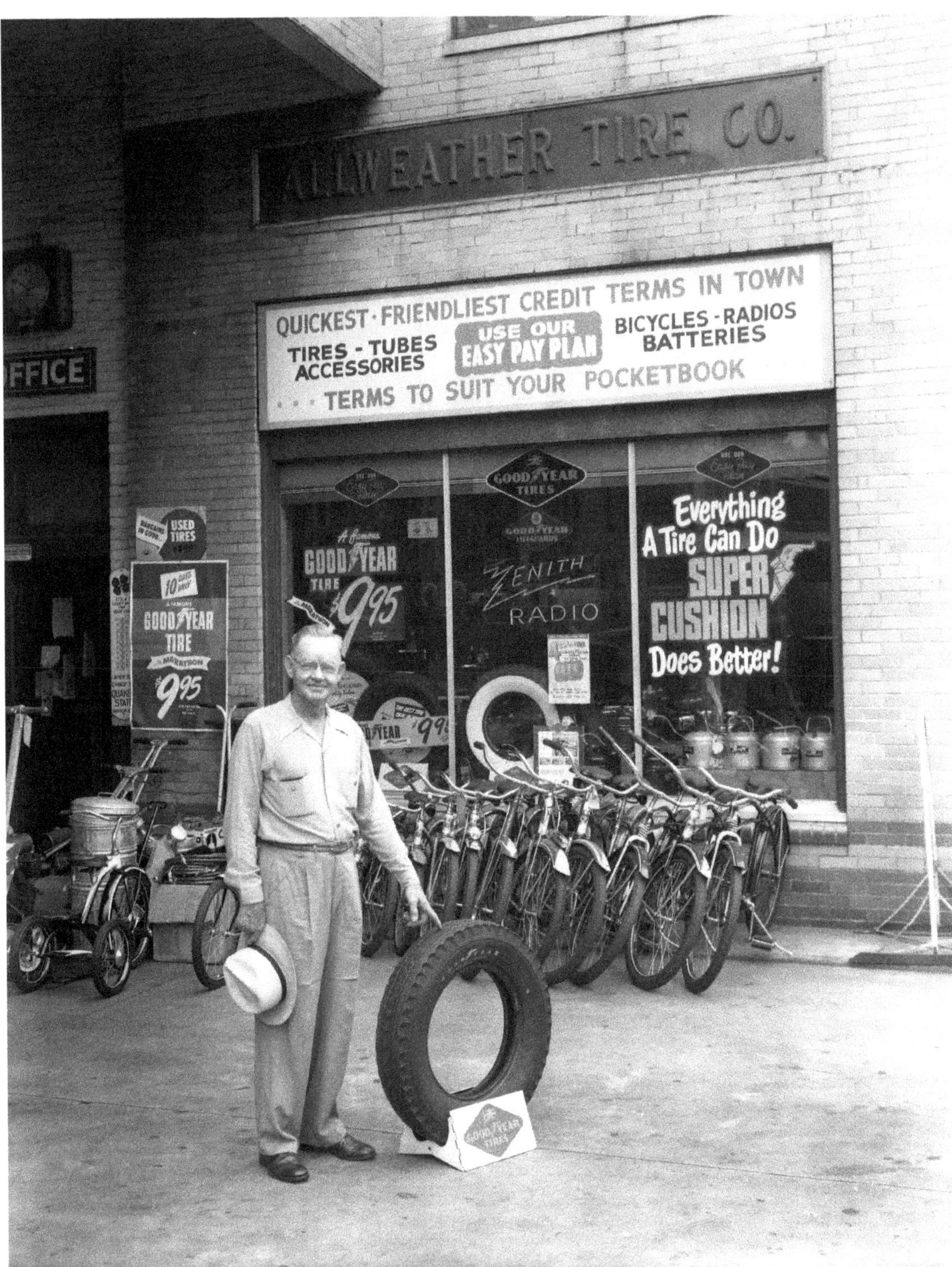

The growing automobile industry led to the growth of tire companies. The Allweather Tire Company advertises a Goodyear tire here in 1949. There were four stores in the city.

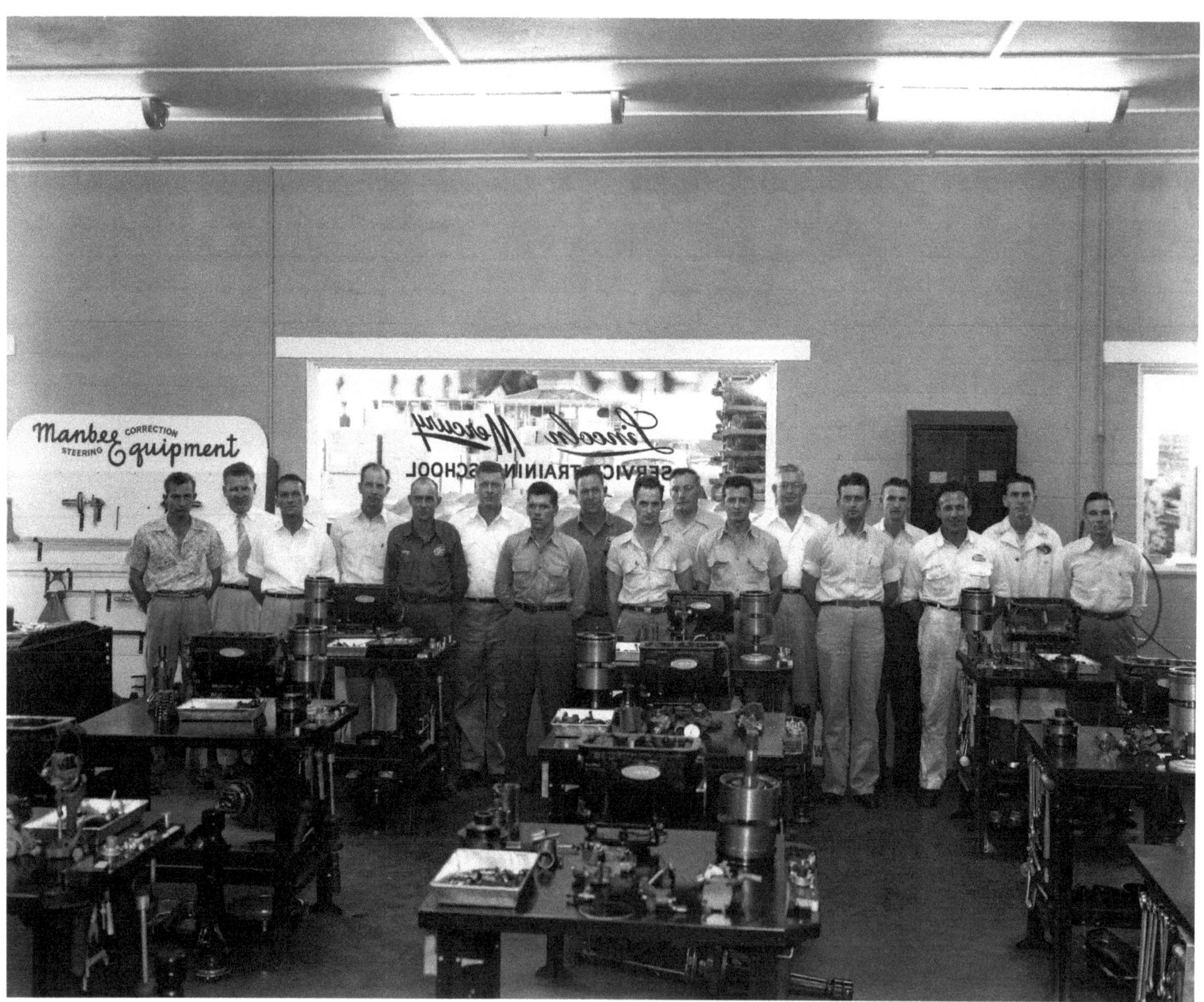

Ford Motor Company employees in training in 1949

Automobile traffic crosses the Main Street Bridge here in 1949.

A Standard Oil Company truck in 1949

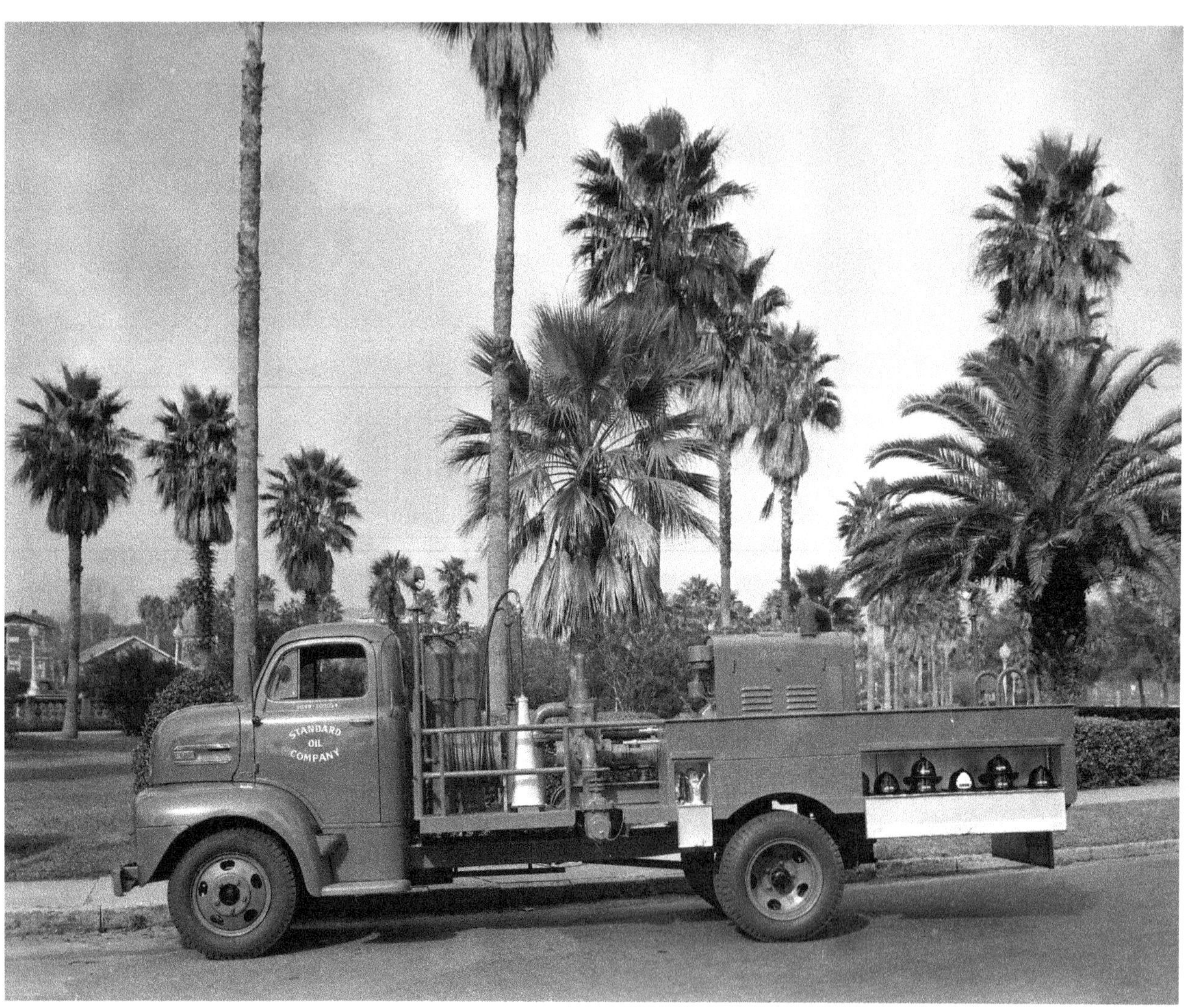

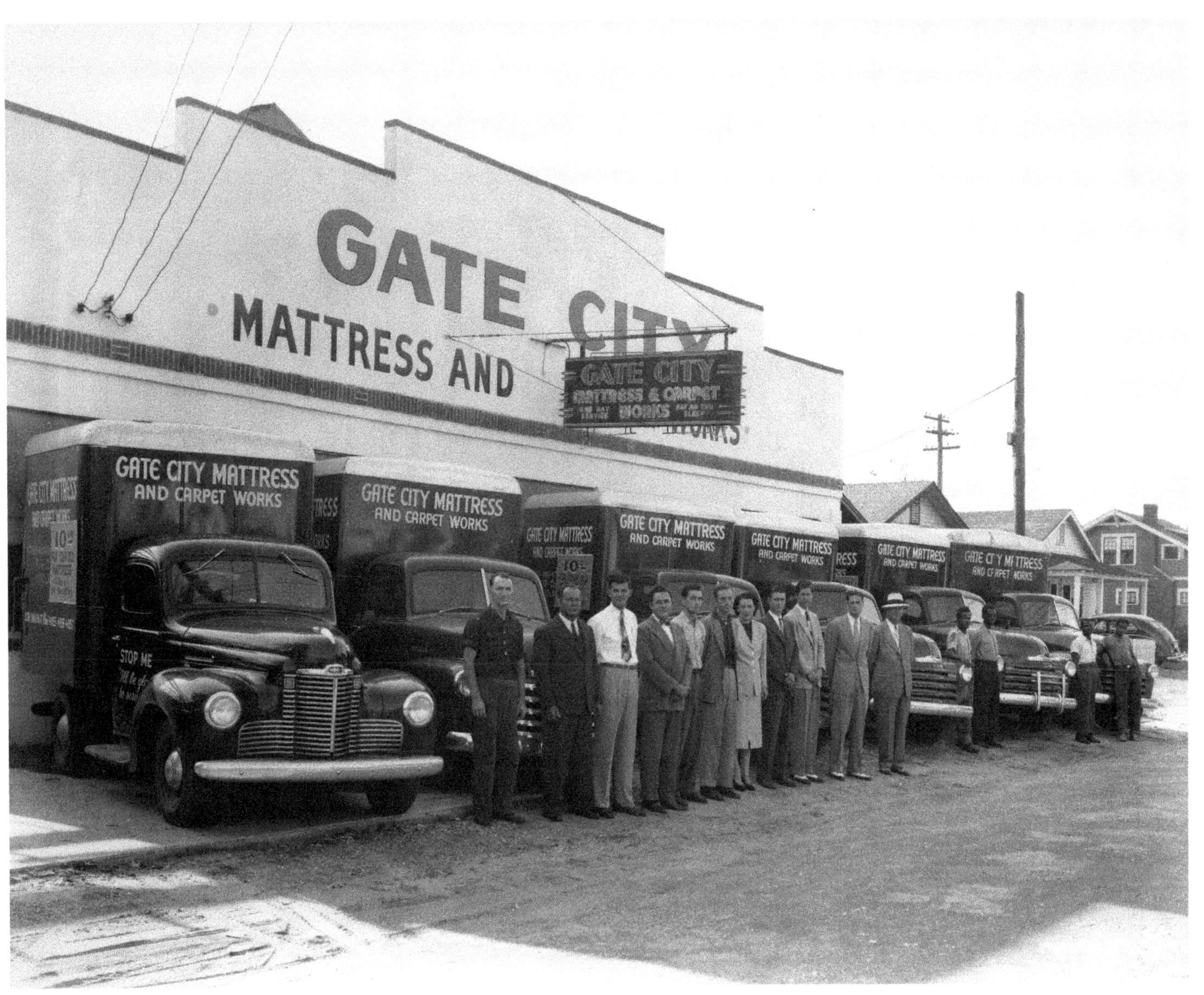

The trucks and employees of the Gate City Mattress and Carpet Works, shown here in 1949

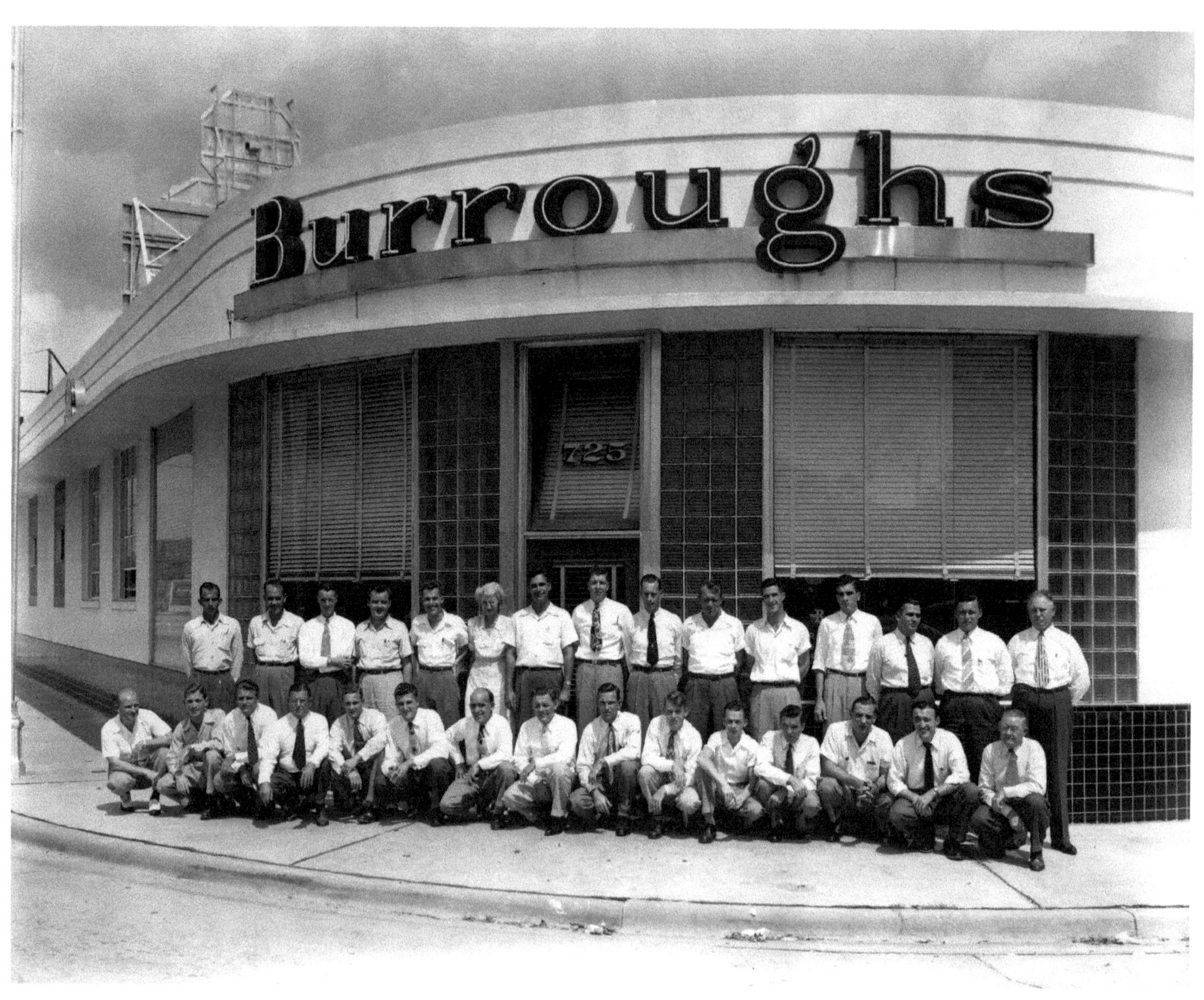

Employees of the Burroughs Adding Machine Company, posing here in front of the building in 1949

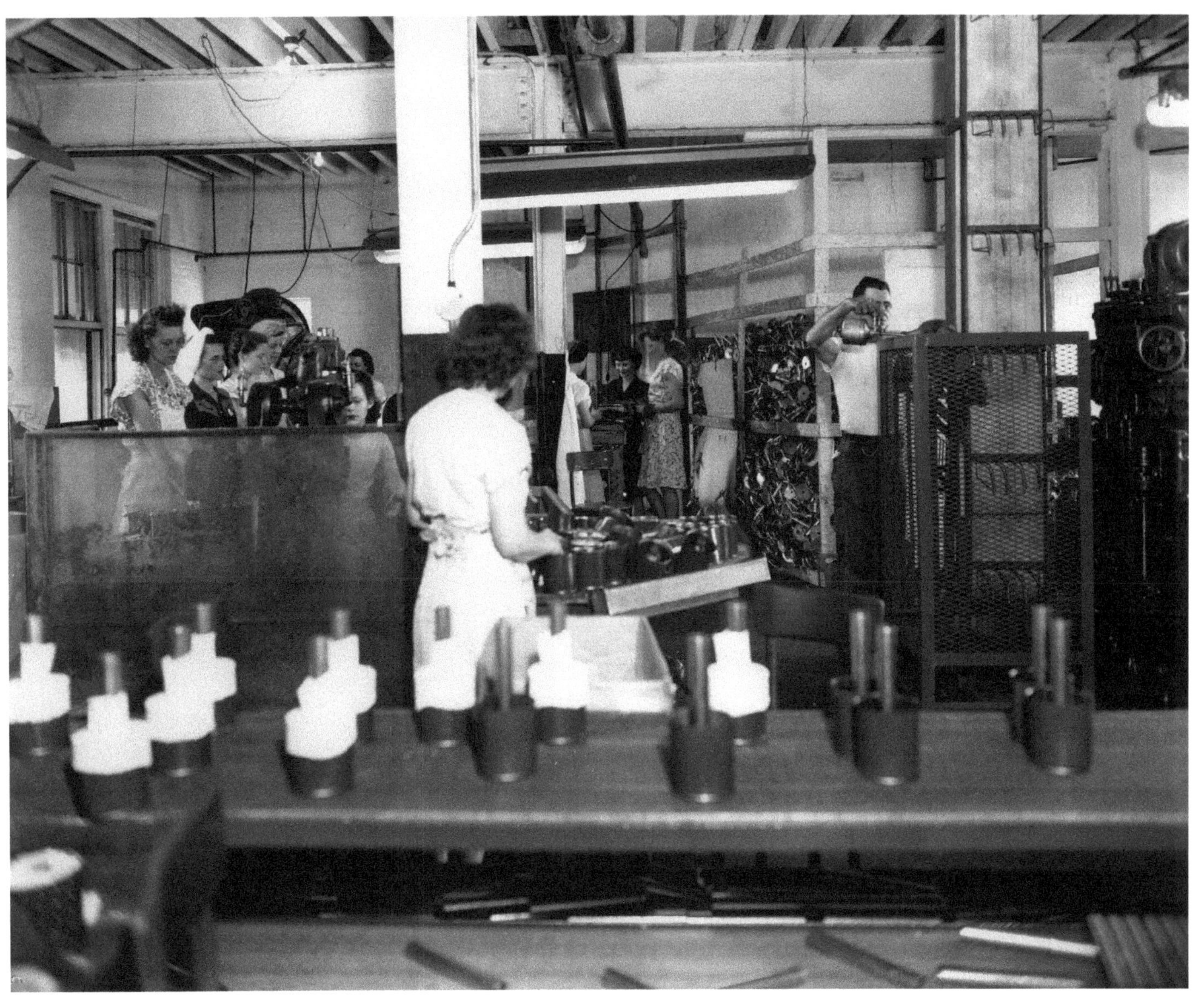

Women employees of Fram Florida can-storage plant, on Stockton Street, shown here in 1949

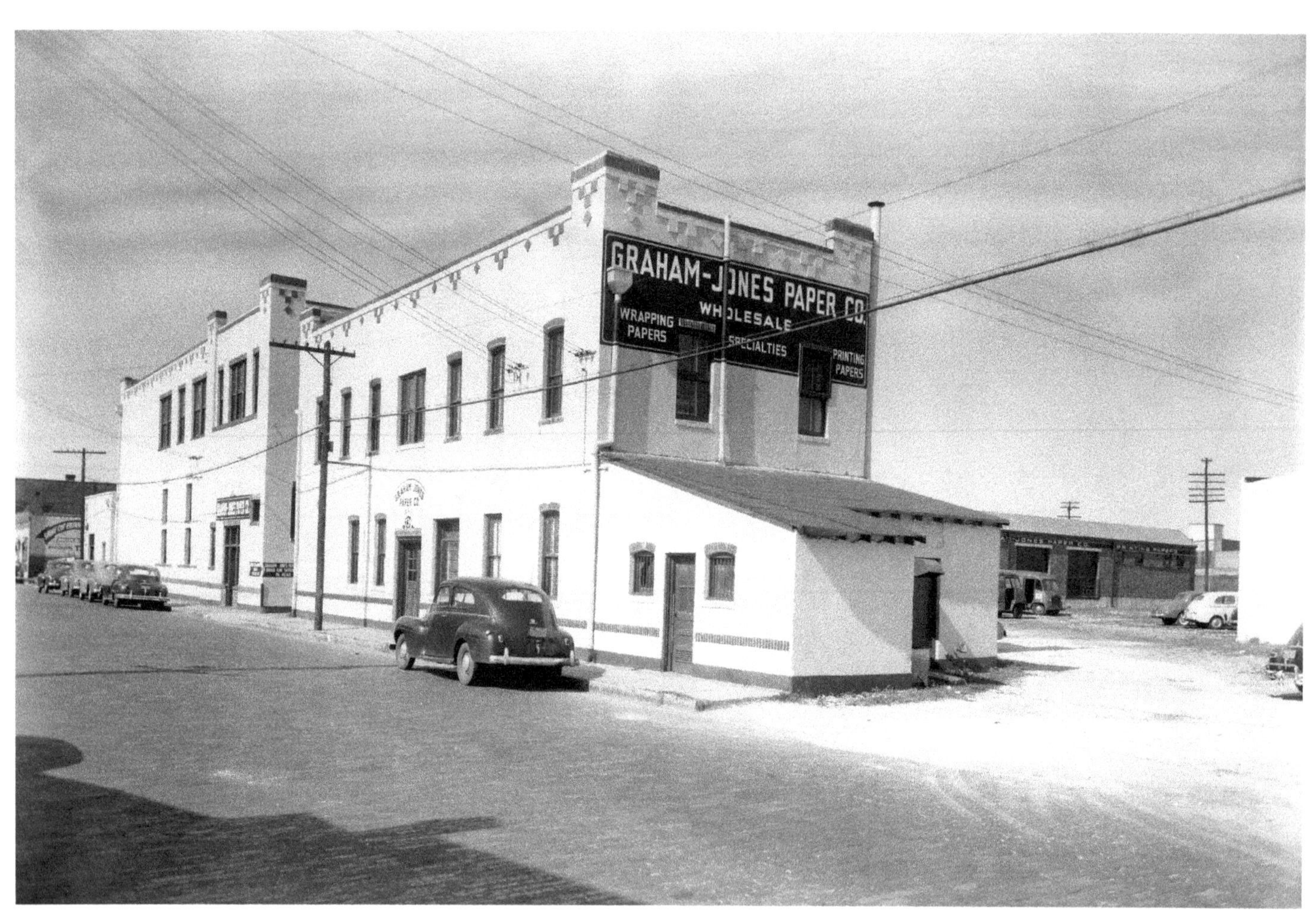

The city became known for its paper companies. Shown here in 1950 is the Graham-Jones Paper Company, on Myrtle Avenue in north Jacksonville.

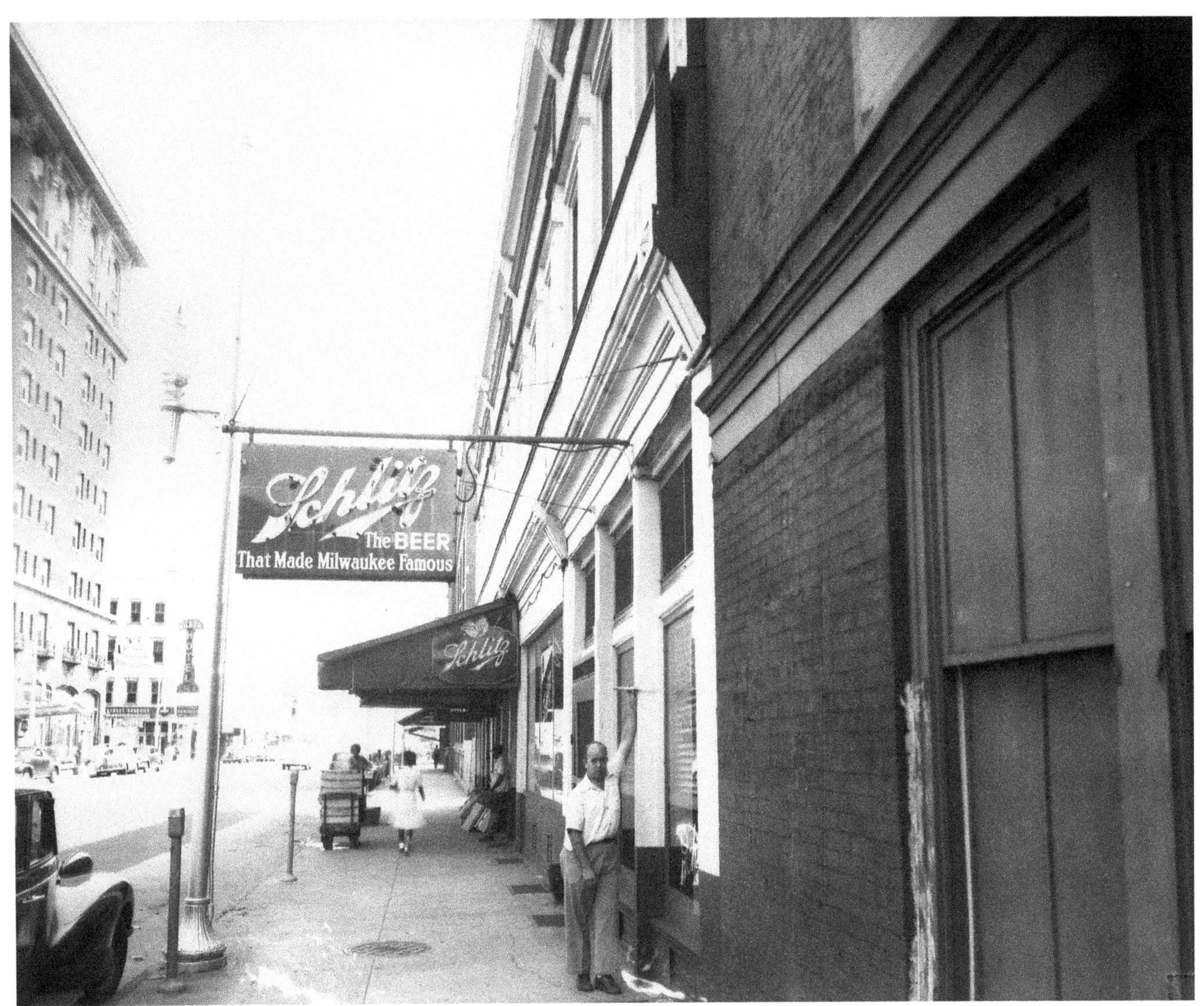

This photo shows the Schlitz Beer neon sign used to attract customers.

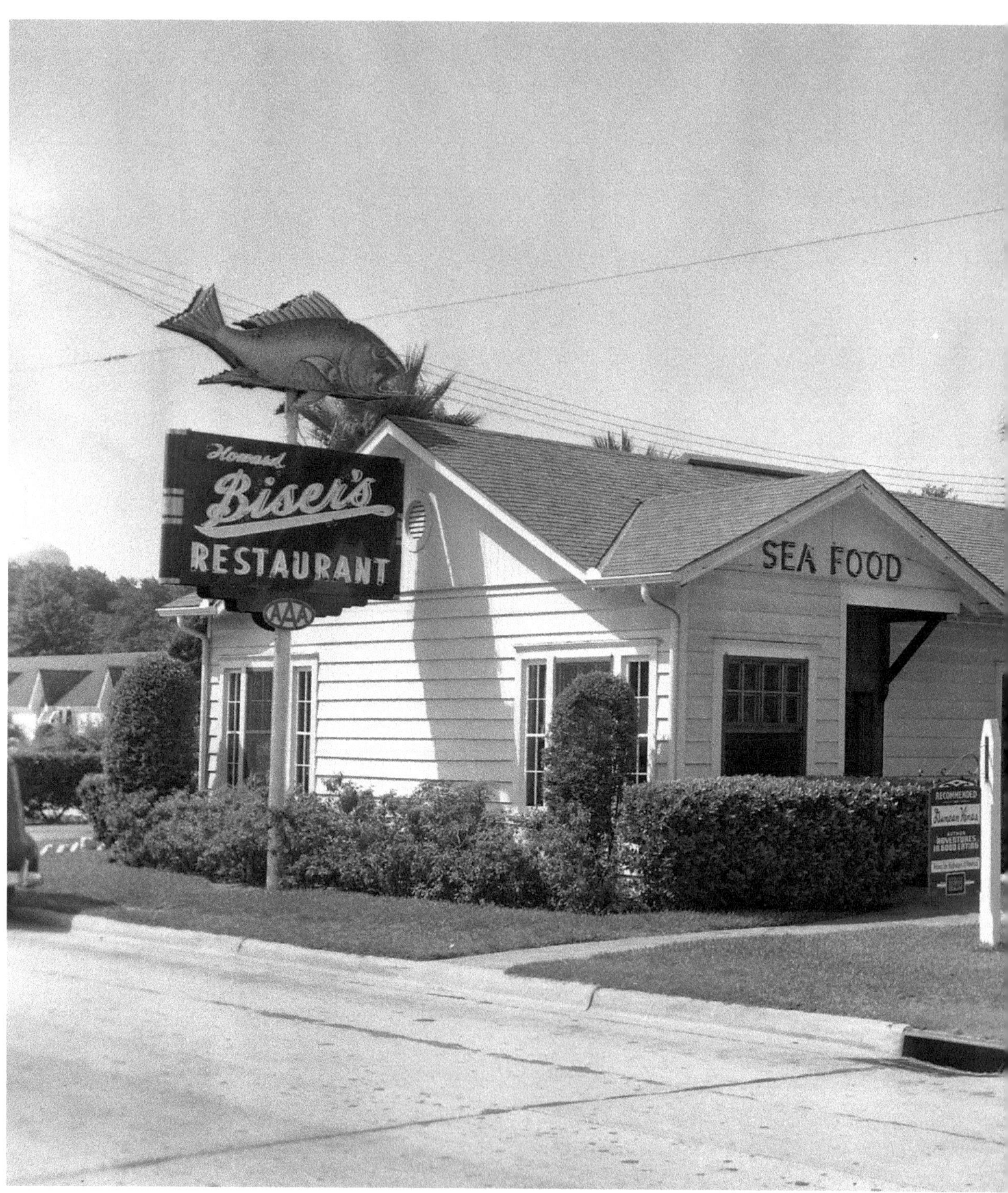

Eating out became possible for more people. Family restaurants like Biser's were becoming common in the late 1940s and 1950s.

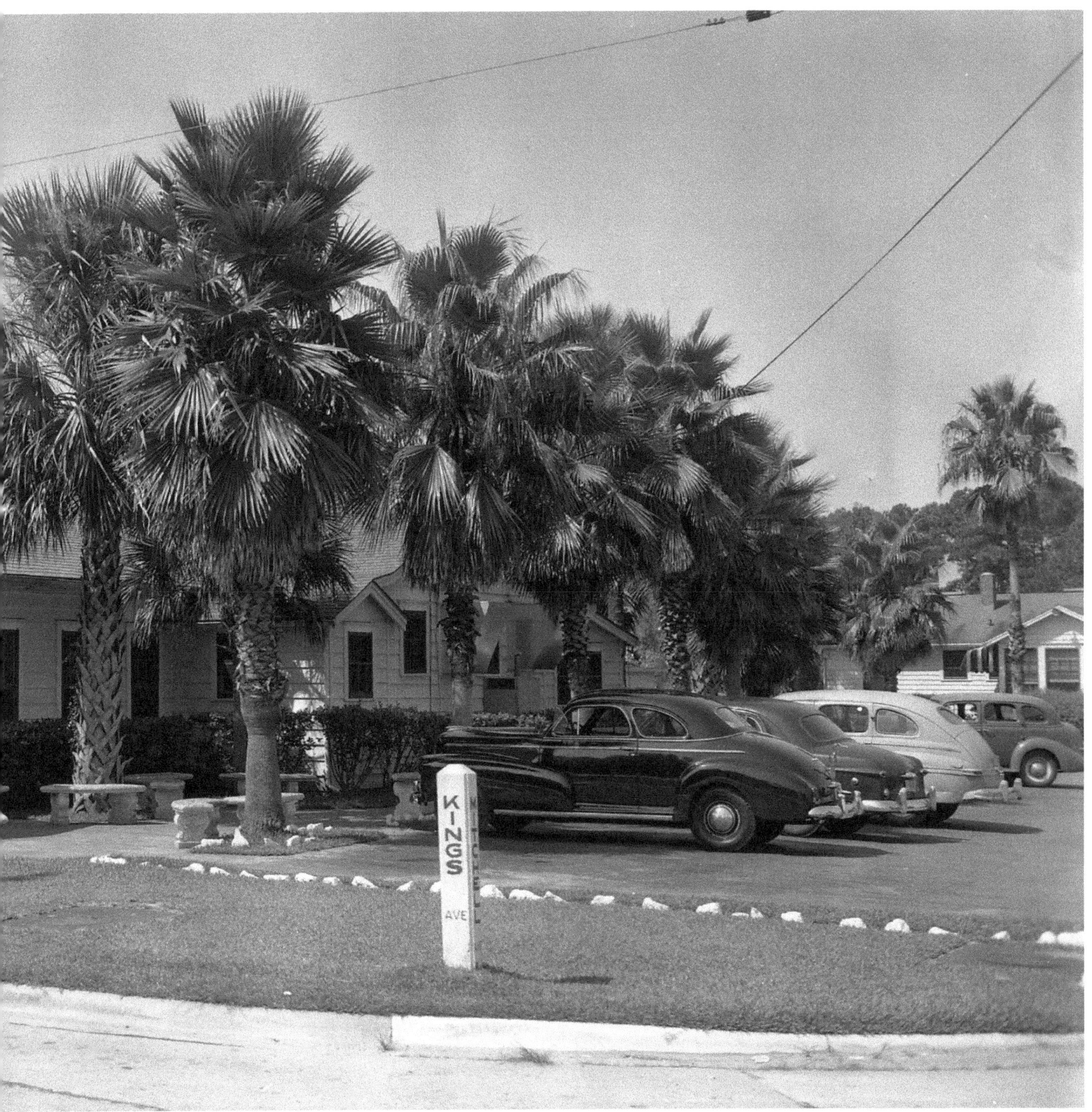
KINGS
AVE

This street scene shows the thriving business district downtown in 1950.

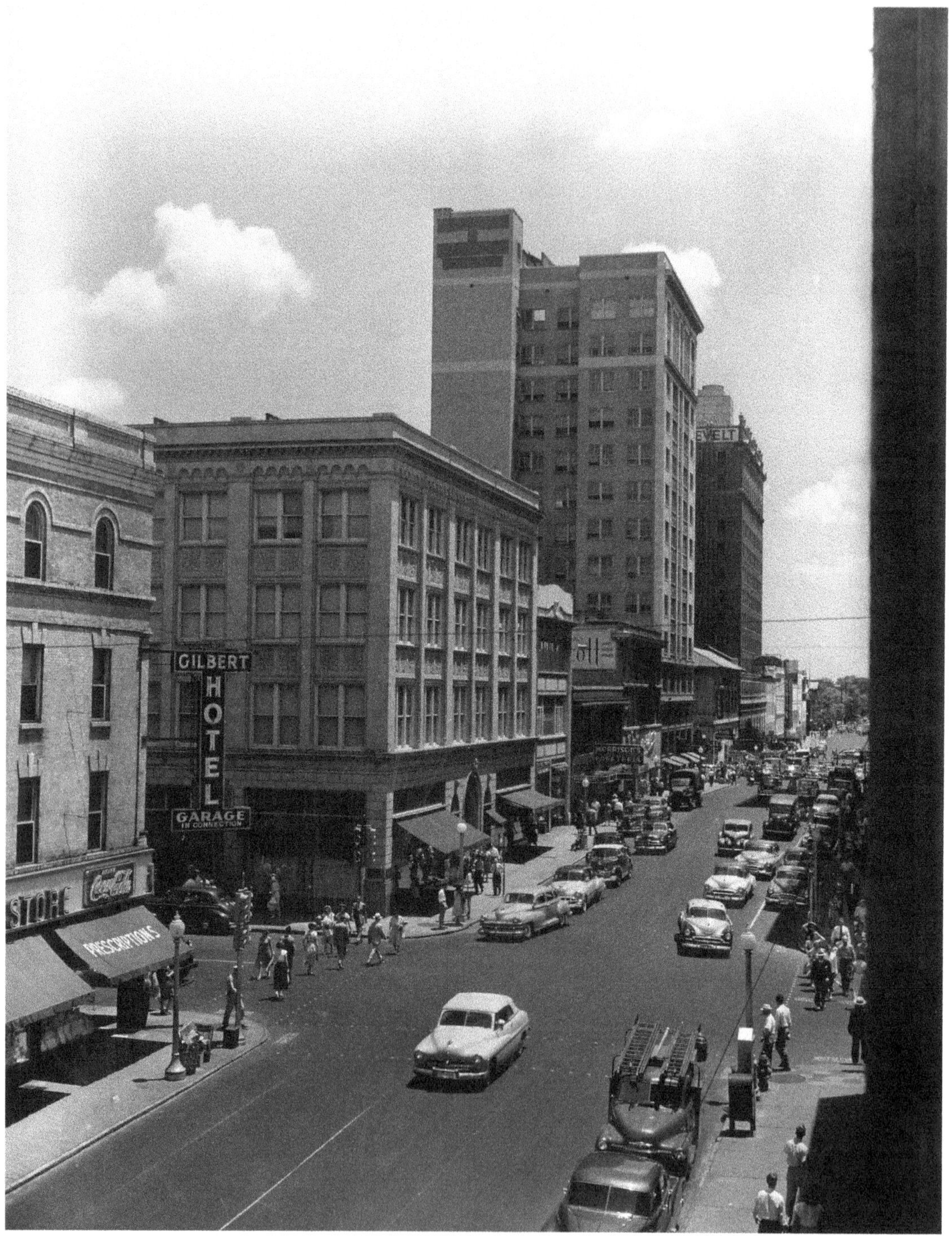

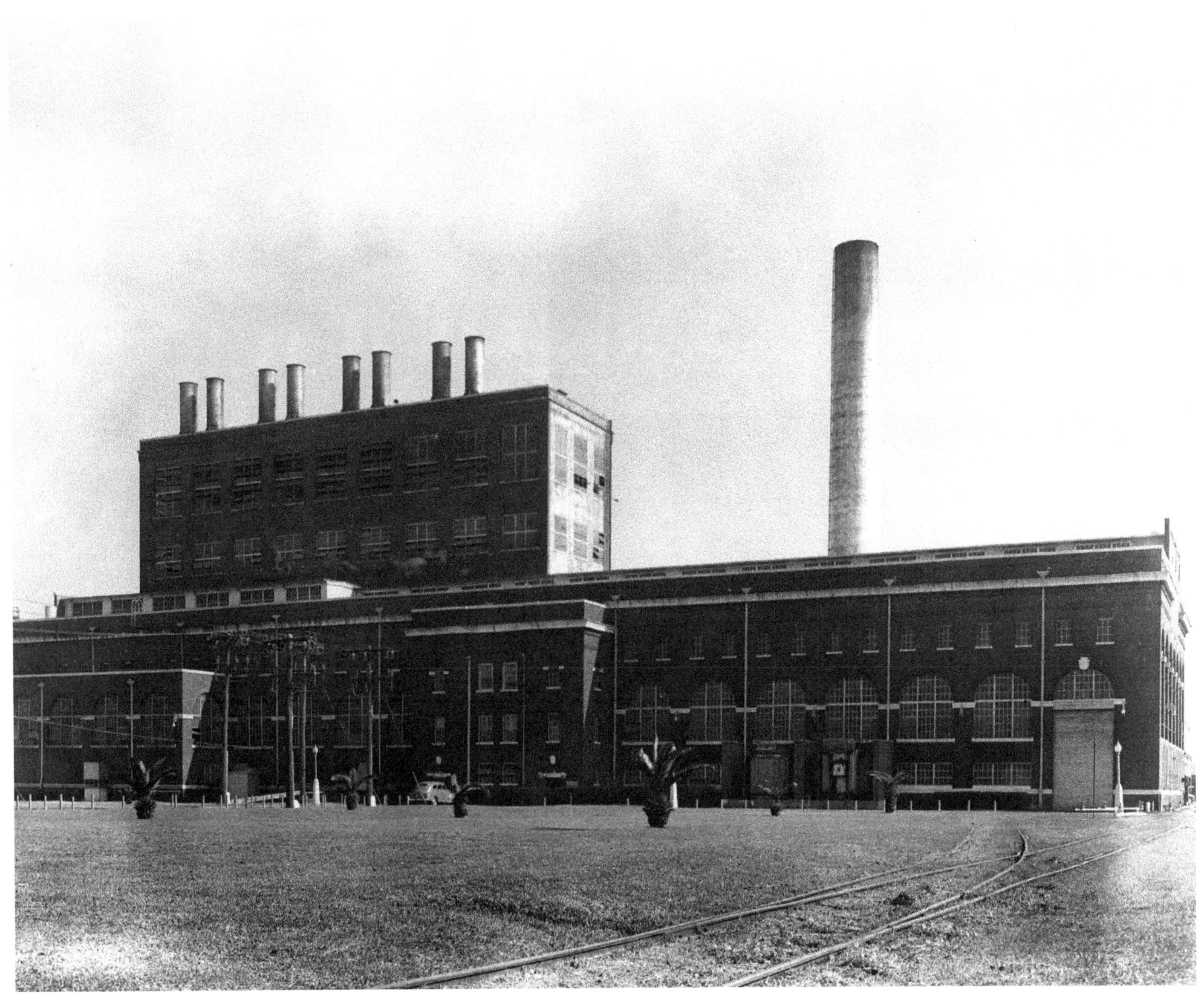

As use of electricity by the expanding railroads, commercial enterprise, and in family homes grew, electric power plants had become more plentiful by the 1950s.

The city's business district on Laura Street in 1949

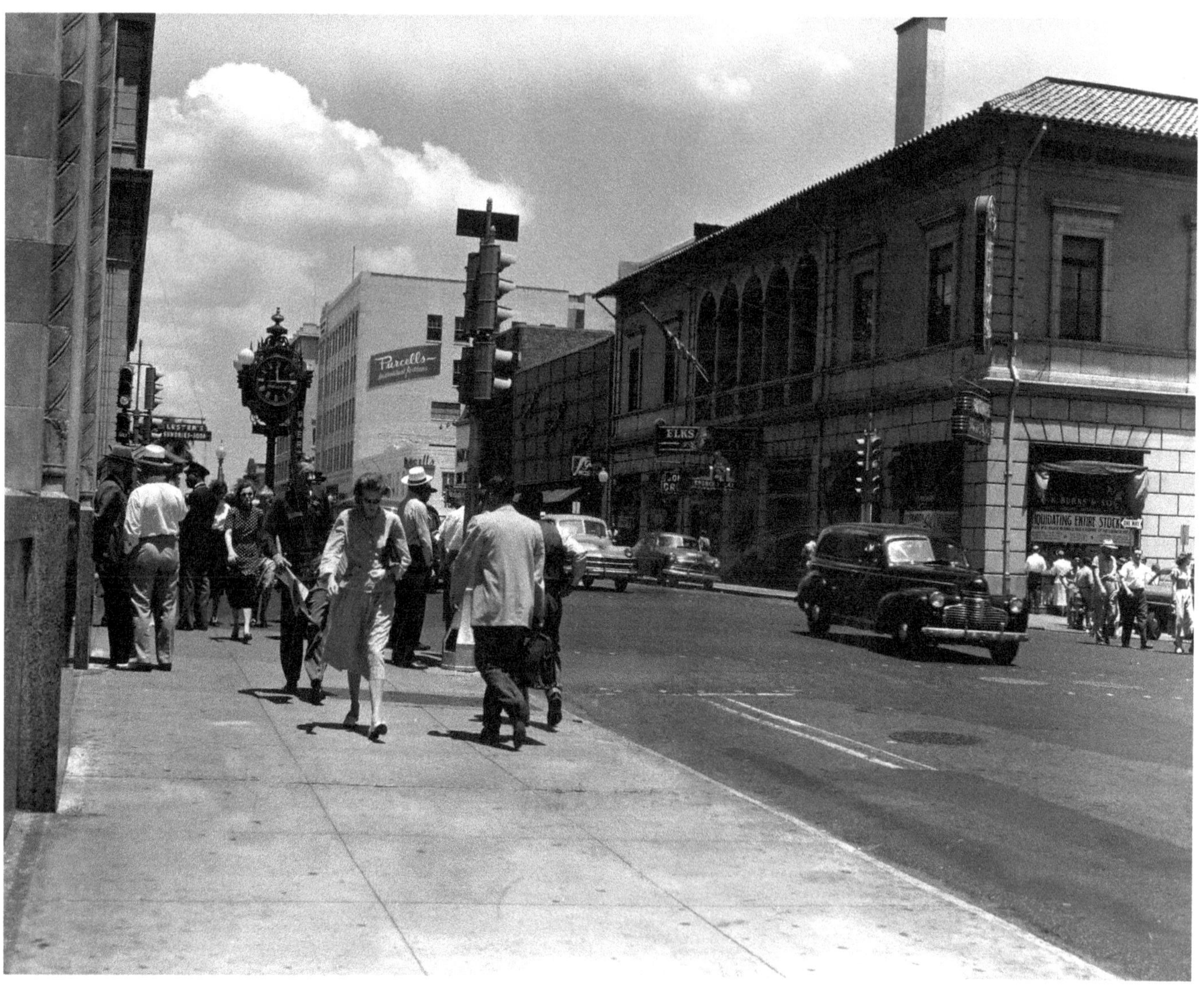

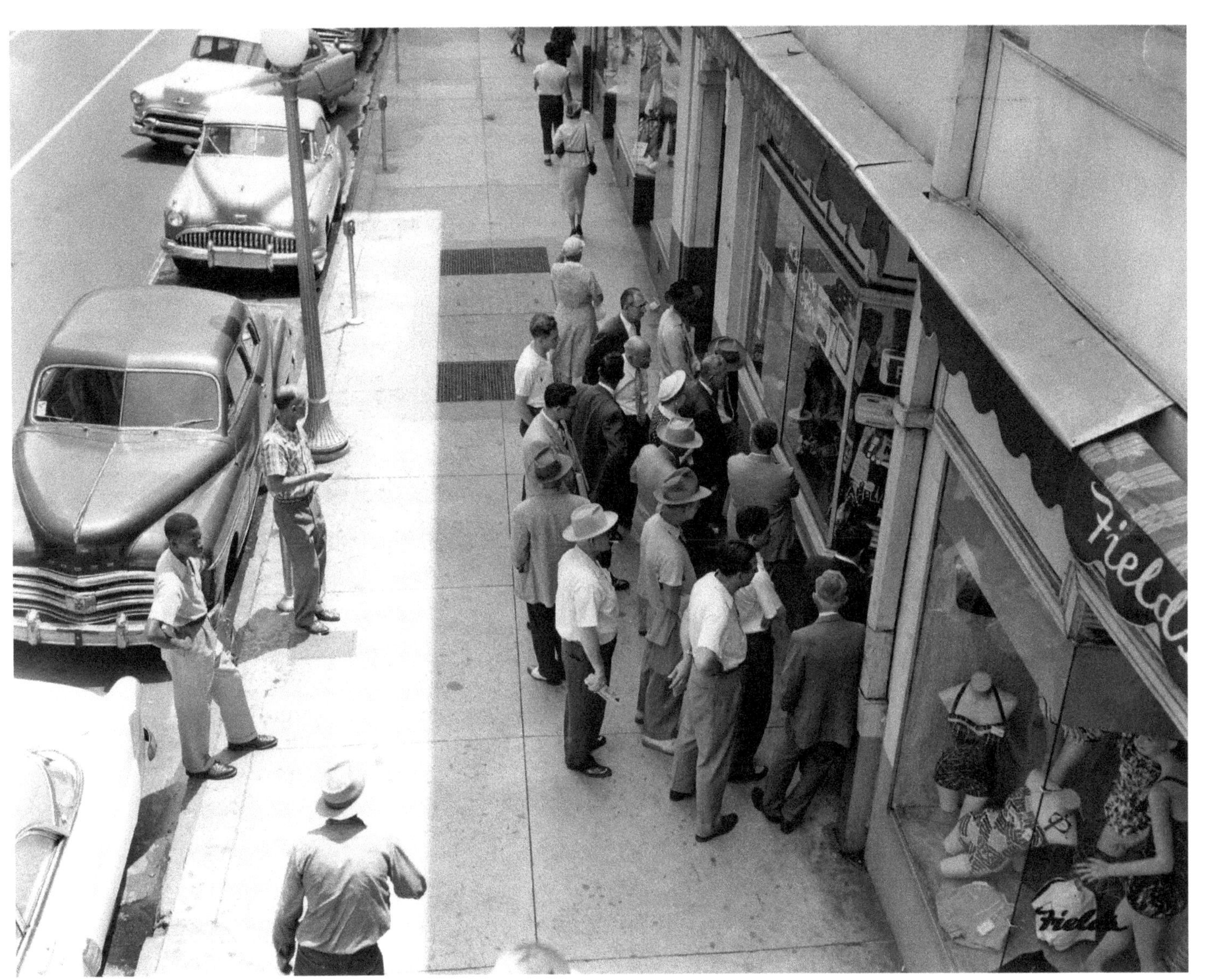

A crowd watches television in a store window in 1954.

Politics was another part of life that continued to serve as mass entertainment in the 1950s. Charley E. Johns' gubernatorial campaign hit town with this parade in 1954. Johns did not succeed in getting elected.

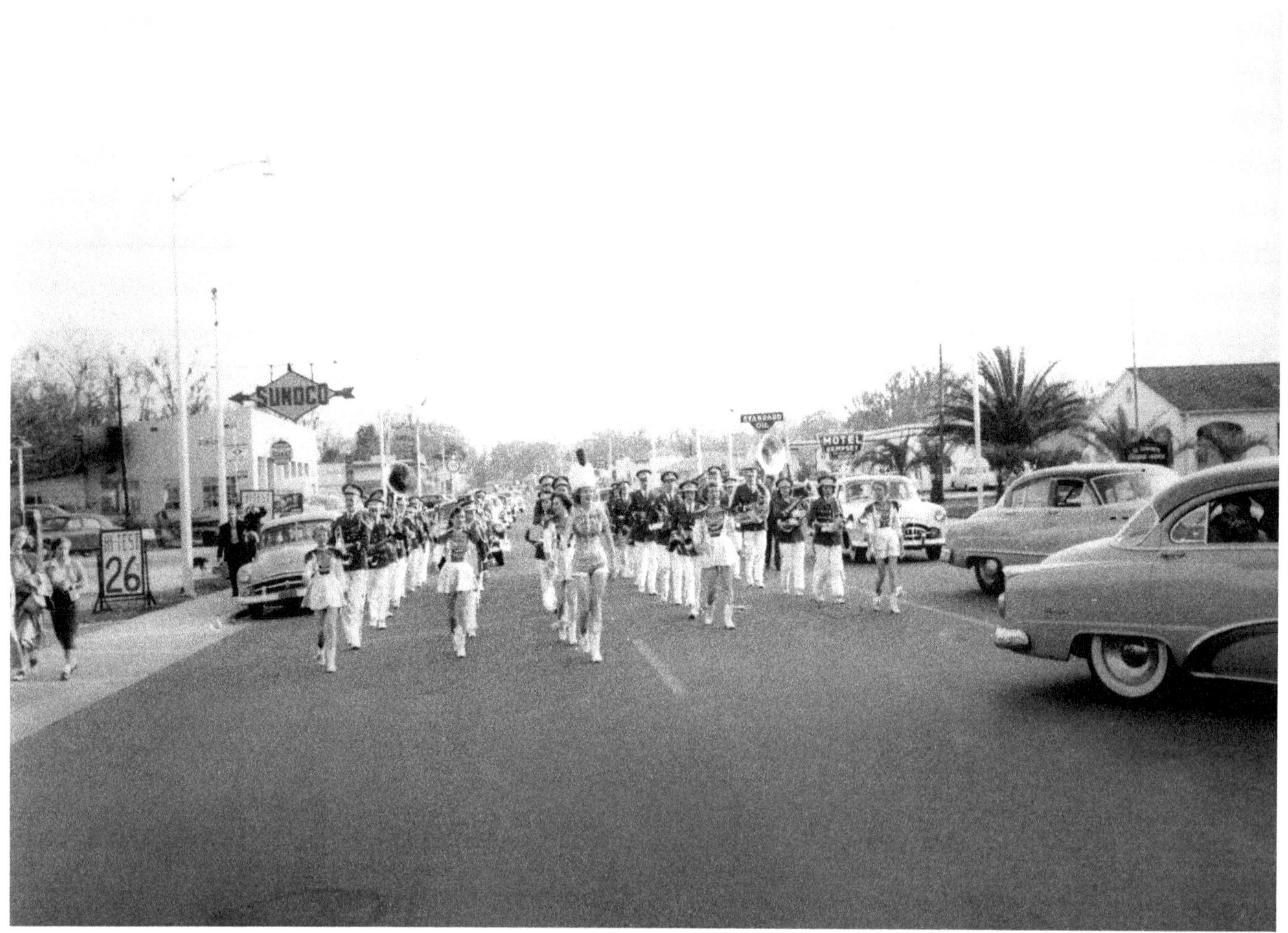

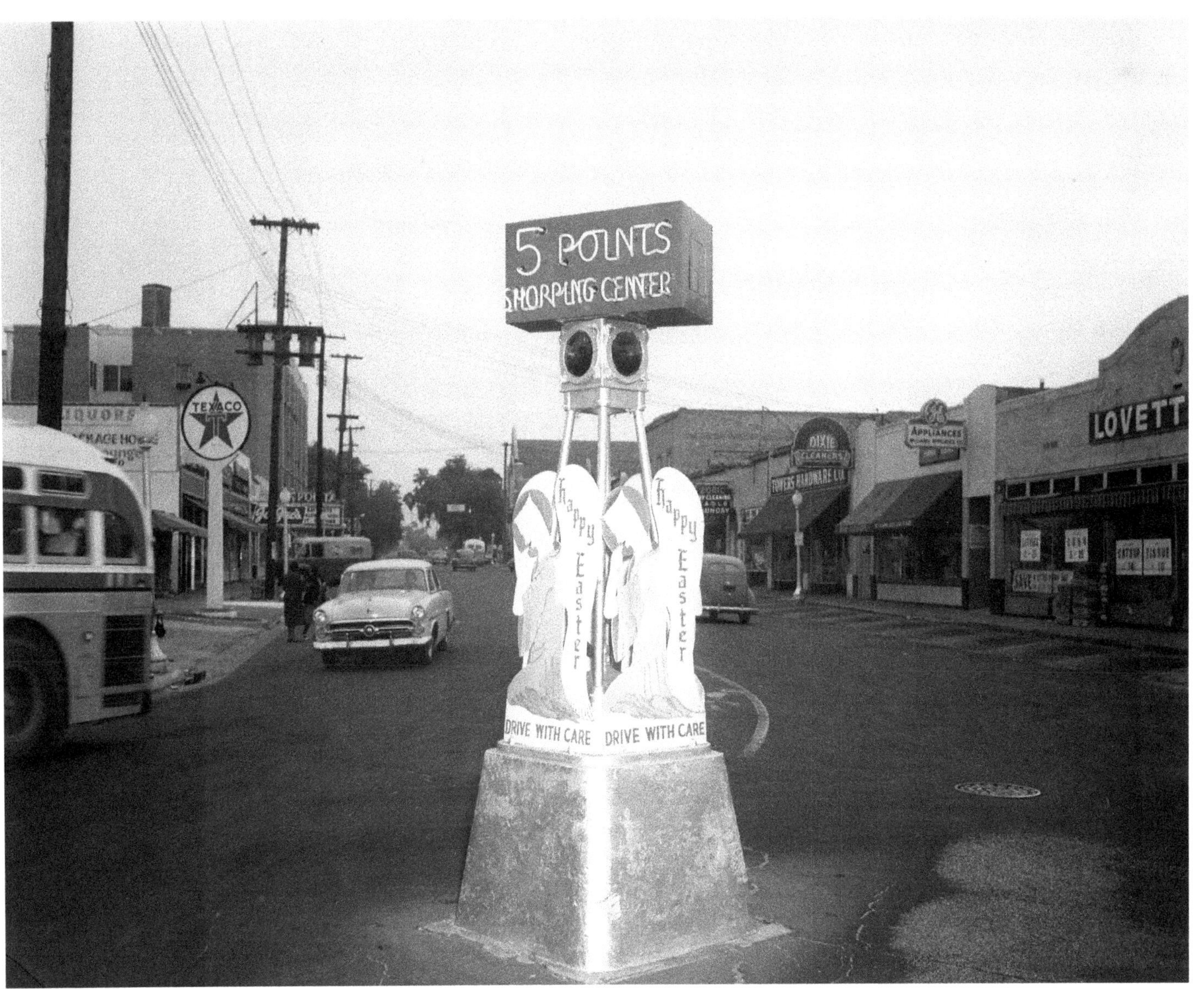

The suburban shopping center of Five Points is highlighted here in this street sign decorated at the intersection.

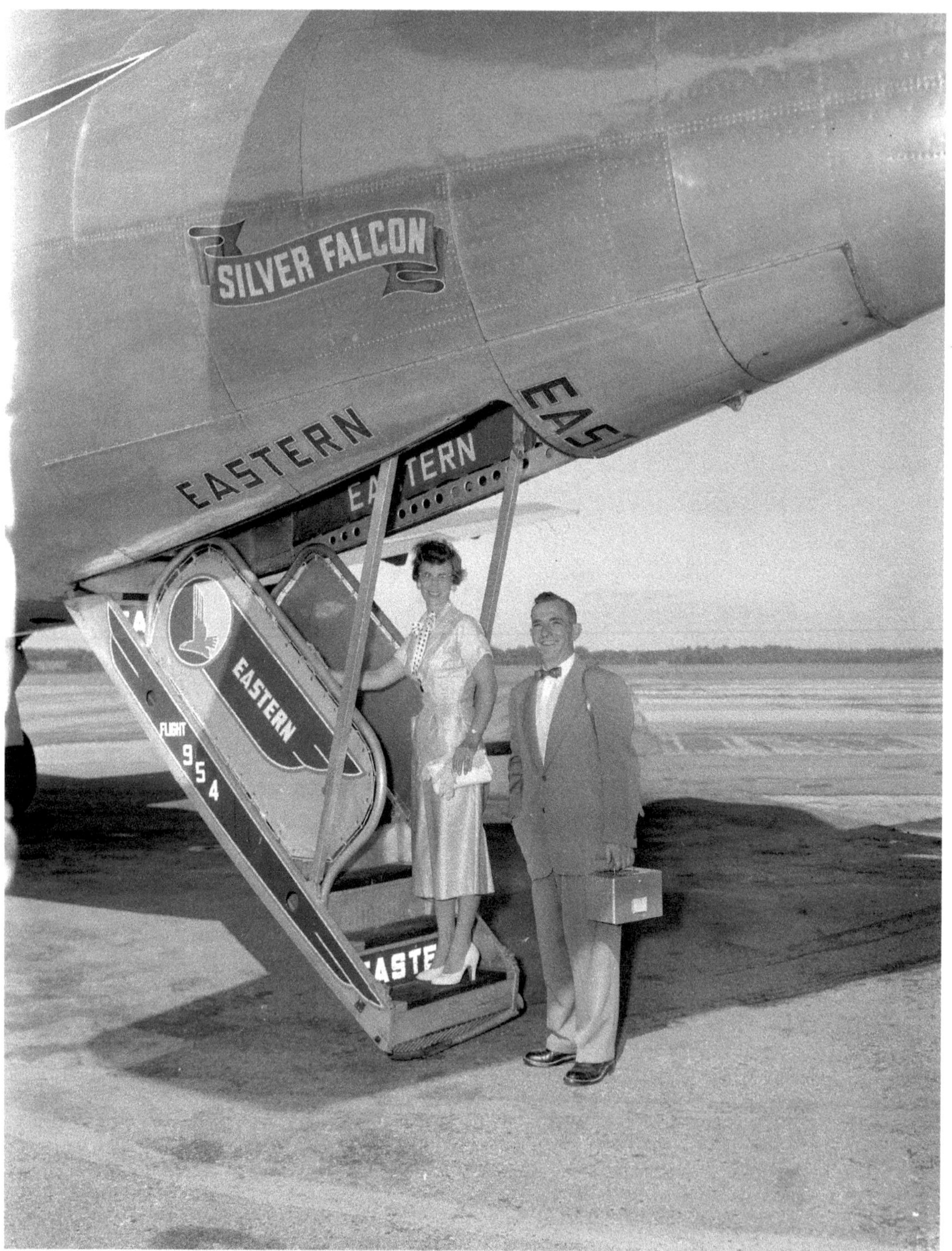

Another form of transportation that became more common among civilians was airplane travel. Shown here is a couple apparently about to board for flight at the Jacksonville Airport in 1956.

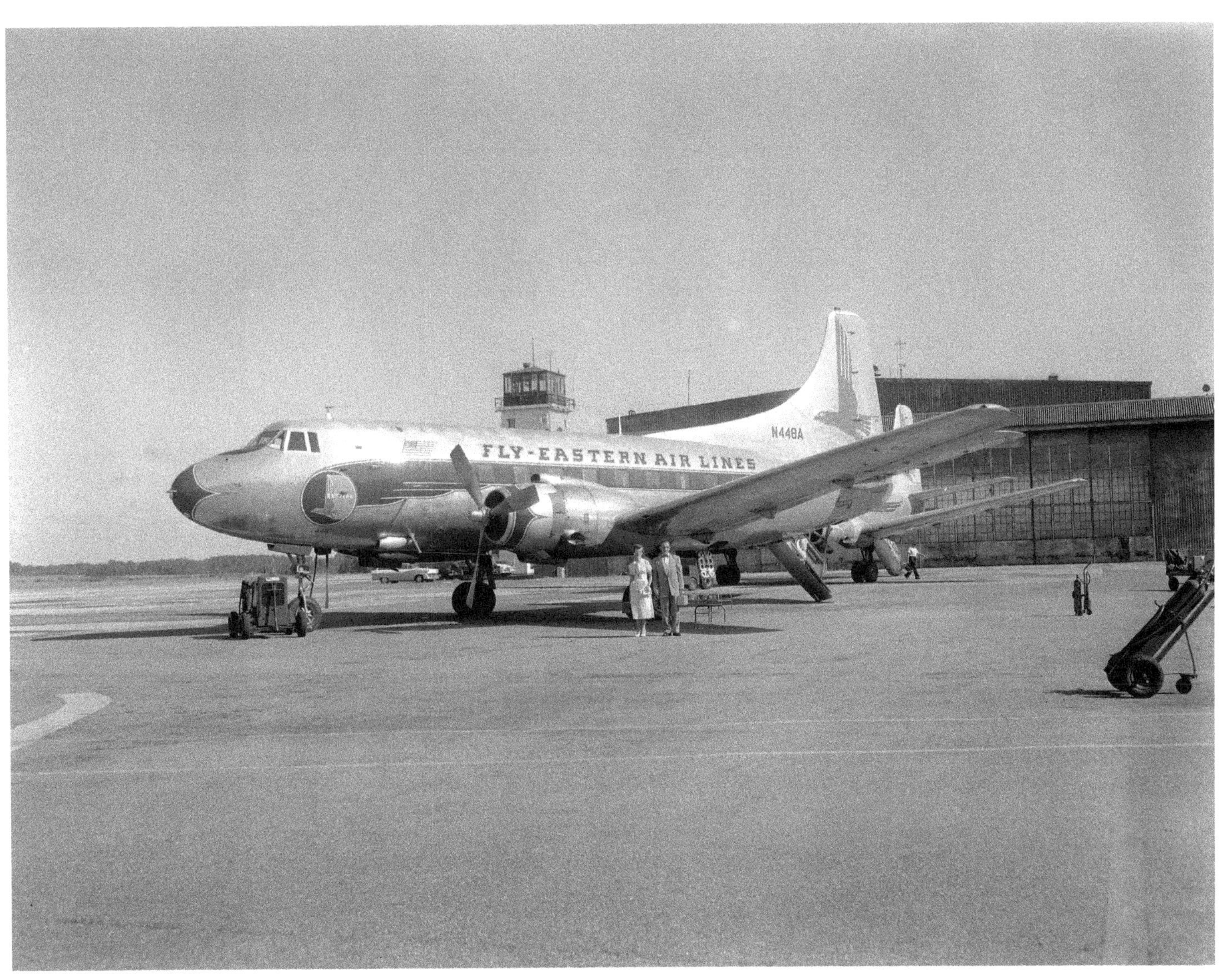

An Eastern Air Lines plane at Jacksonville Airport, 1956

Most people continued to travel by train. The Atlantic Coast Line train is shown here in 1960.

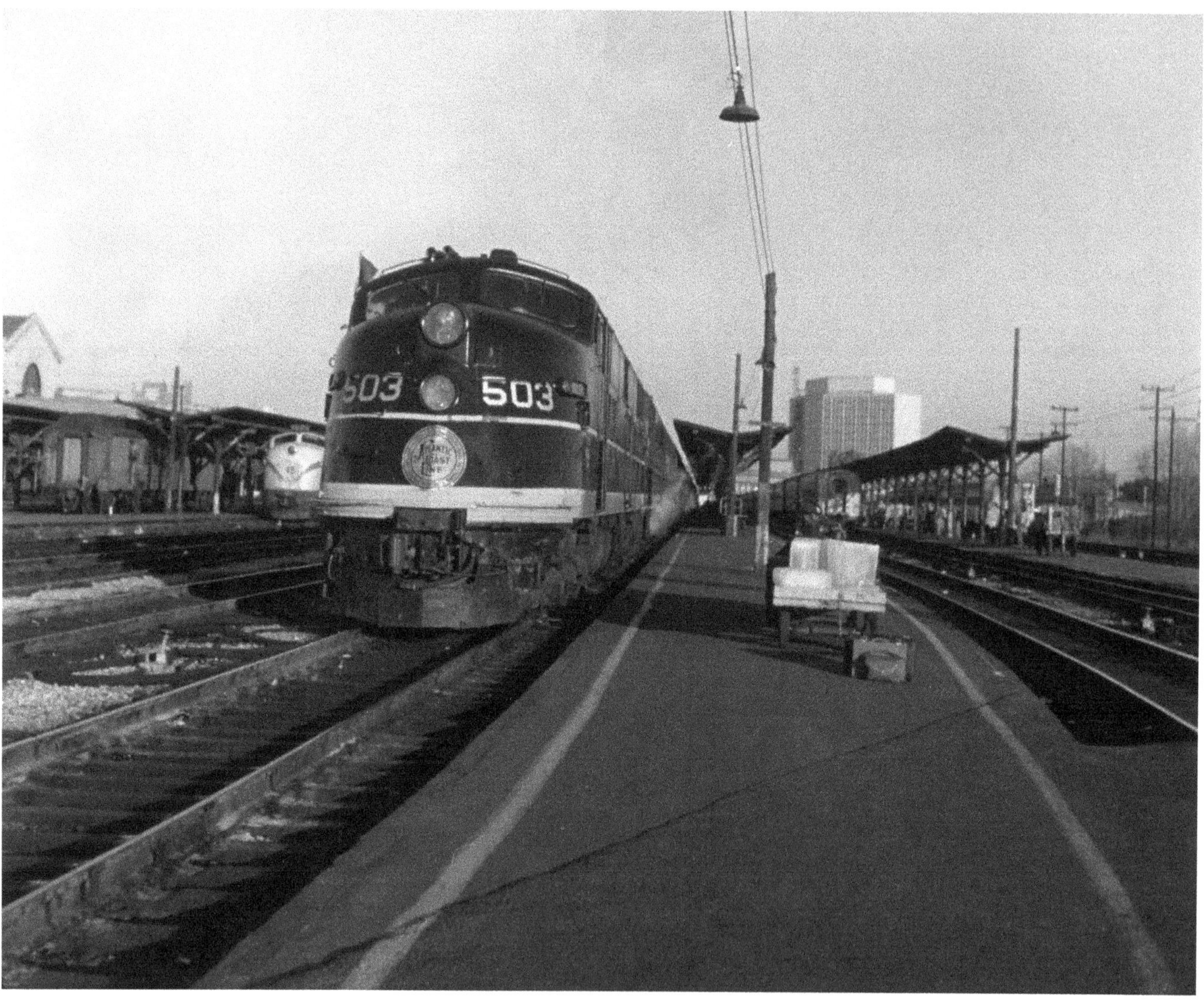

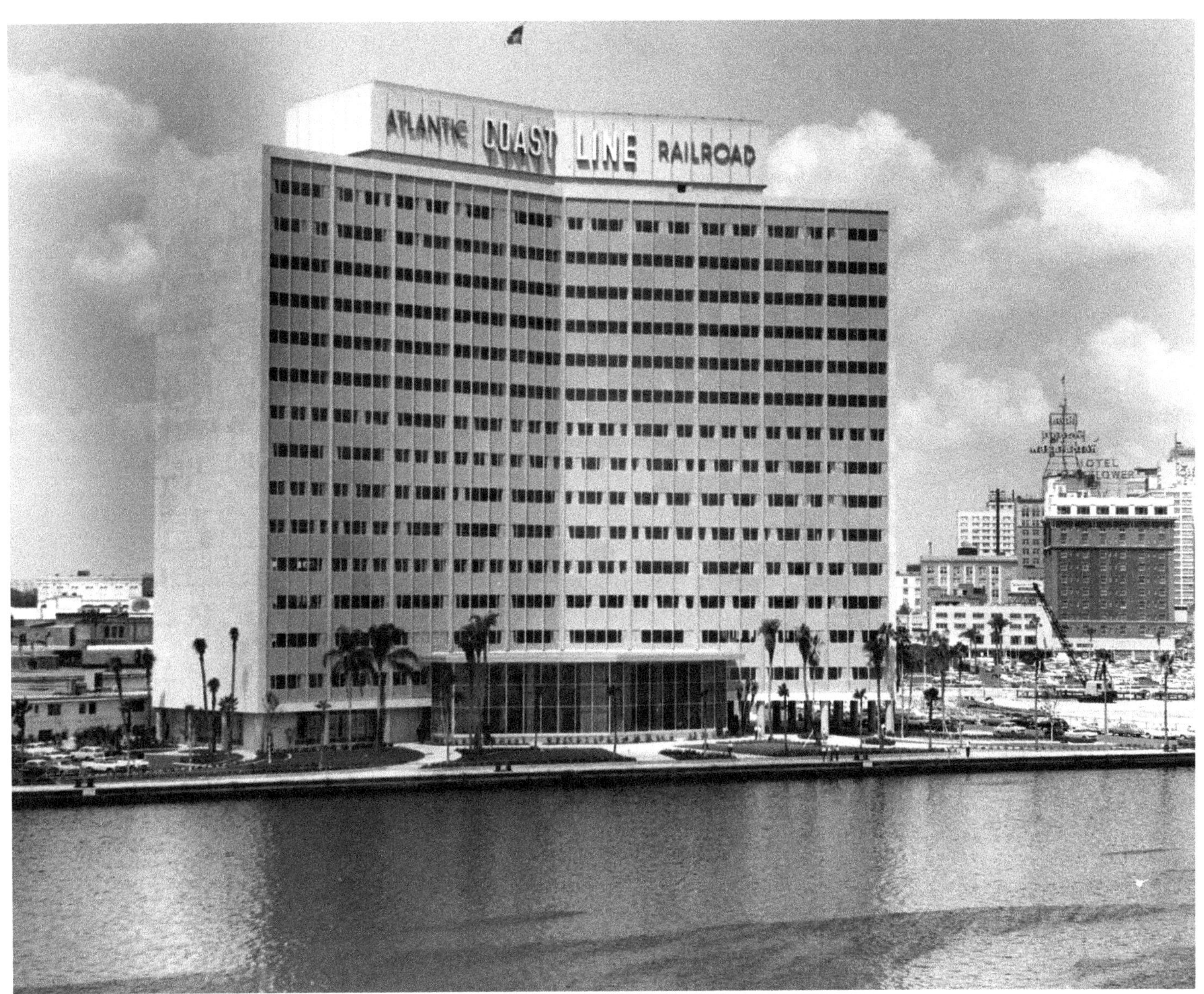

The railroad business was an important part of the corporate structure of Jacksonville. Shown here is the Atlantic Coast Line Railroad Company building near the St. Johns River in 1960.

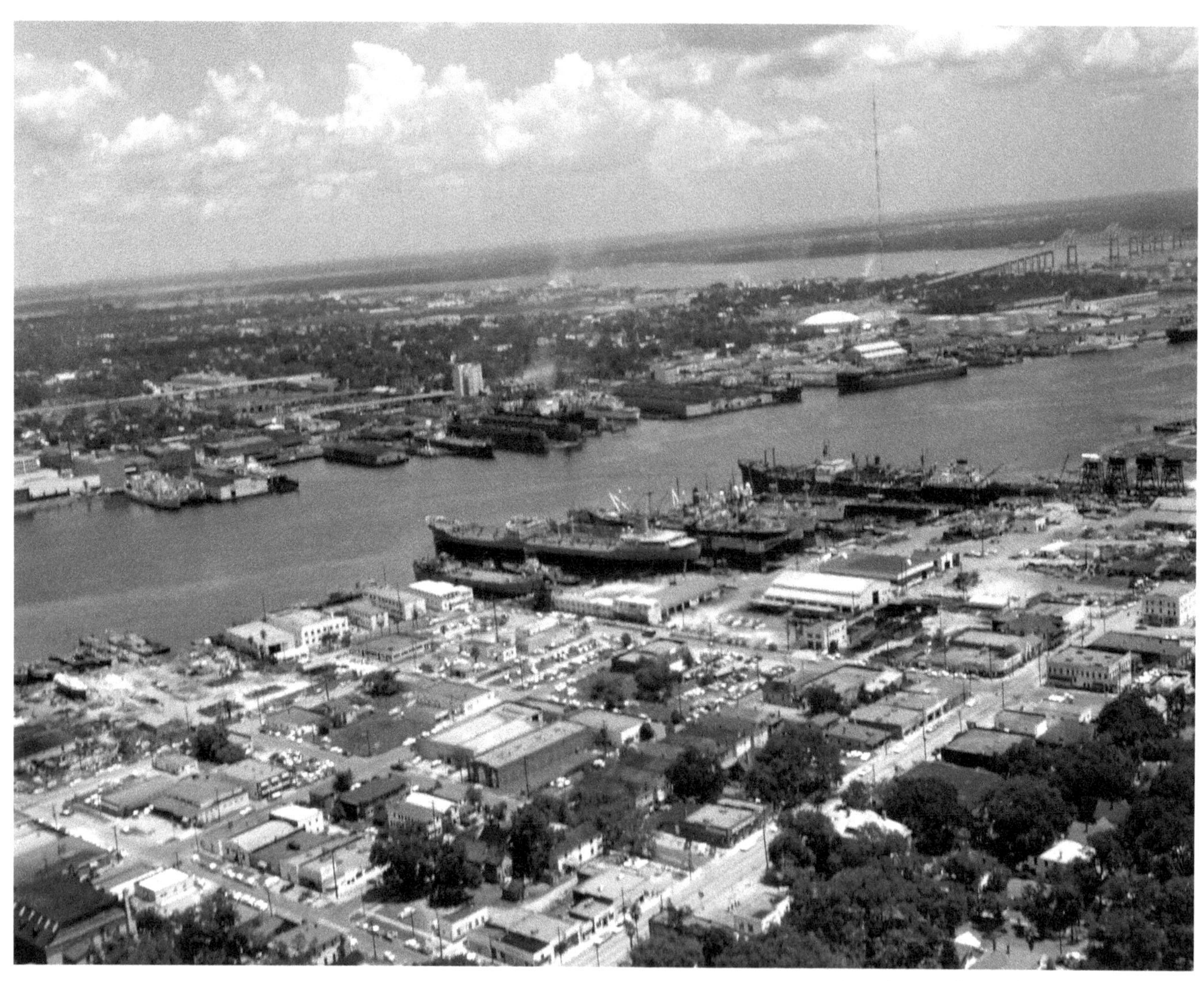

A 1960s aerial reveals the city's progress.

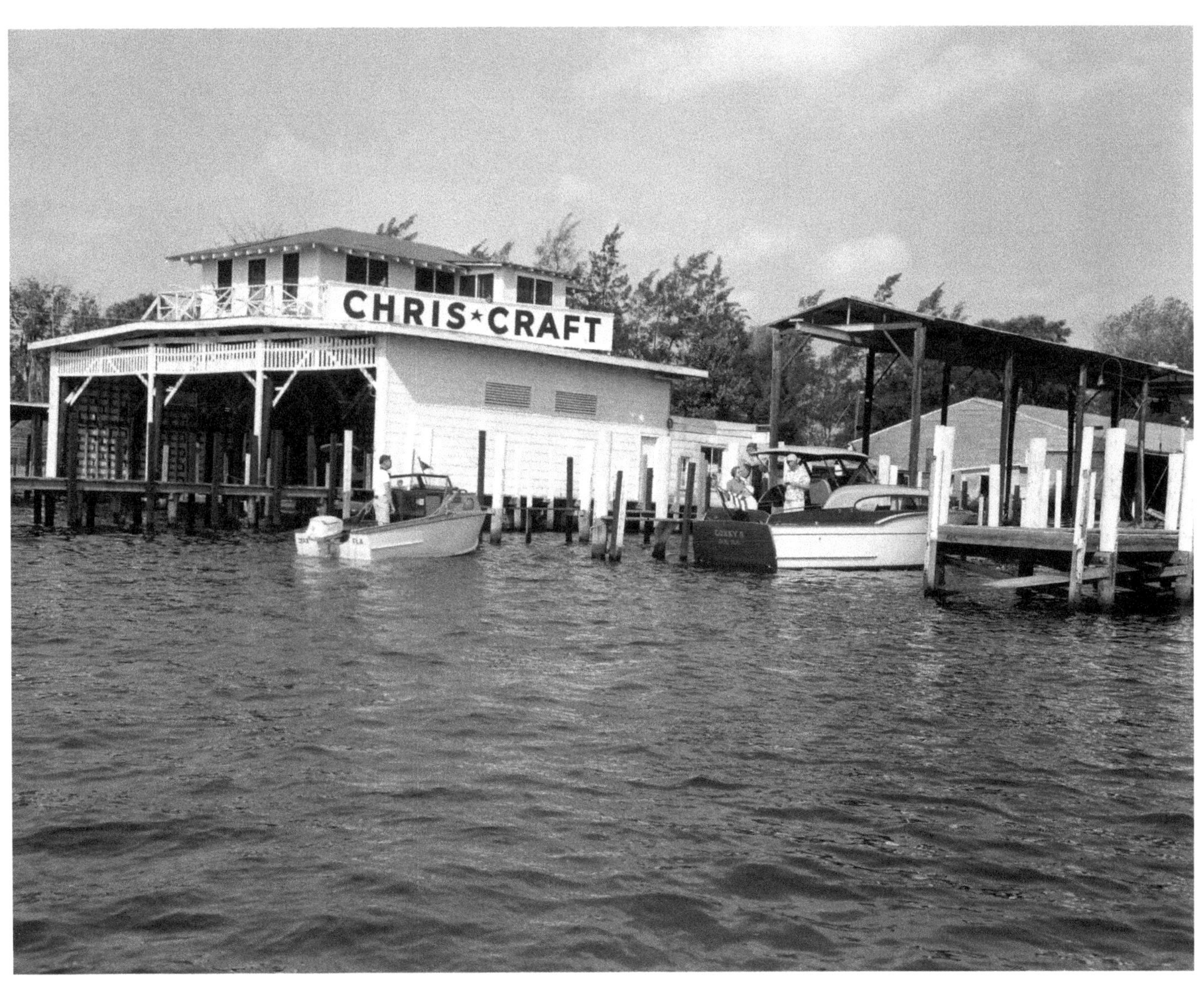

The number of marinas on the St. Johns River grew as river vessels multiplied. Here the *Corky II* rests at Sims Brothers Marina in 1960.

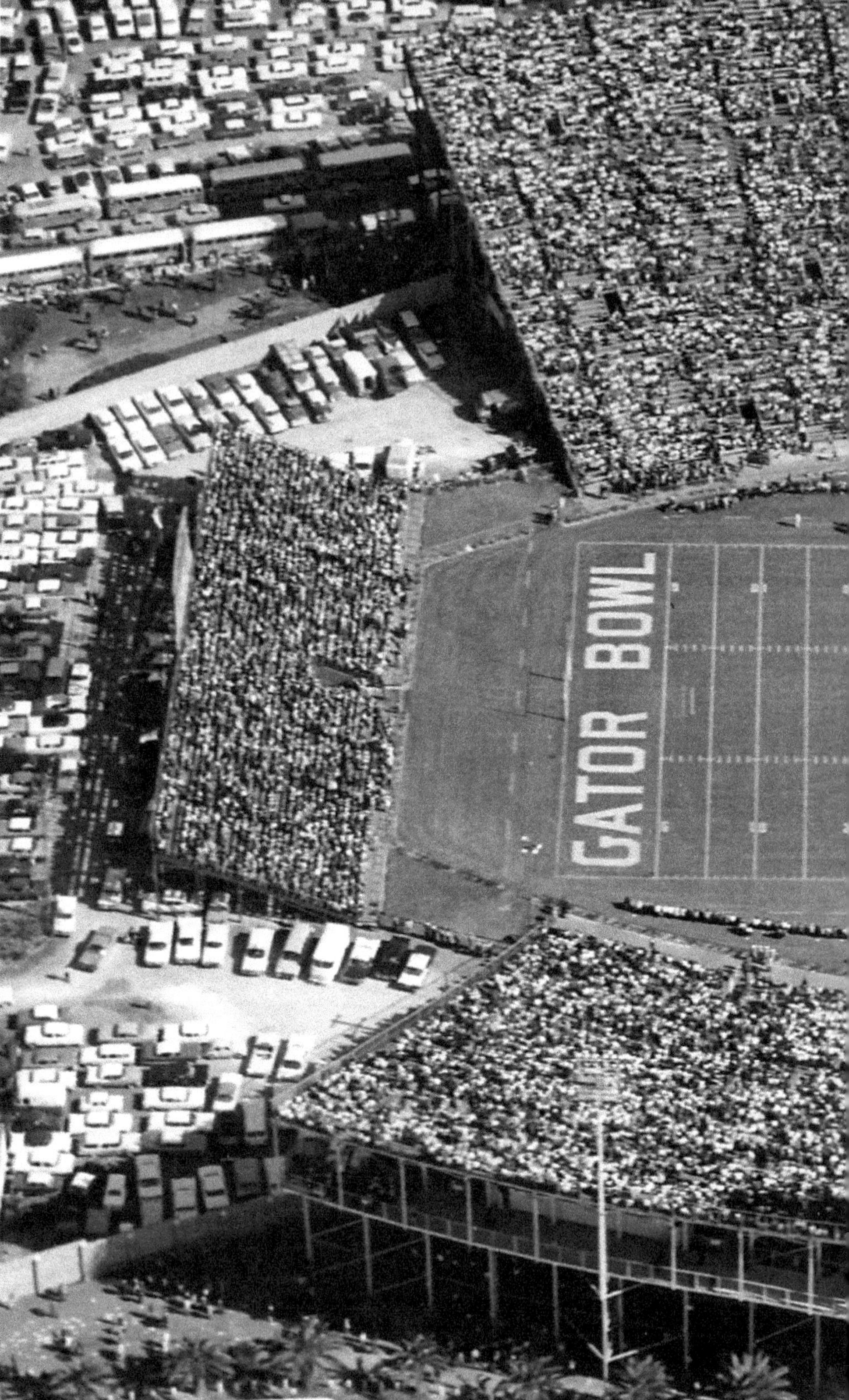

The Gator Bowl served as a municipal stadium for the city beginning in the 1930s. One of the most famous events is the college football rival game, the Florida-Georgia classic. This is an aerial view of the Gator Bowl in 1961.

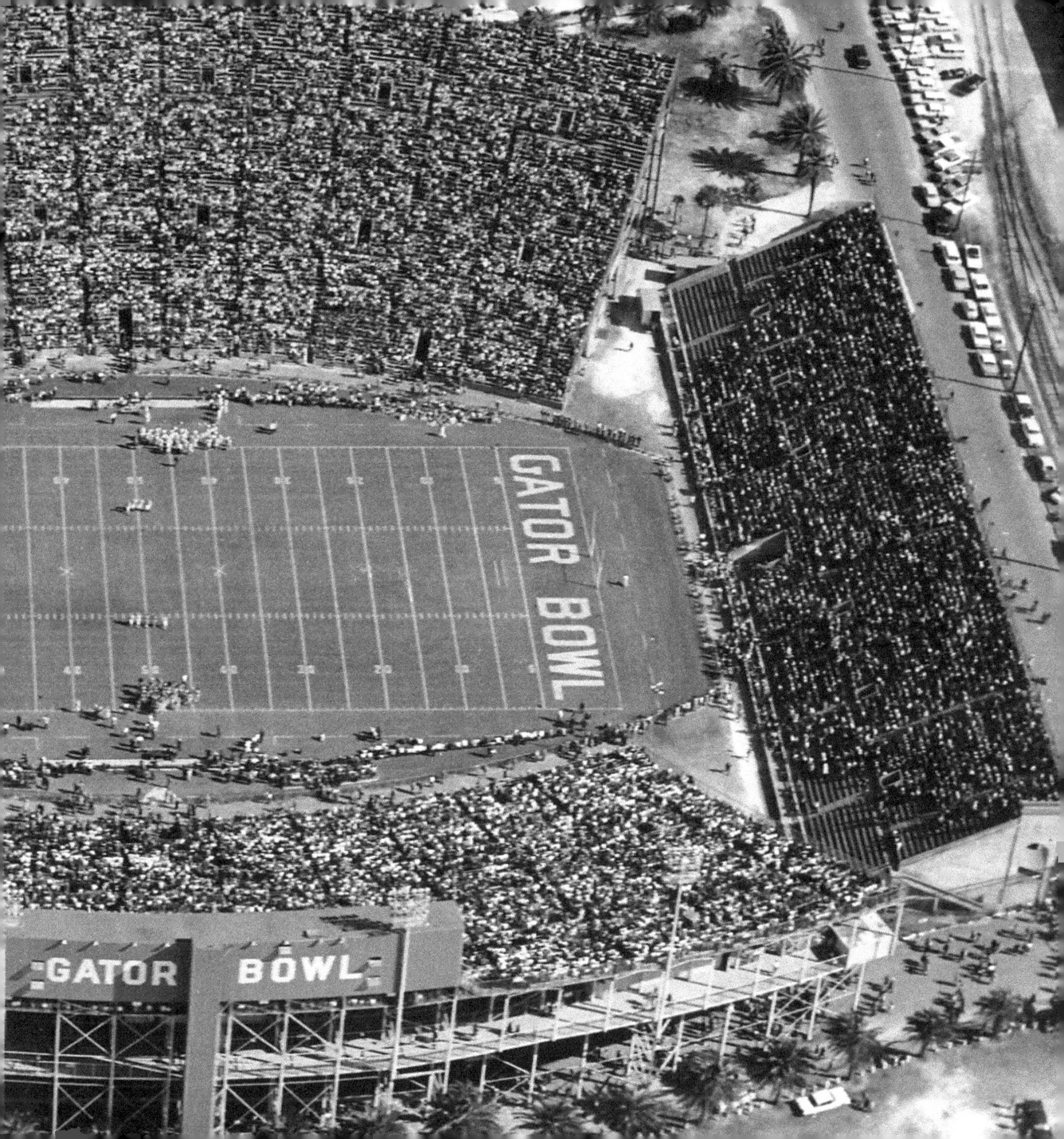
GATOR BOWL
GATOR BOWL

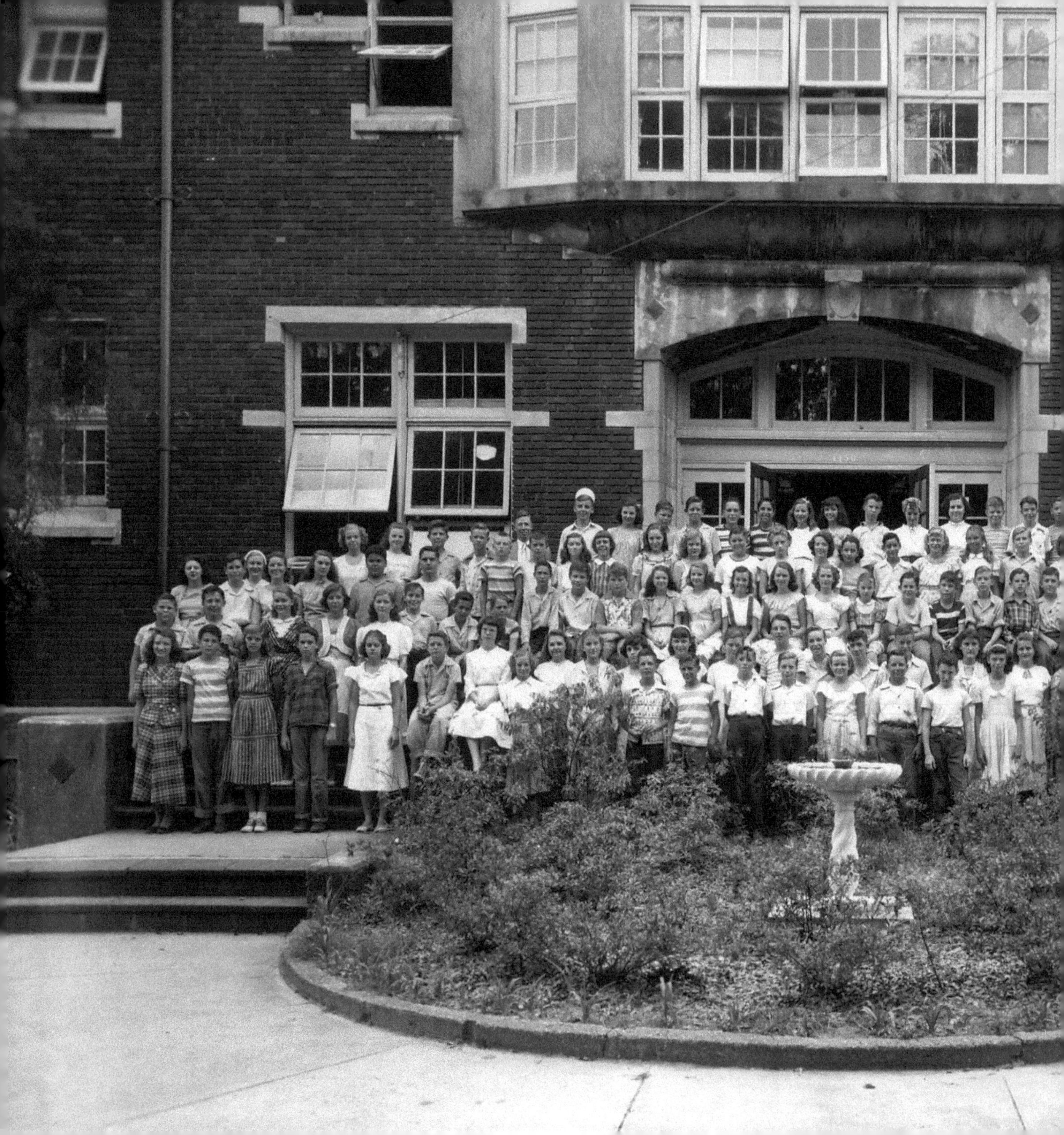

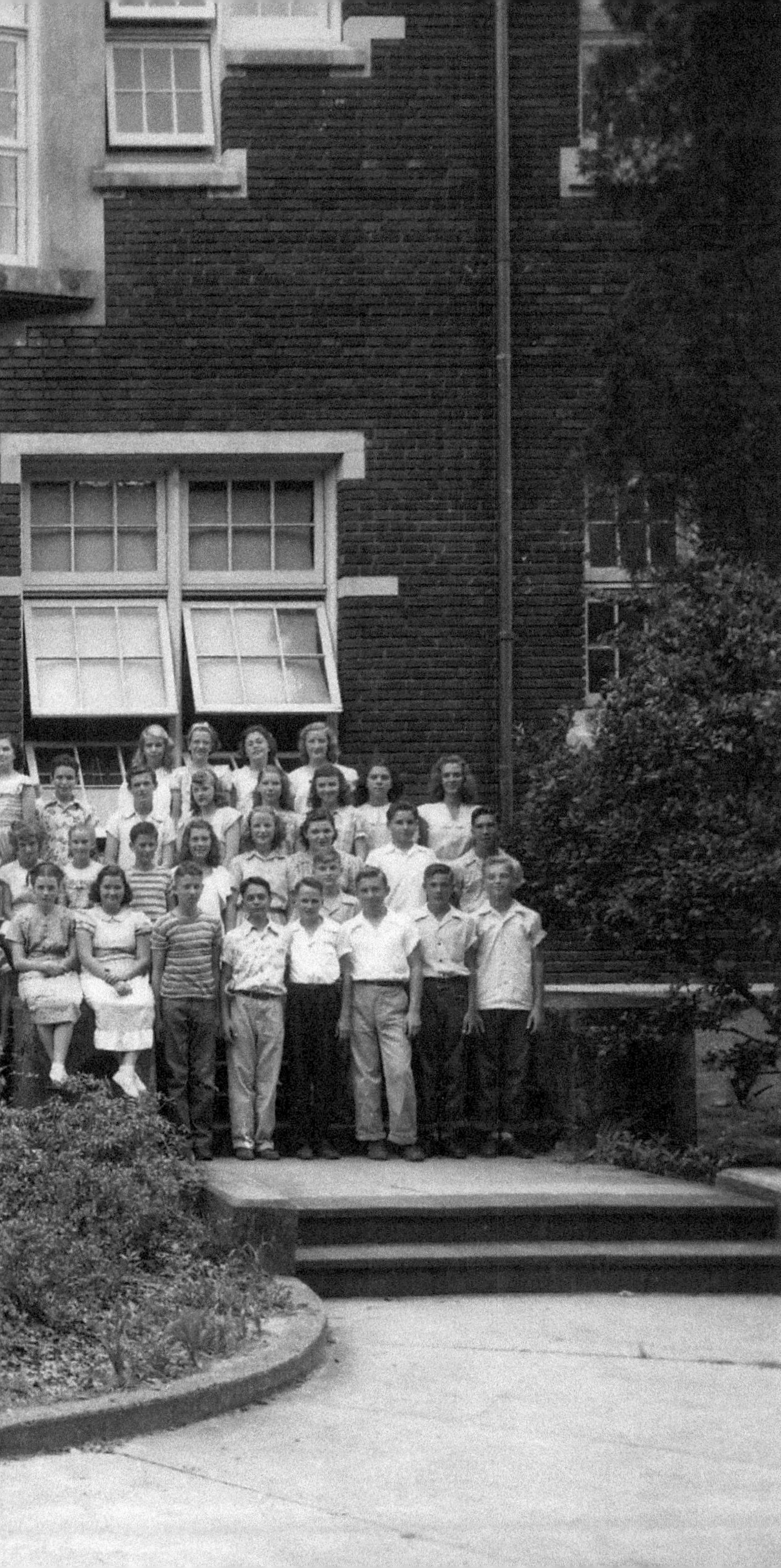

More schools were built during this period. Assembled here is a graduating class at Southside Grammar School on Flagler Avenue.

The Democratic Party was at a crossroads in 1960. Solid support in the South for the Democratic Party was in question as national leaders began to shift emphasis to civil rights. Here the crowd appears attentive as vice-presidential candidate Lyndon Johnson stops to speak in Hemming Park during a campaign sweep.

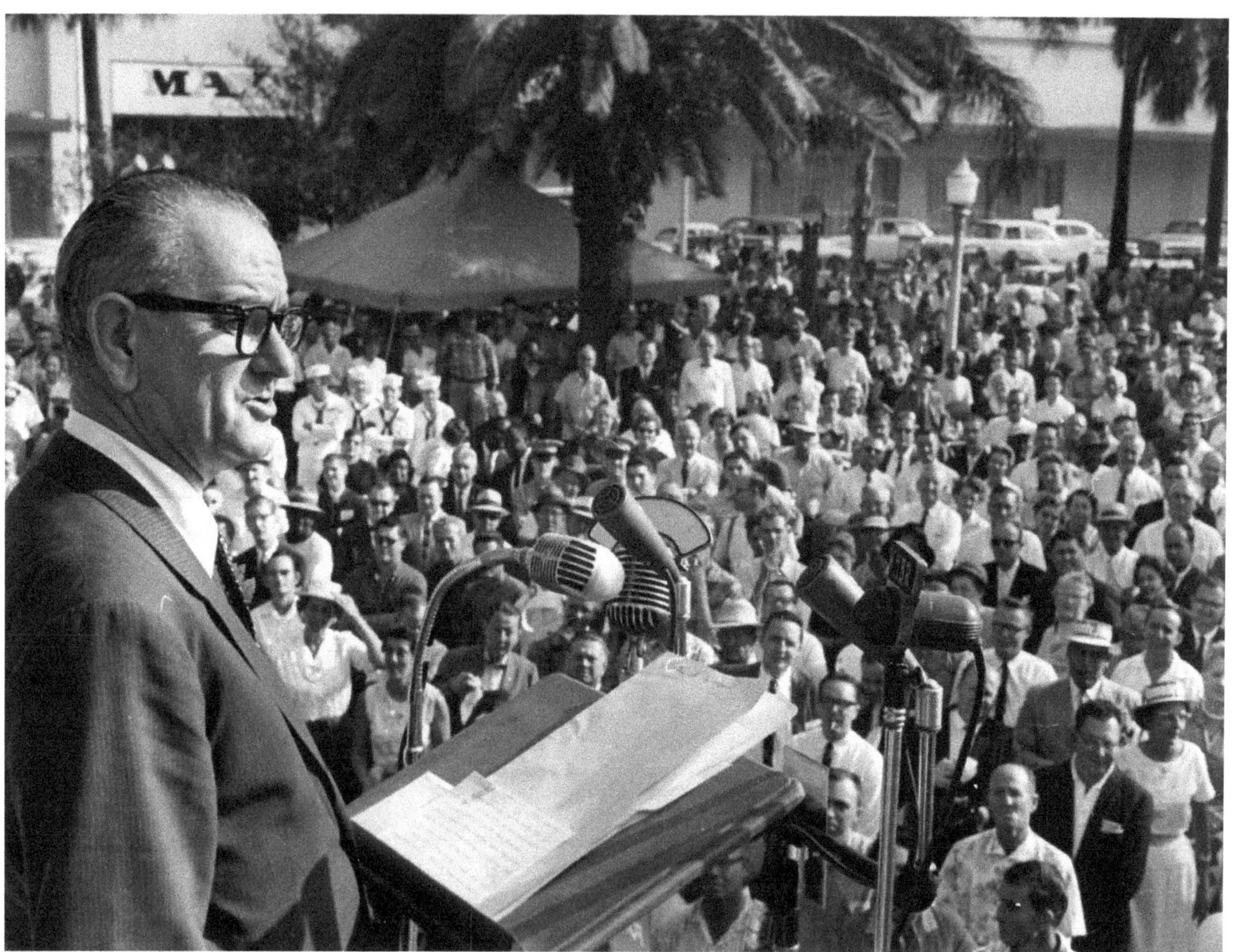

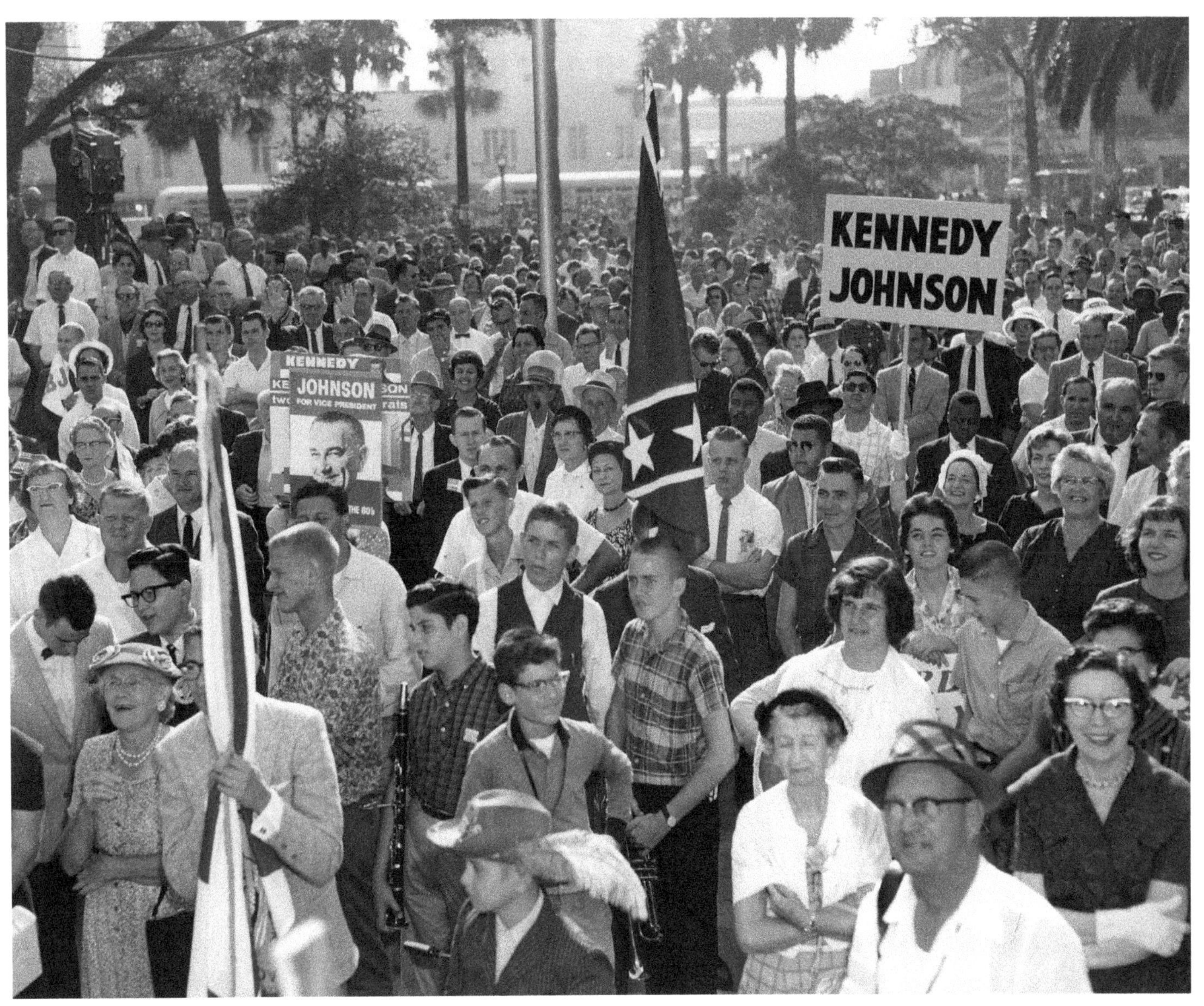

Crowds gather at Hemming Park to listen to Lyndon Johnson speak.

The Foley Lumber Company cranes represent another traditional industry in Jacksonville. This business was located on Main Street near 36th Street.

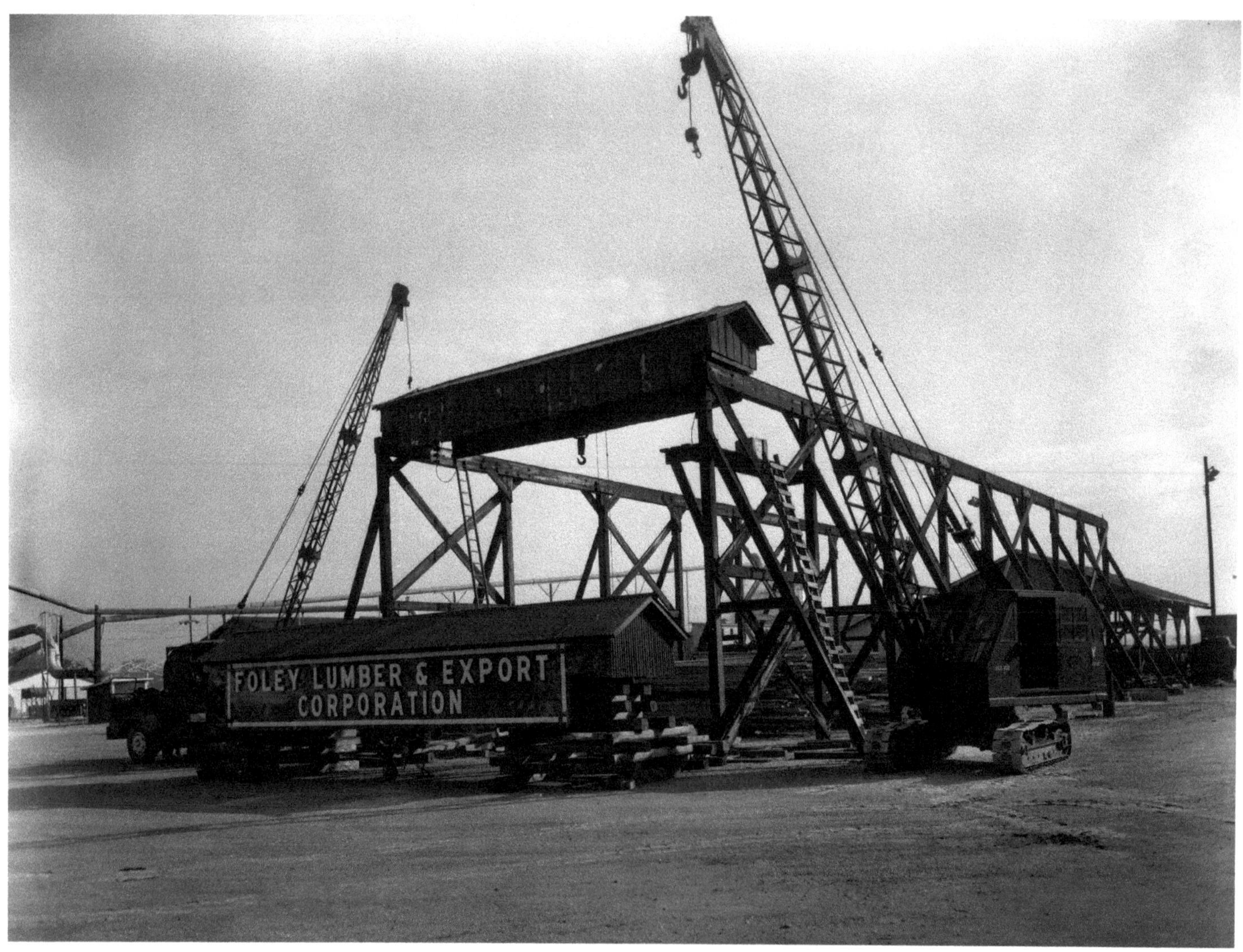

The new city hall building on Bay Street symbolized progress.

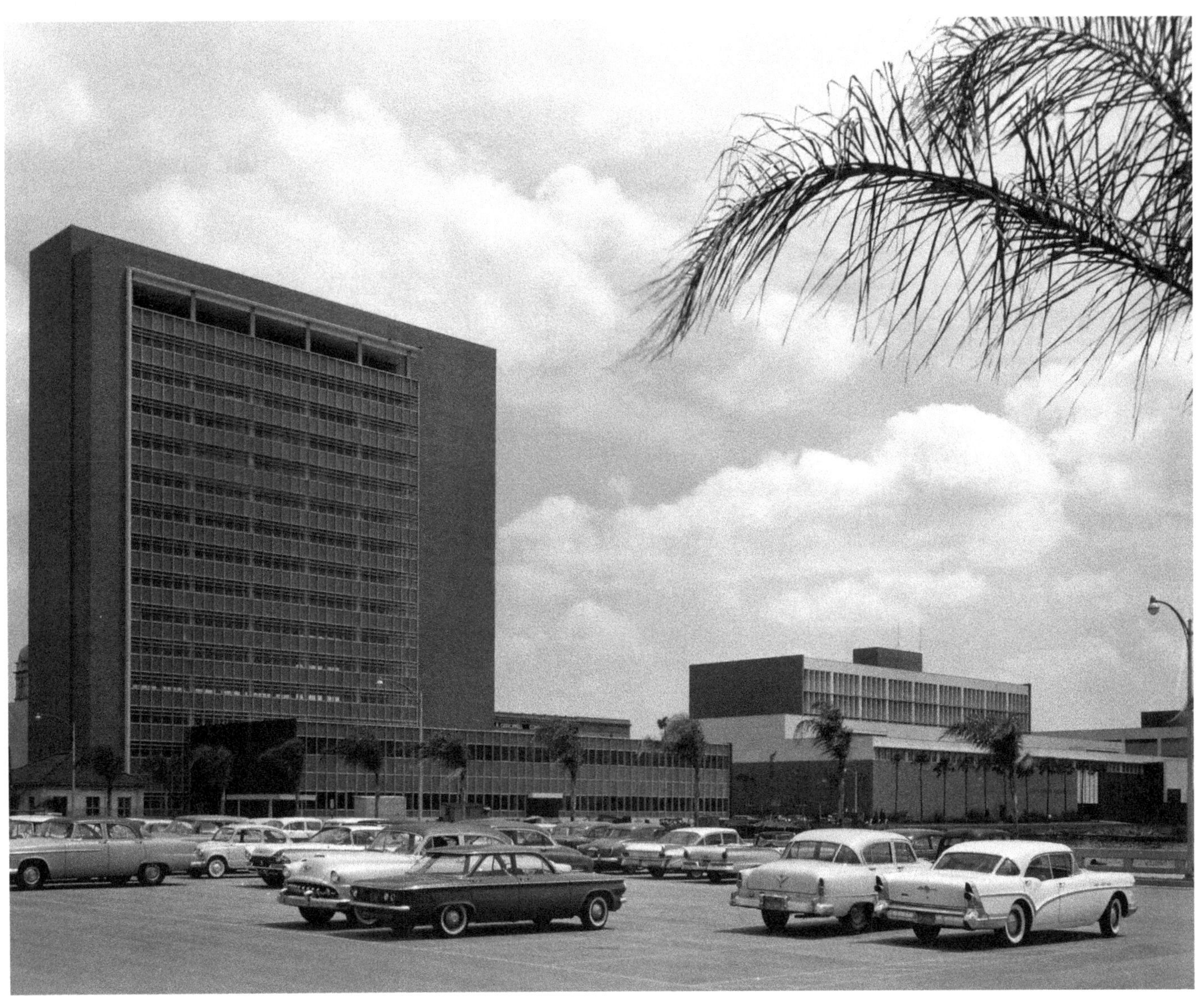

With more bridges to cross and more cars to drive, Jacksonville residents began to frequent the beaches area. These cars on the beach in 1962 reflect the new beach culture of the era.

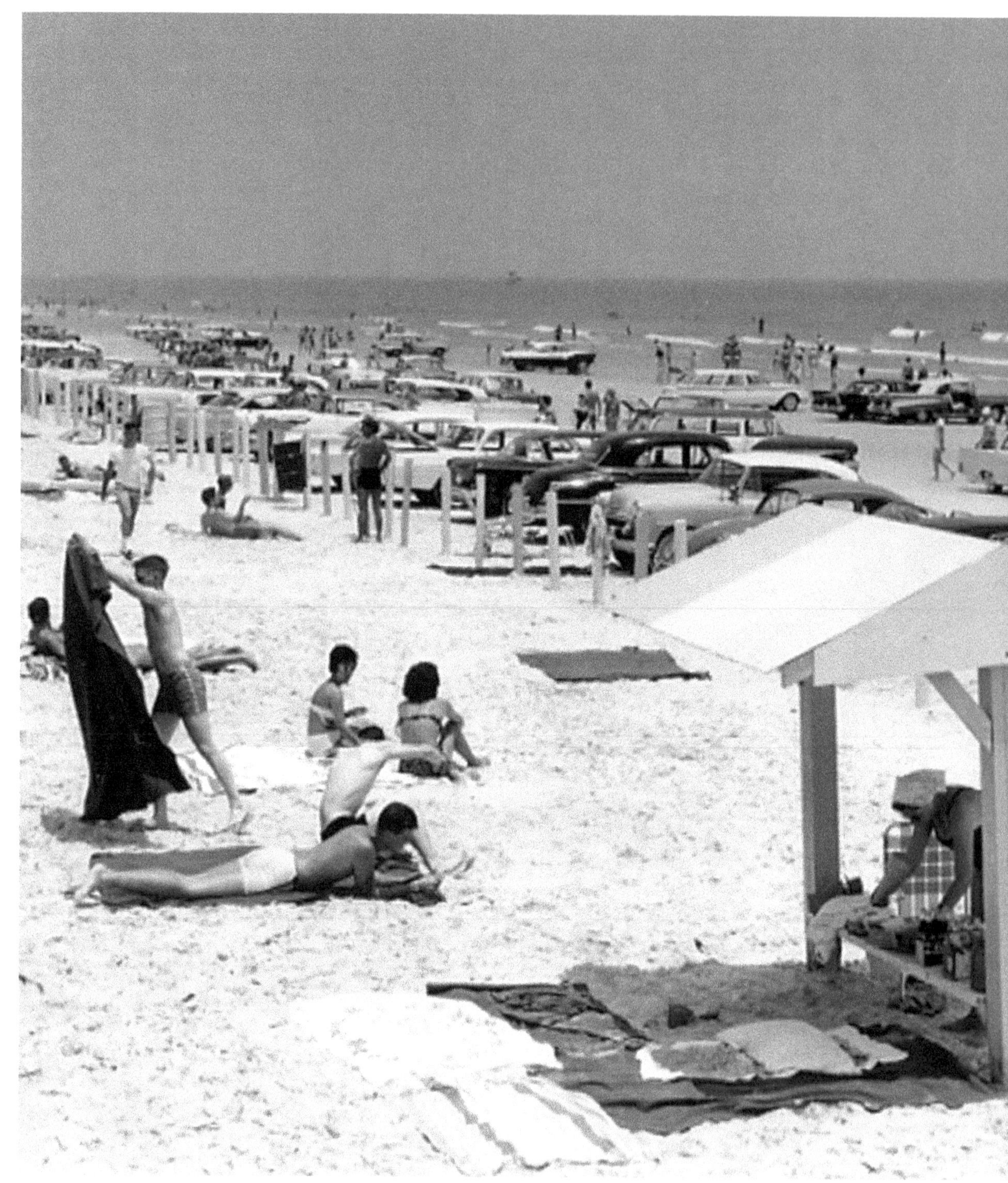

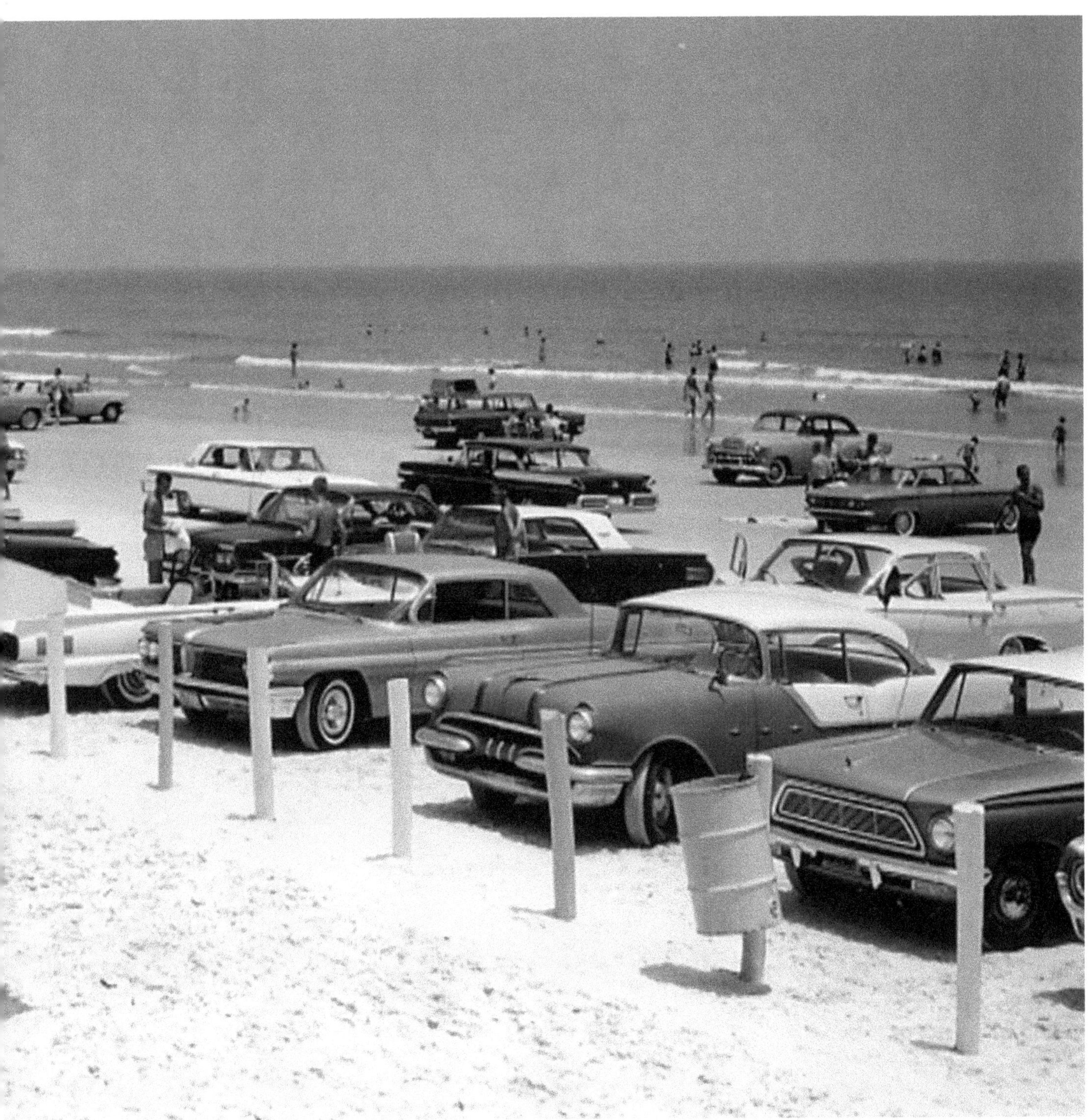

The St. Cloud Hotel in 1949 on Laura Street

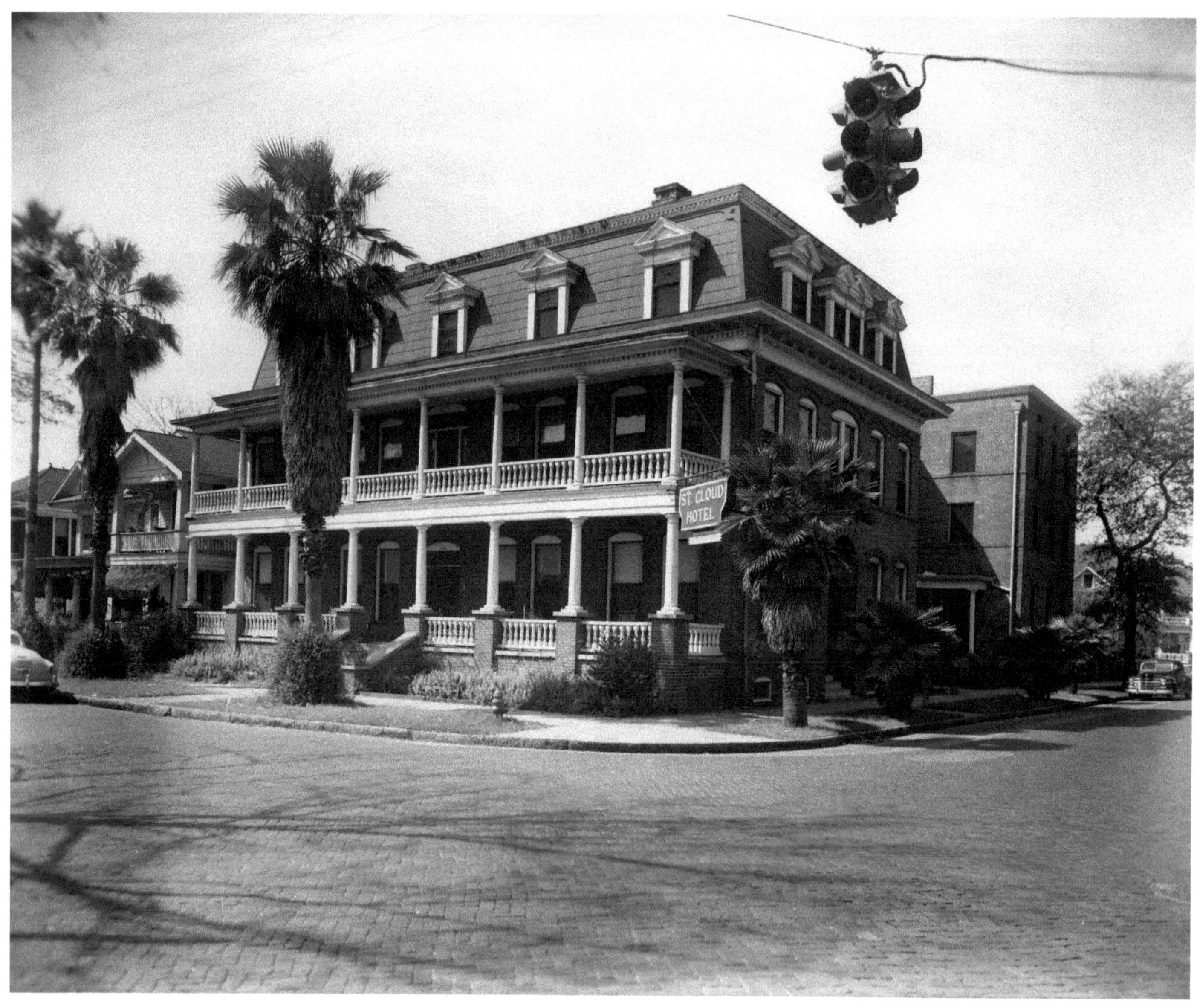

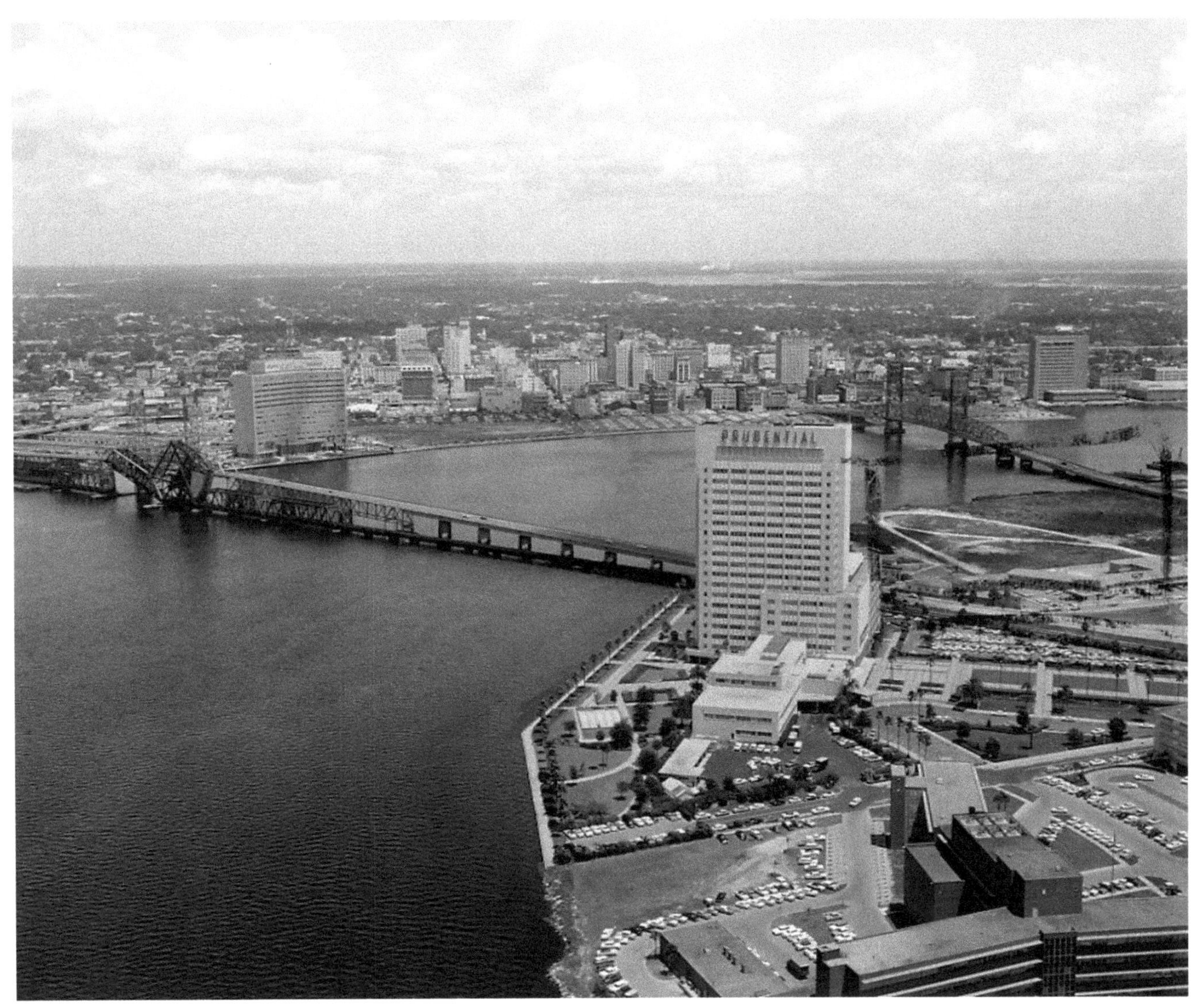

This aerial view of Jacksonville shows how far the city had progressed by the 1960s from the early settlements on the St. Johns River. The high-rise visible is the Prudential Insurance Company building. The decade to follow would bring another leap forward in the city's path to becoming a modern American metropolis by the twenty-first century.

Notes on the Photographs

These notes, listed by page number, attempt to include all aspects known of the photographs. Each of the photographs is identified by the page number, photograph's title or description, photographer and collection, archive, and call or box number when applicable. Although every attempt was made to collect all available data, in some cases complete data was unavailable due to the age and condition of some of the photographs and records.

II **Wharf Along Bay Street**
State Archives of Florida
CC352

VI **Alligator Shot by Captain**
State Archives of Florida
N041288

X **Schooner Lillie of Key West**
State Archives of Florida
N033050

03 **Methodist Church Building**
State Archives of Florida
RC02599

04 **Railway Depot**
State Archives of Florida
RC09671

05 **Bakery**
State Archives of Florida
RC02593

06 **Corner of Bay and Hogan**
State Archives of Florida
N033108

07 **Signal Tower**
State Archives of Florida
RC02601

08 **Provost Marshal's Guard House**
State Archives of Florida
RC02583

09 **Union Soldiers Gathered at Cooley's**
State Archives of Florida
RC17961

10 **Members of the 75th Ohio Infantry**
State Archives of Florida
PR01717

11 **U.S. Boat House**
State Archives of Florida
RC02592

12 **Ocean Street Looking North from Bay**
State Archives of Florida
N033113

13 **S. B. Hubbard Company Office Building**
State Archives of Florida
RC08317

14 **Custom House and Post Office on Bay Street**
State Archives of Florida
RC03324

15 **Sawmill and Lumber Yard**
State Archives of Florida
RC02872

16 **Laying Trolley Track**
State Archives of Florida
N033124

17 **Freedman's Saving and Trust Bank**
State Archives of Florida
RC08384

18 **Stanton Institute**
State Archives of Florida
N033083

19 **Stereoview of Stanton Institute**
State Archives of Florida
N033084

20 **Stanton Institute**
State Archives of Florida
RC11970

21 **View of St. James Hotel**
State Archives of Florida
N032778

22 **Dining Room at the St. James Hotel**
State Archives of Florida
RC08315

23 Residence of S. H. Stowe
State Archives of Florida
N038990

24 Riverside House
State Archives of Florida
RC03049

25 Ocean House
State Archives of Florida
FR0495

26 Grand National Hotel
State Archives of Florida
RC03617

27 Union Passenger Station
State Archives of Florida
RC09131

28 Bull Street
State Archives of Florida
N033132

29 Pine Street from Bay
State Archives of Florida
N033126

30 Bay Street Looking West
State Archives of Florida
N033141

31 Street Scene
State Archives of Florida
RC11991

32 Looking Down Bay Street
State Archives of Florida
RC12006

33 Main Street Looking North
State Archives of Florida
N033106

34 Fruit and Vegetable Display at the Subtropical Exposition
State Archives of Florida
N033199

35 Exteriors of Buildings
State Archives of Florida
PR05305

36 Bootblacking Group Assembled for Portrait
State Archives of Florida
RC08323

37 Group Having a Picnic
State Archives of Florida
RC17822

38 Horse-drawn School Bus
State Archives of Florida
RC04603

39 Lieutenant Stamford at the 7th Army Corps
State Archives of Florida
RC06497

40 Soldiers at the Signal Corps Camp
State Archives of Florida
RC06503

41 Children Having Their Own Parade
State Archives of Florida
RC17917

42 Elizabeth Swaim Memorial United Methodist Church
State Archives of Florida
PR05237

43 C. E. Garner Home
State Archives of Florida
N032999

44 Jacksonville Street Scene
State Archives of Florida
PR12580

45 Democratic Convention
State Archives of Florida
RC01668

46 Marine Guard in Hemming Park
State Archives of Florida
N032724

47 City Going Up in Smoke
State Archives of Florida
RC07423

48 Bell Telephone Gang
State Archives of Florida
N032718

49 Commissary Department of the Women's Auxiliary Committee
State Archives of Florida
N032716

50 Jacksonville Skyline
State Archives of Florida
RC00364

53 Duval County Courthouse
State Archives of Florida
RC17846

54 View of Library from Street
State Archives of Florida
N032933

55 Library Staff on Front Steps
State Archives of Florida
N032921

56 Harry Goldman Posing with His Son Abe
State Archives of Florida
MS26431

57 Looking Down Forsyth Street
State Archives of Florida
RC03638

58 The Florida National Bank
State Archives of Florida
RC14370

59 Forsyth Street Showing Barnett National Bank
State Archives of Florida
N033170

60 Board of Trade Building
State Archives of Florida
N032888

61 Forsyth Street
State Archives of Florida
N033172

62 Yacht Club on the St. Johns River
State Archives of Florida
RC02927

63 Elks Lodge
State Archives of Florida
RC08389

64 Woman's Club of Jacksonville
State Archives of Florida
N032689

65 Steamboat
State Archives of Florida
N040486

66 Railroad Station
State Archives of Florida
RC07295

67 View Down Busy Forsyth Street
State Archives of Florida
RC07012

68 Bay Street from Laura Street
State Archives of Florida
N033159

69 West Bay Street Looking Southward Toward Laura
State Archives of Florida
N033111

70 Windsor Hotel
State Archives of Florida
RC03253

72 Duval Hotel
State Archives of Florida
RC03639

73 Three Men Changing Tire
State Archives of Florida
PR07376

74 People Fishing Off Pier in Jacksonville
State Archives of Florida
CC388

75 Class Portrait of Students Outside One-room Schoolhouse
State Archives of Florida
RC03580

76 Western Union Messenger Boys
State Archives of Florida
RC02485

77 Florida Times-Union Newspaper Advertising Department
State Archives of Florida
RC11825

78 Florida Times-Union Employees Doing Linotype
State Archives of Florida
RC11758

79 Men Testing a Telephone Switchboard
State Archives of Florida
RC20896

80 Firemen and Horse-drawn Fire Wagon of Fire Station #2
State Archives of Florida
RC11505

81 Dinner Hour on the Docks
State Archives of Florida
RC05287

82 Dock and Buildings of Gibbs Gas Engine Company
State Archives of Florida
N032628

83 Laying Water Pipes
State Archives of Florida
RC12018

84 Water Department's Meter Shop
State Archives of Florida
RC12024

85 Looking Down Forsyth Street
State Archives of Florida
RC119675

86 Looking Down Forsyth Street by Intersection of Hogan Street
State Archives of Florida
RC08357

87 Forsyth Street
State Archives of Florida
RC06787

88 Ships in for Repairs
State Archives of Florida
N035232

89 Repairing Ships at a Jacksonville Shipyard
State Archives of Florida
N035234

90 Soldier on Horse Beside Tents
State Archives of Florida
N032542

91 Line of Seated Soldiers
State Archives of Florida
N032544

92 Soldiers at Outdoor Mess
State Archives of Florida
N032535

93 Cooks
State Archives of Florida
N032548

94 Waterfront and Skyline
State Archives of Florida
N0330651

96 Adams Street
State Archives of Florida
N033092

97 Construction of Park Lane Apartments
State Archives of Florida
RC17876

98 Group of Businessmen During Good Will Tour
State Archives of Florida
RC06534

100 Commercial Building with Various Businesses
State Archives of Florida
SP00274

101 Railroad Depot
State Archives of Florida
RC09674

102 Bay Street Near the Railway Depot
State Archives of Florida
RC09668

103 African Americans Began to Mobilize
State Archives of Florida
RC09666

104 Jacksonville Terminal Railroad Depot
State Archives of Florida
RC02736

105 Construction of Double-track Bridge Across St. Johns River
State Archives of Florida
RC06551

106 Municipal Engineering Building
State Archives of Florida
N032914

107 Race-car Driver Sig Haudahl with Mechanic Jimmie Chai
State Archives of Florida
RC10425

108 Line-up at the Jacksonville Fairgrounds
State Archives of Florida
N041975

109 Men Posed in Cadillac Garage
State Archives of Florida
N032611

110 Charles Lindbergh with the Spirit of St. Louis
State Archives of Florida
N027973

111 Young Women Posing on an Airplane Parked on the Beach
State Archives of Florida
SP01276

112 First Annual Woodmen of the World Fair
State Archives of Florida
N034836

113 Municipal Golf Club
State Archives of Florida
RC08356

114 Camp J. Clifford R. Foster: Lt. Col. J. H. Spengler and Major Fred H. Davis
State Archives of Florida
N028585

115 Duval Motor Company
State Archives of Florida
SP01913

116 President Roosevelt in Motorcade Parade
State Archives of Florida
PR08883

117 Laying Railroad Track for Airport Construction
State Archives of Florida
N032903

118 **Florida Theatre and Staff**
State Archives of Florida
N033201

119 **Hotel Mason on a Busy Street**
State Archives of Florida
SP00281

120 **Truck**
State Archives of Florida
SP02440

121 **Truck and Car in Front of an Auto Repair Shop**
State Archives of Florida
SP02435

122 **Arcade Theatre**
State Archives of Florida
SP01936

123 **Street Scene**
State Archives of Florida
SP02717

124 **Crab Plant, with Women Removing Meat from Shells**
State Archives of Florida
SP00436

126 **Duval County High School**
State Archives of Florida
SP01580

127 **Roosevelt Hotel**
State Archives of Florida
SP00396

128 **Baptist Church Building on the Corner of Hogan and Church**
State Archives of Florida
SP00699

129 **Riverside Presbyterian Church**
State Archives of Florida
SP00697

130 **Boy Scouts in the Circus Parade**
State Archives of Florida
SP02894

131 **Student Taking Eye Test**
State Archives of Florida
SP01595

132 **Casa Marina Hotel**
State Archives of Florida
SP00255

133 **Cars on the Beach**
State Archives of Florida
SP02700

134 **People on the Beach**
State Archives of Florida
SP02692

135 **Ferris Wheel and Rides**
State Archives of Florida
SP02688

136 **People Fishing from Pier**
State Archives of Florida
SP02684

137 **Amusement and Shopping at the Beach**
State Archives of Florida
SP02694

138 **Street Scene**
State Archives of Florida
N033091

139 **Levy Building**
State Archives of Florida
SP01921

140 **Roosevelt Inspecting Naval Air Station Personnel**
State Archives of Florida
PR20036

142 **Street Scene**
State Archives of Florida
SP02747

143 **Men Preparing Ribs**
State Archives of Florida
C017866

144 **Epping Forest Mansion**
State Archives of Florida
PR05338

145 **Bridge Opening**
State Archives of Florida
SP02730

146 **J. C. Penney Company Building**
State Archives of Florida
SP00395

147 **Aftermath of Fire at Clyde-Mallory Lines**
State Archives of Florida
N033035

148 **Imperial Theatre**
State Archives of Florida
SP00262

149 **Instructor and Students of VN-11A Primary Training Squadron**
State Archives of Florida
PR20035

150 **Brewster Hospital's Children's Ward**
State Archives of Florida
SP00950

151 **First Presbyterian**
State Archives of Florida
SP00680

152 YMCA Building
State Archives of Florida
SP02679

153 Adams Street After Heavy Rains Flood Jacksonville
State Archives of Florida
C005715

154 Machinists for the Seaboard Air Line Railway Company
State Archives of Florida
SP01309

156 Lovett's Supermarket
State Archives of Florida
SP00345

157 U.S. Naval Air Station
State Archives of Florida
SP00990

158 Truck in Front of Electric Company
State Archives of Florida
SP02314

159 Dollar Motors Presenting a Man with a Car
State Archives of Florida
SP00214

160 Kress Building
State Archives of Florida
SP00076

161 Men Talking on the Showroom Floor at Duval Motor Company
State Archives of Florida
SP00446

162 Jacksonville Dock
State Archives of Florida
C002203

164 Service Attendant with Pump
State Archives of Florida
SP00098

165 Allweather Tire Company Sales with a Goodyear Tire Display
State Archives of Florida
SP00183

166 Ford Motor Company Plant Employees in Training
State Archives of Florida
SP00495

167 Main Street Bridge
State Archives of Florida
C011341

168 Truck
State Archives of Florida
SP02399

169 Gate City Mattress and Carpet Works Trucks and Employees
State Archives of Florida
SP00184

170 Burroughs Adding Machine Company and Employees
State Archives of Florida
SP00234

171 Workers at Farm Florida Can-storage Plant
State Archives of Florida
SP00497

172 Graham-Jones Paper Company
State Archives of Florida
SP00180

173 Schlitz Neon Sign on a Building
State Archives of Florida
SP02031

174 Howard Biser's Restaurant
State Archives of Florida
SP00239

176 Street Scene in Business District
State Archives of Florida
C013235

177 Electrical Power Plant
State Archives of Florida
RC16447

178 Street Scene in Business District
State Archives of Florida
C013232

179 Crowd Watching Television Set in Store Window
State Archives of Florida
RC12850

180 Charley E. Johns' Gubernatorial Campaign Parade
State Archives of Florida
PT00156

181 Intersection Street Sign Decorated for Easter
State Archives of Florida
RC12351

182 Couple Boarding an Airplane
State Archives of Florida
RK0765

183 Couple Near an Airplane
State Archives of Florida
RK0764

184 Atlantic Coast Line Train
State Archives of Florida
PR09220

185 Atlantic Coast Line Railroad Company Building
State Archives of Florida
RC17920

186 Aerial View of Jacksonville
State Archives of Florida
C033854

187 The Corky II at Sims Brothers Marina
State Archives of Florida
C032691

188 Aerial at the Gator Bowl
State Archives of Florida
RC17852

190 Southside Grammar School Graduation
State Archives of Florida
SP01667

192 Lyndon Johnson Speaking in Hemming Park
State Archives of Florida
RC19363

193 Crowd Gathered in Hemming Park to Listen to Lyndon Johnson
State Archives of Florida
RC19364

194 Foley Lumber Company Cranes
State Archives of Florida
SP00198

195 City Hall
State Archives of Florida
C032575

196 Cars Parked on Jacksonville Beach State Archives of Florida
C039075A

198 St. Cloud Hotel
State Archives of Florida
SP00101

199 Aerial View
State Archives of Florida
C033857

HISTORIC PHOTOS OF JACKSONVILLE

By the late nineteenth century, the city of Jacksonville was a vibrant cultural center on Florida's Atlantic coast. Through changing fortunes, Jacksonville has continued to grow and prosper by overcoming adversity and maintaining the strong, independent culture of its citizens.

Historic Photos of Jacksonville captures this journey through still photography selected from the finest archives. From the Gilded Age to the extension of the Florida East Coast Railroad, the Great Fire of 1901 to the installation of three major naval bases, *Historic Photos of Jacksonville* follows life, government, education, and events throughout the city's history.

This volume captures unique and rare scenes as depicted in nearly 200 historic photographs. Published in striking black and white, these images communicate historic events and everyday life of two centuries of people building a unique and prosperous city.

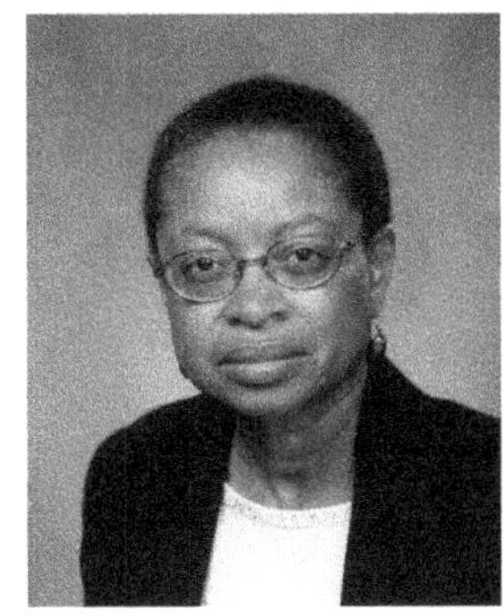

Carolyn Williams, a native of Jacksonville, is an Associate Professor of History at the University of North Florida in Jacksonville.

She is a past member of the Florida Historical Commission and the Jacksonville Historic Preservation Commission. Currently she is the chair of the Northeast Florida Advisory Board and a member of the Florida State Historical Marker Council. She has published articles in *Anthologies of American History* and contributed entries to the *Encyclopedia of American Cultural and Intellectual History* and *The Oxford Companion to United States History.*

WWW.TURNERPUBLISHING.COM

www.ingramcontent.com/pod-product-compliance
Lightning Source LLC
LaVergne TN
LVHW060609110826
845154LV00003B/63
* 9 7 8 1 6 8 3 3 6 9 2 8 8 *